The European Union and the Public Sphere

This book focuses on what the prospects are for a 'citizens' Europe'. It places particular emphasis on the notion of a European public sphere; that is a communicative space that might enable and engender the formation of a transnational or a supranational public. A viable public sphere is a central precondition for democracy because it enables widespread public debate. Analysts have consistently stressed that an important component of the European Union's democratic deficit (that is, its deficiencies in representation and representativeness, transparency, accountability, and support) is the absence of a viable European public sphere. This book lays emphasis on a 'deliberative democratic' perspective, a theoretical conception of democracy particularly well suited to analyse the public sphere and how it relates to democracy. The book addresses the following questions:

- What are the prospects for a European public sphere?
- Is a uniform sphere needed, or are overlapping public spheres a more viable option?
- What do our findings tell us about the EU as a polity?

There is considerable uncertainty – and disagreement – as to the character of the EU as a political system. The book therefore assesses the prospects for a European public sphere by using different models of the EU. It covers three main themes: how to theorise communicative practices in the EU, the working of general publics and the media, and finally the key EU institutions and their implications for the public sphere. No such assessment has been undertaken before.

John Erik Fossum is Professor of Political Science at ARENA, Centre for European Studies at the University of Oslo, Norway. **Philip Schlesinger** is Professor in Cultural Policy in the Department of Theatre, Film and Television Studies, and Academic Director of the Centre for Cultural Policy Research at the University of Glasgow, UK.

Routledge studies on democratizing Europe
Edited by Erik Oddvar Eriksen and John Erik Fossum
ARENA, University of Oslo

Routledge studies on democratizing Europe focuses on the prospects for a citizens' Europe by analysing the kind of order that is emerging in Europe. The books in the series take stock of the EU as an entity that has progressed beyond intergovernmentalism and consider how to account for this process and whether it is democratic. The emphasis is on citizenship, constitution-making, public sphere, enlargement, common foreign and security policy, and social and tax policy.

The European Union and the Public Sphere

A communicative space in the making?

Edited by John Erik Fossum and Philip Schlesinger

Routledge
Taylor & Francis Group

LONDON AND NEW YORK

First published 2007
by Routledge
2 Park Square, Milton Park, Abingdon, Oxon, OX14 4RN

Simultaneously published in the USA and Canada
by Routledge
270 Madison Ave, New York NY 10016

Routledge is an imprint of the Taylor & Francis Group, an informa business

Transferred to Digital Printing 2008

© 2007 John Erik Fossum and Philip Schlesinger for selection and
editorial matter; individual contributors, their contributions

Typeset in Baskerville by Wearset Ltd, Boldon, Tyne and Wear

British Library Cataloguing in Publication Data
A catalogue record for this book is available from the British Library

Library of Congress Cataloging in Publication Data
A catalog record for this book has been requested

ISBN10: 0-415-38456-7 (hbk)
ISBN10: 0-415-47965-7 (pbk)
ISBN10: 0-203-96085-8 (ebk)

ISBN13: 978-0-415-38456-8 (hbk)
ISBN13: 978-0-415-47965-3 (pbk)
ISBN13: 978-0-203-96085-1 (ebk)

Contents

Illustrations

Contributors

Lars Chr. Blichner is Associate Professor at the Institute for Administration and Organisational Research, University of Bergen. His current research interests are juridification and the rule of law, internationalisation and European integration. His publications include *Radical Change and Experiential Learning* (1995); 'The Anonymous Hand of Public Reason: Interparliamentary Discourse and the Quest for Legitimacy', in Eriksen and Fossum (eds), *Democracy in the European Union* (2000); and 'Mapping Juridification', forthcoming in *European Law Journal.*

Deirdre Curtin is Professor of International and European Governance at Utrecht School of Governance, Utrecht University. Her current research interests include constitutionalism, democratic governance and European integration. She has written extensively on issues relating to the constitutional and institutional development of the European Union, including *Postnational Democracy: The European Union in Search of a Political Philosophy* (1997), and is currently working on a book on public accountability of EU executives.

Abram de Swaan is Distinguished Research Professor of Social Science at the University of Amsterdam and director of the *Academia Europea de Yuste* (Spain). His present research interest is transnational society, as it concerns social policy, social identifications and the rivalry and accommodation between language groups. Some of his publications are *In Care of the State: Health Care, Education and Welfare in Europe and the USA in the Modern Era* (1998), *The Management of Normality: Critical Essays in Health and Welfare* (1990), *Human Societies: An Introduction* (2001) and *Words of the World: The Global Language System* (2001).

Klaus Eder is Professor of Sociology at the Humboldt University Berlin, where he teaches comparative macrosociology with particular emphasis on the sociology of culture and communication as well as the sociology of collective action. He is the editor of *European Citizenship: National Legacies and Postnational Projects* (with B. Giesen) (2000), *Environmental Politics in Southern Europe* (with M. Kousis) (2001), 'The Making of a

European Public Space: The Case of Justice and Home Affairs' (with H.-J. Trenz), in Kohler-Koch (ed.), *Linking EU and National Governance* (2003), and 'The Democratising Role of a European Public Sphere: Towards a Model of Democratic Functionalism' in *European Journal of Social Theory* (2004).

Erik Oddvar Eriksen is Professor of Political Science at ARENA, Centre for European Studies at the University of Oslo. His main fields of interest are political theory, democratic governance, public policy and European integration. Recent publications include *Democracy in the European Union* (co-edited with J. E. Fossum) (2000), *Understanding Habermas* (with J. Weigård) (2003), *The Chartering of Europe* (co-edited with J. E. Fossum and A. J. Menéndez) (2003), *Developing a Constitution for Europe* (co-edited with J. E. Fossum and A. J. Menéndez) (2004), *Making the European Polity: Reflexive Integration in the EU* (editor) (2005) and *Arguing Fundamental Rights* (co-edited with A. J. Menéndez) (2006).

François Foret is Lecturer in Political Science at the Université Libre de Bruxelles. He has specialised in research on the European Union, its legitimation and its symbolic dimension. Recent publications include *L'espace public européen à l'épreuve du religieux* (editor) (2007); *Légitimer l'Europe. Pouvoir et symbolique à l'ère du supranational* (2007) and 'Advertising Europe: The Production of Public Information by the European Commission', in A. Smith (ed.), *Politics and the European Commission* (2004).

John Erik Fossum is Professor of Political Science at ARENA, Centre for European Studies at the University of Oslo. His main fields of interest include political theory, constitutionalism, citizenship and identity in the EU (and Canada). Among his publications are *Oil, the State, and Federalism* (1997), *Democracy in the European Union* (co-edited with E. O. Eriksen) (2000), 'The European Union in Search of an Identity' in *European Journal of Political Theory* (2003), *The Chartering of Europe* (co-edited with E. O. Eriksen and A. J. Menéndez) (2003) and *Developing a Constitution for Europe* (co-edited with E. O. Eriksen and A. J. Menéndez) (2004).

Maria Heller is Director of the Institute of Sociology and vice-dean for international relations of the Faculty of Social Sciences at Eötvös Loránd University Budapest. Her fields of research encompass communications theory and mass communications, media sociology, theories of the public sphere and public discourse strategies. Her recent publications include 'The Construction of Collective Identities in Public Discourse: Debates on National Identity and the Media in Hungary', in T. Slaatta (ed.), *Media and the Transition of Collective Identities* (2001); 'Social and Political Effects of New ICTs and their Penetration in Hungary', in K. Nyíri (ed.), *Mobile Democracy* (2003); and 'Le service public en Europe de l'Est', in J. Bourdon (ed.), *Médiamorphoses* (2005).

Ulrike Liebert is Professor of Political Science and Director of the Jean Monnet Centre for European Studies at the University of Bremen. Her research focus is on problems of democracy and integration in the new Europe. Recent publications include *Parliaments and Democratic Consolidation in Southern Europe* (co-edited with M. Cotta) (1991), *Modelle demokratischer Konsolidierung: Parlamentarische Netzwerke organisierter Interessen* (1995), *Verfassungsexperiment: Europa auf dem Weg zur transnationalen Demokratie?* (co-edited with J. Falke, K. Packham and D. Allnoch) (2003), *Gendering Europeanisation* (with S. Sifft *et al.*) (2003) and *Postnational Constitutionalisation in the New Europe* (co-edited with J. Falke and A. Maurer) (2005).

Ágnes Rényi is Chair of the Department of History of Sociology at the Institute of Sociology at Eötvös Loránd University Budapest. Her main research interests are theoretical approaches to the public sphere, public discourse strategies and history of French sociology. She has recently published 'A nyilvánosság problematikája Pierre Bourdieu muveiben' (The Problem of the Public Sphere in Pierre Bourdieu's Oeuvre) (with M. Heller), in Felkai *et al.* (eds), *Forrásvidékek* (2002).

Philip Schlesinger is Professor in Cultural Policy in the Department of Theatre, Film and Television Studies and Academic Director of the Centre for Cultural Policy Research at the University of Glasgow. He is Fellow of the Royal Society of Edinburgh, Scotland's national academy of sciences and letters. His current research focuses on European communicative spaces, cultural creativity policy and the UK film and television industries, and the representation of exile. He is a longstanding co-editor of the academic journal *Media, Culture and Society* and author of *Putting 'Reality' Together* (2nd edn 1987) and *Media, State and Nation* (1991). His most recent books are *Open Scotland?* (with D. Miller and W. Dinan) (2001) and *Mediated Access* (with B. McNair and M. Hibbard) (2003). The *SAGE Handbook of Media Studies* (2004) is his most recent co-edited work.

Andy Smith is Research Director at the National Foundation for Political Science (FNSP) at the University of Bordeaux. His main fields of research are the European Commission, the European Council, social representation and collective identity in Europe. Recent publications include 'Developments in the Academic Study of Public Policy in France' in *Public Administration* (1999), 'French Political Science and European Integration' in *Journal of European Public Policy* (2000), *Les commissaires européens: technocrates, diplomates ou politiques* (with J. Joana) (2002), *Le gouvernement de l'Union européenne: une sociologie politique* (2004) and *Politics and the European Commission* (editor) (2004).

Paul Statham is Professor of Political Sociology at the University of Bristol and Director of the Centre for European Political Communications. His research focuses on politics and the media, the European public sphere, Islam, and immigration and ethnic relations, applying a cross-national comparative approach. His publications include *Challenging Immigration and Ethnic Relations Politics* (with R. Koopmans) (2000), *Contested Citizenship: Immigration and Cultural Diversity in Europe* (with R. Koopmans *et al.*) (2005), 'Becoming European? The Transformation of the British Pro-migrant NGO Sector in Response to Europeanization' in *Journal of Common Market Studies* (2005) and 'Elites and Organized Publics: Who Drives British Immigration Politics and in Which Direction?', in *Western European Politics* (2005).

Hans-Jörg Trenz is Research Professor at ARENA, Centre for European Studies at the University of Oslo. His research interests include European public sphere and civil society, European civilization and identity, migration and ethnic minorities, cultural and political sociology, and social and political theory. Among his publications are *Bürgerschaft, Öffentlichkeit und Demokratie in Europa* (co-edited with A. Klein *et al.*) (2003), *Europa in den Medien* (2005), and 'The EU's Fledgling Society: From Deafening Silence to Critical Voice in European Constitution Making' in *Journal of Civil Society* (with J. E. Fossum) (2006).

Acknowledgements

This book originated in a workshop held at the University of Stirling on 5–6 February 2004. It contains extensively revised pieces from contributors to the meeting as well as specially solicited chapters from other authors. We have been exigent editors, and our contributors have responded magnificently to our comments and requests for redrafts. The work contained in these pages addresses one major theme of the CIDEL project on *Citizenship and Democratic Legitimacy in the EU*, which was funded by the European Commission's Fifth Framework Programme.

CIDEL's central focus was on the prospects for a citizens' Europe. Our book has sought to address this issue by taking stock of the extent to which the EU has become a rights-based post-national union, based on a fully fledged political citizenship, with a democratically viable public sphere. We have approached the question by counterposing distinctive models of the EU as a polity. We believe that these pages provide the most systematic assessment presently available of the implications of different conceptions of the EU for the public sphere.

We owe considerable intellectual debts to our colleagues in the CIDEL network as well as to those at ARENA and Stirling. Both ARENA and Stirling, together with the European Commission, have offered invaluable financial and organisational support, for which we wish to express our appreciation. We are also very grateful to Marit Eldholm for her excellent technical editorial work on this volume.

John Erik Fossum and Philip Schlesinger
Oslo and Stirling, 2007

1 The European Union and the public sphere

A communicative space in the making?

John Erik Fossum and Philip Schlesinger

> The public sphere is a central feature of modern society. So much so that, even where it is in fact suppressed or manipulated, it has to be faked.
>
> (Taylor 1995: 260)

Introduction

After two decades of almost breathtaking integration, the French *non* (by 54.7 per cent) and the Dutch *nee* (by 61.6 per cent) to the Treaty establishing a Constitution for Europe in May and June 2005 underlined that the Union had arrived at a critical juncture. Whatever sense of direction could be derived from a decades-long process of integration has apparently given way to profound uncertainty and heightened contestation over the Union's future development. This has precipitated a 'reflection period', as well as initiatives by the Commission to improve its communication policy (cf. European Commission 2006).

The referendum results have been received and interpreted very differently across Europe. Euro-sceptics have construed the outcome as clear evidence that a European constitutional polity is a dream, a fiction that can never be realised in practice. Euro-federalists, on the other hand, have seen the rejection as testimony to the inadequacy of the Constitutional Treaty (CT) as an instrument for establishing a federal EU polity. This gap in interpretations dramatises current debate over what is, and might be, the character of the EU.

The outcome is directly connected with the concerns of our book, namely, what the prospects are for a European public sphere.

Arguably, a central precondition for a democratic order is a viable public sphere – namely, a communicative space (or spaces) in which relatively unconstrained debate, analysis and criticism of the political order can take place. This precondition applies as much to the EU as it does to any nation state.

In the Union's early stages, the task was to consolidate democracy at the national level and to overcome the legacy of the Second World War.

The EU (like its precursors) has acted as an important consolidator of democracy in post-authoritarian and post-communist states that have acceded to the Union. As the Union has grown, the concern with democracy has been a question posed not only about member states and newly acceding states but also about the workings of the EU itself. There is now a strong onus on the Union to comply with democratic norms. It has become increasingly – and pressingly – relevant to discuss whether there could be a European public sphere in which citizens might simultaneously address common issues *across* state borders and see themselves as the authors of the EU laws they have to abide by. The EU's development as a new kind of polity is therefore closely connected with the range and depth of its development as a public and communicative space. Inasmuch as the Union actually might serve as an exemplar for the development of post-national democracy at the supranational level, surely such a process has to be rooted in the reshaping of the EU as an overarching communicative space (or spaces) that might function as a public sphere.

Traditionally, both political and media theory have conceived of communicative spaces and public spheres in terms of what goes on inside nation states.[1] However, this kind of perspective is rapidly ceasing to be adequate to account for how the EU works as a supranational polity. The integration process has provoked nationalist opposition inside member states as well as reassertions of regionalism and nationalism at the sub-state level. More distinctive spaces below the level of the member state are being reinforced at the same time as the nation-state framework itself is facing new challenges from above.

In addressing the changing political configuration of the EU, this book begins by asking:

- What are the prospects for a European public sphere?
- Is a uniform sphere needed, or are overlapping public spheres a more viable option?
- What do our findings tell us about the EU as a polity?

When considering these questions, first we have to clarify what a 'public sphere' means, and what its functions are. We have to take into consideration that a public sphere is imbricated in a set of legal–institutional arrangements traditionally linked to the nation state. Consequently, it has been quite common to imagine the public sphere in rather monolithic terms.

However, the EU is neither a state nor a nation and, as we shall argue, it remains unclear whether any public sphere at the Union level could be modelled on that presently associated with the nation state. The challenge to democratic theory, therefore, is what kind of conception of the public sphere *might* be relevant to the EU.

In this chapter, first we take, as our point of departure, the Habermasian model of the public sphere and make explicit its presuppositions. Habermas's thinking has been influential in the debate on the contemporary public sphere, and he has also repeatedly sought to apply his theory to the EU. This makes his contribution a natural starting point for any book on the European public sphere. Second, we consider some problems in the workings of the public sphere. Third, we develop two distinct conceptions of an EU still in the making. These differ greatly in their implications for the prospects of a European public sphere.

Conceptualising the public sphere[2]

In conceptualising the public sphere, it is important to deal with three core issues. First, we need to establish its ideal characteristics, so as to bring out the relevant analytical dimensions. Second, we have to spell out its contribution to democracy and its normative value. Third, we identify some key problems that the public sphere is currently facing. Public-sphere theorising has taken the nation state as its point of reference and normative template. However, our investigation of the European public sphere seeks to avoid simply juxtaposing the emergent European reality to a 'model' public sphere based on the template of the nation state.

In Habermas's characterisation, the public sphere:

> can best be described as a network of communicating information and points of view [...]; the streams of communication are, in the process, filtered and synthesized in such a way that they coalesce into bundles of topically specified *public* opinions. Like the lifeworld as a whole, so, too, the public sphere is reproduced through communicative action, for which mastery of a natural language suffices; it is tailored to the *general comprehensibility* of everyday communicative practice.
>
> (Habermas 1996a: 360)

The public sphere has a *triadic character*, with a speaker, an addressee and a listener. In an ideal 'public sphere', equal citizens assemble into a public and set their own agenda through open communication. In Habermas's developmental account, the new spaces of 'public reasoning' that opened up for the political confrontation between state authorities and the public were held to be remarkable and without historical precedent (Habermas 1989: 27). Habermas has conceived the public sphere as non-coercive, secular and rational. A central feature is its reflexive character: it is how a 'society' talks knowingly about itself.

Individual rights that provide citizens with protection from incursions by the state serve as a vital precondition for the public sphere. Habermas's initial account in the *Structural Transformation* (1989) was based on a reconstruction of the ideal features of the bourgeois public sphere. This,

he argued, underwent a subsequent decline in the age of organised capitalism and corporate democracy, which he described as 'a neocorporatist
"societalization of the state" [...], and as a state-ification of society' (Habermas 1992a: 432). In his more recent work, Habermas has linked the notion
of a public sphere more closely to the principle of universalistic argumentation, the principle that forms the core of the theory of communicative
action. Craig Calhoun explains this transition in the following way:

> where *Structural Transformation* located the basis for the application of
> practical reason to politics in the historically specific institutions of the
> public sphere, the theory of communicative action locates them in tran-
> shistorical, evolving communicative capacities or capacities of reason
> conceived intersubjectively as in its essence a matter of communication.
>
> (Calhoun 1992: 32)

This alters the theoretical status of the public sphere: 'The public sphere
remains an ideal, but it becomes *a contingent product of the evolution of communicative action*, rather than its basis' (ibid., emphasis added).

Whereas Habermas's definition cited above locates the public sphere in
the 'lifeworld', this is not the whole picture, as he also seeks to establish
the prospects for communicative action within the political system in
general. After being criticised by, among others, Nancy Fraser (1992),
Habermas has himself acknowledged that *formally* organised institutions
within the system world *also* contain fora that may play the role of publics.
Fraser initially captured this added complexity in a key distinction
between 'strong' and 'weak' publics. Strong publics are spaces of institutionalised deliberation 'whose discourse encompasses both opinion
formation and decision making', and weak publics are spaces 'whose
deliberative practice consists exclusively in opinion formation and does
not also encompass decision making' (ibid.: 134).

In institutional terms, strong publics encompass parliamentary assemblies and other deliberative entities: they are situated in formally organised
institutions imbued with decision-making power and – ideally – should be
constrained by the logic of argument and impartial justification. Weak
publics operate in the wider sphere of deliberation outside the formal political system; in short, in civil society. From this standpoint, it is the interrelations between strong and weak publics that make up the wider
constitutional order associated with the democratic constitutional state.

The public sphere and democracy

The public sphere is intimately linked with democracy. Since it is based on
the tenet that everybody can speak without limitation, it can be considered a precondition for realising popular sovereignty. Legal rights – in
particular, those of freedom of expression and of assembly – secure the

public sphere as a common space for communication. It is the communicative context in which problems are discovered, thematised and dramatised. Here, they are also formed into opinions and wills on the basis of which formal decision-making agencies are empowered to act.

According to Charles Taylor:

> [T]he public sphere is not only a ubiquitous feature of any modern society; it also plays a crucial role in its self-justification as a free self-governing society, that is as a society in which (a) people form their opinions freely; both as individuals and as coming to a common mind, and (b) these common minds matter – they in some way take effect on or control government.
>
> (Taylor 1995: 260)

Plainly, the development of a modern public sphere has profound implications for how democratic legitimacy may be conceived. When citizens become equipped with rights they can exercise against the state, decision makers also face the need to justify their decisions and to gain support in public. In such a setting, power cannot be legitimated solely by reference to divine law or traditional authority. Instead, authority is to be discovered in the public's 'reasonable' discussion. This makes legitimacy precarious but it also becomes an important democratic resource. The speech of power can be turned into the power of speech (Lefort 1988: 38). Within this framework, it is clear that particular institutions or concrete persons cannot guarantee the legitimacy of the law. Only public debate in itself has norm-giving power (Eriksen and Weigård 2003).

A functioning public sphere presupposes basic rights that ensure the autonomy of citizens, both in private and in public terms, and institutions that can relay communicative action originating in the lifeworld to the system world. Such institutions include 'strong' publics with a deliberative vocation as well as executive and legislative institutions that ensure that decisions are made and carried out. Habermas notes that:

> binding decisions, to be legitimate, must be steered by communication flows that start at the periphery and pass through the sluices of democratic and constitutional procedures situated at the entrance to the parliamentary complex or the courts [...]. That is the only way to exclude the possibility that the power of the administrative complex, on the one side, or the social power of intermediate structures affecting the core area, on the other side, become independent vis-à-vis a communicative power that develops in the parliamentary complex.
>
> (Habermas 1996a: 356)

This can be represented in a model of what Habermas terms the 'official circulation of power', i.e. that which is actually set down in the formal

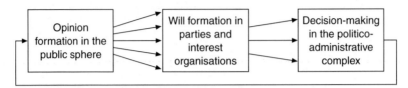

Figure 1.1 The circulation of political power.

constitution of the democratic constitutional state. This is a heuristic device that enables a clearer delineation of both the constitutive elements of the public sphere and its presuppositions. It can be illustrated as in Figure 1.1.

The model presupposes that opinion formation takes place outside the political system, is inserted into the system through 'channels and sluices' and emerges as decisions. How such decisions are justified helps to frame subsequent processes of opinion-formation through a feedback loop.

The application of this model to contemporary reality raises three critical issues of direct relevance for our conception of a public sphere. The first pertains to the types of presupposition that need to underpin a viable public sphere. Do democratic opinion- and will-formation processes have to rest on a set of 'pre-political' values to produce democratically legitimate decisions? Does democracy presuppose a *we-feeling*, a sense of brotherhood and sisterhood akin to that associated with what Benedict Anderson (1991) has famously called the 'imagined community' of the nation? Is a sense of common destiny required for people to consider each other as compatriots willing to trust each other and take on collective obligations?

Communitarianism provides us with the clearest response to such questions and holds that identity is value-based and that notions of the good have priority over notions of justice (Sandel 1998). Without binding norms or shared values, it is argued, societal co-operation cannot come about, and without this it is not possible to explain order as the result of co-operation between free and equal citizens. People need to regard each other as norm-abiding actors in order for solidarity and collective action to occur on a voluntary basis. What is more, communitarians hold that political integration does require a deeper sense of belonging and commonality (Miller 1995). In Amitai Etzioni's (1997) terms, members of a community listen to the same moral voice. The citizens need to regard each other as neighbours or fellow countrymen, or brothers and sisters.

It is this kind of common identification, arguably, that makes for solidarity and patriotism. This type of political integration is held to be the achievement of the nation which, ideally, due to its deep ties of belonging and trust, makes possible the transformation of an aggregation of individuals and groups into a collectivity capable of common action. Communitarianism's position on the character of the circuit of political power is thus clear: an absence of shared norms coupled with increased social scale and heterogeneity will make consensual decisions highly unlikely, causing systemic instability or even breakdown.

The presumption of an intrinsic link between national identity and democracy has deeply coloured the academic and political debate on the EU. Many students of European integration have maintained that a democratic Union must emulate the nation state to promote social and political integration and develop 'pre-political' elements such as a collective identity, common values and common interests (see, for example, Grimm 1995; Miller 1995; Offe 1998). The communitarian perspective requires a high threshold for what constitutes a viable European public sphere – one that the highly diverse Union will find very hard to step across.

By contrast, liberals and deliberative democrats argue that the communitarian position is based on an historical fiction: communitarians are held to underrate democratic systems' ability to accommodate an evolving pluralism and diversity. Furthermore, by stressing the need for a pre-political identity, communitarians may actually overstate the cohesion that modern states require. As Klaus Eder notes in Chapter 3 (pp. 55–56, our emphasis), 'Nationalism distorts the idea of equal citizens into the idea of a *unitary* people. [...] This need for an ontological unity is the central risk of the national variant of a democratic state.'

National public spheres are neither as unitary as communitarians posit nor should we assume that they are paragons of openness and democratic participation. For instance, we may well find that, at the national level, the mediated public sphere operates far from perfectly. In the UK, for instance, there is debate about political communication that emphasises the failure of politicians to communicate effectively or honestly, their recourse to image and news management, the marginalisation of Parliament and the centralisation of executive power. For some critics, media coverage has contributed to a loss of respect for the political class, to electoral disengagement from mainstream politics, and decline in the consumption and credibility of mainstream media (Schlesinger 2006). In related observations on the critical state of the media in France, Jean-Gustave Padioleau (2006) has argued that the constitutional referendum exposed their bankruptcy and the self-delusion that they actually constitute a 'fourth estate'. According to his analysis, the French press is not a spokesperson for the French public and its professionalism is in question as media start to undergo a far-reaching process of transformation.

Most research on political communication at the EU level, and how this articulates with national public spheres, tends to be overwhelmingly concerned with what is eventually represented, with EU-related content that appears and then circulates. Whether the national media are themselves functioning effectively, or the kinds of structural change they are subject to and which might affect media performance, tend to be issues that are bracketed for the purposes of assessing whether or not they are acting as conduits of 'Europeanisation' and therefore of building the nascent European public sphere. However, if there are crises of credibility in the relation between politics and the media at the level of the *national* public sphere, this can hardly be a matter of indifference, for it simply compounds the distinct problems of the functioning of a *European* public sphere.

Contemporary challenges

The second issue connects directly with the argument about national media. It pertains to whether the circulation of power in contemporary political systems follows the ideal conditions of the public sphere model, or actually short-circuits it. Habermas (1989) has argued that the structural transformation of the bourgeois public sphere from the latter third of the 1800s onwards brought about a degeneration of the public sphere through the rise of organised capitalism, the state regulation of social conflicts and the dissolution of the rational public into numerous competing interests.[3] In short, that the ideal conditions (if ever present) no longer apply.

The story of systemic problems in contemporary democracy told in a range of academic fields today focuses both on weak and strong publics. Two stories are often conflated: one of historical decline and the other of a gap between ideal standards and empirical reality. The story of decline runs roughly as follows: the modern state's policy-formulating role – through powerful executives, regulators and autonomous agencies as well as through the dense networks that constitute 'policy communities' – is widely held to have sidelined central representative bodies. Economic relations in society have increasingly taken the form of interest-based politics. Decision-making does not follow upon free and open debate; instead, political questions are decided behind closed doors, through institutionalised bargaining. Public agencies and systems of delegated authority are set up to handle complex technical issues, which helps to increase the public's distance from the substance of decisions. Hence, on this reading, it is not only weak publics in the wider civil society that have been sidelined; the same applies to key strong publics – such as parliaments – whose role is mainly to sanction decisions made elsewhere. This means that the vital link between deliberation and decision-making that should be characteristic of strong publics is severed.

This tendency has the effect of undermining the idea of the public as a forum and as a critical assessor of what takes place inside the political system. The speaker and the addressee are both *inside* the system, whereas the public is left on the sidelines and relegated to the passive role of a spectator or one who reacts to what the system produces. A development that underpins much of the above has been referred to as 'juridification', which 'denotes the tendency toward the increasing expansion of law and law-like methods of formal rules and adjudication to new domains of social life' (Bohman 2004: 321). This contributes to the sidelining of representative bodies as well as to rendering social relations and informally regulated domains of social life increasingly open to state and market imperatives.

The EU – a contested public terrain

The third critical issue concerns the emergence of transnational and supranational organisations such as the EU, which many analysts argue have increasingly sidelined or even *excluded* the nation state from decision-making. This is simply an extension – and exaggeration – of the national story of decline. To the extent that this obtains, the very relevance of the formal circulation of power must be questioned, not only as a description of contemporary reality but also as a regulative ideal. How grave this problem is has been hotly disputed.

The EU as political system

The EU is clearly more than a mere market-type of organisation. According to one widely held view, the Union provides an added layer of decision-making on top of the member states, a process that has given member-state processes of decision-making a strong executive presence, often referred to as 'executive dominance'. In this way, the EU may underpin the existing executive dominance of the member states. This means the net empowerment of the executive branch of states at the expense of parliamentary involvement and control, so that legislative assemblies are effectively unable to control and hold elected officials to account. Some argue that the Union's complex, multi-level structure actually fosters a triple 'democratic deficit' at the EU, member-state and regional levels. This may be amplified by a further element, that of *technocracy*: numerous studies of the Union highlight the central role of non-elected officials in the decision-making process, thereby leading some analysts to conclude that the Union is becoming a closed and self-contained bureaucratic juggernaut (Siedentop 2000). A much-cited example is that of having recourse to the complex system of 'comitology'.[4] This is often presented as a case of extreme *reversal* of the circuit of power (Weiler 1999). From this perspective, the Union's neo-liberal market orientation combines with technocracy and executive dominance to 'feudalise' the public sphere within the multi-level EU system.

Others see the Union less as a creature in the hands of the member states and more as a political system *sui generis*, whose distinguishing trait is its inordinate complexity. Besides being culturally, linguistically, ethnically and socially diverse, the EU is marked by great institutional discrepancies in member states' size and working. It has been labelled a multi-level[5] and poly-centric entity. Poly-centric governance is 'an arrangement for making binding decisions over a multiplicity of actors that delegates authority of functional tasks to a set of dispersed and relatively autonomous agencies that are not controlled – *de jure or de facto* – by a single collective institution' (Schmitter and Kim 2005: 6). Whether the EU fully complies with this designation is a matter of considerable debate. But, however we define it, the precise implications for the public sphere of institutional diversity and of politico-cultural complexity are still not well enough understood.

Cultural diversity adds to this. The EU has not so far produced a collective identity; nor can it draw on the shared norms and values that communitarians find necessary to sustain a community. In communal terms, the EU may be understood less as a coherent community and more as a Union of deep diversity (Fossum 2004). Deep diversity refers to a situation in which a 'plurality of ways of belonging [are] acknowledged and accepted' (Taylor 1993: 183) within the same entity. The EU acknowledges and accepts forms of diversity politically, legally and even constitutionally. However, there is no overarching agreement on *what the Union is for*. This uncertainty and indeterminacy also colours the processes of opinion and will formation within the EU, as the system constantly addresses different collective goals and has to try to accommodate these.

This reading of the EU – as a site of identity struggles – is in tension with the formation of an overarching public sphere. The French and Dutch refusals to ratify the Constitution sent a shock wave throughout the political classes of the Union. The fight now concerns how to define the future of the project. At stake are the relationships between the states and the Union and the economic and social model that is to prevail.

The referenda results have, for the moment, placed a third group of scholars, whom we might label the federalists,[6] on the defensive. They note that the Union has taken measures to rectify some of the defects listed above, with direct implications for the public sphere. For instance, the EU has established a permanent strong public in the shape of the European Parliament (EP); and it has also increasingly relied on other fora, such as conventions, in the process of constitution-making. Over time, the Union has developed civil, political, social, cultural and economic rights that have strengthened citizens' private and public autonomy at the *European* level. The Union has also taken measures to increase transparency, to include citizens more directly in its decisions, and to strengthen the interaction of strong and weak publics within the European framework. These developments help to shape the character of the circuit of power within the multi-level Union.

A number of studies now underline the role of communicative action within the politico-administrative system of the EU. This body of work is generally labelled 'deliberative supranationalism' and raises questions about the relevance of the distinction between 'system' and 'lifeworld'. If communicative action also permeates the system world, what are the public-sphere implications, if any, of such developments?

The temptation of 'methodological nationalism'

The diverse accounts of the Union listed above continue to provoke debate about what type of entity it is. How similar is the EU to the nation state? Ulrich Beck (2003: 454ff.) notes that our assessments are easily distorted by what he calls the hegemonic role of 'methodological nationalism'. Methodological nationalism makes the normative assumption that every nation has a right to self-determination within the frame of its own cultural distinctiveness.

> [Methodological nationalism] assumes this normative claim as a socio-ontological given and simultaneously links it to the most important conflict and organisation orientation of society and politics. These basic tenets have become the main perceptual grid of social science. Indeed, the social-scientific stance is rooted in the concept of nation state. A nation state outlook on society and politics, law and justice and history governs the sociological imagination. To some extent, much of social science is a prisoner of the nation state.
>
> (Beck 2003: 454)

The EU clearly forces us to go beyond the nation state in our search for appropriate conceptual categories. But if we abandon the vocabulary of the national entirely, as Beck seems to suggest, what are we left with? An international order based on the state system still offers a necessary and indispensable point of departure for contemporary political thought. The question is how to recognise this and at the same time not to ignore the relevance of the call to think beyond the national level. The task, in our view, is to *expand and modify* our established political vocabulary rather than to assume that it has completely lost its usefulness. It is in this spirit that we present two distinctive ways of conceiving the EU. Each presupposes the existence of the nation state and therefore stands in a conceptual relation to it. But, at the same time, the conceptualised objects are *not* nation states but are quite different in scope. This is not simply a definitional exercise. Rather, it reflects our attempt to grasp the complex nature of the EU as a distinctive political configuration.

Behind our proposal of the two models that follow is our wish to underline the liminal status of the EU – its unresolved, in-between character. It is precisely this transitional and undecided state of affairs that is so productive of debate, along with the theoretical attempts to grapple with what kind of emergent entity the EU is, that we have already touched on.

The first model we label the 'regulatory', as it conceives of the EU largely as a framework of *transnational governance* made up of a range of specialist agencies and regulatory bodies. This kind of entity takes on board, and compensates for, the declining problem-solving ability of each 'sovereign' member state.

The second model we label the 'federal', as it conceives of the EU as a political community based on citizens' mutual acknowledgement of rights and duties. From this perspective, the Union forms the *supranational level of government* in Europe. Such an entity has a set of overlapping weak publics, rooted in diverse legal–institutional arrangements and supported by a range of strong publics.[7]

Each of these perspectives on the EU entails a conception of a public sphere that differs greatly from that associated with the nation state, namely as *relatively* monolithic, self-contained and closed. The Union is neither a state, nor a nation; and, as current developments underline, it is still on the road to an undisclosed destination. This is precisely the point of identifying the regulatory and federal models. Whatever public sphere we might foresee developing in the EU, this will not necessarily be structured on the model of the modern nation state. The first model is based on de-centred, sectoral publics; the second on overlapping strong and weak publics. And we cannot exclude the possibility of a third model evolving, in which there is a thoroughgoing transformation of the public sphere, in ways yet to be defined.

A regulatory EU?

Polity

The first model is that of the EU as a regulatory entity engaged in problem-solving.[8] This type of organisation is based on an economic–utilitarian mode of thinking. From this standpoint, the EU is best conceived of as a functional type of organisation whose purpose is to promote the material interests of the member states by means of transnational rather than supranational institutions.[9] This comes close to the idea of 'network governance' and links to the idea of the EU largely as an issue-based epistemic community.[10] In this connection, Joshua Cohen and Charles Sabel (1997, 2003) view the EU as having developed a *transnational* deliberative model of democracy, which permits a flexible system of local problem-solving. In this system, the units are linked together through institutionalised discussion; they learn from each other and also seek to improve their learning through institutional reform. Although their reach is transnational, the EU's epistemic communities are served by what are still largely nationally oriented media systems. The dense Euro-communicative spaces of the expert circles in the world of policy-making and debate are not matched by communicative spaces that extend to a wider European public. One of the key reasons for this has to do with the prevalent patterns of mediated communication, a theme addressed at length in this book.

Our regulatory model envisages the multi-level EU as only *partially* transnational. At the level of the Union, a network-based, transnational configuration has evolved above still well-entrenched states.

Democratic legitimacy

The regulatory EU derives its democratic aspect from the practices of the member states. This accords with Robert Dahl's (1999) view that beyond a certain scale, *representative* democracy cannot work. To extend representative democracy to the European level stretches democratic legitimation to such an extent that it may intensify citizens' alienation from the system. The EU's own legitimacy becomes based on its performance. Legitimation is conditional. Support is withdrawn whenever public expectations are not met.

Public sphere

In institutional terms, the regulatory model depicts the EU as a transnational entity with a criss-crossing network of related issue-oriented – and relatively self-contained – epistemic communities. These are involved in practical problem-solving and do not constitute an overarching European public in democratic terms. They tend to be narrowly confined issue communities. They do not constitute weak publics but are considered as groupings that are much more restricted and exclusive in scope.

The foundation in rights of such a regulatory EU is weak, as there is no fully developed supranational level with an independent rights-granting capacity. Citizens have the right to freedom of movement and the right to work, but they are accorded their political rights at the national level and it is from the nation state that they also derive their key collective identities.

The regulatory model of the EU does not correspond well to the distinction made between strong and weak publics in our earlier discussion. The polarity between weak and strong relates to different degrees of institutionalisation. The underlying idea is of a direct vertical relation between an institutional structure (understood as a system of government) and its social constituency.[11] However, this does not easily map onto a complex structure such as the EU, made up – as it is – of member states, each of which has its own well-established historical–institutional relations between strong and weak publics. The member states tend to a relative closure of their political space by way of maintaining national vernaculars, through strong patterns of socialisation, and by way of the deeply entrenched 'channels and sluices' (to use the Habermasian image) between weak and strong publics within their territorial boundaries.

The regulatory model posits an EU made up of distinct political spaces, each of which first and foremost addresses its national citizens. This model is also based on relatively weak central institutions, whose commitment to democratic decision-making, transparency and publicity is often equivocal. It is furthermore assumed that there are no EU-wide institutions able to properly counteract the continuing pull of territorial particularity. Much transnational communication is conducted in relatively closed fora, with limited public engagement across the entire EU territory.

We have sought to capture this territorially bounded publicness, shaped and dominated by the workings of the nation state, by labelling such formations *particular* publics. By contrast, *general* publics are open and extensive, in the sense that they may include all citizens across the entire territory of the EU.

The distinction between particular and general publics pertains first and foremost to the territorial dimension of political life, but it can also refer to sectoral or issue-specific concerns. However, while specific issues, themes and agendas may be articulated across the entire territory of the EU, these do (on the evidence) tend to be refracted in terms comprehensible to particular (i.e. national) publics.[12]

The regulatory model certainly does not exclude the possibility that there may be transnational communication that covers the entire EU territory. However, this is more likely than not to address particular publics, and the extent to which it does so is closely linked to systems of mediated communication that privilege national (particular) modes of address and that address publics overwhelmingly constituted within national public spheres.

What we therefore propose, as one way of developing the debate on the prospects for a European public sphere, is that the concept of the 'public' be discussed along three dimensions: institutional, territorial and issue-oriented.

To sum up, the regulatory model designates a European public sphere that is nationally segmented, in which transnational communication with an EU-wide reach tends to be issue-specific, and is therefore limited to particular topics. This conception of a European public sphere has little obvious capacity to challenge the Union's democratic shortcomings or to generate an overarching public sphere.

A federal EU?

Polity

The second conception of the EU proposed here is that of a rights-based federal Union, based on the core tenets of the democratic constitutional state. The assumption is that the EU will embody these, but with a *post-national* rather than a national vocation and identity. Hence, a wide range of public opinion will be mobilised to influence decision makers and thereby ensure the democratic legitimacy of their actions. This democratic pressure is seen as deriving from broad public debate (European as well as non-European), transnational movements, (I)NGOs, and supranational and international bodies tasked with norm enforcement. Decision makers face the people who are constituted as rights holders cognisant of their entitlements and obligations. In this guise, the public may seek to compel decision makers to pay attention to popular opinion in order for the EU to secure its legitimacy.

Democratic legitimacy

The federal model envisages the EU as a constitutional democracy. A democratic constitutional order claims to be binding on all subjects and to be accepted by the various groups within society, each with its particular and distinctive identity and value. 'Federal' entails complex co-existence, in the sense that certain tasks are carried out jointly, and others singly, in accordance with each subunit's discretion. Federalism both acknowledges and *protects* difference and diversity. At the same time it presumes a measure of comity, generally associated with the 'federal spirit'.

Such a spirit cannot be relied on to ensure cultural integration. For such a society to hang together it will have to rely on political integration, which is necessary to cope with socio-cultural difference and to ensure collective decision-making. To operate democratically, such a society must respect democracy, difference, pluralism, human rights and vulnerable identities.

Constitutional democracy assumes a conception of society that is based on the rule of law. Different groups may continue to live together and resolve conflicts only because they agree on the basic rules and procedures that claim to secure fair treatment for all parties. Only through law is it possible, legitimately, to secure solidarity with strangers in modern pluralist societies (Habermas 1996b: 1544).

The federal model posits democracy and human rights not solely as representative of cultural traditions and shared meanings but also as manifestations of cognitive–moral principles that command respect in and of themselves. They are accessible for rational appraisal and agreement and can be defended and vindicated in rational debate. Such an appraisal assumes that constitutionally entrenched rights will guarantee the freedom of the individual. In addition, the principle of a written constitution, the separation of powers and judicial review impose restrictions on 'the will of the people' and contribute to protecting the *private autonomy* of citizens. Taken together, these measures are necessary for the formation of authentic private opinions.

Democracy presupposes a collective that is made up of equals; it also presupposes that the addressees of the law can participate in the making of the law. Political rights, ranging from freedom of speech and assembly to eligibility and voting rights – and their attendant institutions and procedures – provide citizens with access to public deliberation, collective decision-making and law-making; hence, these contribute to the *public autonomy* of the individual.

The federalists' assumption is that public support will reside in a *constitutional patriotism* (Habermas 1998, 2004), which derives from a set of legally entrenched fundamental rights and democratic procedures, but which also may act as a focal point for political affect and identification. In practice, this should be the outcome of a mutually supportive process. From this standpoint, constitution-making should advance so as to establish an EU citizenship based on entrenched political rights, reformed and transparent decision-making procedures, and clearer divisions of competence – vertically between the EU institutions and the member states, and horizontally among the EU institutions themselves.

Public sphere

A federal conception of the EU does not conceive of the public sphere in monolithic terms, but rather as a set of *overlapping* publics. We should note the importance of strong *and* weak publics, both of which are necessary prerequisites to the proper functioning of the federal model.

Strong publics – such as parliaments – are essential components of democracy because they are tasked to ensure popular representation and executive accountability. Applied to the present-day EU, this model presupposes considerable institutional change, mainly – not exclusively – at the EU level. The EU level would require further parliamentarisation, so that the EP would become a fully fledged parliament and the Council would become a 'second' chamber and co-legislator with the EP. Other institutional measures (in a multitude of increasingly convergent public spheres) might include the use of optional referenda and practices aimed at amplifying the role and scope of public deliberation and the critical scrutiny of decision makers. Such measures would aim to compensate for the enormous institutional complexity and diversity at the national and regional level.

These institutional arrangements depend on the external pressure of weak publics rooted in the wider civil society. Without such pressure, they would atrophy, succumb to co-optation or fall privy to the colonising impetus of instrumental rationality. The federal model thus conceived has the potential to foster a general European public sphere, although this is likely to be constituted as a complexly articulated set of particular communicative spaces whose precise interrelations remain undetermined.

The federal model draws our attention to how the distinction between strong and weak publics operates in a complex, multi-jurisdictional territorial setting. In principle, the EU addresses *general* publics either in areas of federal jurisdiction or where jurisdictions are shared. However, the EU's communications are routinely inflected towards *particular* publics when dealing with matters over which the sub-units (member states and regions) exercise jurisdiction. The potential for constituting a *general* public, therefore, will depend on a host of factors – both institutional and non-institutional.

The federal model, precisely because of its multicultural composition and reliance on political institutions, sees the EU's foundation and its boundaries within a wider cosmopolitan framework. The development of the EU is connected to, and highly dependent on, the support and further development of similar regional associations in the rest of the world, and on a democratised and rights-enforcing UN.

A regulatory versus a federal future?

In this introduction, we have used the two models elucidated above to dramatise the possible alternative futures for a public sphere in the EU. Neither model assumes that the EU will simply reproduce – on a larger scale – a public sphere like that of the nation state. If the EU continues to develop along confined regulatory lines, the prospects for the emergence of a general public sphere look slim indeed. If the EU takes a further federalist turn, the development of a general public sphere is more likely, though not without difficulties that are explored in the chapters that follow.

The two approaches outlined above have shaped the lines of inquiry pursued here: first, into the workings of core political institutions, and second, into the interplay between the institutions and various kinds of public in the EU.

Publics may be thought of as located on three axes: that of institutional scale, that of territorial scope and that of issue specificity (see Figure 1.2).

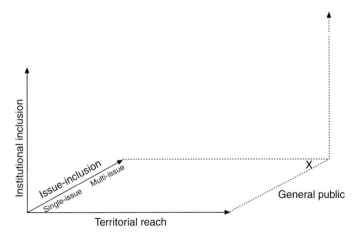

Figure 1.2 Dimensions of the public sphere.

The institutional axis addresses the extent to which an actor may be institutionally enabled, induced or compelled to participate in the activities of a public. The institutional axis runs from low to high degrees of enabling, inducement or compulsion. The territorial axis establishes the spatial reach of the public addressed. This ranges from the general to the particular. That is, it may embrace all citizens in the EU (or beyond) or simply be limited to quite narrowly defined groupings. The third, issue-specific axis ranges across the number of issues attracting public attention and deliberation, from single-issue to many-issue politics. A single-issue focus connects to a particular public, because – by definition – it is highly focused in scope. All three axes intersect, as we show in the three-dimensional Figure 1.2.

Our two models occupy distinctive locations in this three-dimensional space. For simplicity's sake, in Figure 1.3, we have provided an illustration of some of the different conceptions of the public sphere used in this book, presented in a simplified two-dimensional figure, which highlights the territorial and institutional dimensions only.

Within the European setting, the respective end points on the horizontal (territorial axis) are the *national* and *federal* models. The *national* case posits that strong publics are located only at the far left-hand side of the territorial axis, as the European political scene is made up of particular, nationally bounded, publics. The *federal* model, by contrast, positions strong publics on the right-hand side of the territorial axis. Under such conditions, institutionally weak publics, because of their expanded scope, may be transformed into general publics.

Figure 1.3 reveals how difficult it is to precisely locate the *regulatory* model within a distinctive institutional–territorial location. A regulatory system may contain representative bodies at the European level, but these would not be strong publics proper in the sense of being formally representative of, and directly accountable to, the EU's citizens. A regulatory system is best

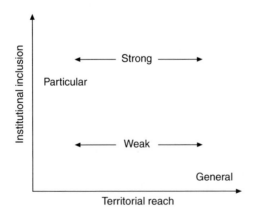

Figure 1.3 Territorial and institutional dimensions.

understood as based on particular publics, either focused on single issues or made up of epistemic (expert) communities.

The remainder of this book is structured into three parts, which elaborate on the questions and themes presented in this introduction. Part I contains chapters that theorise a range of communicative practices and their relation to the public sphere. The chapters in Part II address the workings of specific institutions and what these imply for the creation of a European public sphere. And, in Part III, we have included chapters that discuss how various publics relate to the EU's institutions, with particular consideration given to the role of mediated communication. A concluding chapter brings together some of the main findings of this book and ties these in with the framework elaborated above.

Notes

1 Habermas's classic treatise took the *nation state* as political community as its foundation and point of departure (Schlesinger and Kevin 2000: 208). We are aware that the term 'nation state' is contentious, not least for those living in multinational states. We use it here as a well understood, if imperfect, label of convenience.
2 Parts of this section draw on Eriksen and Fossum (2002).
3 Despite the fact that Habermas (1992a: 430) himself now acknowledges – in response to critics – that he may have exaggerated the magnitude of this decline.
4 Most EU regulation is not enacted as legislation by the Council and Parliament but as implementation measures under the executive duties of the Commission. The pertinent committee procedures are commonly referred to as 'comitology'. See 'Commission proposes reform of comitology procedures', Euractiv.com, 13 December 2002, available at www.euractiv.com/en/governance/commission-proposes-reform-comitology-procedures/article-113831 (accessed 13 September 2006); and Joerges and Vos (1999).
5 See Hooghe and Marks (2003: 237) on multi-level governance.
6 Note that federalism does not presuppose a state. Daniel Elazar (1987: 230) has observed that 'the federal idea and its applications offer a comprehensive alternative to the idea of a reified sovereign state and its applications'.
7 For broader discussions of EU models, see Fossum 2000, Eriksen and Fossum 2004.
8 There is a large body of research on the EU as a regulatory-type entity. See, for instance, Majone 1996.
9 Other analysts have referred to this as a 'special purpose association of functional integration' (Ipsen 1972).
10 Holzner and Marx (1979: 108) define epistemic communities as 'those knowledge-oriented work communities in which cultural standards and social arrangements interpenetrate around a primary commitment to epistemic criteria in knowledge production and application'.
11 A 'social constituency' can be understood as 'people being involved in and being served by an organization (or system of governance) and that this relation has a social reference and social resonance of some sort' (Fossum and Trenz 2006: 58).
12 This issue is addressed by Philip Schlesinger in Chapter 4.

Part I

Communicative practices and a European public sphere

Philip Schlesinger and John Erik Fossum

Has contemporary thinking about the European public sphere been too constrained by the model of the nation state? Of course, it still remains an inescapable starting point. However, the European Union is an emergent transnational space. Therefore, for two obvious reasons, to conceptualise the European public sphere we cannot simply transpose the standard nation-state conception to the European level. First, as shown in the introduction, there are several – not only one – plausible ways of conceiving of the present-day EU. The larger issue is that there is no clear and unambiguous template for this type of system. Second, the EU is still very much a system in the making whose territorial reach, political impact and normative sanction we still cannot determine with great confidence.

This has a number of implications. First, we need a complex conception of the components of the European public sphere and how these might variously impact on broadening deliberation. As outlined in Chapter 1, a variety of publics is in play: strong and weak, general and particular. What is the scope for such publics to participate in the creation of a common European communicative space? These issues are addressed in Erik O. Eriksen's chapter. Second, could it be argued that despite the shortcomings of the EU's democratic order its evolution as a post-national constellation (to use Habermas's phrase) is compelling new ways of learning about collective, transnational endeavour and that these are setting in train a process of democratisation? Given the open-endedness of this, it might also be useful to consider conditions that may obstruct the formation of a European public sphere. Klaus Eder's chapter pays explicit attention to these issues.

Given that a viable public sphere is such a central precondition for a functioning democracy, the character of the European public sphere relates directly to the question of the 'democratic deficit' in the EU. Much debate about this has begun from expectations about how democracy ought to function at the level of the nation state and has been transposed to the supranational institutions of the Union. This move opens space for a critique of how the core institutions are lacking, to varying degrees, in accountability and transparency. A connected argument concerns the relationship between the institutions and the people. Despite the fact that there is a quadrennial EU-wide election process, this does not equate to those that take place in general elections in the member states. The electorate is differently positioned, notably because – in effect – it sends national delegations (divided by party and territorial origin) to the European Parliament and because ideas of a European citizenship (and identity) are not uniformly embraced across the Union.

The process of integration has taken place within a system bereft of major physical means of coercion and without a distinctive collective identity at its disposal for ensuring compliance and cohesion. This represents a theoretical challenge. Arguably, communication may be accorded a more significant role in the forging of European integration than was the case in state formation. Analysts have therefore been looking outside the main representative institutions for the democratising potential of communicative processes.

Such processes are central to democratic debate and development. All the authors in Part I lay considerable stress both on the conditions that best conduce to open discussion and criticism in the public domain and on the role of mediated communication in shaping the wider political culture. Is the 'Europeanisation' of both publics and mediated communication conducing to an emergent cosmopolitanism? How might this be assessed in comparison with the continuing robustness of the national public sphere? These questions are considered in Philip Schlesinger's chapter.

2 Conceptualising European public spheres

General, segmented and strong publics

Erik Oddvar Eriksen

Introduction

In its widest sense, the public sphere is the social room that is created when individuals deliberate on common concerns. It depicts a relationship between the speakers and the audience that is created by social actors experiencing the by-products of cooperation, which in turn prompts the inclusion of affected parties.

The European Union's development as a new kind of polity is closely connected to its development as a communicative space. Traditionally, political theory and media theory have thought of communicative space and public spheres as what goes on inside nation states. But this kind of perspective is rapidly becoming deficient, as the EU manifests more and more the characteristics of a supranational polity. Furthermore, regionalism and nationalism at the sub-state level are leading to the creation of more distinctive spaces below the state level. The upshot is a fragmentation and differentiation of national publics. How are we to conceptualise the public sphere in sites beyond (and below) the nation state? Is it merely a communicative space or can it develop into a democratic sovereign – a collective entity able to act?

The public sphere is a precondition for the realisation of popular sovereignty, because, in principle, it entitles everybody to speak without any limitation, whether on themes, participation, questions, time or resources. The idea of a public sphere provides the sort of deliberative arrangement that fits the requirement of discourse theory, namely that a norm is deemed legitimate only when all affected have accepted it *in a free and rational debate*. A deliberative public sphere has problem-solving functions as it increases the level of information and understanding between co-operators, but more importantly, it is a sphere of political justification intrinsic to democracy.

The main problem with the development of a European public sphere is held to be the lack of a cultural substrate required for collective will formation. The forging of a collective identity, so to speak, presupposes certain social underpinnings presently lacking in the EU. Can there be a public sphere without a collective identity? A collective identity above the level of primary groups and a collective we-feeling are needed in order for the EU citizens to acknowledge the 'sacrifices' imposed in the name of the European collective good (Scharpf 1999). At a minimum, the members must recognise each other as being members of the same group. According to Bernhard Peters (1993: 117), collective identities do not merely depict the successful integration of a social entity, but also, and specifically, 'social communities based on defined member-ship and a shared collective self-conception, shared convictions and aspirations'.

The second question to be addressed picks up on the epistemic value of deliberation and its putative democratic quality. The epistemic interpreta-tion of deliberative democracy holds that deliberation is a cognitive process for the assessment of reasons, in order to reach just decisions and establish conceptions of the common good. But can such a variant of public deliberation be sustained in normative terms or does it merely amount to 'governance without democracy'? What kind of notion of the EU polity does this concept of the public sphere speak to – the EU as a regulatory, problem-solving entity or a democratic government? I start by addressing Jürgen Habermas's seminal work on the public sphere and focus on the public sphere as a normative category. Thereafter, I examine the prevalence of a European public sphere, the communicative space of Europe, and distinguish between a *general public sphere, transnational seg-mented publics* and *strong publics*. The last part contains a discussion of the trust put into network governance based on transnational publics – delib-erative governance – from a democratic point of view.

Conceptualising the public sphere

The public sphere is the place where civil society is linked to the power structure of the state. It is 'the informally mobilized body of nongovern-mental discursive opinion that can serve as a counterweight to the state' (Fraser 1992: 134). Habermas is the founding father of the most influ-ential concept of the public sphere.[1]

The norm-generating power of reflective argument

The notion of a 'public sphere' signifies that equal citizens assemble into a public and set their own agenda through open communication. Histori-cally speaking, the citizens immediately lay claim to this public sphere through confrontations with public authorities over the general rules of coexistence in the fundamentally privatised, but publicly relevant sphere for exchange of goods and societal work. The medium for this political confrontation is remarkable and without historical precedent: public rea-soning (Habermas 1989: 27). The public sphere that sprang forth in

British coffee houses from 1680 to 1730 – and correspondingly in drawing rooms and clubs in France – was first literary, then political.

The essence of the modern public sphere is *rational* debate. There are no elevated dogmas to be protected or a meta-standard according to which conflicts can be resolved. In this type of public sphere, actors have to seek support on a broad basis and across established convictions, religions and status hierarchies. The modern concept of a public sphere is larger and wider than one formed on a particular ethical basis, i.e. that of the state or the Church. It spread to all of civilized Europe (Taylor 1995: 266). It became possible to appeal to a public that was greater than the nation state. In this sense, the public sphere predates the modern state.

In conceptual terms, the public sphere is non-coercive, secular and rational. It is established through freedom rights – political and civil liberties – that provide citizens with protections from state incursions and with the right to speak freely. Further, the modern public sphere is founded on rational debate and is antithetical to coercion and dogmatic modes of conflict settlement. This idea of the public sphere is, then, closely linked to the principle of universalistic argumentation. The discussion can go on indefinitely, and the participants can address an indefinite circle of interlocutors, who are scattered in time and space. The public sphere is reflexive; it is a sphere in which 'society' thematises itself.

The development of a public sphere has profound implications for the conception of democratic legitimacy.[2] It alters the power holders' basis of legitimacy, as citizens are equipped with rights against the state. Decision makers are compelled to enter the public arena in order to justify their decisions and to gain support. They cannot allow themselves merely to pose for the masses, as the Emperors in the ancient world did (and some tyrants have tried in recent times). This forms the background to speaking of a modern public sphere that is critical of power. There are no external bodies that guarantee the legitimacy of power – neither divine law nor traditional authority. Authority is established through public discussion. Legitimacy consequently becomes not only precarious, but also a critical resource – something 'outside of the reach of individuals'. We see a transition from the speech of power to *the power of speech* (Lefort 1988: 38). It is neither a given set of institutions nor concrete persons that guarantee the legitimacy of the law. Only public debate in itself has norm-giving power. Hence, democracy has become the sole legitimation principle of government in modern, post-conventional societies based on an inclusive public sphere, entitling everyone affected to take part in deliberation on common affairs.

One may, however, ask whether this depends upon the institutionalisation of one overarching, unifying public sphere. Historically, a single authoritative public sphere, representing one collective identity has never existed. There were many and they were stratified. The dominance of high culture and the *Bildungs-Bürgerschaft* (or *Gelehrtenöffentlichkeit*) were successively challenged by the lower classes and popular publics. The contention between elitist (high culture) and popular (plebeian) publics was manageable because of the existence of a well-developed collective identity – a prevailing value consensus (Giesen 1999; Eder and Giesen 2001; Eder 2003a). The process of fragmentation and dissolution of given identities based on, for example, nation, religion, class and ethnicity has been due to the processes of globalisation and Europeanisation.

A complex public sphere

According to Habermas's revised theory, the public sphere is a common space in society, but it is a space presently divided into different types and categories (1996a: 373ff.). It consists of different assemblies, forums, arenas, scenes and meeting places where the citizens can gather. Today the public sphere is a highly complex network of *public sphere segments*, which stretches across different levels, spaces and scales. There are subaltern public spheres – municipal, regional, national and transnational. There are different arenas, where elite and mass, professionals and lay people, prophets and critics can meet and cooperate with various degrees of intensity and passion. The public sphere extends from episodic café and street gatherings, via organised professional, cultural and artistic public spheres, to abstract public spheres, where listeners, readers and viewers are isolated and spread in time and space. There are strictly situated public spheres, where the participants meet face to face; there are written public spheres, and there are anonymous, faceless, public spheres made possible by the new electronic technologies.

Habermas thus adjusts to the critique that his early, 'bourgeois' concept of a public sphere involved a fixed, ontological distinction between res publica and res privata – between the common good and special interests respectively.[3] Further, the criticism has been that the original use of the concept involved *one* uniform and national public sphere, and that the increasing division and duplication of the public sphere which followed in the twentieth century (for example, as represented by the labour and feminist movements) consequently had to be regarded as a decline and not as a contribution to the democratisation of society. Already, in the early modern period of Europe, the *Vielstimmigkeit* (multivocality) of the popular publics and the level of contention are striking (Tilly 1986; Eder 2003a: 92). This is even more so in well-developed *modern societies*, characterised by dominant discourses, worldviews and established forms of understanding coming under pressure, and where more unconstrained patterns of communication emerge. New forms of communication develop; new discourses emerge and are in constant flux and contestation. The public sphere has become polymorphous, polyphonic and even anarchistic. Today, according to Habermas, it forms '*einen wilden Komplex*', which is vulnerable to perversions and communication disturbances. On the other hand, this open public sphere is a medium for *unlimited* communication, and is hence sensitive to social pathologies. However, the question is whether this variety of public spheres, which creates different identities, does not also disrupt and fragment the political community, that is, lapse into 'identity politics': the disruptive effect of groups demanding recognition for their difference. How is order possible in this cacophonic symphony?

One should note that there are different kinds of publics with different functions. While anonymous mass publics or *silent publics*, according to Klaus Eder, are conducive to merely a statistical aggregation of preferences, *speaking publics* may be able to integrate opinions and form a collective will. The first subverts established orders through *scandals*, whereas the latter organises morally motivated *campaigns* (Eder 2003a: 104).

Antenna and sluice

The public sphere is 'a communication structure rooted in the lifeworld through the associational network of civil society' (Habermas 1996a: 359). *Civil society* is a common space for free communication secured by legal rights to freedom of expression and assembly, where problems are not only discovered, but also thematised and dramatised and formed into opinions and wills acted upon by formal decision-making agencies. The public sphere 'sluices' new problems into the political system. In Gramscian terms, *it besieges the parliamentary system without conquering it.*

Bernard Peters models the circulation of political power upon a centre-periphery scheme (1993: 327ff.). The parliamentary nexus consists of formal political institutions, such as the parliament, political parties and different types of bodies that influence choices and decision-making – such as expert committees, boards and councils including neo-corporativist arrangements. It makes up the *centre*, with the authority to take binding collective decisions, and is the focus of attention and enjoys the highest degree of legitimacy. It is connected to the periphery of civil society – consisting of associations, social movements, pressure groups, clients, organised interests, non-governmental organisations (NGOs), etc. – through a set of channels of political influence such as elections, neo-corporatist lobbying, interest aggregation and public debate. For collective decisions to be regarded as legitimate, it must be demonstrated that they started with a communication process originating in the periphery – in non-distorted areas of civil society – and were channelled into the formal power apparatus in a procedurally correct manner (Habermas 1996a: 356). While the centre controls instruments of power and decision-making competence, the public sphere is the only possible channel of influence for the periphery. It lacks formal instruments of power, it does not make decisions, and it does not address all aspects of a problem.

However, if we look at the public sphere in a longer time perspective, we are struck by its positive role as a *sensitive sensor* or antenna vis-à-vis new questions and problems visualised and verbalised by civil society organisations and social movements.[4] Neither détente politics, minority rights nor third-world problems were taken up by the established system. Instead, they were advocated by the new social movements and their extra-parliamentary actions (Dalton and Kuechler 1990; Offe 1990). To explain this ability to influence politics, we must see the public sphere not merely as a 'warning system' with sensors (Habermas 1996a: 359). This points us to *strong publics*: institutionalised deliberation close to the centre of the political system that is legally regulated, that is, sites in which there is a requirement to provide justification and a stronger regulation of discourses. Nancy Fraser (1992) distinguishes between *weak* and *strong* public spheres. The latter concept alludes to parliamentary assemblies and discursive bodies in formal institutions that have obtained decision-making power, while the concept of weak public spheres signifies deliberation outside the political system. For the latter, I prefer the term *general public sphere* because it entails free and open access to opinion-formation processes, and has in many instances proven to be both 'strong' and powerful, as in revolutionary situations, constitutional moments and when bare public opinion has forced corrupt leaders out of office. Will formation and decision-making, as opposed to mere opinion formation, are reserved for institutionalised discourses in the political system. Such bodies transform the influence of civil society and the general public sphere into *communicative power* and this in turn serves to justify political decisions in parliament. Parliaments are quintessential strong publics, but there are also others. Historically, strong publics have existed within the nation state, but now, especially since the Second World War and the establishment of the United Nations, there are also transnational strong publics, such as panels, tribunals, committees and conventions (Brunkhorst 2002).

The discourse-theoretical proceduralisation of popular sovereignty not only makes a conceptual space for a distinction between general and strong publics, but also makes visible transnational communicative spaces; spheres above and between the nation states in which the actors affected can reason about common affairs but where access is limited. These can be seen as *nascent general publics*. However, the problem of collective identity, which is seen as intrinsic to the democratic deficit, lingers.

A European public sphere?

The EU in its present form is held to suffer from a democratic deficit due to a weak parliament, the absence of European-wide parties and the absence of a European public sphere based on a symbolically constructed people. It can only be indirectly legitimated, through the member states.

The rights and procedures in place do not suffice to ensure a proper hearing for the voices of the citizens.

Collective identity and the public sphere

Fritz Scharpf (1999: 187, 1994: 220) maintains that the EU has to overcome 'the triple deficits of the lack of a pre-existing sense of collective identity, the lack of a Europe-wide policy discourse, the lack of a Europe-wide institutional infrastructure that could assure the political accountability of office holders to a European constituency'. As there is a lack of collective identity, the prospect for a viable European public sphere is rather bleak. There is no agreement on common interests or values, and different languages and disparate national cultures make opinion formation and coherent action unlikely. The intermediate structures of civil society in the form of a Europeanised party system, European organisations, social movements and European media are lacking as is a common language making possible a transnational binding debate (Grimm 2004). A common public debate – on the same themes and issues under the same criteria of relevance – is, thus, not achievable.

There is a communitarian underpinning to this kind of critique, as public debate is seen as something quite different from a discussion of private concerns, i.e. it appears as if a common will prevails from the outset. This view presupposes a homogeneous culture, a populace and a united people that come together in public spaces to deliberate and decide about common concerns. It pictures the public sphere as something rather distinct and stable, as a place where enlightened and equal citizens can assemble to discuss public matters and come to discover a shared pre-existing good. This is the concept of the *res publica* handed down from the Greeks, where citizens meet in the *agora* as friends and brothers to deliberate before decisions are reached in *ekklesia*, resurrected in medieval, Italian republicanism and in seventeenth century England, France and Germany. The Greek model of the public sphere, which for example Hannah Arendt (1958) makes use of, presupposes a homogeneous political community (Benhabib 1992: 90ff.). The formation of a *volonté générale* is seen as possible because citizens are equal and share common values and notions of the public interest. In cases of conflict, parties can reach an agreement on the basis of a hermeneutic interpretation of historic tradition and collective self-conception about who they are and who they would like to be, and then, develop into a collective subject – a nation – capable of action.

In this model, there is no distinction made between deliberation and decision-making, between opinion formation and will formation. This conceptualisation does not capture the way the modern public sphere is institutionalised in opposition to government, the manner in which it is situated in civil society and rendered possible by the fact that the citizens have rights that they are entitled to use against the state. Thus, this communitarian reading of the public sphere is one closely associated with the rise of nation-state democracies. The idea of a collective identity based on a common origin, heritage, language, memory or remembrance, goes together with the conception of citizenship-based government in which the sovereign people via law can form a collective will and rule themselves. The democratic sovereign is created in a public room in which the people lay down the law authoritatively and make it binding on every party to the same amount and degree. This republican view is also basic to discourse theory which, however, opposed to communitarian readings of republicanism, posits that a *post-national identity* is possible. It is based on a reading of the procedural nexus of the modern constitution and the continuing voluntary recognition and appreciation of this, which is conducive to the accommodation of difference and plurality, and a form of solidarity (also with strangers) that is founded on mutual respect. The underlying assumption, then, is that the lack of pre-political identification with the emerging political community can be recompensed by a public debate with catalytic effects on enlarged citizenship, solidarity and plural identities (Kleger 1998). Public debate is held to lead to opinion formation, the forging of a common identity on the basis of which collective decision-making can take place, namely an identity-shaping process strong enough to enable the solving of the collective action problem. But how 'thick' a collective identity is required?

A communicative network

The public sphere is constituted by *freedom of communication*, which makes the public use of reason possible. We should, however, conceive of the public sphere not as an institution or as an entity unto itself, existing prior to decision-making bodies, i.e. as a place where 'the people' come together and deliberate upon who they are or would like to be, and then form a collective will of 'the nation' or 'the class'. The public sphere should also not be seen as existing prior to, or independent of, decision-making agencies but as emerging in opposition to them – as a vehicle to test the legitimacy of legal provisions and as a counterweight to governmental power. This view of the emergence of the public sphere is based on the contention that the state originated, more or less, through war or brute force. All democracies have non-democratic roots (Offe 1998: 116).[5] Only subsequently was state authority subjected to the rule of law and democratised. In brief, first came the state, then the nation and democracy. Collective identity, thus, has to be made rather than merely discovered.[6] It is from this assertion that the contention 'no European demos without a European democracy' is derived.

The public sphere is not an institution, but rather a *communication network*. This network of 'subject-less interaction' based on informal streams of communication is not aimed at achieving particular results. The public sphere is that social space which is created by communicatively acting operators who are bearers of opinions and interests. The public sphere is a forum where what happens is determined by what can be made generally understandable, interesting, believable, relevant and acceptable through the use of everyday language, subject only to the procedural constraints of discourse.

This is a very thin concept of the public sphere as it consists of actors united merely on the basis of dealing with the same topics and problems.[7] How can a collective opinion come about unless there is *one single public sphere* where people discuss the same issues, at the same time and with the same frames of interpretation, and unless certain commonalities are in place? In other words, how can a collection of actors be transformed into a group with a distinct collective identity capable of collective action unless there is a sense of common mission or vision? A certain minimum of unity and solidarity is necessary for actors to come together at all in public spaces to struggle for the realisation of collective goals and be prepared to take on new obligations, as well as being prepared to surrender some of their own sovereignty and possessions. Naturally, this 'cultural substrate' – the collective 'we' – can be created through inclusive processes of opinion formation and law-making. However it comes about, it is a precondition for collective action and redistributive measures to be undertaken in the name of all.

The symbolic establishment of a demos – a people – founded on a sense of unity and belonging, is a precondition for a democratic sovereign capable of regulatory as well as redistributive measures, for the people to obey the law out of duty as well as to pay for the misfortune of their compatriots. Such a 'culturalist substrate' depicting societal bonds is required for the formation of a collective identity strong enough to ensure that compatriots not only see themselves as members of a community based on liberty but also as one based on equality and solidarity. While the concept of the public sphere as a communicative network may be too thin, and although a single European space revolving on common concerns is needed for a general political debate on major European decisions, there is no reason to 'essentialise' it. Collective identities as well as nations are not natural entities but are constructed from the social categories that unite and divide people. Rather, what is needed is to see the public sphere as presupposing a certain dosage of solidarity along with norms of tolerance and respect making up a liberal-democratic culture that are conducive to a *reflexive identity*, i.e. a self-confident identity that also recognises *difference*.[8] Even though everyone is entitled to equal respect and concern, there is, in normative terms, a need to distinguish between what we owe each other as human beings – as citizens of the world – and what we owe each other as compatriots – as fellow citizens of the same polity.

One polity – many publics

There are many public spheres in modern states and they are not confined to national borders. There are subaltern counter publics and there are overarching publics transcending limitations of time and space made possible by new media technologies and audio-visual spaces. New forms of communication are evolving and citizens' involvement in public debate may rather be seen as voluntary and elective than obligatory and 'native'.

Conceptually, then, we may distinguish between three types of public, as outlined in Table 2.1:

* *overarching general publics*, which are communicative spaces of civil society in which all may participate on a free and equal basis and, due to proper rights entrenchment, can deliberate subject only to the constraints of reason;
* *transnational segmented publics*, which evolve around policy networks constituted by a selection of actors with a common interest in certain issues, problems and solutions;
* *strong publics*, which are legally institutionalised and regulated discourses specialised in collective will formation at the polity centre.

A general European public sphere?

A general public in Europe is not totally missing as there are new European audio-visual spaces – newspapers, television, Internet and English (maybe) as an eventually unavoidable first language – and new social movements and identity politics across borders. The multilingual TV-channel *EuroNews* operates on a large scale. In addition, the *Financial Times, International Herald Tribune, The Economist, BBC World, ARTE, European Voice, Deutsche Welle* (broadcasting in English) and *Le Monde Diplomatique* with editions in most major European languages – and certainly not least the Internet – create audio-visual spaces in Europe. Many of these efforts are market driven (Schlesinger 2003), but address the broad political and economic issues of the continent. Many NGOs, such as Attac, keep Internet pages in several languages and thus facilitate transnational European debate.[9] Some media operate as a motor for Europeanisation and the European debate is catching on (Trenz 2005a). In comparison with other actors – civil society actors, state and party organisations –

Table 2.1 Typology of public spheres

Type of public	Participation	Legitimacy basis	Function
General	Open	A sovereign demos	Opinion formation
Segmented	Restricted	Common interests	Problem-solving
Strong	Specialised	Delegated authority	Will formation

Ruud Koopmans and Barbara Pfetsch (2003: 30) find that the German quality newspapers 'emphasize the collective identities, norms and values that Europe should stand for'. There are also traits of a Europeanised public debate. The 'Haider affair' reveals that even though transnational events are still viewed through national lenses, they lead to common and simultaneous types of debates within the different national public spheres. There is, in other words, a Europeanisation of events (see Chapter 6). The same can be said about Joschka Fischer's famous speech in May 2000, which was widely reflected and commented upon by journalists in 12 newspapers of six EU member states that were studied (Trenz 2005b).[10] We should also not forget the large demonstrations that took place in all major European cities against the war in Iraq on 15 February 2003. Habermas and Derrida (2003) suggested this event was the birthday of a European public sphere. However, these demonstrations were world wide and universalistic principles are not confined to Europe.

Even though there are spaces for the creation of collective identity through a pan-European press and media and English as a lingua franca, these still fall short of meeting the criteria of a public sphere. There is a long way from the kind of debate and information dissemination currently taking place in Europe to the kind of committed public deliberation needed for collective opinion and will formation, namely the requirement of a general debate on identical topics and policy proposals under the same criteria of relevance throughout Europe, rendering collective decision-making possible on the basis of a broad mobilisation of public support effectively sluiced into the governmental complex by intermediate organisations and political parties. A general European public sphere required by a fully democratic government still remains latent.

Segmented publics

Common communicative systems of mass media facilitating real public debates conducive to collective will formation are to a large degree lacking at the European level. However, there are transnational public spheres emanating from the policy networks of the Union. Networks are joint problem sites based on common issue orientations and knowledge – so-called epistemic communities (Haas 1992). Such issue communities, constituted on the common interests of actors in certain issue areas, fluctuate, grow and shrink, sometimes in cycles. In Europe, networks of transnational regulation are conducive to a Europeanisation of policies and deliberative governance beyond the nation state (Zürn 1999; Burkard and Grande 2003).[11] Networks represent 'the *institutional software* for the reflective treatment of discourses' (Dryzek 1999: 35). They take the form of publics inasmuch as there is a coupling between the collective actors and the audience, in the sense that the actors not only communicate among themselves but are also heard by others. As far as communication can be heard by an 'undetermined audience' – a public – this takes the shape of *transnational resonance* (Trenz and Eder 2004: 8–9).[12] Scandals and campaigns are pertinent vehicles (Ebbinghausen and Neckel 1989).

Philip Schlesinger and Deirdre Kevin (2000: 219) testify to this kind of public-sphere formation by pointing to the prevalence of campaigns in the EU, such as the 'Citizens First' campaign on the four freedoms, 'the Building Europe Together' campaign prior to the 1996 Intergovernmental Conference (IGC), and the 'Euro' campaign. Hans-Jörg Trenz (2002a) demonstrates how European security discourses evolve and revolve on a European community of solidarity and are propelling human-rights discourses. *Scandals* and *campaigns* are the legitimating and de-legitimating functions of the silent and speaking publics respectively. The public-sphere effects of (the criticism of) Schengen, of the European campaigns against racism, of mad cow disease [bovine spongiform encephalopathy (BSE)], of the charges of corruption and fraud in the Santer Commission which developed into a scandal in the eyes of the public – resulting in the dismissal of the Commission in 1999 – are all examples of events creating transnational but segmented public spheres. These cases show that no one unifying form of discourse develops but rather discourses that vary according to the issue fields that reflect the institutional structure of the EU. The ability to manipulate or homogenise the European public discourse is rather limited. The bare suspicion of manipulation in fact leads to a delegitimising critique and is conducive to the broadening and pluralisation of public communication (Trenz 2002a: 193). Still, it is a form of elite communication where experts and the well-educated speak to one another and stage communicative noise and protest. It falls short of reaching the level of mass communication in a 'homogenised' political public sphere. But segmented publics also fall short of complying with the democratic proviso of openness and equal access.

The European public space is currently fragmented, differentiated and in flux. In the place of the sovereign people, there is the noise of anarchic and polyphonic communication. The public sphere, nevertheless, has effects on governance as it subjects the decision makers to protests and 'communicative noise' – '*kommunikativer Lärm*'. Such 'noise' can be anticipated and thus discipline decision makers *ex ante*.[13] The informal and unruly streams of communication that characterise the European public debate take place in scattered fora and arenas. From a democratic viewpoint, the lingering problem pertains to the lack of ability to form collective identities on an equal basis in order to facilitate collective decision-making as well as solving the (de facto) problem of holding the rulers to account. But what about the deliberative and democratic qualities of the *institutional 'hardware'* of the EU?

Strong publics in the EU

The EU is a highly complex institution with many points of access and sites for deliberation, negotiation and decision-making. It displays a conglomeration of organisational forms geared towards integrating policy fields and establishing consensus ranging from the hard-core decision-making units such as the Council, the European Parliament (EP), the Commission and the European Court of Justice (ECJ), via the nexus of adjacent committees – expert committees, Committee of Permanent Representatives (COREPER), Comitology, the Conference of Community and European Affairs Committees of Parliaments of the European Union (COSAC) – to the two Conventions on constitutional matters. The deliberative scope of these varies, but some of them amount to strong publics, as a brief look at the institutional forms makes clear. There are institutionalised deliberative spaces, in which deliberation takes place prior to decision-making, and in which decision makers are held to account.

The EP is directly elected by the peoples of the member states, and can, hence, claim to be an institutional expression of the will of the people. It is the only EU institution endowed with direct democratic legitimacy through Europe-wide elections. Further, the EP is the world's only supranational parliament, and has over a longer period of time been effectively empowered by the member states (Rittberger 2003, 2005). Multiparty parliamentary systems are generally consensus oriented and prone to deliberation, but in the EU there is even more scope for open deliberation as there is no clear-cut division between government and opposition. Majorities can therefore more easily form around a number of dimensions, but in fact positions mainly follow party cleavages.

The EP is a multilingual body – there are 23 working languages in the present assembly. The political groups are made up of representatives from different countries, which means that Members of the EP (MEPs) must actively interact with representatives from different language and cultural backgrounds. Achieving proper understanding and agreement in such arenas requires comprehensive and genuine argumentation. The EP fosters such deliberation and seeks to ensure rational and transparent decision-making. It has also been a firm promoter of the development of a more representative and accountable EU system:

> In addition to its role in granting the budgetary discharge to the European Commission, the Parliament is involved in other, less spectacular, scrutiny activities. It may put oral and written questions to the Commission and the Council committees, hold public hearings, set up temporary committees of inquiry and discuss the EU's performance with the Council's presidency.
>
> (Maurer 1999: 6)

As Andy Smith argues in Chapter 12, according to the *investiture procedure* of the Maastricht Treaty there is 'a requirement for Commissioners to present themselves and their respective portfolios to sessions of parliamentary committees open to journalists and other interested members of the public' (p. 229). This new appointments procedure has contributed to establishing a kind of parliamentary government in the EU. The EP conducts major monitoring functions, which now also include supervising compliance by the member states with the provisions of the Charter of Fundamental Rights. Initially, the EP was a consultative body – a talking shop – with very limited powers and made up mostly of representatives of national parliaments. Over time, and in particular after the introduction of the direct election of MEPs in 1979, its decision-making powers have grown. The EP increased its status and power with the Single European Act, which marked a watershed as the cooperation procedure was introduced. Then, reinforced by the Maastricht and Amsterdam Treaties, it moved from being a secondary institution to become an important actor in law-making. It changed from being a Parliament in name to acting like one. It has achieved the power of co-decision with the Council in many areas and is increasingly curtailing the power of the Commission. Although it has become an important legislator, its role in shaping the constitutional and institutional development of the EU is still more that of an *auditor* than originator or constructor (Eriksen and Fossum 2002).

The EP is hampered as a democratic sovereign not only because of deficient popular support (low turnouts in elections) but also because it lacks proper law-making power. It is 'the masters of the Treaties' – in the intergovernmental Council – that are in charge of Treaty changes. Such changes pertain to the basic structure of the Union – its constitution – and are the ones most in need of popular input and democratic enactment. Two recent developments have changed this: the Charter of Fundamental Rights of the European Union (2000) and the Laeken Convention on the Future of Europe (2002–2003). These suggest a more open constitutionalisation process. Conventions are deliberative bodies or settings set up to deal with constitutional matters in which the power of the argument should prevail. 'The procedure must go beyond the simple recording of votes and allow for communicative interaction. Also the setting must steer this interaction toward arguing and away from threat-based bargaining' (Elster 1998: 105).

The Charter Convention was important. It was not only the first case, at the European level, of the direct inclusion of parliamentarians in a process of a constitutional nature, but they also made up the majority of the representatives (45 out of 62). This stands in marked contrast to IGC-based processes for Treaty change, which are the sole preserve of executive officials. The strong presence of parliamentarians greatly added to the legitimacy of this body. The Convention's deliberations were also affected by the fact that all the participants were legally trained. This probably made it easier to reach agreement on a Charter essentially based on existing law.

The Charter process was different from the previous IGC processes. Whereas IGC processes were closed and secretive, the Charter process was open and set up as a co-operative argumentation process. The drafting process ran from December 1999 to October 2000, and the Charter was proclaimed in December 2000. The timeframe was therefore quite tight. The Convention held open hearings and received written submissions (a total of 1,000). It almost unanimously adopted the Charter. No final vote was held, but participants' accounts reveal that 60 out of 62 supported it. This process did, to some extent, contribute to the sparking off of 'an authentically European-wide debate among the organizations of civil society'. The mobilising effect of this process, however, should not be overestimated but it certainly did compare favourably with the intergovernmental approach that had preceded earlier Treaty changes (de Schutter 2003).

The Charter Convention, which was deemed a success, established a procedural precedent for constitution-making. It became a model for the second Convention. The Laeken Convention's composition largely duplicated that of the Charter Convention; it was made up of a majority of parliamentarians (46 out of 66 voting members, and 26 out of 39 from the candidate countries). It also had appointed representatives from the member state governments, but these were in a clear minority. Their deliberations resulted in a draft Treaty establishing a Constitution for Europe. The subsequent Constitutional Treaty has now been ratified by 15 states,[14] but was rejected in two referenda – in France and the Netherlands in May and June 2005. The European leaders thus resolved that there should be a 'reflection period' and postponed the time for the final ratification.

The missing link

Conventions are communicative sites where citizens or their representatives assemble to propose the basic principles and rules of a legal community – the constitution – and they conduct their affairs through an open and deliberative process. To be legitimate, the ensuing proposal has to be subjected to a comprehensive public debate in the general public sphere and be enacted by popularly authorised bodies such as a Parliament, a Congress or a Senate.

The Conventions at work in the EU were fairly representative and were open to public scrutiny. The deliberative imprint was also clear. Positions moved and standpoints changed. The agreements rested on *reasonable reasons*, not only on threats and compromised interests (Eriksen 2006). Participants portrayed the draft as the best that could be achieved under the given circumstances, but they also underlined that this was a result that had been forged through a lengthy argumentative process. However, these conventions have not yet triggered a larger Europe-wide political debate over the constitutional essentials. They did not spur a *constitutional moment*, in the sense that a broad spectrum of the population 'took to the streets'. It is this that is demanded for the constitutional draft to find public justification, but it is also much needed to foster and bolster the collective identity of Europeans.

With regard to the concept of the public sphere, the link between institutionalised debates and general public debate is largely missing. In fact, the problem is not the lack of public spaces in Europe that are capable of holding decision makers responsible. What is lacking is the ability to link and filter themes and topics, the problems and solutions aired in civil society and verbalised in the general public, and sluiced into the decision-making units via transnational networks and strong publics.

The plethora of transnational publics increases the information level and the contestation of different viewpoints. They also enhance the rationality of decision-making and may even enable holding supranational power holders effectively to account, but they do not suffice to constitute a democratic sovereign. Access to *one* common public – one single European public space – is necessary to enable citizens to address the same political issues and be exposed to the same information, arguments and counter-arguments. To develop common opinions and wills requires common themes, shared interpretative frames and inclusive fora. Only these can establish the preconditions necessary for a rational opinion-formation process among all that are affected. In particular, this is required for the proper legitimation and justification of the basic ruling principles of society – of the constitutional essentials. Since such a discussion revolves around deontic norms or principles (e.g. democracy, the rule of law, equality, solidarity), there are prospects for consensus. Whether these discussions can bring about an identity strong enough to make possible collective action is the decisive point for the EU to develop beyond a regulatory regime in legitimacy terms.

What kind of legitimation?

Given that the findings testify more to a segmented, transnational rather than a supranational public sphere in Europe based on equal citizenship and a well-developed civic infrastructure, one may question its putative democratic quality. As mentioned, proponents of deliberative governance see networks as the *institutional software for the reflective treatment of discourses*, and see its epistemic value as conducive to democratic legitimacy.

Deliberative governance

Public debate can have epistemic value even if the ideal requirements of communication have not been met because deliberation forces the participants to justify their standpoints and decisions in an impartial manner. This kind of deliberation takes place in transnational networks and institutionalised deliberative settings, contributes to a more rational way of solving problems and to increasing the epistemic quality of the reasons in a justification process. Deliberation, according to followers of John Dewey, is seen as a co-operative activity for intelligent problem-solving in relation to a *cognitive standard* and not as an argument about what is correct, in the sense that it can be approved by all. It is substantive, not procedural. Publicity, then, is to be understood as a democratic *experimental device* for detecting and solving social problems – including the identification of unintended consequences or by-products – and not as a political principle of legitimacy.[15]

In this perspective, the EU is read as an example of transnational governance. Policy-making in committees and networks supplemented with civil society organisations, (I)NGOs and social movements have created communicative spaces in and between states. As no one possesses absolute power within these structures, they, for some analysts, represent functional equivalents to democracy. Government is not needed because networks are available and are an appropriate 'institutional expression of a dispersed capacity to engage in deliberation that helps determine the terms of discourse in the international system' (Dryzek 1999: 48). Deliberation substitutes, so to speak, for government. Pluralism, disaggregation, interest contestation and deliberation in the criss-crossing public sphere are seen as facilitating *multi-perspectival inquiry* and democracy in a multi-centred world of diverse, non-governmental actors.[16] The EU amounts to a *direct-deliberative polyarchy*:

> Consider now a world in which sovereignty – legitimate political authorship – is neither unitary nor personified, and politics is about addressing practical problems and not simply about principles [...]. In this world, a public is simply an open group of actors, nominally private or public, which constitutes itself as such in coming to address a common problem, and reconstitutes itself as efforts at problem solving redefine the task at hand. The polity is the public formed of these publics.
>
> (Cohen and Sabel 2003: 362)

Deliberation as a mode of problem-solving may enhance the effectiveness and efficiency of the decision-making system and help targeting policies, as qualitatively good discussions lead to more enlightened actors and more rational decisions. However, the problem of democratic *legitimacy* lingers on. Legitimacy is the crucial criterion to be met for a political system to be recognised as valid. The institutional *nexus* of the EU should thus be tested with regard to legitimacy and not merely efficiency. In modern post-conventional societies, democracy is the sole remaining

principle of legitimation. It pertains to public accountability and congruence between the law abiders and the lawmakers, namely the entrenchment of political, participatory rights: *the rights of rights.* Experimental
deliberation cannot bear the burden of legitimacy in the latter variant, as
there is no possibility that the laws that all have to obey are consented to
in a free, open and rational debate by all the affected parties. It is an
unstable solution as the polity has to rule in the name of all, not in the
name of a section of the public. Such a concept of the public sphere may
suffice for a regulatory entity or international organisation, but not for a
power-wielding polity like the EU whose actions have a profound influence on the citizens as well as on the member states.

A democratic sovereign capable of action?

Central to the discourse-theoretical notion of the public sphere is a distinction between opinion formation, which is the domain for the public
sphere, and will formation, which is the domain for decision-making units
within the political system. Publics do not act, as they possess no decision-
making agency in a constitutional state with a division of powers. The
public may be seen to act in revolutionary moments, as in the storming of
the Bastille, but generally, in public spheres it is only possible to deliberate and as such form opinions about what should be done. In pluralistic
and complex societies, public opinion is 'anonymous' – it is 'decentred'
into the network of communication itself. It is dispersed and has no power
to govern. This corresponds to a *desubstantialised concept of popular sovereignty.* Popular sovereignty resides in the dispersed process of informal
communication and not in a substantively defined demos. That is also why
Habermas (1996a) maintains that popular sovereignty has to be located in
the interplay between institutionalised and non-institutionalised bodies
for deliberation and decision-making.

Transnational bodies of governance and deliberation may, in this
perspective, be able to tackle normative and politically salient questions in
a qualitatively good manner. 'The public use of reason' enhances the
problem-solving capacity and political rationality also at the supranational
level where 'soft power may push hard power' (Habermas 2001). This
assessment draws on the epistemic value of deliberative democracy, which
underscores the rationality presupposition and not merely the institutional or participatory presuppositions in conceiving of democratic
legitimacy.

Legitimacy, then, first and foremost stems from the deliberative process
itself. Under modern conditions, it cannot stem from direct and full participation in collective decision-making as the people are rarely present to
make choices in modern complex states.[17] It is also hard to see how democratic legitimacy can be based merely on votes, as voting procedures are
loaded with aggregation problems and as the principle of a majority vote

does not guarantee full political equality. Moreover, thanks to the new role of media and more public criticism, politicians have to define and refine their mandate on a continual basis, and to drum up support in the general public sphere. Their mandate is 'unbound', it is barely transmitted via elections but has to be struggled for by communicative means, and this underscores the epistemic value of deliberative democracy.

> [T]he democratic procedure no longer draws its legitimizing force only, indeed not even predominantly, from political participation and the expression of political will, but rather from the general accessibility of a deliberative process whose structure grounds an expectation of rationally acceptable results.
>
> (Habermas 2001: 110)

The implication of this is to lower ambitions in respect of popular rule and normative space for transnational network governance. The basic problem with the epistemic approach to democratic legitimacy is the lack of commitment that follows when law is not laid down authoritatively by a people or their symbolic representative, and made equally binding on every part. The authority of the law stems not only from discursive processes but also from participatory processes – such as elections – in the shaping of a common will or the common good. This constitutes the link to the people, complying with the credo that all political power stems from the people, which authorises the polity to rule in the name of all and sanctions non-compliance unilaterally.[18]

Conclusion

The public sphere is the place where civil society is linked to the power structure of the state. It constitutes the basis for deliberative politics because it is here that power must find its justification. It is in this space that binding decisions must be justified to the citizens who are bound by them, according to standards they agree upon. The public sphere, which is based on communicative freedom, gives citizens the right to discuss the general conditions for the common weal as well as to form opinions about what is just. As far as counter-arguments are voiced, this is a test as to whether political decisions are correct.

The public sphere has, in general, become fragmented, polymorphic and polyphonic. In the EU there are transnational communicative spaces in which all the citizens of the EU can take part, but more salient are segmented publics evolving around policy networks and legally institutionalised discourses – strong publics – specialised in collective will formation. Hence, the situation speaks more to the EU as a regulatory, problem-solving entity than to the EU as a democratic government. The assessment of the EU from a democratic perspective should take heed of different kinds of public and be aware of their different functions and spheres of validity. Generally, the existence of many publics fosters democracy as these enhance the possibilities for popular participation in opinion formation. Even though the problem of fragmentation and communication disturbances prevail, and make opinion and collective goal formation difficult, it is fair to say the more publics, the more debate and critique. Fewer voices are excluded and more questions are asked. More publics provide more possibilities for testing the legitimacy of power. They contribute to criticising and deconstructing hegemonic 'truths' and prevailing consensuses and force the decision makers to provide more general and universalistic justifications for their positions. Publics are the vehicles of democratisation, also in the sense of making conscious earlier wrongdoings and coming to grips with the past – or *Bewusstmachung* and *Vergangenheitsbewältigung*, as it is termed in the German debate.

However, when deliberative networks in communicative spaces are seen as exhaustive of the democratic tenet, there is a renunciation of the idea of rule through public, collective reasoning. In modern societies, it is the law that establishes unity: participation in law-making constitutes the collective identity. What hampers democracy at the European level today is the lack of a common, law-based identification and the possibility for transnational discourse – *a single European space* – in which Antonio in Sicily, Judith in Germany and Bosse in Sweden can take part in a discussion with Roberto in Spain and Triin in Estonia on the same topics at the same time.

Notes

This is a revised version of a paper read at the CIDEL Conference 'One EU – Many Publics?', Stirling, 5–6 February 2004. I am grateful for comments received from the participants and from the CIDEL members at ARENA. A different version of this chapter was published in the *European Journal of Social Theory*, Vol. 8, No. 3, 2005, pp. 341–63.

1 This part of the chapter draws on Chapter 9 in Eriksen and Weigård 2003.
2 It is a principle of political justice: 'All actions relating to the rights of others are wrong if their maxim is incompatible with publicity' (Kant 1996 [1797]: 347).
3 He now carefully points out that 'We must distinguish *procedural constraints* from a constraint or limitation on the *range of topics* open to public discourse' (Habermas 1996a: 313).
4 Such social movements have added dynamism to modern politics. They have forcefully advocated new causes, come up with new arguments, and put matters in a new light. Popular protest movements develop and help realise new collective goals and new forms of rule by making modern norms and values acceptable to wider social strata in modern societies (Eisenstadt *et al.* 1984). They have not taken over from established parties or established interest organisations, but have forced them to relate to new problems. Gradually, this pressure, through demonstrations, campaigns and argumentation, has exerted influence and considerably changed the political agenda and programmes of

the political parties (Olsen 1983). The new social movements represent a form of *intellectual mobilisation*, which has its source in international relations. They constitute an independent explanation of social change (Bendix 1978: 266; Loftager 1994, 2005). On the epistemic function of discourse, see Habermas 2006.

5 'Democracies cannot establish states, but they impose new forms upon pre-existing non-democratic states upon whose previous existence they are parasitic' (Offe 1998: 116).

6 According to Claus Offe (1998: 119) the stability of the political community rests on the 'reflexive homogeneity' in which citizens are integrated 'through an understanding of the communality of their fate'. See Guéhenno 1996 and Miller 1995 for a similar position; Stie 2002 and Peters 2005 for a discussion.

7 'The core is formed by a political sphere which enables citizens to take positions on the same issues at the same time under similar aspects of relevance' (Habermas 1998: 160). See also Kantner 2002: 60.

8 The German public debate about making earlier wrongdoings conscious – *Bewusstmachung* – and coming to grips with the past – *Vergangenheitsbewältigung* – provides an instructive example of such an endeavour.

9 One may even hint at examples on the global level, and the non-publicly funded www.zmag.org that has sections based on voluntary translations.

10 Fischer's speech also spurred a transnational European debate within the academic community (Joerges *et al.* 2000).

11 Cf. the Commission's White Paper on Governance (European Commission 2001a) and its urge for partnership models and the Open Method of Coordination (OMC). For the latter, see Eriksen 2001, and further contributions in Eriksen *et al.* 2003.

12 This is inspired by Luhmann's model, in which the public sphere is a mirror of societal self-observation – the observation of the observed – and where the handling of the problem of suspicious intentions rather than rationality/non-rationality constitutes the decisive difference through which the public sphere is established and every so often collapses (Luhmann 2000: 291; cf. Trenz 2002a: 28, 29, 34).

13 'They compel the checking of decisions, in that protest at decision-making is being anticipated, or that elitist communicative noise is put before popular communicative noise, thus the elitist public sphere itself takes part in the staging of communicative noise' (Eder 2003a: 104, see also 106). Author's translation.

14 For an overview of the constitutional ratification process, see europa.eu.int/constitution/ratification_en.htm (accessed 13 September 2006).

15 For this conception of the public, see Dewey 1927; Brunkhorst 1998; Kettner 1998.

16 See Rosenau 1997, 1998; applied to the EU, see Cohen and Sabel 1997; Dorf and Sabel 1998; Gerstenberg and Sabel 2002; Bohman 2005.

17 Rather, collective decision-making is conducted through programmed systems and professionals specialised in self-justificatory deliberation and the management of mass loyalty. Hence, '*Wer würde es merken, wenn es gar kein Volk gäbe?*' ['Who would notice if there was no such thing as a people?'] (Luhmann 2000: 366).

18 On this basis it may also be argued that democracy requires a government or a state – a Leviathan – as there must be a body endowed with the capacity and authority to act on behalf of 'the people', which in turn can be held publicly accountable. See Eriksen 2005, 2006.

3   The public sphere and European democracy

Mechanisms of democratisation in the transnational situation

Klaus Eder

The issue revisited

From prerequisites to mechanisms

Whether we need democratic procedures at the European level can be contested. There are good arguments why democracy might interfere with the requirements of steering complex systems. This certainly holds at the transnational level where the problem of steering a society of nation states requires forms of politics that do not easily go together with the idea of democratic politics. The theory of the regulatory state (Majone 1994) states that democratic procedures that maximise participation may become incompatible with the functional task of supranational institutions to regulate social and economic processes beyond the national level. A way out of this dilemma is to give back to national institutions as many regulatory functions as possible, thus reducing supranational regulatory institutions to the minimum possible in order to simultaneously maximise efficiency and democracy. The nation state thus returns as the best container for having both efficiency and democracy. This is a possible path which reduces transnational institutions to their instrumental function and links their durability to their capacity to provide efficient solutions.

Such a developmental path, however, runs into the problem that such institutions cannot avoid being 'political'. The more market globalisation advances, the more political solutions to its consequences are required. Such solutions presuppose the coordination of nation states, and any form of coordinating collective actors is political. This implies that democratic procedures are unavoidable at the transnational level and may even be required more than ever before (assuming the normative premise that politics is to be based on some kind of democratic process of consensus-building). This claim needs to be defended against the idea of reducing transnational institutions to mere regulatory agencies such as proposed by Majone.

Recently we argued that there is a functional necessity to base a complex social order on democratic procedures (Trenz and Eder 2004). This theory of democratic functionalism argued that political communication is increasing with the complexity of societies. The decisive argument is that the more political communication is triggered by the complexity of issues, the more those involved are exposed to the force of counterarguments, thus fostering normative claims of equal participation. From this we concluded that the European Union (EU) will need even more democracy than the nation state if it is to continue in the future. Thus we have to expect that the more the integration process goes on, the more processes of democratisation will be set off (which does not imply that they will succeed).

This functionalist explanation has to face the deficiency of any functionalist argument. It leaves in the dark what really produces the functional relationship. However, it already goes beyond what can be called the classic approach to explaining the process of democratisation, which is to ask for the 'prerequisites' of democratisation. This approach, canonised in the political sociology of Seymour Martin Lipset (1994), extended by authors like Robert Putnam (1993, 2000), starts with the question of what are the necessary conditions (and maybe even the sufficient conditions) that explain processes of democratisation? Comparative research has added evidence of the particular configurations of prerequisites which trigger or block processes of democratisation or the 'democratic performance' of nation states.

This approach underrates the shifting configuration determining the democratic performance as soon as a series of such prerequisites is given. Democratised societies will certainly generate different configurations of 'prerequisites' for explaining further democratisation. In this way, the explanation finally will not provide a good theory, which explains why democratisation is a necessary outcome of 'variables' that in some combination 'explain' democratisation. We still do not know *how* democratisation takes place. Thus the 'why' question generates a black box: what is it that transforms, e.g. a market economy into a factor of democratisation? We might have common-sense guesses, but we have no theory that tells us what it is that pushes in the direction of democratisation. This is the question of the *mechanisms* of democratisation. From prerequisites to mechanisms – this is the theoretical change needed in the field of explaining democratisation.[1]

Applied to Europe, such a shift is unavoidable: it does not make much sense to look for prerequisites of democracy in Europe – they are there everywhere. But what we do not know is how these prerequisites can be transformed into a process of democratisation. It is the 'how' question which we have to answer.

The issue of the democratic deficit of the EU revisited

Public debate has recently raised the issue that the democratic deficit of the EU is to be explained by the lack of a European public sphere. This debate has provoked contradictory descriptions of the reality, arguing either that there is none or that there is one.[2] Empirical research has shown that there is more than what everybody would have expected, given the common-sense perception and description of Europe.[3] The presence of a public sphere can be described empirically in an increasingly refined way, ranging from media presence through emerging linguistic frames to practical organisational forms at the national and transnational level.

So we have a prerequisite of democracy in Europe, yet we still claim that there is no democracy in Europe. We could argue that it will come by itself, as a functional consequence of these prerequisites. This argument provides an intermediate step: it claims that we should expect functional pressures towards democratisation, given the series of prerequisites we have in Europe. Focusing this 'how' question on the problem of a European public sphere forces us to rethink the problem of democratisation in terms of the mechanisms that drive it forward or that block it. This dynamic perspective can substitute for the static, in the best case, comparative view of democratisation of our forefathers in political sociology.

A theory and a model for explaining democratisation

Extending the functionalist argument and introducing the normative argument

Our functionalist argument concerning democratisation identified a general process underlying it: political communication. When political communication takes place, several mechanisms start working which push for democratisation. This is not really a new argument. The theory of the public sphere as the locus of democracy (Habermas 1989) points to a learning mechanism resulting from people arguing with each other in public. In its strong version, this theory says that those entering a situation of free and equal discussion are bound by the force of the argument. Thus a theory of democratisation through public debate can start (but should not end) with the identification of a learning mechanism built into public communication.

A particular version of this theory can be framed in system-theoretical terms. To the extent that a polity conceives of itself in democratic terms, it builds into its *autopoiesis* a mechanism that pushes towards democratisation.[4] Paradoxically enough, the causal link made in public debate between the lack of a public sphere and a democratic deficit in Europe is part of this self-observation, which we as social scientists take as an indicator of the self-production of a democratic polity.

This system-theoretical perspective brings back the normative question in terms of a standard that is used in public debate. But what do normative theories tell us regarding this problem?[5] Normative theories optimise normative arguments. Social scientists act as civil society experts who want to shape the argumentative universe (in which they sometimes succeed). Often they use normative arguments as benchmarks for evaluating the quality of democratisation processes. Then they become the official intellectual critics of the existing state of a polity. There is also a third way, arguing that normative theories are part of the public debate that is constitutive of democratisation. Using normative theories as self-descriptions of ongoing processes of democratisation (or de-democratisation) allows us to see them as an instance of a mechanism of democratisation. This means taking an observational stance towards such debates and asking for their function in the making and reproduction of a civil society.

The theory of democratic functionalism moves us towards an explanation of the function of political theory for the dynamics of democratisation. The challenge is to move beyond a theory of democratic functionalism towards a theory of the mechanisms of democratisation that holds not only for the national but also for the pre-national as well as transnational situations.

A parsimonious model of explanation

The model proposed for explaining democratisation is based on a series of mechanisms which tell us *how* public political communication leads to democratisation in a given situation. Taking up a proposal made by McAdam *et al.* (2001), I start with three mechanisms that make assumptions about the link between political communication and democratisation. These are, first, *cognitive mechanisms* that emerge in political communication, leading to claims of the free and equal participation of citizens in the political decisions that concern them; second, *relational mechanisms* that bind together those involved in political communication into networks of free and equal citizens (such as mutual recognition, trust and solidarity); and third, *contextual mechanisms* which explain why these cognitive and relational mechanisms are triggered or blocked at a given point in time and space.

Contextual mechanisms explaining the process of democratisation can draw on research on the prerequisites of democracy. They provide opportunities or threats for actors involved in the dynamics of political communication. What has to be clarified is, in what sense political communication entails the mobilisation of cognitive and relational mechanisms that generate democratisation? This also opens the possibility of explaining failures of democratisation, which are cases of the perverse effects of the mechanisms that propel democratisation, i.e. undemocratic outcomes of the dynamic of democratisation. This model of mechanisms is applied to the categorical triad of state, market and what is variously called civil society, public sphere, or associations. Contextual mechanisms refer to this triad as a series of opportunities and threats for relational and cognitive mechanisms. The theoretical focus for explaining the dynamics of democratisation is on the role of the third sphere, where cognitive and relational mechanisms have stronger normative implications than in the sphere of the market and the state. People learn – this is the assumption – because they participate in public affairs and argue about it. People succeed in acting together because equal participation creates reciprocal obligations. Finally, there is a basic normative goal that these people pursue: to realise a *res publica* through self-governance. Self-governance is considered to be the royal road to good governance where common goods are created by free and equal people.

The argument in a nutshell

In the first part, I look into the specific 'original situation', namely the take-off of democratisation in a situation where democratic institutions do not yet exist. This is the original situation where unbounded political communication leads to claims and actions for the democratic control of power.[6]

In a second step, I describe an analytically different situation: how do such mechanisms work once democratic forms of the control of power have been established? The particular feature of this situation is the embeddedness of democratisation in a nation state, which provides particular cultural and institutional restrictions on the dynamics of democratisation. This situation has been described as the fall of public man, or as the decay of public space.[7] In other versions, it has been described as the fulfilment of the democratic ideal in the modern nation state. Such contradictory observations point to the ambivalence of what we call a public sphere in this second national phase.

In a third step, the transnational situation is described, namely democratisation beyond and outside the nation state.[8] In this situation, arguably, the fall of public man continues at an accelerating speed culminating in the assumption that a public sphere beyond the nation is (empirically and/or normatively) impossible. This contrasts with the observation that the European public behaves like a watchdog. Instead of continuing this debate, I look into how the mechanisms of democratisation work where the nation no longer provides the exclusive container for political communication. The claim of ontological primacy for the nation is replaced by an observation of the self-constitution of a people in the transnational situation.

In the conclusion, I discuss some implications for the constitution of a demos capable of controlling political power. This clarifies the question of how we understand democratic governance.

The original situation

Public communication as a starter of democratisation

That public communication has particular effects has been the central claim in the theory of a public sphere by Habermas (1989). It is a theory of the take-off of democratisation. His observations follow those of de Tocqueville, who found the cause of democracy in America in intermediate groups, in which people came together beyond their private sphere to discuss things that were of concern for all. This concern for collective goods to be taken up in public debate explains – as de Tocqueville concluded – the take-off of democracy in America.

Habermas added a systematic explanation by describing first the process of the constitution of public space that was separated from the private world of the household. Public political communication brings together people as equal individuals. To do so, these individuals have to leave the private realm and enter a public space. In this space they encounter each other as political beings, stripped of their private social relations, as equal citizens. Habermas reports on the debating clubs and societies where interaction was based on equal access for everyone. Public communication triggers a relational mechanism: those who talk with others about politics in public have to accept – *uno actu* – the other as an equal.

There is a second mechanism identified by Habermas. Those communicating on political matters engage in a process of collective will formation; they learn collectively. This is a cognitive mechanism triggered by political communication. People cannot escape the force of the better argument as soon as they engage in public argumentation.

Finally, Habermas introduces the absolutist state and the emerging capitalist economy as contextual variables. Thus, in the early work of Habermas we can reconstruct an explanatory model which distinguishes between situations (the economic and political situation of classes of people) and mechanisms of associating and learning which provide an explanation for the take-off of democratisation. Only one empirical assumption is needed: that there is some public political communication going on.

What is the advantage of reconstructing an old argument in this way? First, we avoid crude, causal reductionism – taking the economy or polity as determining factors in the process of democratisation. Rather, we have to find additional mechanisms that can explain this process, given some contextual mechanisms. The historical assumption is that these mechanisms have something to do with the process of public political communication that was triggered in the course of the economic and political changes of the eighteenth and nineteenth centuries. Thus the hypothesis is that mechanisms of civil interaction and collective learning are at work. Public communication sets off mechanisms of collective will formation in collision with the will of the traditional authorities. Here the model becomes recursive: contextual mechanisms may foster or block the other mechanisms of democratisation.

Democratic governance as outcome – the logic of democratisation

These mechanisms are indissolubly linked to normative criteria of their appropriateness. We call this the 'logic of democratisation'.

This logic is linked to the symbolic side of the process of democratisation. No change takes place without being perceived and reflected in ongoing communication. This situation forces those involved in the processes, which are triggered by diverse mechanisms, to take contingent perspectives on what happens. We simply have to reckon that actors consider what is happening as purposeful. There is an evolution of meaning in the dynamics of democratisation. Mechanisms of learning are forces for consistency and coherence. Relational mechanisms are forces for fairness and reciprocity. Contextual mechanisms either force or block the future opened up by cognitive and relational mechanisms.

Democratic self-governance is a possible, but not a necessary outcome of the mechanisms that are triggered as soon as public communication expands beyond a critical mass. Democratic self-governance is defined here as an institutional arrangement that gives a prominent position to the third sphere in the triadic relations with the market and the state. It describes the capacity of a people to act collectively upon itself, thus creating a political body capable of creating a *res publica* beyond the realm of private interests and of constraining the power of the state.[9]

These mechanisms thus produce an outcome that can be qualified normatively. Democratic governance is contingent upon three principles. The first is that everybody concerned should have a voice, in short, that of the free and equal participation of all. The second is the principle of deliberation: all should engage in exchanging arguments, taking into account the conflicting perspectives of all concerned. Finally, there is the principle of rational decision-making: when people participate and deliberate, they should be able to make rational decisions. This is the principle of governance.[10] By combining these three principles, the outcome is democratic governance: decision-making by people who participate and deliberate when public issues are to be decided. Democratic governance means controlling the power of decision-making by the people concerned. The outcome can be measured in terms of rights that follow from the first principle: rights that guarantee individual freedom, rights to have a voice in public and equal rights of participation framed by institutions (constitutions) that guarantee their application.

The three principles of participation, deliberation and governance are those that oriented the political observers of the times. The history of modern political theory is a variation on these three themes while designing institutions that would best fit the three principles.[11] This double process, describing a mechanism of change and analysing its functioning by looking into what the observers then considered as new, provides a powerful analytical framework. Any theory of a good democracy is a variation of the combination of these three normative criteria.

It is obvious that fulfilling all three principles simultaneously, thus creating democratic governance (or 'self-governance' by the people), requires an idealised situation. In the original situation this could be the case: equal citizens meeting in associations and debating and thus forming a collective actor capable of controlling political power. In non-idealised situations, we have the problem of maximin or minimax situations. This has led to competing normative theories on how to realise a democratic polity. Some plead for maximising participatory democracy, which raises the problem of how to create enough deliberative spaces and the capacity of collective action.[12] Others plead for maximising deliberative democracy, which raises the problem of securing the participation of all in decisions concerning them and the problem of binding political power to deliberative outcomes.[13] Finally, there have been political theories emphasising the capacity of collective action over participatory or deliberative concerns, doing away with the latter as bourgeois attempts to destroy the capacity for action of the people, or as institutional blocks to the capacity of collective action to come to the fore.[14]

These normative theories struggle with the problem of finding an institutional design for democratic governance which guarantees an ideal mix between the three principles. None of the proposed institutional designs is without cost regarding democratic governance. The central issue in the search for an adequate institutional design is the question of representation. Who participates, who deliberates, and who decides? Debating this is itself part of the process of democratisation: it is democratic governance regarding constitutional issues.

All this makes democratisation a vulnerable endeavour. It can easily end up in pathological dynamics leading away from democratic governance.

The openness of the original situation

The ideal model of individuals coming together, deliberating and governing a *res publica* can be distilled from the situation of a democratic take-off. Habermas for Europe and de Tocqueville for America provide historical case studies for this original situation.

Thus we have mechanisms built into political communication that link participation and deliberation to governance. Their outcome can be democratic governance, but not necessarily so. Contextual mechanisms come into play, producing configurations of cognitive and/or relational mechanisms that determine the outcome, i.e. whether the form of governance is democratic or left to the state or to the market or to some missionary collective actor in civil society. Democratic governance is therefore a rather improbable outcome, due to the incompatibility of maximising simultaneously the underlying principles for democratic governance.

Pathologies of democratisation

The dynamics of democratisation do not guarantee rational results. A first form of failing democratisation is to justify particular interests by recourse to an authority that represents the group as a whole. This maximises participation while minimising deliberation and is successful to the extent that deliberation is handed over to representative bodies. The extreme case of a pathological path would be deliberation by one and participation by all: the *Führerdemokratie*, where the *Führer* thinks for all, and all participate in the appreciation of his arguments (a pathology that has happened more than once). This is democratisation turned 'authoritarian', separating governance from free and equal participation by those affected by it.

A second form of failing democratisation is the reduction of democratic participation and deliberation to a strategic game, minimising both deliberation and participation. Acting together consists in the strategic balancing of interests. This is a world of people relating to each other as 'idiotes' in the Greek sense of the word. In this world, you do not argue, you bargain; you do not participate, but you act in your self-interest. This pathology puts a premium on minimising argumentative and participatory costs. This is 'marketised' democratisation; democratic governance gives in to the market.

A third form of failing democratization rests on maximizing participation and/or deliberation while disregarding the consequences for the common good. This is democracy without an efficient state. Political life is contingent on confession (*gesinnungsethisch*). This is 'ideological' democratisation (Max Weber would have said 'material rationalization'); democratic governance becomes a missionary enterprise in which other arguments no longer count and others are excluded from being part of the chosen people.

Such a conceptualisation of failing processes of democratisation allows us to evaluate the democratic performance of a polity. The explanatory strategy is not to argue with the absence of mechanisms of democratisation, but to argue with pathological configurations of the mechanisms of democratisation.

Interlude: democratisation with ontological illusions

Political communication in a liberal society

How do the mechanisms of democratisation work for existing democratic nation states? This is the situation of the 'interlude' of 150 to 200 years at the most: a nationally integrated society struggling to avoid the built-in tendencies towards pathological forms of governance.

In this interlude, those engaging in political communication no longer act against those in power, i.e. the original situation of society versus state. We have a co-evolution of political institutions and a nationally defined society.[15] Claims of societal actors against political organisations and legal obligations put on these societal actors go hand in hand, creating an isomorphism between what we formerly called state and society.

First, this situation changes the effects of contextual mechanisms: opportunities and threats are reconfigured along the axis of democratic and antidemocratic protest, of conventional and unconventional action, of voting and protest. Second, this situation changes the effects of relational mechanisms: it provides a container, the nation, that restricts the number of participants; and it moves deliberation to representative bodies, speaking in the name of individuals, thus creating a new relational effect: an interorganisational field of political action. Third, this situation changes the effects of cognitive mechanisms: the public is reduced to an observing public, which acts at times as an arbitrator (by voting), whereas learning takes place on the stage, watched by the public.[16] Learning lies in rewriting the scripts actors play on the stage. The key to an understanding of the effects of the mechanisms of democratisation in this interlude is the separation between the stage of public space (with front and back stages) and the place occupied by the public. On the stage we have the collective actors playing alongside each other; and then we have the public watching the actors on the stage. This theatre creates what I would like to call the illusion of collective will formation.

The theatre provides a particular situation of political communication, which is no longer tied to confrontation with somebody who does not share the principle of negotiating competing claims (as is the case in the take-off situation of democratisation). We rather have the institutional form of a script that regulates the exchange of arguments in front of a third person, the observing public.

The transformation of the dynamics of democratisation is fundamental. We move from the situation of double contingency where an actor coordinates his views with other actors, to a situation of triple contingency where actors communicate while being observed by a public. The public space, here, is the nation observing collective actors searching for efficient solutions for providing the common good.

This situation forces those enacting their script on the front stage to adapt it continuously to a by-standing public. The better argument is the winning argument. Since no decision lasts forever, the winning argument can always be questioned by new arguments that enter the process of political communication. This is the institutionalised variant of the ideal model of the speech situation.[17]

Normative principles of nationally bounded interorganisational fields

Within the context of nationally bounded interorganisational fields, the principles of participation, deliberation and governance take on a different and ambivalent shape. The participating public judge continuously. This invites certain forms of strategic behaviour: withholding communication, keeping parts of communication secret or off the record or mobilising public attention, which creates communicative biases through media communication. All these are typical strategies that emerge as the basic formative processes of political decision-making in such institutional environments.

The deliberative principle is moved to front stage when political decisions have to be justified to a public. The principle of governance is moved to back stage where the script presented on front stage is negotiated, a process defined as 'policy-making'. The modern nation state provides a form in which policy-making and democratic participation are coordinated in a system of public performance. Staging politics is mediating between policy-making and the people watching what is going on on the (visible) stage. In normative terms, this means that we still have participation, deliberation and governance, but they rest increasingly on a theatrical illusion: of actors on the scene acting in the name of the public, which is a homogeneous body of people (a 'demos'). The public and the actors on the stage remain in the same space, the theatre, and play the game of government by the people. There is a direct link between actors and the public – the public's (and media's) positive or negative reaction to the play on the stage either by showing disagreement or by not renewing the prepaid regular ticket for the next season (which equates to weekly opinion polls or to electoral votes every four years).

The limits of the institutional design of the interlude

Why does the metaphor of the theatre work so well?[18] Because the nation state is based on a narrative which binds the actors and the public together in the production of a *récit* that is structuring the scripts, regulating the events on the scene, and recognised by those listening. This creates the self-enclosure of the public in their theatre. The nation state is based on a *récit* which needs to be enacted permanently to be effective. The front stage serves for the enactment of this script. The back stage is protected from the observing public by this script. In this triple relationship between back stage, front stage and spectators (the public) a situation of triple contingency emerges: the back stage and the public mediated by the front stage playing the game of left versus right, of good and bad, of right and wrong. The outcome of this triple game is that democratisation rests less on the public than on those on the front stage.

In the theatre, we make an idealising assumption: that the world coincides with who is present in the theatre. This is done by an ingenious device: to unite the people into one public sitting in the theatre. Analogously, outside the theatre, in the nation state, national mass media create a particular national world distinct from the rest of the world. National media systems have traditionally supported this illusion of one public. The globalisation of the media undermines this idea and thus the solution to the problem of triple contingency built into the process of democratisation. This phenomenon points to a discontinuity of the process of democratisation produced by constituting media publics that no longer coincide with the nation. The advent of transnationalism is a turning point in the process of democratisation.

The benefits and costs of the national model are clear: it is good for mobilising legitimacy, and it is risky because it rests, to a high degree, on an illusion, since the theatre requires some idealising assumptions to be made about the players in the game. Those on the stage are bound to keep the illusion and are therefore vulnerable to even minor deviations from the scripts. The public presentation by those on the stage as the representatives of those sitting in the public generates risky consequences because the performances not only have to provide the legitimacy of political decision-making, but also have to re-enact the moral and affective coherence of the people that make up the public, i.e. the nation. The nation is re-enacted in the 'public' – the public performance has to provide the ontological basis for democratic nation states.

Comparative differences in good and bad democratic governance

Historical comparative institutionalism (Jepperson 2000) has produced insights into the differences in the national performance of the political representation of a people. Differences appear to be the result of contextual mechanisms: whether a society is shaped by corporate or by associational structures and whether collective agency is conceived in terms of statist or societal capacities of agency. In this way, the different institutional traditions of France, Germany, the UK, and the European North and South can be assessed comparatively and provide some contextual mechanisms for democratisation within the national boundaries.

To explain democratic performance in the national 'theatre-state', relational mechanisms provide further insights into the process of democratisation and tell us about the social capital that is available for getting people involved in public debates (Putnam 2000). This determines whether people take part in politics. The quantity of social capital is a decisive parameter in determining the impact of relational mechanisms on democratisation.

Finally, there are cognitive mechanisms shaping not only the process of collective will formation but also the possible paths of 'pathological democratisation', such as nationalism (ideological democratisation), fascism (authoritarian democratisation) or neo-liberalism (marketised democratisation). We could call these phenomena pathologies of democratisation. The cognitive core of democracy is turned into an illusion, which makes people believe that they live in a democracy. Nationalist dynamics of democratisation mobilise the people as a whole for the collective good in the name of the nation. This even implies a readiness to die for the collective good in the name of the nation. Nationalism distorts the idea of equal citizens into the idea of a unitary people. Fascist forms of the dynamics of democratisation result in authoritarian governance, mass participation and the substitution of deliberation by ideological statements of 'truths'. Neo-liberalism takes democratisation as the outcome of the competition of individuals for power. Everybody who is interested in power should participate and compete on the market for political power. The conditions are a weak state, which reduces its task of governance and enhances self-help, and the transformation of deliberation into a strategic game by actors, who follow rational interests, but not reasonable grounds, i.e. 'reasons'.

This triad of pathological forms of national democracies tells us about failing learning processes in the course of democratisation. They have a common characteristic element: they produce an illusory unity of a people united by nothing but by their capacity to communicate with others as free and equal beings. This need for an ontological unity is the central risk of the national variant of a democratic state. Such underpinnings and the illusions they require change when the nation-state model no longer defines the situation of democratisation. The emergence of transnational situations marks the end of the interlude.

The transnational situation – democratisation beyond national ontology

Democratisation in a situation of social integration by negotiation

Europe was once a case of a democratic take-off. Europe was then the locus of the national solution: creating the public as a nation and adding elections and organisational competition among institutionally privileged and constitutionally recognised collective actors. The EU today is a totally different case. It is based on a democratic tradition, on functioning democratic unities such as local governments or nation states. What makes it distinctive is its being a case of democratic self-organisation outside the national container. It is a social situation in which membership in a polity is no longer based on submission to a cultural form, but based on negotiation.[19] This moves the issue of the dynamics of democratisation to the question of how democracy is reorganising itself beyond the nation state, i.e. beyond a national ontology.

How then does democratisation proceed beyond the nation state? I sketch this out in terms of a transnational public generating resonance, then in terms of collective actors entering an open interorganisational field no longer fixed by strict constitutional rules such as the national 'interorganisational game', a situation which invites 'reflexive' institutionalisation. I finally take up the question of how learning mechanisms are built into this situation, thus identifying the particular mode of collective will formation at a transnational level.

This invites a further change in the metaphor of the theatre. We still have the theatre of the nation state, but now there are many theatres with different publics, yet they all want to participate in the same play. Thus, an additional stage is necessary which differentiates the public: the public is no longer the people, but their representatives; so it turns into a representative public watching the plays on the front stage. The people turn into observers of the representative public – they become the public watching the selected theatre public entering the theatre (like at the Wagner festival in Bayreuth). In order to be part of the public watching the performance, you need tickets that are difficult to get. This does not exclude the outside public from evaluating the performance, however, they have to rely (if there are any) on what the participating critics tell them, or what they can see in mass communication: the (normally highly selective) theatrical performance in the mass media.

The transnational public – a public beyond national ontology

Taking these changes of the situation into account, the mode of democratisation can be assessed more adequately. In Europe, there is a lot of political communication going on, inside political organisations as well as outside, by collective actors as well as by diverse publics. To understand the democratising potential and the pathological potential of this situation, it is not sufficient to repeat the lamentation over Europe's democratic deficit. This discourse should rather be the object of our observation and analysis.

I propose a different way of formulating the question. Do mechanisms of democratisation work, and if so, in what ways? Are there democratising effects of public communication at the transnational level? All this presupposes empirical data: that public political communication really takes place in Europe, measured as follows: (a) how much of it takes place; (b) how often it takes place; and (c) how many actors engage in it. Research on these questions has produced interesting answers. Suffice it to say that there is enough political communication going on that is capable of setting off mechanisms of democratisation beyond the nation state.[20] The European case is a polity composed of liberal nation states. We could even go further and argue that the mode of creating the EU, the process of entering contractual agreements and adding new ones, this form of negotiated membership, provides the context for institutional forms relating to the ideal speech situation much more than the national context in which membership has been forced upon the people.[21] Membership is negotiated, and is thus not equivalent to a national demos. It lacks a particularising collective identity. Thus the limiting mechanism of participation is softened. A key question is again opened up. Who participates in the public space?

There is a public of the people's voice in Europe that has started to address claims towards Europe: either as responsible for bad outcomes or (less often and organised by particular publics of activists in Europe) as an ally against the nation state. A considerable amount of research has looked into the claims of farmers, fishermen, consumers, public interest groups, environmental groups and antiracist groups addressing European institutions (Imig and Tarrow 2001; Balme *et al.* 2002; Eder 2004).

The public resonance of European issues exists and increases. This is, however, a public that no longer has a unitary character. The diversity of resonance is necessitated by the diversity of publics. The unity of the will of the people is spatialised and temporalised. We have the universal public of formal members and the particular publics (in the plural) of the concerned. We have many demoi of people who have entered the EU by means of a contract (which differs fundamentally from the national situation). This diversity of the public in Europe does not lead to a common front stage of political debate. The national arrangement – linking decision-making on the back stage through front-stage scripts to a public conceived as a people – no longer works. The public as well as the actors at back stage find themselves on diverse stages on different occasions and in different locations. This undermines the taken-for-granted validity of a well-institutionalised script. Instead of deploring this, we could argue that this is the opportunity for creating public performances that force the tri-partite constellation of actors (back stage, front stage, public) into varying and volatile performances. The transnational situation leads to more public performances, which could be read as a mechanism fostering democratisation or – where there is no democratic procedure – creating strong claims against those making decisions.

Thus, triple contingency increases. The public becomes more incalculable, adding an element to collective learning that could inhibit the neutralisation of participation that has accompanied the process of democratisation since its inception.[22]

The interorganisational system of transnational institutions

The increasing isomorphism among collective actors

The public space is peopled not only by a public but also with an increasing number of collective actors, more than the national context permits. Such collective actors who represent a voice in Europe comprise more than just the functionaries in Brussels and the national representatives in European bargaining. It is rather an open interorganisational field that continuously expands and sets its own institutional rules. It is not by chance that Weiler (1999) called this the real European invention: to build a polity on a set of normative rules that reproduces itself through the continuous addition of further procedural rules. It is this positivisation of constitutional rules that allows us to speak of reflexive institutionalisation.

This open interorganisational field produces collective actors with their own internal publics. These organisational publics maximise the second aspect of the mechanism of democratisation: deliberation. There are elite publics in Europe that can be considered learning entities. There are expert publics (epistemic communities) in this emerging system, which are by definition learning organisations, the Commission being one such case. Thus the mechanism of deliberation extends beyond organisations into the interorganisational field. The mechanism of collective learning is fostered in the emerging transnational situation. There is a democratic functionalism working in this evolving space of interorganisational communication.

This enhances the importance of group rights. The public no longer represents individuals but groups claiming the legitimate support of a constituency. The most important group is the 'national group'. They speak in the interorganisational field for nations. This marks the disenchantment of the nation as a group based on ideal markers, on strong collective identities in the process of transnationalisation. Nations turn into interest groups that fight for advantageous gains in distributive struggles coordinated by supranational institutions. Any claims that are justified as being in the economic interest of the nation blur the differences between groups which base their social bond on strategic interests and groups which claim loyalty to a transcendent unity based on a 'we-feeling'.

The isomorphism emerging among the contending groups within the EU has been explained by organisational theorists (DiMaggio and Powell 1991) as resulting from increased participation in the interorganisational field. It is the result of relational mechanisms within the context of transnational competition among members of a supranational entity.

How do these different mechanisms, the cognitive mechanisms of learning and the relational mechanisms of creating multiple public stages interact in the transnational context? How do they continue the process of democratisation that has taken place within the national container? The assumption made above is one of discontinuity in the process of democratisation. In addition, we have to reckon with a plurality of paths of democratisation after this turning point. The theoretical argument therefore will have to move from reconstruction to the construction of possible paths of democratisation.

Alternative models for democratisation in the transnational situation

Three models for Europe can be identified that take into account the triad of mechanisms of democratisation. All three mechanisms are at work, yet the outcome of the dynamics is open. We can observe particular conditions in the *participatory* dimension, mainly due to the specific form of a European public. We can also observe particular conditions in the *deliberative* dimension, mainly due to the problem of the interorganisational culture of interested collective actors. There remains the dimension of *governance*, which is at the core of the legitimacy of a supranational arrangement, overcoming the lack of regulatory capacity of national governments due to the challenge of globalisation.

The paths of democratisation that are opened in the transnational situation by European integration can be described as different modes of making compatible the three mechanisms distinguished above. These are linked to models of normative legitimation specifically suited to each of these modes. They can be named the *Majone-type solution*, the *Habermas-type solution* and the *Arendt-type solution*.

The Majone-type solution

According to Majone, the central task of politics is to raise the capacity of governance by the state while taking into account as many interests as possible (achieving Pareto-optimalities), in order to find the most efficient solution to contradictory interests. To do so, a fourth branch of government emerges, which acts as a neutral proxy for reaching such solutions. For democratic processes, this needs the consideration of as many interests as possible, in a way that maximises the advantage of all and implies some criterion of fairness. Deliberation is fostered, while participation is defined in functional terms.

The Habermas-type solution

The Habermas solution is based on the model of the public beleaguering political institutions. A strong civil society is needed to debate issues that have to be taken into account by decision makers. This option obviously emphasises participation. In this model, the conflict among the three aspects is resolved through participation. Deliberation is the outcome of free participation, and efficiency will emerge as a systemic side effect of these actions.[23]

The Arendt-type solution

In the last model, those who enter the space of political communication should be those competent to do so. In the neo-liberal world, a normal man or woman is incompetent since he or she is estranged from dealing with a *res publica*. This model in fact provides a rather close-to-reality image of Europe. European institution-building is based on a highly selective procedure of choosing actors to act on the European scene. They are engaged in learning processes (a fact that early integration theorists noticed). It is an elitist solution in which the public space is constituted by political organisations dealing with the common good in Europe. This solution to the democratic organisation of processes of political communication obviously emphasises deliberation at the expense of participation (leaving open the degree of efficiency).

The three solutions put their emphasis on good governance either by informed and deliberating experts, or by a deliberating public, or by chosen political actors deliberating in public among themselves. Deliberation seems to be the key to the transnational situation, which is tempered by aspects of participation (Habermas) or of expert knowledge (Majone). In the Arendt-type solution, deliberation remains a self-justifying form of democracy. The three solutions offer feasible paths of transnational democratisation that mark the discontinuity with the national past of democratisation in different ways. They can be presented as 'better' because they are either more efficient or more deliberative or more participatory than the models of the national past.

Three pathological dynamics

There are no scientific grounds to prefer one solution to the other. What sociological analysis can do is to tell which solution is more probable than the other, given the constraints of the mechanisms that feed the dynamics of transnationalisation. What systematic analysis can do is to evaluate the risks tied to these solutions. Each solution has its particular risks, namely, those of authoritarian, ideological or elitist paths to democratisation.

The authoritarian path: maximising efficiency at the expense of participation and deliberation

This path is indicated by the strong role that expert bureaucracies play in the transnational situation, a real possibility in the European case. Rational bureaucracies tend to minimise the participatory and deliberative processes and maximise the strategy of rational legitimation in the Weberian sense. The pathology of this solution was remarked upon by Weber: that the gods, polytheism, will come out of the iron cage of rationality, thus undermining the rational basis of formal administration and making it vulnerable to irrational politics.

The ideological path: maximising participation at the expense of deliberation and efficiency

Participation is a close companion of populism, a danger that grows with the intensity of political communication. Participation fosters the marketisation of politics. This option is also a real possibility at the European level, where the strategy of referenda on the borders of the Union has given a particularly strong voice to xenophobic sentiments and fostered references to primordial and traditional visions of what constitutes the identity of Europe.

The elitist path: maximising deliberation at the expense of participation and efficiency

This is the case of deliberative structures where unending debates side-step the common good while excluding the mass of people from access to deliberative procedures. This is a possible path to democratisation in Europe. It may be traced in the formation of a civil society in Europe that resembles the model of enlightened absolutism where enlightened subjects joined the emperor to create a common good for all subjects. This is the model of democracy from above – the democracy of deliberation by proxies and advocates.

Conclusion

Europe appears to be a learning entity, providing a plurality of spaces to act and interact and fostering the collective good of Europeans. Against such an idealisation, the explanatory model outlined above provides a critical perspective by identifying the possibility of pathologies of learning. Instead of deploring the fact that the EU is not democratic in the same way as the nation state, it is proposed that we focus on the emerging forms of collective learning as elements of a possible process of the self-organisation of a democratic society. This can fail, and here social scientific critique can start, to identify the events that block learning processes.

Pathologies of the mechanism of democratisation are easily imaginable in Europe. But this is different from the question of the democratic deficit. It is rather a question of whether the EU can avoid the traps of pathological learning processes, which are a real possibility in any collective will formation in whatever kind of democratic polity. It is on these real possibilities that we should focus our critical eye.

Notes

This chapter has gained from criticism after presentations at the Conference on 'Debating the Democratic Legitimacy of the European Union' at the University of Mannheim, 27–29 November 2003; at a seminar presentation at the European University Institute, Florence, 10 December 2003; and at the conference on 'Governance and Civil Society' at the University of Trento, 11–12 December 2003.

1 Regarding the argument for mechanisms substituting for a variable-oriented explanation, see Hedström and Swedberg 1998; McAdam *et al.* 2001.
2 For the argument that there is none, see Gerhards 2001; for the argument that there is one, see Eder 2000; Eder and Kantner 2000; Trenz and Eder 2004.
3 For empirical results of research on media coverage in Europe, see Trenz 2004a and 2004b.
4 This theoretical perspective takes up the arguments made by Luhmann (1990, 1995) in his theory of the autopoietic character of social systems. In his theoretical exposition of the reality of the mass media, the self-observation of society by the media is turned into a mechanism of autopoietic self-reproduction (Luhmann 1996).

5 An excellent overview discussion is found in Eriksen and Fossum 2000.
6 The notion of 'original situation' alludes to Rawls (1971) in the sense that the people experiencing change in their time did not know what was coming. They acted historically under the veil of ignorance, only guided by the enlightenment idea that all men are equal and will do well when they act together as a people. On the other hand, many were afraid of the outcome – and had good reasons to be so, given the experience of the French Revolution as the central event for thinking about new times.
7 This holds for the early Habermas (1989), a position he revised later (Habermas 1992a), and in particular for Sennett (1977).
8 The term 'transnational' avoids the implication of postnational and the strong institutionalist perspective linked to the term 'supranational'. It focuses on the movement of ideas and people across national boundaries and on the forms of crystallisation of groups and ideas across national units.
9 Another concept that could be used here is 'civil society'. This is, neither society nor the state, but also a third space in-between. Democratic governance captures more adequately what is going on: the process of the democratic organisation of governing a society. In the end, this might turn out to be a mere terminological issue resulting from different traditions of political thought.
10 Note that I use the concept of governance as a principle of the rational and efficient organisation of a *res publica*, not as a particular form of a real polity.
11 The major part of Habermas (1989) is concerned with this aspect of the semantics of *Öffentlichkeit* in the political theories that tried to make sense of its emergence and function.
12 Some of the classics are Pateman 1974; Barber 1984; Dahl 1994. Whitley (1995) offers a discussion of the rationalist foundation of political participation.
13 See Habermas 1992b; Benhabib 1996; Cohen and Sabel 1997; Bohman and Regh 1998; Elster 1998; Dryzek 2000. See also Eder (1995) on the structural prerequisites of deliberative democracy, and Young (1996) for a critique of deliberative democracy.
14 In this category belong Leninist theories, which however, have fallen into disregard. Alternative versions are theories that give a central political role to social movements, such as Touraine 1981.
15 In this situation, it does not make much sense to distinguish between civil society and society, since society is coextensive with the people as a political collective. It is no longer a *bürgerliche Gesellschaft*, since workers have joined the ranks of national society, thus making it an all-class society.
16 The metaphor of the theatre makes sense. Whether the public is stupid or intelligent is an irresolvable question and also irrelevant regarding the explanation of the dynamics of democratisation. However, it does play a role when looking into pathological paths to the democratisation of the nation state.
17 It should be clear that such an arrangement of triple contingency is highly improbable. It emerges under rare conditions and is hard to stabilise. But once stabilised (in institutions and/or political culture), this constellation is hard to do away with: it will be remembered as a world that is better than the non-democratic constellation. Thus the counterfactualism of the ideal speech situation can be transformed into the evolutionary improbability of democratic arrangements.
18 There is a good argument concerning the 'theatre state' by Geertz (1980), relating to the state in nineteenth-century Bali. This does not exclude the applicability of the concept to the nation state in nineteenth- and twentieth-century Europe.
19 Eastern European countries are experiencing the simultaneity of making a

nation (post-1989, these countries continued the tradition of anti-colonial struggles to gain national sovereignty) and the making of a transnational Union of nation states. Thus they are torn between adherence to the national idiom and to the dynamics of European integration. This is situational *Ungleichzeitigkeit* (non-synchronicity).

20 For empirical data, see Trenz 2004a, 2004b.
21 Federal systems come closer to such a model context than unitarian systems.
22 Since transnational solutions logically follow national solutions, we can assume cumulative experience regarding democratisation and its pathological variants. This might be a reason why the people of Europe are so upset about the form of democracy that is offered to them in terms of a constitutional treaty between them and those that will have to govern in their name.
23 Habermas could also be labelled as a defender of deliberative democracy in the sense of arguing for a deliberative public beleaguering the institutions. This is, however, an idealisation of the original situation. Deliberation no longer takes place in the public that is the 'demos'. Thus his approach has a strong participatory aspect. It is not surprising that the idea of participatory democracy has not fared so well in the recent debate on democratic institutional design (Cohen and Sabel 1997; Joerges and Neyer 1997; Dorf and Sabel 1998; Neyer 2000).

4 A fragile cosmopolitanism

On the unresolved ambiguities of the European public sphere

Philip Schlesinger

Introduction[1]

The idea of communicative space is central to how we think about the workings of the contemporary public sphere. This is typically conceived of as a domain of argument – of writing, publishing, visualising, talking, listening and deliberation. In the era of the modern state, the principal space of political communication is commonly equated with the territorial boundaries of a national community in which the mediated discourse of political actors has a key role.

By contrast to the trope of a national home, for contemporary cosmopolitanism, communicative space is potentially global in scope. The world community is the interlocutory oyster. And so, the key stage for much political action (and relevant forms of discourse) is now properly transnational. In significant measure, action and discourse are relocated to a different plane and cosmo-communicative action is boundary-transcending rather than nationally bounded.

That said, states – long considered to be the modal, modern frameworks of political communication and the idealised homes of national cultures – have not yet been transcended as the principal controllers of citizenship, the purveyors of key collective identities, or the deliverers of a myriad of services and demands that shape the everyday lives and experiences of their inhabitants. Nevertheless, from a cosmopolitan viewpoint, they have become decidedly relativised as communicative spaces and containers of political action. Cosmopolitans, therefore, as opposed to national citizens, are involved (potentially, if not actually) in a global conversation about the good society.

When it comes to conceptualising the public sphere, two broad perspectives – the statist and the cosmopolitan – are the polar grand variants in play. True, this dualistic characterisation may simplify and dramatise; but it does offer us a clear entry-point into the arguments that follow.

If the state and the globe describe distinct conceptions of political space, polities that are neither clearly the one nor the other become objects of considerable analytical interest and challenge. In a binary framework, their ambiguity simply cannot be resolved. The European Union is a conceptual anomaly. It is less all embracing than the globe, yet also more far-reaching than the state.

The interesting questions that then arise concern the scope and scale of the public sphere and what this might signify for the politico-cultural identities and cohesion of different kinds of collectivity. Whether we frame the problem in terms of an international system of states and nations or, alternatively, that of a global community *in statu nascendi* becomes a matter of utmost significance. Each differs radically in how it imagines the spaces of political action, addresses their significance and locates processes of communication. Each, moreover, conjures up diverse views of human possibility and the political constraints within which this unfolds.

In Chapter 1, we have explored the implications for the public sphere of the EU remaining either a regulator or becoming a federation. Could the EU constitute a communicative space on the model of the nation state? Or is it rather an increasingly interconnected grouping of overlapping communicative communities with the potential to become a loosely integrated, transnational communicative space?

The EU's communication policy

As well as being fundamental to how we theorise the public sphere, these questions are of practical import for the EU's bureaucratic problem solving. In the wake of the June 2005 constitutional impasse, the eyes of the European Commission quickly turned to remedying shortcomings in communication. The 'democratic deficit' was plainly accompanied by a 'communications deficit'. The Commission's White Paper on a European Communication Policy (published in February 2006) illustrates the point especially well. This demonstrated a renewed – and much needed – interest in how to improve the effectiveness of the EU's communication with Europe's publics. The White Paper adopted a self-critical tone and ostensibly signalled an end to top-down communication. To 'close the gap' between the institutions and the disenchanted publics of the member states, what was needed was a 'partnership approach', aiming to bring 'all the key players' into its embrace: 'the other EU institutions and bodies; the national, regional and local authorities in the member states; European political parties; civil society' (European Commission 2006: 2). This required a mobilisation of forces that went with the grain of subsidiarity in the EU. 'Dialogue' and 'decentralisation' were the buzz-words. As Hans-Jörg Trenz and Klaus Eder (2004: 14) point out, the broad outlines of this approach had already been articulated in the White Paper on European Governance in 2001, when 'networking' was all the rage. Of particular note is the explicit reference to a 'European public sphere'. The adoption of such terminology demonstrates a striking congruence between a key term in longstanding academic debate and current bureaucratic terms of reference.

This is not altogether surprising as, encouraged by the successive European Commission Framework Programmes for research, as well as by other bodies such as the European Science Foundation, added impetus has been given to investigating the European public sphere in the early years of the millennium.[2] The horizontal research networks that have grown up in the EU's academic circles do not enjoy a public presence equivalent to that of national intelligentsias. But they are, nevertheless, a resource with the potential for shaping debate over policy.

Research on the public sphere is formed by an intellectual field. This is centred on a specific set of themes and problems in which definite strategies are pursued (Bourdieu 1993). In the calls for the Fifth and Sixth Framework Programmes, the European public sphere was mooted as a topic for research. As James Wickham has noted:

> the problems are not mainly generated internally by academic disciplines but stem from public debate and from what are perceived to be emerging issues by the Commission. Of course, there is a two-way flow here. Commission staff consult the research community informally and formally; issues that enter 'public debate' sometimes derive from, or are reformulated by, particular disciplines.
>
> (Wickham 2004: 192)

Given the negotiated character of what is researched, the research community is neither simply a heteronomous problem taker acting at the Commission's behest nor is it always an autonomous problem maker. How the research community has dealt with the tensions between supply and demand is a proper topic for the sociology of knowledge.[3]

Not surprisingly, there are echoes of academic discourse in the White Paper into which research-based arguments that emphasise the continuing importance of states and nations have also found their way into official thinking, as is evident in the following remarks:

> [T]he 'public sphere' within which political life takes place in the EU is largely a national sphere. To the extent that European issues appear on the agenda at all, they are seen by most citizens from a national perspective. The media remain largely national, partly due to language barriers; there are few meeting places where Europeans from different Member States can get to know each other and address issues of common interest [...]. There is a sense of alienation from 'Brussels', which partly mirrors the disenchantment with politics in general. One reason for this is the inadequate development of a 'European public sphere' where the European debate can unfold.
>
> (European Commission 2006: 4)

The continuing strength of the public sphere at a national level is coun-
terposed to the weakness of the 'pan-European political culture', largely
limited to the elites of member states. Linguistic and cultural diversity are
also rightly recognised as potent, ensuring a diversity of discourses, imagi-
naries and mentalities. It is also acknowledged that beyond the Rue de la
Loi and its environs, most Europeans do not engage in the routine
encounters and talking-shops that shape the intense micro-world of the
governing elites and the policy communities.

The proposed solution is to build the 'European dimension into the
national debate' (ibid.: 5). The chosen means is a 'communication policy'
to serve the common interest and obey principles of freedom of expression, inclusiveness, diversity and participation.[4] Fine words; but – in the
end – old reflexes die hard. By a communication policy is meant a top-
down, supply-side transmission of political information to recalcitrant citizens, using traditional media instrumentally and new media expediently
on the assumption that this will close the 'gap' and end the 'alienation'
detected. The Commission's approach is focused on content and content
carriage. It is centred on creating fora for debate and exchange as well as
working on media performance, which is seen as offering only a fragmented and episodic account of the EU, and therefore as inadequate in
informing the citizen.[5] The solutions are entirely focused on shaping the
production end of mediated communication, as questions of reception
are hardly susceptible to policy intervention.

There is no reason to suppose that such instrumentalism will resolve
the problem of producing a European public sphere, even if decanted
through subsidiary structures.[6] Daniel Dayan (2005: 44) has remarked that
'[t]he construction of collectives involves architects'. The White Paper
acknowledges that the primary and indispensable building blocks are still
the member states.

Social communication and the state

It is precisely the European nation state, addressed as a political community, that Jürgen Habermas's early theory took as its framework (Habermas
1989). But how are we to think of publicness in the multi-level complexity
of the EU? Both national and 'European' discourses and institutions
coexist. The EU's policy-making is a constitutive part of member states'
domestic political agendas and also of their legal and economic frameworks. Yet – and here the alienation detected by the Commission figures
in the form of the 'democratic deficit' – the Union is also still another
place, a different political level and, for most, an external locus of
decision-making. Herein lies the essential ambiguity of the European
public sphere. The evolution of the EU has ensured that the state-
bounded context no longer completely defines the political scope of communicative communities. Consequently, to analyse emergent European

communicative spaces, the focus needs to shift outwards to the supra-national arenas centred on Brussels and to consider how these try to address their constituent publics.

The challenge, therefore, is to develop a social communication theory capable of addressing the EU's complexity, by which is meant 'the number of elements in interaction and the number of different states that those interactions can give rise to' (Boisot 1999:5).

Social communication encompasses the gamut of distinctive signifying practices that defines and delimits a communicative community, operating within the framework of a broadly anthropological idea of a culture as a 'distinct whole way of life' (Williams 1981: 13). It is more extensive in scope than political communication, although political institutions and mediated communication about these have a focal importance for our contemporary understanding of social communication. Arguably, a European public sphere presupposes a theory of social communication because the relations it entails go beyond how citizens qua citizens interact with political institutions. Indeed, there is clearly some recognition of this question in the Commission's White Paper, where the envisaged 'partnership' encompasses 'civil society' across the member states. Civil society is only in part to be conceived as operating in the political domain. It is also simultaneously a socio-cultural hinterland and a realm of everyday life. Thus, a theory of social communication encompasses 'thick' social relations – not least those productive of a sense of belonging and emotional attachments – that continue to be integral to national life, despite its conflictual dynamics.

In this connection, we should consider one line of inquiry that is deeply rooted in the *longue durée* of European experience. Karl Deutsch (1966) first explicitly outlined a social communication theory of nationalism half a century ago. However, its origins, doubtless, lie further in the past. Some 50 years before Deutsch, the Austro-Marxist theorist, Otto Bauer (2000), wrote his seminal account of the 'national question'. This is the likely precursor of Deutsch's theory. Bauer and Deutsch together have exercised a remarkable – and virtually unacknowledged – influence over some of the more significant recent theorising about the communicative dimension of the nation (and therefore of the public sphere). Their central contention – still virtually an axiom – continues to have a bearing on how we might understand the contemporary, multinational EU. Such, now venerable, Austro-Marxist thinking is more than of passing coincidence. Finding a pluralistic solution to communicative complexity inside the EU has a strong family resemblance to Bauer's wish to give due recognition to national cultural autonomy in a multinational empire. The intimate connection between 'language' (in effect, social communication) and nationality was central to his analysis – not least the passions and emotions that linguistic and cultural claims could – and did – generate within the creaking imperial order that Robert Musil satirised as *Kakania.*

Bauer (2000: 34) contended that a modern democratic nation should be seen as a 'community of culture'. In contemporary conditions, it has been more common to think in terms of a community of *cultures*. Although, that said, particularly since 9/11, multiculturalism itself has increasingly come under pressure as questions of social cohesion and political loyalty rise up the agenda. Bauer also famously observed that the nation was a 'community of fate' (*eine Schicksalsgemeinschaft*) engaged in 'general reciprocal interaction' (ibid.: 100), thereby sharing a common language and culture. He remarked:

> The culture's sphere of influence extends only as far as the communicative possibilities of the language. The community of interaction is limited by the scope of the linguistic community. Community of interaction and language reciprocally condition each other.
>
> (Bauer 2000: 102)

The nation qua linguistic community, then, is conceived as culturally self-contained or, at the very least, as tending towards communicative closure. This was an early statement of a social communication theory of the nation. It came from trying to think through a strategy for ensuring cultural autonomy within a wider political order. The effort to address the *Kulturkämpfe* of the declining years of the Austro-Hungarian Empire has left its conceptual imprint on contemporary theorising about the public sphere in the EU.

An influential proponent of such thinking was Karl Deutsch – appropriately enough an early theorist of European union.[7] Central to his argument is the view that nations and nation states are strongly bounded by their patterns of interaction: 'People are held together "from within" by this communicative efficiency, the complementarity of the communicative facilities acquired by their members' (Deutsch 1966: 98). Social communication, in other words, produces collective cohesion and identity – and invites us to share a common fate. Bauer and Deutsch, therefore, had a fundamentally similar approach to how communicative and cultural practices and institutions (to which language is central) might strengthen the collective identity of a national group by creating and maintaining boundaries.

This simple – but compelling – idea is reproduced in a number of influential theories of nationalism. Ernest Gellner's (1983) view that culture is 'the distinctive style of conduct and communication of a given community' and that it is 'now the necessary shared medium' of the nation is likewise, at root, a social theory of cohesion. Cultural boundaries become defined by national cultures, which diffuse a literate 'high culture', in which the key agency is the national education system. Media are seen as sustaining that political community, providing it with its deep codes for distinguishing between self and other. For his part, Benedict Anderson (1991) has contended that mechanically reproduced print languages have unified fields of linguistic exchange, fixed national languages and created idiolects of power. So, by going to Gellner's schools, cultured nationals acquired the competence to read Anderson's novels and newspapers, and entered the public sphere endowed with cultural capital. For each of these writers, the collective consumption of mediated communication (based on a common 'national' language) creates and sustains a sense of common belonging. Michael Billig (1995) has endorsed and extended this broad argument. As nationals, he suggests, we live less in a state of perpetual mobilisation than one of the banal assimilation of everyday symbolism and categorisation: flags, anthems, distinctions between home and foreign news, national histories and languages, a particular sense of political geography. National identity – outside of crises – is unremarkably reproduced in the routines of everyday life. Culture holds us together: it both conditions and informs our conceptions of national identity. Although social communication theorists may differ on the key mechanisms or processes that produce cultural cohesion, all agree that some or other dimension of communication is central to how the nation should be conceived.

Of course, no culture is an island. All ostensibly national systems of communication are influenced by what lies outside. National cultures are usually permeable, however much they may be censored and controlled, and in the age of the Internet, mobile devices and satellite broadcasting, such relative openness is necessarily greater than ever before. I have argued elsewhere (Schlesinger 2000) that the main thrust of classical social communications theory is to concern itself with the *interior* of the national culture and communication, with largely endogenous explanations of what makes us what we are, with how boundaries are drawn around us. Look at Bauer's *Fragestellung* and such interiority is not at all surprising: it is congruent with the assertion of the right to have a national communicative space within a wider imperial constitutional framework of competing national cultures. It represents both the quest for, and the defence of, cultural space. But it is obvious that such a neatly demarcationist theory of social communication and public space is no longer tenable. It is especially the case, in a 'globalised' world, that its limitations are thrown increasingly into relief by the rapid development of new forms of public electronic connectedness through information and communications technologies, although the emergence of such spaces does not mean we should now regard the continued shaping role of the state in social communication at the national level as irrelevant (Hjarvard 2001; Street 2001; Sinclair 2004).

The evolution of the EU poses Otto Bauer's century-old problem afresh: how may many diverse national, ethnic, linguistic and other cultural communities achieve autonomy *within* a single, overarching political framework?[8] The old Habsburg empire had to adjust to nationalist claims to autonomy from below and it did not survive these. By contrast, the EU is an importer of already formed nations shaped by (more or less well) established states.[9]

But there is a second question that reverses the terms of Bauer's conundrum. If Bauer was trying to find a solution to nationalist demands within an overarching framework, current cosmopolitan writers emphasise the transcendent potential of the emergent European framework to connect to a new global order that needs a public sphere to match.

The gradual emergence of a supranational formation such as the EU (as a distinctively developed instance of wider trends towards supranational governance) has unsettled how we might now conceive of established communicative relations between national publics and state-centred systems of power. It makes us intensely aware of the diverse levels at which publics might form, the horizontal ties that bind across state boundaries, and how our communicative competence needs to make appropriate adjustments.

The present picture is contradictory, as Abram de Swaan illustrates in Chapter 7. For him, the lack of a European intelligentsia, with all the supporting apparatus of journals, academies, prizes, career opportunities, and crucially for him – a common, synchronous debate about key matters – is at the heart of the EU's democratic deficit. As he rightly points out, there are indeed multiple interrelations at the expert level – in short, particular micro-publics do exist – but at the level of the routine general debate that still characterises the national public sphere, there is a decided lack of purchase. De Swaan also notes how the EU's linguistic diversity – alongside the de facto rise of English as 'the vehicular language of Europe' – has underpinned the pull of the national. Multilingual democracy on a large scale is not an impossible dream, he notes, citing the cases of India and South Africa. But in the European context, to counteract the continuing robustness of state systems, the material underpinnings of a new 'cultural opportunity structure' are now needed. Thus, he maintains, the necessary conditions for sustaining a European public sphere are not yet in place. However, as noted, micro-publics created by the problem-oriented theorising, empirical research and consultancy accompanying the growth of European institutions do exist. Whether they will constitute part of a cosmopolitan, European intelligentsia is an open question.

While, presently, linguistic diversity and a fragmented intelligentsia do stand in the way of a common public sphere, the question of cultural complexity extends further, into the state itself. First, as is self-evident, the EU's member states cannot be treated as the simple expression of the nation. Statehood does not entail monolingualism or monoculturalism. Regional or minority languages, often with supporting institutions and media systems, operate at a sub-state level, perhaps most potently in regions that are also self-consciously 'stateless nations'. Publics do exist at the sub-state level, and are constituted on the basis of linguistic or cultural distinctiveness (Moragas Spà *et al.* 1999; Cormack 2000). Aside from this, continuing migration and diasporic links have ensured that, as elsewhere, linguistic and cultural diversity – in part sustained by transnational media consumption – are part of the contemporary landscape of the member states (Jouët and Pasquier 2001).

Second, the EU's enlargement has meant that national questions held in check during the Cold War are increasingly the inheritance of the EU to manage. As Rogers Brubaker (1996) has observed, post-communist Europe became a space of 'nationalising states'. These legacies are an inherent part of the discussion about how a European public sphere might evolve.[10] In many cases, national minorities without citizenship of the new nationalising state constitute a significant component of a neigh-bouring state or states.[11] The implosion of Yugoslavia has left ethno-national problems that eventual accession for its successor states might resolve. And, there is the moot question of Turkish accession to the EU, which is embroiled in the recurrent debate over whether or not the Union should underline its Christian heritage as an integral part of its identity (Schlesinger and Foret 2006 and Chapter 10).

Towards a cosmopolitan communicative space?

The debate over spiritual values in the EU shows that we cannot escape from politics, high or low. This means that we do have to take the EU's institutions seriously. On this score, cosmopolitans divide into two main camps: institutional and post-institutional.

Institutional cosmopolitans use the language of rights and duties and take seriously the means by which these might be enforced. Habermas's rights-based, supranational conception of the EU connects to a global perspective. He portrays the public sphere as potentially unbounded, as shifting from specific locales (such as the nation) to the virtual co-presence of citizens and consumers linked by public media.

Habermas (1996a: 373–4) argues that communicative space is to be understood in terms of 'a highly complex network [that] branches out into a multitude of overlapping international, national, regional, local and subcultural arenas'. He envisages that 'hermeneutic bridge-building' will occur between different discourses. A European communicative space conceived in open network terms has become the new political play-ground (ibid.: 171). A European public sphere would therefore be open-ended, with communicative connections extending well beyond the continent. Contemporary cultural flows and networks ensure that commu-nicative autarchy is unachievable.

What this leaves unresolved is whether or not convergent communica-tive practices might, in the end, produce some kind of cultural cohesion, resulting in a European community of fate. Habermas's answer to this question is to propose that EU citizens become 'constitutional patriots'. This post-nationalist, rule-bound form of identification implies an order of preference and (however fluid) at least some distinction between an 'us' and a 'them'. It still carries inescapable echoes of an older, interstate conception of political order. If a social communications approach to the public sphere insists on the 'thickness' of what sustains the political culture, constitutional patriotism presumes 'thin' relations. However, it does also presuppose affinities with other patriots. So the EU's cosmopolitan potential is still anchored in a web of affiliations.

Habermas (2004) emphasises the importance of a European constitution. This demarcates a distinctive political space and provides a common value orientation. Constitutionalism remains central to how a European public sphere might be imagined: linked upwards to more general structures of governance and downwards to more particular ones. Habermas has argued that 'the making of such a constitution represent[s] in itself a unique opportunity of transnational communication' (ibid.: 28). He has stressed the key role of a 'European-wide public sphere' and 'the shaping of a political culture that can be shared by all European citizens' (ibid.: 27). Quite how this is to be achieved is still a moot point. We may question whether the constitutional process was an effective form of transnational communication. More striking was the national framing of the debate and how national considerations played into rejection of the Constitutional Treaty in France and the Netherlands in May and June 2005 (Dacheux 2005: 129).

Although the ratification process ran into the sands and still has to recover its momentum, it remains of key importance for the development of the EU's political identity. Aside from its directly legal and political significance, a constitution also defines the limits within which 'European' patterns of political culture and communication may be encouraged to emerge at the EU level.

Habermas's attempt to navigate between the free flight of cosmopolitan potential and the gravitational pull of institutions is akin to Manuel Castells's (1996, 1997, 1998) approach. For Castells, the new communication technologies contribute to the formation of a novel kind of society, the 'informational'. He sees the EU as a precursor to a new political order, to new forms of association and loyalty. The emerging European polity epitomises what Castells terms 'the network state'. The EU is imagined not only as a political–economic zone but also as a specific kind of communicative space.[12] Castells focuses on how networks, facilitated by Information and Communication Technologies (ICTs), transcend borders, thus in effect providing an infrastructure for cosmopolitanism.

The boundaries of the putative European communicative space – and therefore the potential public sphere – are produced by the nexus of political institutions that constitute Union Europe, the dealings between them and growing 'subsidiary' horizontal links across the member states (Castells 1998: 330–1).[13] Castells argues that the EU has different 'nodes' of varying importance that make up a network. Regions and nations, nation states, EU institutions, together constitute a framework of shared authority.

Castells's approach implies that complex interconnected 'communicative complementarities' – as Deutsch put it – may emerge out of the informal processes of making the union. The potentially globalising pull of communications technologies is countered by emergent patterns of social interaction in the EU's space. These are polyvalent: simultaneously, they knit together diverse actors economically, politically and communicatively. Cosmopolitans are challenged to recognise the varying significance of particular fora linked by networks.

With a quite different emphasis, David Held (2004) has sketched an institutionally oriented cosmopolitan conception of citizenship and the kind of public sphere that accompanies this. He envisages a citizenship that goes beyond 'exclusive membership of a territorial community' to

> an alternative principle of world order in which all persons have equivalent rights and duties in the cross-cutting spheres of decision-making which affect their vital needs and interests [...]. Citizenship would become multilevel and multidimensional, while being anchored in common rules and principles.
>
> (Held 2004: 114)

To think of the political community as no longer bounded by the sovereign nation state is highly pertinent to the EU, which Held – like many others – sees as an example of the 'reconfiguration of political power' (ibid.: 87). Political communities, he suggests, no longer 'correspond in any straightforward way to territorial boundaries' (Held 1995: 225). In consequence, '[t]he cultural space of nation-states is being rearticulated by forces over which states have, at best, only limited leverage' (ibid.: 126). Held argues for an international order based on cosmopolitan democratic public law (ibid.: 227) because 'the regulative capacity of states increasingly has to be matched by the development of collaborative mechanisms of governance at supranational, regional and global levels' (Held 2004: 15).

In this vision of a 'social democratic multilateralism' we find an echo of Otto Bauer, since for Held the world consists of 'overlapping communities of fate' (2004: 107). Such diversity requires the establishment of 'an overarching network of democratic public fora, covering cities, nation-states, regions and the wider transnational order', working along the lines of rational deliberation, argued for by Habermas (ibid.: 109). However, in Held's argument, the EU is just another node in the institutional network envisaged, and not therefore a principal focus of interest. He adheres to a worldview in which articulation between fora (more or less institutionalised communicative spaces) is emphasised over the internal elaboration of territorially bounded spaces. So it is entirely understandable that the detailed workings of a European public sphere will be a matter of relatively minor interest.

This is a point of connection to post-institutional theorists of cosmopolitanism who argue that it is essential to think of Europeanness *beyond* the limiting institutional framework of the EU and rather to locate it in its global context.

For Ulrich Beck (2006: 164), the EU's struggle with its political future is actually an 'institutionalized failure of the imagination' that does not live up the cosmopolitan dreams of its founding fathers. The Union, he maintains, lacks political pragmatism and radical openness. The present tensions between the regulatory and federal models, which are actually of vital explanatory importance, are swept aside by Beck (rather oddly) as denying Europe's diversity (ibid.: 171–2). Instead, Beck argues, 'The political union must be conceived as a cosmopolitan union of Europe, in opposition to the false normativity of the national' (ibid.: 167). Indeed, the prospect that is held out is variously that of a 'cosmopolitan state' or a 'cosmopolitan cooperative of states'. But beyond these slogans it is not at all clear how power would be exercised, how post-territorial politics would function or how ethnocultural diversity might be secured. Thus, while I would not dissent at all from Beck's view that European states must cooperate to survive in the context of global risks, there is little but exhortation to help us on our way in his analysis. There is certainly little realistic engagement with institutional politics.

For instance, according to Beck, the EU has inaugurated 'a struggle over institutions with the aim of confronting European horror with European values and methods'. Thus, after the Second World War and the Holocaust, he believes, one of Europe's most positive achievements is to stand for the protection of human rights. He further asserts that commemoration of the Holocaust is an institutional foundation for the EU's identity and indeed for a wider Europe. However, Beck's position takes no account of Holocaust denial, or of the way in which opposition to acts of commemoration is now connected to the politics of the Middle East, or of the differences between official acts and popular sentiment, or, indeed, of present-day competition over victimhood throughout Europe.

Gerard Delanty and Chris Rumford (2005: 20), who have taken an even more radical post-institutional line, maintain that 'the state does not define a people's imaginary. New conceptions of peoplehood can be found in the cosmopolitan currents that are a feature of Europeanization' and that the emergent social construction of Europe should be understood in the wider context of globalisation. The conception of identity involved here is seen as 'thin' and dialogical and as rooted in 'a system of relations and a capacity for communication' (ibid.: 68). The argument is a boundary-transcending and transformative one, taking its distance from political science models, so that Europe is seen as a space of possibilities for new cosmopolitan attachments in which the challenge for the EU is to 'create spaces for communication'.

Communication is judged valuable principally in articulating connections *beyond* the EU, rather than in building it as a political community or a collective identity. The 'emerging' European public sphere is characterised as 'European-wide forms of communicative competence, discourses, themes and cultural models and repertoires of evaluation within different national contexts'. Its uniqueness is held to be 'based on certain common issues and interconnecting debates in which the community of reference becomes increasingly diluted and, as it does so, reconfigured [...] it is a medium in which new expressions of cosmopolitanism are taking place' (ibid.: 103–4). From this point of view, the European public sphere is not so much an institutionalised space that might democratise the Union – and also deal with Europe's chequered past – as a post-institutional launching pad for a new orientation to the world that increasingly sheds its European cast.

However, bounded relations surely still remain important because, as Christer Jönssen *et al.* (2000: 184–5) argue: 'social communication is most effective between individuals whose mental worlds have been "formatted" analogously over lengthy periods of time'. Strikingly congruent with Deutsch's principle of communicative complementarity, the argument is that 'human thought requires boundaries', based on proximity, likeness and linkage, so that 'place, neighbourhood and region will continue to play important roles as realms of experience and epistemic communities'. This, in turn, 'fosters local anchorage and regional identity' so that even '[i]n the age of electronic networking, conversation therefore continues to have a major role, as does the face to face meeting' (ibid.).

In an analysis of such meetings, Catherine Neveu (2000, 2002) has adopted a processual approach to 'becoming European', exploring the internal dynamics of Euro-networking. Investigating what happens when European institutions invite various categories of people to participate in transnational activities, she suggests that the resulting acculturation may have a 'return effect' once participants go back to their places of origin. Involvement in networks and exchanges are seen as building an important path to the formation of a European public sphere. Interaction with European institutions constitutes a kind of 'training process' that may impact on people's notions of citizenship and identity.[14] Neveu's anthropological approach reveals how background models and representations grounded in national discourses come into play and are modified. It remains an open question whether such encounters can build up a common sentimental basis for a nascent cosmopolitanism.

To sum up, the development of a European public sphere may be conceived as based on interaction between Euro-institutions and Euro-networks. Not all institutions have the same centrality; not all networks have the same intensity of interaction. Although a relatively weak, transnational public space has indeed evolved around the policy-making actors in the EU institutions, states, nations and regions remain crucially important as locales for debate and sources of identity. Castells's Euro-networker has not completely forgotten how to wave Billig's national flag and most of the EU's citizens still maintain a wary distance from Habermas's ideal of constitutional patriotism. Unevenly, over time, the EU is developing a special interactive intensity that, in some sectors of public life, favours internal communication and creates an internally differentiated referential boundary with stronger and weaker forms of institutionalisation. This may, and does, coexist with global networking and the development of transnational governance.

The public sphere and mediated communication

Because EU policy-making and political direction impinge increasingly on member states, the European dimension impacts on the agenda of the mediated political discourse of national polities. How should we interpret this? Not surprisingly, a fault-line runs through contemporary theorising about the role of political communication in the public sphere. This reflects the Union's liminal status – poised, as it is, between being a regulator and a federation. The dividing line is over how political communication impacts on citizenship, collective identity and patriotism. Are these now shifting from their longstanding and often exclusive alignment with the member states (and nations) into a more inclusive cosmopolitan 'European' citizenship, collective identity and constitutional patriotism?

Consider one current of contemporary debate about the media and the public sphere – well represented in this book – that identifies the EU's dynamic as chronically enlarging the common public communicative space.[15]

In Chapter 3, Klaus Eder has presented a 'democratic functionalist' argument for the role of political communication in conditions of complexity. He suggests that 'the more political communication is triggered by the complexity of issues, the more those involved are exposed to the force of counterarguments, thus fostering normative claims of equal participation' (p. 45). Must the dissemination of argument and diverse perspectives across the borders of member states produce more democratisation in the EU as a whole by stimulating action in the public sphere? Not necessarily. Eder recognises that deliberation and participation do not invariably lead to democratic governance, as there can be systemic obstacles to this. Nevertheless, he does consider that 'there is enough political communication going on that is capable of setting off mechanisms of democratization beyond the nation state' (p. 57). Eder argues for a kind of spill-over effect of 'emerging forms of collective learning' (p. 62). This breaks with the idea of a single public sphere and single collective identity as necessary to the process of Europeanisation. European identity is seen as an emergent property of the process of negotiation between the peoples of Europe.

Trenz and Eder (2004), in related vein, have suggested that it is 'media-tized public spaces' that best conduce to the prospects of collective learn-ing: the governing elites are driven to account for themselves, and the public demands greater accountability from its rulers. Trenz and Eder therefore consider the European public sphere to have a 'self-constituting dynamic'. However, despite their argument that the very discussion of the democratic deficit is a kind of remedial action, a 'self-help therapy' that begins to fix the problem, they do – in the end – have to accept that 'the self-reflexivity of the EU institutions is not automatically transformed into the reflexivity of the European public' (ibid.: 19). If the process of general social learning with a democratising outcome is not in the end routinely guaranteed, it is hard to see how Trenz and Eder can then conclude that the very working of the unfolding European public sphere conduces to a 'process of permanent democratic transition' (ibid.: 21). Consequently, it is surely questionable to assume that the mediatised public sphere must continually 'Europeanise' the constituent national publics in the long term. It is much safer to conclude that this might happen, given numer-ous conditions.

In analyses of two key phases of the constitutional debate by Trenz in Chapter 5 and Fossum and Trenz in Chapter 11, the emphasis shifts. Trenz argues that in the initial phase of the constitutional debate in May 2000, rather than sustaining national public spheres and anti-Euro-peanism, 'the quality press has become a dynamic forerunner of Euro-pean integration, promoting the deepening and the constitutionalisation of the EU' (p. 90) so that collectively such publications have a 'European voice'. His analysis of the constitutional debate in 13 'quality' newspapers is premised on the view that '[t]he central function of the newspaper commentaries on the EU thus consists in allowing for the imagining of a "European society" as a collectivity of political self-determination' (p. 91). Trenz concludes that the press commentaries studied promote an active, progressive consensus in favour of a federal vision of the EU.[16] In this version of the argument, there is now less emphasis on the reciprocal learning process of the EU institutions and the wider public and a clearer recognition that there is no linear relationship between editorial comment and the formation of public opinion and, moreover, that the 'constitutional debate does not automatically transform the permissive consensus expressed in the media into the permissive consensus of the people of Europe' (p. 107). Nor, Trenz accepts, does the public necessar-ily share in the European imaginary he finds in the press.

The people's continued reluctance to think of themselves as Europeans is even more pronouncedly identified by Fossum and Trenz in Chapter 11. Reflecting on the rejection of the Constitutional Treaty in France and the Netherlands in May and June 2005 and asking whether a failure of communication played a role in this, they argue that the constitutional debate became 'decontextualised' throughout the Union – in other words, that it was not interpreted in the terms intended. In particular, rather as is recognised in the Commission's White Paper on a European Communication Policy, they draw attention to the 'national patterns of media framing' (p. 215) that have shaped the ratification debates. Fossum and Trenz take one step further in the direction not only of recognising the key importance of the national dimension but also of acknowledging that the vast majority of news media output is part of the entertainment business and that attention paid to EU questions is at best episodic and mostly of brief duration. In short, assumptions about the quality press as an instrument of enlightenment, even if correct, refer only to a minor part of the system of news production and distribution.[17] As media systems increasingly fragment under the pressures of economic competition and digital convergence, and the Internet more and more poses questions about the conditions under which traditional media reporting will evolve, for political classes everywhere the challenge of credibly addressing general publics is likely only to increase.

Given the 'rational commitment' of European institutional actors, argue Fossum and Trenz, they end up speaking to the wrong audiences through inappropriate means. Most citizens are not readers of the elite press. Moreover, as Andy Smith shows in Chapter 12, commitment to a rational communications strategy by the Commission is really rather questionable, given Commissioners' diverse interests and the well-documented shortcomings of media management capacity in the Commission itself. Neil Gavin's (forthcoming) analysis of the inadequacies of the EU's communication strategies underscores these points. It is particularly instructive, therefore, to see how exponents of the democratic functionalist line, which has been exemplary in stressing the Europeanising potential of mediated communication, have increasingly concluded that the EU's institutions risk speaking to themselves alone, thereby failing to effect the necessary process of democratisation.

Even if the 'Europeanisation' of public spheres is conceived of as an unfinished process, its rolling out, as Ruud Koopmans and Jessica Erbe (2004) have acknowledged in a study of the German press, is rather uneven in impact, depending not only on the specific policy arenas but also on the characteristics of the media culture in which debate occurs (cf. Kevin 2003: 174).[18] In Chapter 6, arguing from a similar perspective, Paul Statham suggests that although 'Europeanisation' means that (to varying degrees) certain EU policy issues are now routinely reported, in France debate about Europe is directly connected with the EU level, whereas in the UK it remains far more distanced and self-contained. His analysis underlines the continuing weight of national political systems in shaping the scope of debates in the public sphere and, moreover, that these tend to be dominated by elites, whose own relationship to the EU is crucial. While this body of work shows that elite media are addressing similar issues at the same time, this thematic convergence does not necessarily equate to producing a shared European perspective (cf. van de Steeg 2002). Even if – to a lesser or greater extent – news agendas have become 'Europeanised' across the EU, for national publics this has not translated into an irresistible invitation to become European.

Inasmuch as a media-sustained, transnational communicative space is emerging because of EU integration, this is class-inflected and predominantly the domain of political and economic elites, not yet that of a general European public. I have argued elsewhere that in the European communicative space today some media are, in effect, creating specialised audiences and readerships by seeking markets (Schlesinger 1999, 2003; Schlesinger and Kevin 2000). Examples include *The Economist*, the *Financial Times*, the *International Herald Tribune* and, perhaps, in the audiovisual sphere *Euronews* and *Arte*. Traditional print journalism centred on Europe has not easily transcended national boundaries, as the short life of *The European* (London) and the much briefer one of *l'Européen* (Paris) have shown (Schlesinger 1999; Neveu 2002).

European journalism is geared to the EU's intergovernmentalism, its continuing role as a regulatory rather than federal entity. In the member states, national editorial values continue predominantly to shape coverage of European themes and issues (Kevin 2003: 179), not least because the established paths of source-media relations underpin the national discourse. National governmental sources are still of paramount importance for journalists covering EU issues (Morgan 1999), even if other voices are also gaining access to news agendas. Research in Brussels suggests that some weakly transnational forms of exchange have developed at the EU level between journalists and their sources. Christoph Meyer (2000) has argued that there is an increasing tendency for transnational investigative journalism to emerge, thereby contributing to the accountability of the institutions. Occasionally, but not so far systematically, this can have political effects, particularly in the exposure of scandal and corruption. But such alliances still appear to be a transient rather than a systemic feature of the Euro-political scene. Olivier Baisnée (2002) also refers to the co-operative context of Brussels reporting. Although he claims that journalists have been socialised into being 'Europe's only real public' (ibid.: 112), diverse orientations and patterns of coverage prevail in British and French news media, with the EU seen as not very newsworthy (Baisnée 2003a). Even at key moments – such as a focus on constitutional developments – coverage is framed principally in terms of national politics, although openness to other EU perspectives may vary cross-nationally (Gleissner and de Vreese 2005). Much the same may be said of the row triggered by European Council President Silvio Berlusconi's address to the European Parliament in 2003. His insult to a German Member of the European Parliament was widely reported as 'a clash of (ethnic) nations' rather than a moment occasioning European deliberation (Downey and Koenig 2006: 184).

If we are attentive to the cosmopolitan potential of social interaction, we certainly should not discount the transnational relations and negotiations that have become part of the everyday reporting experience. But nor should we over-estimate it. The Euro-journalism network remains divided by diverse national ideas of professionalism, serving domestic markets and principally meeting nationally rooted audience expectations. These still hold the key to career success. The continuing national pull of journalistic practice and frameworks of reference explain the sheer difficulty of developing journalism either for a Europe-wide general public or, indeed, for a particular public oriented to the EU contained within a given member state.[19] But this is merely a microcosmic illustration of the tensions that still persist between the national principle and Europeanness. Theorising the evolution of the EU requires simultaneous recognition of the relative robustness of national public spheres and of the relative fragility of the cosmopolitan, transnational dimension.

Notes

1 This chapter departs from, and extensively reshapes and revises my essay 'The Babel of Europe?' (Schlesinger 2003).
2 The CIDEL project (Citizenship and Democratic Legitimacy in the European Union), from which this book originates, is one such example.
3 This book itself derives directly from the opportunity created by the Commission's concern with its lack of democratic legitimacy. For two divergent views of where research should be going, see Golding (2007), who focuses on comparative journalism research, and Slaatta (2006), who argues for taking a cultural turn.
4 These principles are not as straightforward as may be supposed. For instance, insistence on respect for diversity and inclusiveness may well conflict with freedom of expression.
5 The European Parliament has followed up by suggesting that we need citizens' agoras. See the report 'MEPs Plan Citizens "Agoras" to Boost EU Debate', *EU Observer*, 23 May 2006.
6 See Trenz and Vetters (2006) for a brief critique of the White Paper. In a seminar on the proposals held at the University of Lugano in May 2006, professional European communication managers found the Commission's conception of the audience to be unsophisticated and the project itself to be very under-resourced.
7 Deutsch seems not to have acknowledged fully his own debt to Bauer's conception of the nation as a cultural community.
8 With the 2004 enlargement, and those still in prospect, the EU is incorporating more and more of the old Habsburg lands.
9 This is an oversimplification, of course. It is certainly not the case that all EU states are to be regarded as homogeneous, as the politics of devolution and/or separatism in, for instance, Belgium, France, Italy, Spain and the UK shows.
10 As is demonstrated in the analysis of the Hungarian accession debates outlined by Maria Heller and Ágnes Rényi in Chapter 9.
11 The Hungarian minority in Romania and Slovakia is a well-known case in point. But many more examples could be cited.
12 Mattelart (2000) has given us a detailed intellectual history, situating Castells in

relation to his key precursor, Daniel Bell. Garnham (2000a: 61) reminds us that we should treat this version of the idea of a new information society with scepticism. His critique of Castells's account of the network is rooted in a political economy of communication that underlines how relations of power are embedded in networks and their uses. Networks operate as 'systems of collaboration and not of competition' (Garnham 2000b: 70). Looked at from the standpoint of a political system, however, competition *between* networks becomes a key matter of interest and so Castells's analysis remains suggestive.

13 Castells's more recent work has moved beyond this position. However, his utopian vision of an 'Internet Galaxy' as a zone of citizen freedom still has to contend with a world of states that combine to regulate threats to their control over information (Castells 2001: 178–85).

14 This parallels Olivier Baisnée's (2002, 2003a) findings: Euro-journalists share some features, but the needs – and models – of different national political systems presently impose insuperable limits.

15 The next paragraphs consider work connected to the europub.com project, which is one of the most systematic studies of the European public sphere.

16 Trenz rightly notes discordant British exceptionalism in the European chorus – which runs against his thesis and requires the kind of explanation given by Statham that we find in Chapter 6, where the historical particularity of national public spheres is stressed.

17 The focus on the quality press echoes earlier expectations of public service broadcasting in contributing to political rationality (Garnham 1986). Kevin (2003: 180) finds that public service broadcasting channels' output plays 'a greater role' than that of commercial competitors.

18 Perhaps Germany is a special case. Kevin (2003: 165) suggests that German television 'appears to feature the most representative range of participants' and that comparatively across eight countries, 'most [EU] news appears in the German press' (ibid.: 170), which also has the most comprehensive cultural coverage (ibid.: 174).

19 Journalistic production in the EU is overwhelmingly oriented to national consumption. Fiction in the five main media markets is also overwhelmingly nationally produced and consumed – unless it comes from the USA. Cross-border circulation of films and TV programmes is very low or non-existent (Lange 2003).

Part II

Assessing Europe's general public(s)

Philip Schlesinger and John Erik Fossum

'General publics' operate in the associational domain of civil society. They can take a wide variety of forms, ranging from what Nancy Fraser (1992) calls 'subaltern counterpublics' that produce counter-discourses in opposition to the established order, to a wide variety of interest groups and voluntary associations that also seek to make their voices heard and, at times, to affect public policy.

Due to the Union's still open-ended character, a crucial issue is how EU institutions might in future articulate with general publics. This requires us to pay attention to general publics, as these are crucial to how the public sphere is conceptualised:

> the expectation deriving from a discourse-centered theoretical approach, that rational results will obtain, is based on the interplay between a constitutionally instituted formation of the political will and the spontaneous flow of communication unsubverted by power, within a public sphere that is not geared toward decision-making but toward discovery and problem resolution and that in this sense is *nonorganized.*
>
> (Habermas 1992a: 541)

Consequently, our assessment of the prospects for the formation of a European public sphere should ask, first, what the social preconditions are for the formation of a European general public or publics; and second, what might be the desired democratic effects of public spheres. A third question, posed from the standpoint of the public, concerns the current state of the Union.

On the first issue, social preconditions commonly educed include a common language (whether vernacular or political), a common identity (national, post-national, religious, etc.) and shared media. We might also add the role of intellectuals and research communities and networks. The European Union – with its strong onus on recognising various forms of diversity – is based on the tenet that a polity can be established and function without 'thick' sociocultural presuppositions. But how can the Union forge a sense of commonality sufficient to sustain it as a polity? Abram de Swaan considers the obstacles to the formation of a European cultural and intellectual space, whereas Lars Blichner addresses the shortcomings of public language in the EU. For their part, François Foret and Philip Schlesinger examine the potential divisiveness of religion. Religions – typically self-referential entities – offer excellent examples of particular publics. And Maria Heller and Ágnes Rényi show how EU debates are shaped by the intellectual field in an accession state.

Media are crucial players in any debate on a European public sphere. Assessments of the media performance often start by referring to ideal conditions, such as those sketched out by Blumler and Gurevitch (1995). From one normative standpoint, therefore, virtuous mediated communication might offer features such as meaningful agenda-setting, dialogue across a wide range of views, ways of engaging citizens' interests, and robust resistance to censorship and news management. Of course, such ideals have to be played out against contemporary debate about actual media performance, which rarely conforms to fine principles.

Mediated communication has been – and remains central to – thinking about the public sphere and the formation of public opinion (Habermas 1996a; Mayhew 1997; Splichal 1999). For some two decades now, a growing body of work has addressed the complex relations between media and public spheres in the EU, whether at the national or supranational level (for discussions, see Schlesinger 2000, 2003; Kevin 2003). There is also relevant empirical research into the relations between EU institutions and the Brussels press corps (e.g. Morgan 1999; Meyer 2000; Baisnée 2003a; Bastin 2003).

Mediated communication is often assigned a key role in providing links between EU institutions and general publics. Consequently, in significant measure, Part II addresses how communicative processes *relate to* general publics and what we might judge their impact to be.

This connects directly to the second issue we have identified above, namely that of the *desirable effects* of public spheres. Writing about mini-publics, Fung (2003: 347) has identified various factors relevant for judging the contribution of the public sphere to democracy. These are no different from those typically invoked for general publics and include civic engagement and popular involvement, the quality of deliberation, open access to information and robust processes for ensuring official accountability.

Mediated communication is commonly held to contribute to the good functioning of a democratic culture. Media performance is variously addressed in several of the chapters that follow. Hans-Jörg Trenz focuses on the role of the 'quality' press within the broader integration process, whereas Fossum and Trenz seek to explain why there were negative outcomes in the ratification process and how media contributed to these. For his part, Paul Statham explores the continuing importance of national frameworks for media coverage.

On the third issue, the current state of an EU public sphere, the various contributions differ and thereby properly reflect the present state of debate occasioned by the EU's unresolved status.

5 '*Quo vadis* Europe?'

Quality newspapers struggling for European unity

Hans-Jörg Trenz

Raising the 'European voice': the quality press as a public entrepreneur

Within the diversified media landscape of Europe, mass media attention given to the European integration process is still quite unequally distributed. The prospects for the development of a European public sphere depend on the building of organisational capacities and degrees of specialisation as a guarantee of regular news coverage of the European Union. So far, this kind of know-how has been built only by specific media segments, principally by the quality press and by public broadcasting.[1] The selective attention to European integration obviously creates a biased European space of public communication. In practice (though not in principle), it implies a limited access of only higher-educated publics that develop a special interest in following the particular kinds of debate that accompany European decision-making processes.

This chapter analyses the quality newspapers' active role as the principal mediator of European political communication. As will be claimed, quality newspapers have not only developed their own rules for selecting and processing political news about the EU but also become engaged in public opinion-formation processes at the EU and member state level. According to their own ethical standards, newspapers apply a common distinction between news reporting and news commentating, the latter being allocated to specific editorial pages and set apart in style and format from the main information pages. The quality press is thus not simply to be considered as the passive mediator of European political communication facilitating autonomous opinion and will-formation processes of the public. On the editorial pages, the quality press is also becoming engaged in overtly shaping and structuring public opinion. This latter role of the media is of particular importance for preserving or overcoming the fragmentation of public spheres that results from the selective amplification of political communication within nationally biased media systems.

The mass media are generally held responsible for preserving the national bias and sometimes even for spreading hostile and anti-European attitudes among the public. In contrast to this general wisdom, it is claimed here that the quality press has become a dynamic forerunner of European integration, promoting the deepening and the constitutionalisation of the EU. In short, quality newspapers raise the 'European voice' against the undecided, hesitant and particularistic attitudes of the national governments and sometimes even against the Euro-scepticism of their own readers.

The debate on the future and the constitutionalisation of the EU is one of the outstanding trans-European media debates of recent years. In the course of the debate, newspapers are neither neutral observers nor passive amplifiers of political statements. What we observe, instead, is an active role of the newspapers in supporting the deepening of integration and in staging the consensus on EU constitutional values. The particular place for raising the 'European voice' is reserved to the newspapers' commentaries.

Meta-communication in newspaper commentaries

Commentaries[2] have been identified as a 'neglected subject in mass communication research' (Eilders 1997). Their analysis has been guided by two main concerns. First, to what extent the 'voice of the media' is heard in the political process, i.e. to what extent newspaper commentaries can exert influence on decision-making (Eilders *et al.* 2004)? Second, to what extent commentaries are used for political mobilisation by the newspaper. Commentaries are the place in which the newspaper itself mobilises public opinion, entering the arena as a political actor, putting aside the professional standards of impartiality and objectivity. In the editorial, the journalists turn into essayists who dissociate themselves from daily events and unfold a more reflexive position and evaluation of long trends and contextualised problems. It is above all this last function that is to be exemplified in this study. In the debate on the future of Europe, the possible impact of the media on political decision-making is only of secondary importance. The emphasis lies, for the most part, on the question of how far press commentaries reflect consensual ideas and values of European integration.

In accordance with the overall framework of this book, this chapter analyses different conceptions of the EU as a political entity as they appear in newspaper commentaries. By focusing empirically on the early stage of the constitutional debate we expect newspapers either to retain the particular national model of a political body and to propound a differentiated conception of the EU as a regulatory entity engaged in problem-solving, or to advocate an integrated federal model of the EU as a membership community based on a mix of rights, values and identity. We expect newspaper discourse thus to be marked by a tension between a traditionally nationalist and a newly promoted trans- or supranationalist vision of the EU. This will help us to clarify to what extent commentaries on the future of Europe refer to the EU as a collective undertaking, i.e. as a community of shared destiny and belonging of those Europeans to whom the urgency and necessity to solve the present problems are called upon. The premise is that commentaries are used systematically to promote such visions of the future of Europe, which are expressed not simply as the personal opinions of the journalist but as the collective opinion of the editorial board.

Our own research interest on the debate of the future of Europe analyses this ideological role of newspaper discourse further: we believe that commentaries are systematically used to turn the *collective opinion* of the newspaper into the *public opinion* of Europeans. This difference has been elaborated in a classic study by Hall *et al.* (1978: 63) who distinguish between two different modes for a newspaper to express its own voice on an issue. One common type of editorial judgement consists of expressing its own statements and thoughts on an event by translating them into the paper's public language (*using a public idiom*). The other type 'goes beyond expressing its *own* view in a public idiom and actually claims to be expressing *the* public's views' (*taking the public voice*). The essence of the difference lies between two kinds of commentary. The first says 'we believe that the EU has to be democratised' whereas the second says 'the public believes that the EU has to be democratised'. For obvious reasons, the editorial that claims to speak *for* the public contains a much stronger claim: it represents the collective voice of the public.

At first sight, our emphasis on the ideological role of the mass media in 'orchestrating' public opinion (Hall *et al.* 1978: 120ff.) resembles the undertaking of critical media theory in identifying and accusing the 'consciousness industry' of capitalist societies (Enzensberger 1962).[3] We claim indeed that the mass media generate something to be called 'ideologies', but we do not conclude that these 'ideologies' manipulate the public in any meaningful sense. Instead, in the course of political communication, the function of the mass media lies in producing and reproducing the semantic representations of society as a political unity. The imagined unity of society as a political community of collective belonging and self-determination is transmitted through the mass media which open up the most generally accessible and farthest-reaching arena for communicating between the most differentiated sectors of society and for attending to communication by separate and distant publics (Luhmann 1996). The central function of the newspaper commentaries on the EU thus consists in allowing for the imagining of a 'European society' as a collectivity of political self-determination.

This function of the media in reflecting collective belonging and identities between the nation and Europe has been highlighted in Díez

Medrano's (2003) long-term study which analyses press commentaries in the German, Spanish and British quality press for the period 1946–90. Diéz Medrano identifies a shared cognitive framing of the integration process, which is taken as a solid basis for the formation of a European *imagined community*. Similar findings of an affirmative attitude towards European integration are also reported by Eilders and Voltmer (2003), who analyse EU-related commentaries in German quality papers between 1994 and 1998. The principal consensus over European integration conceals the partisan conflict that is dominant in national news coverage.

The consonant orchestration of public opinion becomes of particular significance in newspaper commentaries on the future of Europe. Commentators do not advocate national interests but a European collective good. European public opinion is intoned by the small choir of media advocates who do not care much about the dissonances and noise outside. Instead of debating the possible contents and potential innovations of a European constitution, media commentaries perform a kind of ritual act in replicating the well-known hymn of the European value community based on a catalogue of fundamental rights that have been long enshrined in the national constitutions and became a kind of supranational collective property of all Europeans after the Second World War.

Research design

The empirical research is based on a representative sample of commentaries from the following newspapers: *Frankfurter Allgemeine Zeitung* (*FAZ*), *Süddeutsche Zeitung* (Germany); *Le Monde, Libération* (France); *Guardian, The Times* (UK); *La Repubblica, La Stampa* (Italy); *Die Presse, Der Standard* (Austria); *El País, ABC* (Spain); and the *New York Times* (*NYT*) (USA). Our total sample of 128 articles includes ten commentaries for each newspaper that discuss at full length the issue of the future and constitutionalisation of Europe. The period covered is from 11 May 2000 (Joschka Fischer's speech at Humboldt University) to the end of December 2000 (the Nice summit).[4]

Our selection of newspapers follows the general criterion of representativeness. The underlying criteria are the ideological alignment of the newspaper (left–right), nation-wide distribution and a leading role in opinion formation in the relevant country. The application of such a selective procedure implies several hypotheses about the expected cleavages and conflict lines that structure media discourse about the future of Europe. First, we take the existence of national media systems for granted, assuming that there is a content bias between quality papers along national cleavages. Second, we take the existence of cross-national ideological cleavages for granted, assuming that ideological preferences make a difference in discussing European issues. Third, we take for granted the existence of cross-national quality standards that are applied by newspapers in selecting and framing European news.[5] We expect divergent patterns of news coverage of the first national cleavage and a convergence of preferences and opinions between national media of the second and third cleavages. Despite persisting patterns of divergence, we will also find sufficient grounds for questioning the taken-for-granted view of national media as closed systems of meaning and will identify an overall trend of national quality papers becoming engaged in a common European debate.

The qualitative coding of the articles has been completed with the help of the computer package ATLAS.ti. In the standardised code book, particular attention was paid, first, to the models of European integration that are underlying the newspaper discourse; second, to the policy actors linked to it; and third, to the particular conceptualisations of issues or general expression of values and identities.[6]

Issue cycle and event history

The question of whether media coverage on the future of Europe was triggered by the same events can be answered positively. All newspapers except the *NYT* selected the constitutional debate for regular commentary, which can be taken as a strong indicator of the converging thematic relevance of the issue. The issue cycle reveals a clear convergence of media salience which points to a kind of 'natural history' of the debate. The media debate was launched with extensive commentary on the 'Humboldt Speech' given by the German Minister of Foreign Affairs, Joschka Fischer.[7] The subsequent debate was marked by an ongoing event production in the form of various responses to Fischer by the heads of state and government. In September 2000, the issue cycle converged on the occasion of the conclusion of the Convention on the Charter of Fundamental Rights. In October, decision-making was prepared at the Biarritz summit. Finally, the chain of events culminated with the Nice Intergovernmental Conference (IGC) of December 2000.

Actor coalitions

At this early stage, the debate on the future of Europe is a representative debate between governments and not between anonymous institutional actors or between citizens. Governments which decide about the collective destiny of Europe are the central carriers of the conflict. European institutional actors, members of the European Parliament (MEPs), and even the President of the Commission step back or even disappear.[8] Moreover, the debate on the future of Europe does not lead to the Europeanisation of domestic debates: in fact, no national non-governmental or sub-national actors, such as members of the parliaments, speakers of the opposition, of political parties or of non-governmental organisations (NGOs), are found

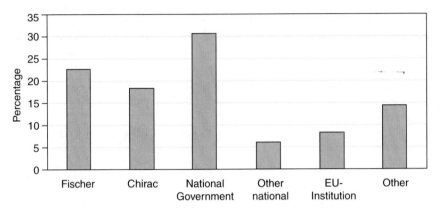

Figure 5.1 Types of actor.

Note
Actors were coded only as contributors to the specific debate on constitutionalisation through their directly or indirectly quoted statements in the commentaries.

in the media. Joschka Fischer and Jacques Chirac alone are referred to in 42 per cent of all the statements, with 23 and 19 per cent respectively (see Figure 5.1). They are clearly visible as the two protagonists who 'make the new Europe' and set the agenda for the completion of the integration project. Other members of the various national governments are together responsible for 30 per cent of the actors' statements,[9] in most cases intervening and responding to previous contributions by Fischer and Chirac.

The repetitive constellation of actors in an identical thematic context is a central carrier of meaning and interpretations used in commentaries. We distinguish between three different schemes: (a) the *friend–enemy constellation*; (b) the *conflict constellation*; and (c) the *partnership constellation*.

The *friend–enemy constellation* is evocative of a Europe of sovereign states within the framework of traditional nationalisms. In the early constitutional debate, we find only occasional references to such a constellation, which is used as a mode of excluding the internal other in domestic politics rather than excluding the external other in the field of external relations. The Europhile British *Guardian*, for instance uses this constellation when referring to British Euro-scepticism. Other examples refer to French *souverainists* (Jean-Pierre Chevènement, Charles Pasqua) and right-wing populists (*Lega Nord*, Haider's *Freiheitliche Partei Österreichs* – FPÖ) and, in some exceptional cases, general references to a whole country (like the Euro-sceptical Danes or the Austrian government). The fact that the role of the 'other' is mostly limited to notorious troublemakers provides some evidence of a highly consensual approach to European integration among European quality newspapers. An exception is the British press, which has partially 'domesticated' the debate, carrying out partisan conflict about deeper integration and constitutionalisation.

The *conflict constellation* is evocative of a multiple transnational Europe in which different legal traditions, particular interests and conceptions of the public good have to be accommodated. It is typically evoked in newspaper discourse when reflecting on the desirability and viability of alternative models of (or paths to) integration. Two main dimensions of conflict can be distinguished. The first is the conflict between the different political cultures of French centralist Republicanism and German Federalism. The second emerges from the common law tradition in Britain as distinct from continental constitutionalism. One could expect such different constitutional traditions to be an important obstacle in agreeing about the future shape of the EU polity (Jachtenfuchs *et al.* 1998). However, the newspaper commentaries avoid expressing fundamentally different views on these issues. In most cases, the constitutional conflict is not framed as a conflict between opposing models but as personalised controversies between national protagonists.

Strikingly absent is the explicitly mentioned conflict between the two main alternative models for the future institutional shape of the EU, namely the federalist and the intergovernmental perspectives. These are not presented as two alternative scenarios or possible solutions to the conflict in the commentaries. The authors clearly prefer exclusive reference to either the one or the other solution: the federal model in the majoritarian perspective of the continental countries (France, Germany, Italy and, to a lesser extent, Austria) and the intergovernmental model in the minority position of the more peripheral countries (UK and Spain).

The *partnership constellation* speaks to a supranational entity in the making that is based on a collective will and a shared understanding of how to proceed with European integration. To our own surprise, this constellation is the most recurrent mode of framing the debate on the future of Europe. This can be interpreted as an indicator of the high consensus expressed in newspaper commentaries. The most frequent references are made to the Franco-German tandem ('motor' or 'locomotive') as the driving force of European unification from its first days. Most commentators stress its importance as an enduring alliance and not merely as a tactical one. With the Euro-sceptical British conservative press being the only exception,[10] this leads to a positive evaluation of the Franco-German partnership as the core for the whole integration project, which is carried not only by shared interests but also by the idea of a shared responsibility towards the past and a mission towards the future.

Another alliance mentioned frequently in opposition to the Franco-German partnership is the more Euro-sceptical group of EU members formed by the UK, Spain and/or the Scandinavian countries (Denmark and Sweden). This partnership has a much more rational base, formed by opposition to the idea of a European Federation launched by Fischer and Chirac. Other constellations of partnership do not appear in our sample. Peripheral EU member states, partisan actors, national parliaments, NGOs and European institutional actors are not presented as relevant partners in the game of modelling the future of the EU.

The general story line

The speech given by Fischer on the future and constitutionalisation of the EU, held at Humboldt University on 12 May 2000, was a masterpiece of media agenda-setting. The German Foreign Minister explicitly spoke as a private man but nevertheless arranged for the invitation of correspondents from the major European newspapers to attend the event. In evoking a fateful moment in European history, Fischer presented himself as the saviour who was fiercely determined to rescue European integration from its present crisis and to master the great challenges of the future. Fischer openly and emphatically identified with the supranational model of the EU as a political community based on popular sovereignty and citizens' rights and duties.[11] All newspaper commentaries about the future of Europe are based on this plot. They either associate themselves with the model of the EU as a supranational entity or try to defend an alternative vision. The general story line contrasts the glorious past of European integration with its present crisis and outlines some visionary perspectives and future prospects. The drama consists in a fight among the heads of state as the heroes who take up the lance against the windmills of the lasting Euro-sclerosis. The tragedy consists in their weakness and vulnerability as single actors who must build coalitions and partnerships out of lasting conflicts and differences.

In this fateful moment, newspapers explicitly declare their readiness to support the struggle for European integration and to do their best not to lose this 'unique historical chance for the constitutionalisation of Europe' (*Libération*, 15 May 2000, p. 13). In commenting on the past, present and future of European integration, an essential consensus emerges which is based on (a) shared memories of a glorious past; (b) the identical diagnosis of the present crisis; and (c) on the identification of shared values and principles for modelling the future. In opposition to this overall consensus, newspaper commentaries are only rarely the place to carry out conflicts and debates among ideological or national cleavage lines. The resistance to the constitutionalisation of the EU is either suppressed or, as in the case of the British and Spanish positions, not reflected by the other newspapers. The general story line in the debate on the future of Europe is outlined in Table 5.1.

Evoking memories of the collective past

Mobilizing memories is an integral part of modelling a social space of exchange and experience. It adds a temporal dimension to the collective horizon of problem-solving. The general expectation is that the mobil-

Table 5.1 The future of Europe debate: general story line

	Past	Present	Future
Evaluation	Success story of European integration	Euro-sclerosis	Confidence versus scepticism
	Glorious past	Crisis	
Typical rhetorical references	Founding fathers	Irony/indignation about	Avant-garde
	Founding zeal	European bureaucracy	Motor
	Milestone decisions		
Models	Elite Europe	Functional integration	European federation (majority)
	Moral community	Economic *Zweckverband*	Confederation of states (minority)
Cleavages	Consensus	Consensus	Suppressed conflict

isation of memories would lead to a new fragmentation of political communication. Memories can only be mobilised within a particular community with its own history. Against this restrictive assumption, the newspaper commentaries analysed become strongly engaged in a collective elaboration of memories across the European space. The result is a common frame of historical references that facilitates the coordination of collective action and identities. At this point, the reaffirmation or the reinterpretation of the national past is of less importance (these can be parallel and intervening processes). Rather, newspaper discourse on the future of Europe builds on the lessons of a common European past.

What kind of European memory can be mobilised as a collective point of reference for European nation states? The hypothesis that has been put forward by Giesen (2002) is that the particular historic constellation of Europe only allows for a *negative identification* with the past. The traumatic experience of Fascism and Nazism has given birth to the project of European integration and continues to shape contemporary practices of mobilising collective identities. Overcoming the national past (*Vergangenheitsbewältigung*) would thus be the strongest legitimation for a postnational or supranational European future.

Our data do not provide sufficient evidence for this strong hypothesis. European integration has consolidated so far that its negative delimitation from fascism and militant nationalism can be taken for granted.[12] Most commentaries opt instead for a *positive identification* with the past. The particular past that is remembered is the glorious history of European integration consisting of the heroic actions of the founding fathers of Europe who brought the divided continent together. The material underpinnings of this history are the different Treaties from Rome to Maastricht and the milestone settlements linked to them. This reveals a new identity practice in which the experience of successful integration is turned into collective memories (Eder 2003b). The common horizon of problem-solving and governance with their undeniable effects on the wealth and strength of the continent are a new source of pride and confidence. It is this common horizon of problem-solving and the belief in governance that creates the *political* community against the purely economic *Zweckverband*.

The founding myth of European integration has a normative authority that is taken as the yardstick for all those who want to step forward with new proposals for the making of Europe's future. At the same time, this particular post-war setting of the foundation of European integration restricts the discourse to what can be called the post-revolutionary consensus of European modernity. The particularity of this post-revolutionary Europe is that it never experienced its own revolution and therefore has to revert to the ideals of the French or even of the American Revolution.[13] The collective memory of Europe constructs a history of shared ideas and not of particular historical moments. It incorporates the ideals of the

French and American Revolution but at the same time strongly rejects any attempts to go beyond these (the failed experience of socialism) or to fall short of these (the failed experience of ethno-nationalism). This post-revolutionary consensus explains the striking absence of religious expressions of collective identity in the newspaper discourse. The concern expressed by liberal French newspapers about whether Europe should continue the lay tradition of the French Republic is in fact unfounded.[14] The Christian heritage does not play any role in newspaper commentaries on the future and constitutionalisation of Europe.

By the end of 2000, the debate on the future of Europe had created its own history. The speeches delivered by Fischer and other heads of state were not treated as political nine-day wonders that briefly impressed the media – soon to be forgotten. They left their imprints in the collective memory of Europe and were kept in mind as milestones, which could be used, for instance, for evaluating the reform steps taken at the Nice summit.[15]

Diagnosing the crisis and reaffirming shared values and principles

As the glorious past of European integration is taken as a general source of consensus among the newspapers, it allows the journalists also to take a critical attitude towards the present, and to open a perspective for a better future. The positive evaluation of the past is turned into a negative diagnosis of the present crisis and Euro-sclerosis.

The feeling of unease and concern with the present state of European integration is thus another source of consensus that unites newspaper discourse on Europe. Notably, this frequent Euro-criticism of the media is not linked to expressions of Euro-scepticism or Euro-hostility. It is rather to be understood as a critique of the present management, which still characterises the whole enterprise. Here, frequent reference is made to the functional model of European integration, which is unanimously discarded as inappropriate with regard to the ambitious zeal of the founding fathers and with regard to the challenges the EU has to meet in its proximate future.

To illustrate the present crisis of integration, newspapers often adopt an ironic style, consisting in exposing the bizarre results of EU decision-making procedures or the labyrinths of European bureaucracy. A quite common practice also consists in 'Commission-bashing' (Trenz 2002b) or in accusing key actors of European integration of idleness or selfishness.

In this desperate and languishing situation, Fischer's attack on the deadlock in European integration was highly welcomed by the newspapers. Apart from the contributions made by the heads of state, the newspapers were also given the opportunity to comment on some current institutional developments and negotiations in anticipation of forthcoming decisions by the IGC. The Convention on the Charter, which published its final draft in September 2000, was taken by all newspapers as an opportunity for the reaffirmation of a principled consensus of values that unites Europe. At the same time, latent conflicts between the majority of those commentators who consider the Charter of Fundamental Rights as a draft constitution, and the minority of those who fight against its legally binding status, become visible. Here, the consensus about the present crisis of integration is transformed into a conflict about its possible future.

Modelling the future of Europe

The appeal by the European statesmen to recover together the founding zeal of Europe and to build the future of Europe was unanimously taken up by the media. The confidence in the future is derived from reflection on the past: 'It is not the question of ignoring what has been achieved in the last 50 years but of continuing on the basis of these achievements' (*El País*, 21 May 2000, p. 15). However, this shared evaluation of the past and the present of European integration does not necessarily lead to converging interpretations about the reforms to be taken. The thematic and interpretative relevance of the issue determines the motivational relevance in the form of a high consensus expressed by the media that something has to be done urgently. However, major differences still remain over the particular solutions offered.

The success story of media-framing is highly dependent on the newspapers' capacities to offer key concepts that schematise the instrumental and normative expectations of the public. Such models work as schemes that put the central ideas in a nutshell, namely what the EU is about and how it should be changed. Media schemes of interpretation are highly selective with regard to the more comprehensive policy or scientific debates about the shaping of European integration. Even the quality press has only limited capacities in illustrating the complexity of alternative choices for EU polity-building. Instead of coherence, journalists will opt for a pragmatic ad hoc arrangement mixing the incompatible in the form of pre-framed pieces of interpretation.[16] On the whole, such media discourse can be grouped along three basic journalistic visions of the EU: (a) the *federal model* of a supranational union with a unitary constitutional order; (b) the *intergovernmental model* of a union of states without a constitution; and (c) the *mixed model* of a compound system of governance with a flexible treaty arrangement. The three general models are outlined in Table 5.2.

All constitutional models are linked to outstanding actors as the architects of Europe: the federal model to the Franco-German motor of integration, the intergovernmental model to the British (or Spanish) brake and the functional model to the institutional bodywork (Commission). The evaluation of the role of these actors changes along the Franco/German–British cleavage line. The three models further distinguish three different modes of allocating sovereignty: in the first model,

Table 5.2 The future of Europe debate: general models discussed in the media

	Federal Europe	Europe of states	Functional integration
Attitude	Progressive	Regressive	Pragmatic
Form	Constitution	Statement of principles	Flexible treaty
Order	Legal order	Political order	Institutional order
Allocation of government	Supranational government	National governments	Institutional governance
Speeds	Different speeds	Parallel speeds	Different but slow speeds
Sovereignty	Supranational allocated delegation of sovereignty	Divided sovereignty of governments	Shared sovereignty of multi-level governance
Evaluation	Positive: Germany, France, Italy, Austria Negative: Spain, UK	Positive: Spain, UK Negative: Germany, France, Italy, Austria	Negative: all

the supranational delegation of sovereignty is promoted; in the second model, sovereignty remains with the national governments; and the third model prefers the shared allocation of competencies between different levels of governance.[17]

Commentaries are not the place for weighing up the merits and weaknesses of each single model. Most story lines give clear preference to one of the models with only marginal and pejorative references to the others. In this sense, editorials are sermonising rather than debating about Europe's essence and future destination. Only British media come close to a discursive style in defending their minority position against the hegemony of the federal model.

The *federal model* is represented by Fischer's speech, which opted for the constitutionalisation of Europe. It is clearly the hegemonic model defended by the media. This hegemony of the constitutional model is remarkable. At first sight, Fischer's speech in Humboldt appeared to be highly provocative and almost subversive (which accounts also for its successful agenda-setting). Fischer proposed nothing less than the supranational delegation of powers against the sovereignty of the nation states. The riddle is that a storm of indignation did not break out. The only indignation was expressed by the French Minister of the Interior, Jean-Pierre Chevènement, who associated Fischer's proposal with the old German dream of the Holy Roman Empire and accused the Federal Republic for not having banished Nazism and sticking to a '*voelkisch*' tradition of nationalism. The French press, however, clearly dissociated itself from the quick response of their minister and instead opted for being outraged about those who did not join the overall consensus over Fischer's proposal.

The *intergovernmental model* of a union of states is highlighted by parts of the British and Spanish press. It consists in the explicit refusal of the Fischer model, opting instead for a confederation of states and seeking the solution in a reallocation of powers with the national governments. The British position is as simple as possible: 'to negotiate toughly and to get our way'.[18] The same applies to Spanish newspapers that stress the necessity of unanimous EU decision-making as the only guarantee to secure Spanish interests in a wider Europe. Proposing a 'statement of principles' instead of a constitution, as a political and not as a legal document, Blair's answer to Fischer opened a different normative dimension on the debate on the future of Europe, in which the transfer of power to supranational institutions is seen as non-democratic and counter-productive. Thus, the EU would become 'judge-governed' and not 'self-governed' (*The Times*, 5 June 2000, p. 18). A legally binding Charter would become a source of never-ending conflict and not of expected harmony. Instead of defending the EU, it would destroy its precarious unity.

In advocating an intergovernmental model of European integration, the British and Spanish press break the continental consensus on the federal model. Newspaper commentaries open an international conflict, which has both an instrumental and a normative dimension (the interests at stake and the two constitutional models are opposed, not simply seen as alternative ways to realise democracy in Europe). In addition, British newspapers opened up an internal partisan conflict about different ideological preferences linked to the project of European integration. The *Guardian* identified the European superstate as 'Tory propaganda' much more concerned with short-term calculations of soft targets than with the long-term future of Britain or Europe. Moreover, the *Guardian* accused the 'Tory press' of spreading an anti-European xenophobic discourse (21 May 2000, p. 3; 16 November 2000, p. 25) and took a much more supportive and distinctive view on European integration:

> To call this a quest for a superstate is mere propaganda. Endless repetition in the hyperbolic output of British anti-EU politicians has given the word bogus recognition, but that is what it is: bogus. Portrayal of the EU as a demonic conspiracy against the people, especially the British people, by a bureaucratic SS has become a substitute for thought and a suppressor of creative speculation about how the experiment might best move forward.
>
> (*Guardian*, 16 November 2000, pp. 24–5)

Apart from the fear of supranational domination, resistance to Fischer's model is motivated by the mistrust of the Franco-German motor and the fear of being pushed into a disadvantaged position. Italy and Spain are highly sensitive towards the idea of an integration process at different speeds. Italian commentaries are rather self-confident that Italy would be among the front-runners. In Spain, however, newspapers opt for open resistance against Franco-German 'manipulation' of the EU.

The *model of shared sovereignty* is little represented in the media. It is held responsible for the present crisis of the EU and discarded as a future option for the EU. The *sui generis* model of shared sovereignty of a multi-level governance system is also rejected as being particularly opaque, elitist and undemocratic. Actors such as former Italian Prime Minister Giuliano Amato, who try to defend the particular architecture of the EU in the media, are misunderstood and criticised for their lack of vision.[19] The third way of a Europe *sui generis*, which would consist in a stabilisation of the present model of functional integration, is held to be impossible.

Here, the disadvantages of framing become visible with regard to the predominance of the federal model in the media. It is difficult to sell the conception of a *sui generis* European system to a general public which needs simplified visions and explanations. Functionalism is only accepted as the last resort of European integration. If the worst became true and the governments were to fail in their role as the creators of the united Europe, there is still one consolidation: 'that history will do it alone' (*Libération*, 19 June 2000, p. 8).

Images of Europe: unity in diversity or diversity of units?

Commentaries in opinion-leading newspapers about the future and constitutionalisation of the EU could be characterised by the high reciprocity of their underlying ideas and concepts. As will be argued, the parallel account of the past, present and future of European integration points to a fundamental consensus about what makes for the unity of political Europe beyond the diversity of its elements. In raising the 'European voice', media discourse creates discursive representations of this unity that can be condensed into images and symbols of the unity of European political society (Soysal 2002).

To treat the collective representations of Europe not as fixed images and symbols but rather as semantic self-ascriptions of the European polity points to a changing practice of collective identity formation. In contrast to the symbolic repertoire of the nation, the semantics used for the representation of European integration remain highly flexible, open and comprehensive. The mass media look at the unity of political Europe and at the same time at its own contingency. This is what we identify as the major difference between traditional identity discourse within the nation state and European semantic representations. The media's view on the unity of political Europe is based on a second-order observation: unlike traditional identity discourses which have to repress the contingency of their underlying concepts, the semantics of the self-description of European society unfold through the observation of the multiple practices of identity formation within the political space of Europe. In doing so, the quality press constitutes a European second-order observer which builds a new semantics of unity from a reflexive view of the diversity of units.

The semantic field is further characterised by a lack of vision and of promises for a better future. The future of Europe is not particularly spectacular, attractive and appealing. There is nothing to worship or to fight for. The lowest common denominator is that a visionary Europe does not exist. Instead, the media take a highly pragmatic attitude towards the future of Europe. Either Europe is linked to functional institutionalisation or it is a necessary part of the realpolitik of governments. As such, the future of Europe is very much a reiteration of the same theme: it is applying the Community method and, at best, expanding it with new (democratic) elements.

As there is no visionary Europe of the future, a particular form of the unity of Europe derived from the past also does not exist. A common European cultural heritage, European civilisation, and even Christianity, are only occasionally referred to in the media as possible elements of a European identity. The same applies to the negative demarcation from the collective trauma of the past (Communism, Nazism). Instead, media tend to make use of a new practice of commemoration in turning the good old success story of European post-war integration into the shared history that constitutes the European community of memory and experience. At the same time, this practice of commemoration is becoming rather negative in evaluating the past and the future. The collective Europeanism of the media is rather defensive and conservative in protecting major achievements of the past against the present crisis of Euro-sclerosis, and against the challenges and insecurities to be met in the future.

In retrospect, this reluctance of journalists to pin down the substance of a European collective identity could be interpreted as a particular trait of the early stage of the debate on the European constitution. The intention was precisely to avoid politicisation and to suppress fundamental conflicts (such as the role of Christianity) that were seen as detrimental at this stage. In the absence of an external voice, journalists could successfully maintain such a gatekeeper function of public discourse. As a matter of fact, the monopoly of journalists as the interpreters of European integration was slowly broken by the amplification of the constitutional debates through the Laeken process, in the course of which debates about the substance of a European identity revealed to be unavoidable.

This particular attitude of journalists in reflecting the 'unity of Europe' points to a new mode of 'postnational' identity construction. With no fixed points derived from the past or projected towards the future, the unity of Europe was treated as a by-product of the present practice of cooperation, as something to be constantly in the making through common debate and dispute. The unity of Europe remains obscure, but as the Italian newspaper *La Repubblica* (14 May 2000, p. 15) writes, 'it is certainly something worthwhile to be discussed and express divergent opinions on'. If nobody else cares about the unity of Europe, newspapers offer themselves as the constructors of European unity from diversity and dispute. In the absence of a public voice, their original contribution cannot lie so much in processing the different inputs and contributions but in 'simulating' the debate on European integration and promoting the reflexive self-understanding of its putative disputants and their publics.

The political society of Europe forms the core of this discursive practice of self-ascription. Its genuinely political character consists in imagining the unity of society in the form of a collectivity of self-determination. The imagined European society is at the same time the political community as well as the potential carrier of democracy (Nassehi 2002). The belief in self-government as the fundamental leitmotif of European integration is thus becoming the major identity marker of political Europe. It implies a political community that expresses its neutrality towards the plurality of ideological and religious beliefs of society, the supremacy of politics over the market and confidence in its steering capacities. It is also a political community held together by the principal affirmation of building supranational institutions and delegating powers to them.

The process of reflecting this model of self-governance is one that reflects the unity and diversity of Europe. 'Unity in diversity' is an old mythos and a recurrent theme of European religious, philosophical and political thought. There is already a collective historical experience of Europe in dealing with its unity in diversity and there are ready-made semantics that can be applied by media discourse.[20] More than a mythos, the '*Concordia Discors*' (unity in diversity) and '*Discordia Concors*' (diversity of units) remain an open paradox. The debate on the future of Europe is filled with such paradoxes and newspaper commentaries are the place to unfold them.[21]

From a traditional perspective, it might be hard to accept that there cannot be any substance but only a recurrent discursive practice to defend the unity of Europe. Not so for the quality newspapers. For them, Europe is commonly referred to as the 'open institutional construction site' (*La Repubblica*, 4 July 2000, p. 17), as the 'patchwork quilt' (*FAZ*, 5 May 2000, p. 7), or as 'the eternal god Janus' (*Le Monde*, 12 September 2000, p. 21). Over time, newspapers have become quite acquainted with this strange construction and developed their own vocabulary for designating the paradoxes of the unity of Europe and expressing their astonishment, that 'despite all, it works' (*La Repubblica*, 19 October 2000, p. 16).

The contingency of the European integration project as a 'compromise of compromises' (ibid.) has to be constantly renegotiated; not only its success but also its permanent failures are thus becoming the last resort of collective identity formation. For the self-imagination of the political society of Europe, such a bizarre construction also has clear advantages. Europeans who want to find themselves together in a political community must not learn to love each other as members of the nation, but they must learn to love these paradoxes. The search for the *finalité* of European integration that is achieved through constitutionalisation is itself one of these paradoxes. And the Europeans, who observe this never-ending game through the media, are gradually getting used to the idea that the genetic laboratories of the EU are apparently trying to invent the 'egg-laying wool-milk-sow' (*Eierlegende Wollmilchsau*) (*Der Standard*, 15 September 2000).

Conclusion: constitutional reform and the new permissive consensus of the EU

This chapter has shed light on the impact of the mass media on articulating a new consensus on the EU in the early stage of the constitutional debate. Throughout Europe, the quality press became an active entrepreneur in promoting a vision of a democratic union of citizens and rights corresponding to the second, federal model outlined in the introductory chapter. This federal union is seen as relying strongly on cultural integration, i.e. on commonality, affiliation and commitments that emerge in the history of European integration and that assume a moral value of their own ('progressive Europeanism'). The general expectations that European newspapers are divided by national cleavages, representing their nations as closed systems of meaning, were not verified. The journalists' look at Europe was taken through a pair of European glasses. Only the British newspapers' vision of Europe was split by internal partisan conflicts.

Opinion-leading newspapers turned the general consensus on values into a permissive consensus that authorises political representatives to take further steps in deepening integration. The European value community is not visionary and innovative. It is based on universal principles that have been long enshrined in national constitutions. The core contents can be found in the promise of freedom, equality and fraternity of the French Revolution with their expressions of civic and political rights. Possible sources of conflict emerge either from attempts to go beyond the ideals of the French Revolution (e.g. by expanding social rights) or from attempts to retreat to earlier times (in remembrance of pre-revolutionary Christian Europe). Although they constitute part of the political debate and negotiation on the Charter, such attempts are clearly dismissed by the media.

The overall support for European integration by newspapers contributed to a Europe-friendly climate as a solid and comfortable basis for initiating the constitution-making process of the EU. Progressive Europeanism became the general code of conduct for political actors to appear in the media. In the ritual of European speeches that was initiated by German Foreign Minister Fischer, other heads of state (such as Chirac) were encouraged to step forward and join the chorus.

Progressive Europeanism breaks up the old permissive consensus that was based on non-communication about Europe. The old permissive attitude towards functional integration is replaced by a new permissive attitude towards democratic integration. Progressive Europeanism is also a moral attitude that takes the integrity of the European value community for granted. The deepening of European integration itself is the central moral value of this ideology. Hence, the new intensified communication about Europe resembles a sermon from the high pulpit rather than a debate in the public sphere. It is heard only by the small community of the faithful that gathers together for that purpose but is still based on weak knowledge and information on the part of the public.

There is obviously no linear relationship between the opinions expressed in newspaper commentaries and the public opinions of the Europeans. Newspaper commentators step forward to speak in the name of uninformed citizens, but they themselves lack information about the preferences and attitudes of their audiences. When media become engaged as a public entrepreneur in moral discourse, they risk decoupling media opinion from public opinion. The constitutional debate does not automatically transform the permissive consensus expressed in the media into the permissive consensus of the people of Europe, even if opinion surveys such as the Euro-barometer upheld this illusion of a favourable public until early 2005.

We might conclude, therefore, that this misunderstanding of progressive Europeanism as speaking in the name of the public has ultimately added fuel to the present impasse of constitution-making. The new permissive consensus of the uninformed citizens has concurred in applying the discourse of European democracy but not in the modalities of becoming engaged in a shared democratic practice. The constitution of a European democracy lacks constituents in the form of the voice of European citizens who are linked together by their capacity to carry out conflict and debate. However, the deadlock of European constitution-making should not be taken as the breakdown of European democracy linked to the project of an unfolding public sphere. The challenge is rather to make sense of the new spaces of politicisation that are breaking with the consensus culture of the EU.

Notes

1 The organisational features of this specialised media sector and their contribution for promoting a Europeanised public sphere are described in detail by Meyer 2002 and Trenz 2004b.
2 In this chapter, no further distinction is made between commentaries written by the editorial board of the newspaper and opinion editorials ('op-eds') written by single journalists. As far as possible, the research focuses on 'home editorials and commentaries', assuming that 'guest commentaries' have to be considered as less representative of the newspaper's voice.
3 For a recent elaboration, see Bourdieu 1996.
4 Only in one case (*Standard*) could the maximum of ten commentaries not be reached for the period. The *NYT* did not address the topic of the 'future and constitutionalisation of the EU' in any of its commentaries.
5 The ideological alignment of the newspaper – as far as known – is generally measured with regard to domestic news coverage (Kriesi 2001). We do not know whether these assumptions hold for the case of European news [Eilders and Voltmer (2003) claim that they do not]. It is always possible that a national newspaper has a conservative alignment with regard to domestic news and a progressive alignment with regard to European news.
6 The coding was done by two coders, which guaranteed sufficient controls through double coding and cross checking of articles.
7 In comparing commentaries in European newspapers with our control sample, one could thus conclude that the European space is clearly demarcated from the outside in giving relevance to particular issues selected for common debate. For similar findings regarding the demarcation of a European space of political communication, with reference to the Haider debate, see van de Steeg 2004.
8 Only 11 per cent of all statements could be attributed to European institutional actors (mainly Günter Verheugen and Romano Prodi).
9 This includes mostly unspecific notions like 'the French government said ...' or 'London wants to ...' The most frequently quoted actors are UK Prime Minister Tony Blair (7 per cent), French Interior Minister Jean-Pierre Chevènement (5 per cent) and French Prime Minister Lionel Jospin (4 per cent).
10 *The Times* (3 June 2000, p. 23) writes of 'those two Governments [that] still make the running in the EU, just as they have always done', i.e. as dominating the other countries and disrespecting their national interests.

11 For the ambivalence and contradictions of the Fischer speech, see the contributions in Joerges *et al.* 2000.
12 Negative identification with the past only becomes relevant to a certain extent in arguing for Eastern enlargement, when the promise of European democracy is held against state socialism.
13 The American Revolution obviously has a modelling character for the EU that is frequently discussed (and mostly rejected) by the media.
14 As stated by the French newspaper *Libération* (6 October 2000, p. 10): 'Europe will be lay or it will not be'.
15 For instance, *Libération* on 27 December 2000 and *FAZ* on 30 December 2000.
16 This also distinguishes our media models of the future of Europe from the conceptual framework elaborated in the introduction to this book.
17 See the comparative analysis of constitutional models in partisan discourse by Jachtenfuchs *et al.* 1998.
18 A formula attributed to Blair (*The Times*, 15 November 2000, p. 22).
19 *La Repubblica* (16 July 2000, p. 15) considers the reflections of the Italian Prime Minister about the multiple structures of Europe as a 'post-Hobbesian, post-statal order without a sovereign but only flexible aggregations of power', as 'terribly intelligent, but maybe a bit too much'.
20 Giesen (2002: 201) summarises this historical experience as follows: 'This unity [of Europe] did not repress or ignore the diversity of its elements. To the contrary: European culture was aware of its internal tensions and able to turn its polycentrism and internal inconsistencies into a major impetus for change. Thus, the coexistence of unity and diversity marks the core of European cultural dynamics.'
21 Here, the role of intellectuals must be highlighted not only as one of the major sources used by the journalists but also as guest authors of many commentaries.

6 Political communication, European integration and the transformation of national public spheres

A comparison of Britain and France

Paul Statham

Introduction

The decline of the 'permissive consensus' over European integration and its democratic consequences are central themes of this book. The European Union's failed attempt at 'constitutionalisation', in 2005, brought issues about its perceived or real 'crisis of legitimacy' to a head. Rejections of the Constitutional Treaty (CT) in referenda by citizens of two founder members, France and the Netherlands, marked a watershed, indicating that integration could no longer advance without popular consent. It dealt a possibly fatal blow to an idea that was already in decline: that political elites could simply proceed by 'building Europe in the absence of Europeans', as Jean Monnet succinctly put it (Tsoukalis 2003). It also exposed as overly optimistic the assumption, promoted by early scholars of integration, especially Ernst Haas (1961), that political engagement would automatically follow from Europe's supranational institutional developments. Haas visualised a 'process whereby political actors in several distinct national settings are persuaded to shift their loyalties, expectations and political activities towards a new political centre' (ibid.: 196). Such functionalism has been criticised and mostly rejected in the academy for several decades but retains a pervasive influence in the Commission's thinking. Even after the constitutional crisis, Brussels officials sometimes give the impression that they use Eurobarometer opinion data to determine whether European peoples' consciousness has sufficiently 'evolved' to be ready for EU citizenship in its full sense. Instead, it is perhaps time to consider the public sphere, where politics is mediated to citizens, and the dilemmas posed by European integration. This chapter therefore addresses the emergent 'Europeanised' political communication in national public spheres.

The constitutional crisis highlights that it is increasingly crucial to examine to what extent Europe's advancing institutional integration is

also matched by emergent forms of politics that are mobilised by collective actors and mediated to broader public constituencies. This is
addressed by studies on actors' positions over European integration, for
political parties (Hooghe *et al.* 2004), interest groups (Wessels 2004),
voters (Van der Eijk and Franklin 2004) and protestors (Imig and Tarrow
2001). The growing body of research on political communication and the
possibility of an emergent European public sphere also take this as a
central research question (Gerhards 1992; Schlesinger 1999; Koopmans
and Statham 2001; Eder and Trenz 2003; see also Chapter 1). Such
approaches emphasise the importance of communication for the emergence of the EU, as Calhoun states:

> If Europe is not only a place but a space in which distinctively Euro-
> pean relations are forged and European visions of the future enacted,
> then it depends on communication in public, as much as on a distinc-
> tively European culture, or political institution, or economy, or social
> networks.
>
> (Calhoun 2003: 243)

In this view, political communication and the construction of a public
sphere are essential prerequisites for a meaningful process of European
integration. However, a participatory public sphere will not emerge automatically in response to advancing integration. It will only emerge to the
extent that it is built by the actions and interactions of collective actors
who politically engage over European issues, between, across and within
levels of national polities. To be a genuinely 'public' sphere, it is also
essential that political action by collective actors be made visible to citizens, which allows for wider public scrutiny and deliberation, thereby
conferring accountability, responsiveness and legitimacy on the political
process (Koopmans 2007). To a large extent, the public visibility of European politics depends on the extent to which it is carried by the mass
media.

Although there are many theoretical contributions on a European
public sphere, empirical evidence on the patterns of Europeanised political communication that are shaping such emergent processes is thinner
on the ground. This chapter, along with the Europub.com project from
which it is derived, takes a step towards redressing this balance. It aims to
identify some basic cross-national and cross-actor variations in the patterns
of political communication over Europe that are mobilised by collective
actors and become visible to citizens, in the two national public spheres of
Britain and France. The approach is primarily exploratory, inductive and
analytic-descriptive. We use an original data set on public acts of claims-
making over European integration retrieved from newspaper sources.
When aggregated, this data set allows us to describe the overall pattern of
Europeanised communication that characterises a national public sphere

and claims-making by different types of actors within it. It thus facilitates a linked cross-national and cross-actor comparison. This evidence can then be used to assess three key questions regarding the extent and type of emergence of a European public sphere.

First, has European integration produced similar or different national responses with regard to the acts of political communication that constitute a public sphere? Here Britain and France are selected as contrasting cases of nation states. France is a founder member and 'pace-setter' for advancing European integration, whereas Britain is a latecomer, opting out of several key aspects of integration, including monetary union. Are these differences reflected in the way that Europe is mobilised and communicated in the national public sphere?

Second, to what extent is Europeanised political communication participatory? Here we examine the extent and type of civil society engagement in political claims-making over Europe and, then, how political parties 'represent' Europe to citizens through their claims-making within national public spheres.

Third, it is possible to ask to what extent the regulatory and federal models of a public sphere, as outlined in the introduction to this book, find empirical support in our data, or alternatively, are we left with the 'old' national public sphere? Here, we interpret our findings following the important theoretical insights set out in the introduction. In general, the two models predict the following patterns of claims-making: the *regulatory* model presupposes a weakly developed European public space where political claims mobilised by collective actors will occur mainly within the geopolitical boundaries of a nation state, combined with a restricted and issue-specific imprint (that is, speaking to particular publics), that may stretch horizontally across other EU states, and vertically with respect to the EU. By contrast, the *federal* model presupposes strong vertical links, leading us to expect patterns of claims-making that build important channels of communication linking nation states to the supranational EU.

Given that this is a data-driven chapter, we now outline our methodological approach, before turning to our analyses.

Conceptual and methodological approach: political claims-making

Political claims-making analysis is an established approach for examining the public dimension of politics (Koopmans and Statham 1999; Koopmans *et al.* 2005) from newspaper sources. Following 'protest event' analysis (Rucht *et al.* 1998), the unit of analysis is not an article, but an individual act of claims-making. In contrast to media content analyses which often study journalists' representations of actors and events, claims-making analysis takes news as a 'source' for claims-making by reported 'third-party' actors. Claims-making analysis sees reported news as a record of public events, and retrieves information on this aspect. A political claims-making act is a strategic action in the public sphere. It consists of intentional public speech acts which articulate political demands, calls to action, proposals and criticisms, which, actually or potentially, affect the interests or integrity of claimants and/or other collective actors in a political issue field. For this study, acts are included if their claims relate to the regulation or evaluation of events in relation to European integration, irrespective of which actor made the claim.[1] Regarding territorial criteria, we included acts in the United Kingdom and France, respectively, and those in the EU, even if they were made by foreign or supranational actors or addressed to foreign or supranational authorities.

The method codes a wide range of actors including civil society groups, such as employers, trade unions and non-governmental organisations (NGOs), and state actors, such as courts, legislatures, governments and supranational institutions. To give an idea of the type of information coded, claims-making acts are broken down into seven elements, for each of which a number of detailed variables are coded (see Koopmans 2002 for the codebook):

1   location of claim in time and space (WHEN and WHERE is the claim made?);
2   actor making claim (WHO makes the claim?);
3   form of claim (HOW is the claim inserted in the public sphere?);
4   substantive issue of claim (WHAT is the claim about?);
5   addressee of claim (AT WHOM is the claim directed?);
6   justification for claim (WHY should this action be undertaken?);
7   constituency actor: who would be affected by the claim if it were realised (FOR/AGAINST WHOM?).

In a simple form: at a time and place (1) an event occurs, where an actor (2) mobilises a speech act (3) that raises a claim about an issue (4) which addresses another actor (5) calling for a response, on the basis of a justifying argumentation (6). The claim is made with reference to a public constituency, whose interests are affected (7).

Our sample is taken from three years – 1990, 1995 and 2000 – and drawn from editions of the *Guardian* and *The Times*, for Britain, and *Le Monde* and *Le Figaro*, for France. These papers are chosen as broadsheets of public record. We take two newspapers per country with different (left/right) political affiliations, in an attempt to control for possible selection biases in the type of reported actors and events. LexisNexis versions of the newspapers are coded using a standardised codebook. All articles in the home news section of the newspapers are checked for relevant acts, i.e. the search is not limited to articles containing certain keywords. We retrieve our cases from a sample determined by specific days selected in advance at regular time intervals within each year. This retrieval strategy is preferable to sampling around key events of European debate, such as the Haider controversy, or the launch of the European Monetary Union (EMU), because our findings are more able to represent general trends instead of issue-specific occurrences whose importance, though significant, may be limited to a contingent time period.[2] Conventional inter-coder reliability tests are used for article selection and coding.[3]

We now turn to the cross-national comparison of the overall structure of political communication over Europe in the two national public spheres.

Communication over Europe in a national public sphere: Britain and France

It is necessary to see claims-making acts as *communicative links*. Claims-making acts may link across different political levels (EU supranational, EU foreign, national domestic) and national borders. For example, the British Prime Minister may make a demand regarding the proposed Constitution on the European Commission. In this case, a vertical link is mobilised from Britain upwards to the supranational EU. By aggregating the sum total of communicative links that are mobilised by claims-making over European issues, it is possible to reconstruct the pattern of communication in a national public sphere.

If we take the three basic levels of polity (national domestic, foreign EU and supranational EU) and state that a claims maker, or the addressee of a claim, is an actor who may belong to one of these three polities, then logically, there are nine possible relationships between claims makers and addressees. These are represented in Table 6.1.

Each of the nine relationships is produced by a claims-making act which links the polities through communication. By distributing the sum total of claims-making across the nine possibilities, it is possible to demonstrate variations in the patterns of communication between two public spheres. At the same time, each cell represents a specific type of claims-making that carries a specific form of 'Europeanisation' for that public sphere. These forms of Europeanisation in a national public sphere are listed as (a) to (i) in Table 6.1 and require comment because they define the ways in which Europeanised political communication may vary.

We propose to focus principally on the five claims-making relationships in which national domestic actors are actively engaged as claims makers or addressees ((a)–(e)). Such types of claims-making can be expected to have a more *active* transformative impact as carriers of Europeanising trends in a national public sphere, because they purposefully engage national domestic actors in communicative political relationships over Europe. Conversely, the four 'externalised' types ((f)–(i)) are more *passive*. They simply represent the reporting in British and French public spheres of 'outsiders' – the external interactions between foreign EU and EU supranational actors – to national publics.

Table 6.1 Types of 'Europeanised' political communication carried by claims-making acts in a national public sphere

Claims maker	Addressee		
	National domestic	Foreign from other EU country	EU/EEC supranational
National domestic	(a) National claims-making over Europe (domestic actors target domestic actors)	(c) Horizontal claims-making on foreign EU actors (domestic actors target actors from other EU states)	(e) Bottom-up vertical claims-making on EU/EEC (domestic actors target the EU)
Foreign from other EU country	(b) Horizontal claims-making by foreign EU actors (actors from other EU states target domestic actors)	(f) 'External' transnational horizontal claims-making between actors from foreign EU states in domestic national public sphere	(h) 'External' bottom-up claims-making on EU/EEC actors in national domestic public sphere
EU/EEC supranational	(d) Top-down vertical claims-making by EU/EEC (EU actors target domestic actors)	(g) 'External' top-down claims-making by EU/EEC on actors from foreign EU states in domestic national public sphere	(i) 'External' supranational claims-making between EU/EEC in domestic national public sphere

The five possible types of 'active' claims-making in national public spheres are the following:

a   *National claims-making over Europe.* National actors mobilise demands over European issues on other national actors. This is evidence for 'internalised' national political debates over European issues, including contestation, as a form of Europeanisation.

b   *Horizontal claims-making by foreign actors from European member states on domestic actors.* Actors from other EU member states enter national domestic politics demanding responses over European issues from national domestic actors. This contributes to Europeanisation by linking the national politics of two or more EU states.

c   *Horizontal claims-making by national actors on other EU member states.* This is the reverse of (b). Demands are mobilised by national actors over Europe on actors from other EU member states. These horizontal types of claims-making ((b) and (c)) depict a Europe of interacting nation states whose politics are being more closely interwoven with one another by conflict over, or collaboration in, European integration.

d   *Top-down vertical claims-making by EU institutions on national actors.* Supranational European institutions are the driving force behind Europeanisation by calling for a response from national domestic actors over issues of European integration. This creates a top-down vertical 'Europeanising' relationship from the supranational to the national domestic polity.

e   *Bottom-up vertical claims-making by national domestic actors on EU institutions.* This is the reverse of (d), whereby claims-making by national actors calls on EU supranational institutions to respond to demands.

The crucial difference is that 'nationalised' communication over Europe has a less direct engagement with the supranational EU institutions (vertical) and with other foreign polities (horizontal). The national public sphere is effectively 'closed' to the claims-making of the EU and other EU member states, and mediated only through interaction between domestic national actors. If the EU does not make demands, nor have demands directed towards it, then European institutions are not 'opened up' and made visible in a public sphere. This inhibits possibilities for political engagement by collective actors, and wider processes of deliberation by citizens, with regard to EU politics. Conversely, vertical and horizontal claims-making transform the national public sphere by linking upwards and across, respectively, to other polities. It creates new channels and paths for politics linking the nation state to the supranational level and to other EU members' polities. The national public sphere is 'open' as a forum for multi-level and transnational political engagement, as well as making such relationships visible to national publics.

The models outlined in Chapter 1 lead to the following expectations. The regulatory model presupposes the *closed* variant (a), but also the presence of some horizontal, transnational forms of Europeanised communication between the domestic nation state and states beyond national borders (b and c). The federal model is based on *open* Europeanised communication; it therefore presupposes strong vertical links across issue-areas (d and e), as well as horizontal forms, although the defining characteristic of the federal model is vertical communication. A third alternative is the standard national model of claims-making over Europe (a), which is a *closed* variant, where Europe becomes a topic for politics between actors only within the national domestic framework, and without carrying any direct transnational or supranational communicative links.

We now use the data to test the nature of the British and French public spheres. Tables 6.2a and 6.2b show distributions across the types of claims-making for Britain and France.[4] In addition to the shares of claims-making, for each cell we show a score for 'position' over European integration. Each claims-making act is coded +1, if the claim is in favour of European integration, −1 if it is against, and 0, if it is neutral or ambivalent. By aggregating and calculating the average position score for a given category, we are able to give a first indicator for the position, on a scale ranging from −1 against, to +1 in favour, of European integration.

A first general observation is that the positions expressed in the French public sphere are significantly more pro-European than those in the British, for claims-making by, and on, national domestic actors (all British claims makers +0.03, all French claims makers +0.32; all British addressees +0.16, all French addressees +0.40). This indicates that the French political debate over Europe occurs on an axis that is generally more favourable to integration than the British. In France, the country with the longer and deeper institutional involvement in European integration, political debates over Europe are less sceptical than in Britain.

Starting with top-down 'vertical' claims-making, where EU supranational actors make demands on British and French actors (d), we find relatively modest amounts in both countries (Britain 5.5 per cent, France 2.5 per cent). This indicates a limited penetration of European institutions as a visible and 'active' political actor addressing national domestic politics, even in the field of claims about European integration. The EU appears to be a poor communicator, though it could be that the national media are poor at picking up EU demands. However, the effect is the same: although the EU is an increasingly powerful actor, there are relatively few opportunities for citizens in both countries to see the EU as an initiator of political demands on national actors. In terms of top-down patterns, the federal model figures weakly in both countries. Not surprisingly, when it does reach national public spheres the EU is a strong advocate of European integration (Britain +0.62, France +0.58).

Conversely, for 'vertical' claims by national actors on EU institutions

Table 6.2a The distribution and position of 'Europeanised' communication in the British public sphere (1990, 1995, 2000)

Claims maker	Addressee								
	British		Foreign		EU supranational		All	
	Share (%)	Position (+1/−1)	Share (%)	Position (+1/−1)	Share (%)	Position (+1/−1)	Share (%)	Position (+1/−1)
British (a)	35.2	+0.12	(c) 1.6	NA	(e) 15.5	−0.24	52.2	+0.03
Foreign EU (b)	4.2	+0.38	(f) 7.9	+0.40	(h) 14.4	+0.35	26.5	+0.36
EU/EEC supranational (d)	5.5	+0.62	(g) 2.1	+0.13	(i) 13.6	+0.42	21.3	+0.44
All	44.9	+0.16	11.5	+0.30	43.9	+0.20	100.0	+0.20
Number of cases (N)	171		44		166		381	

Note
NA, not applicable ($n < 5$).

Table 6.2b The distribution and position of 'Europeanised' communication in the French public sphere (1990, 1995, 2000)

Claims maker	Addressee							
	French		Foreign		EU supranational		All	
	Share (%)	Position (+1/−1)	Share (%)	Position (+1/−1)	Share (%)	Position (+1/−1)	Share (%)	Position (+1/−1)
French	(a) 12.6	+0.39	(c) 3.1	+0.40	(e) 26.6	+0.29	42.3	+0.32
Foreign EU	(b) 2.3	+0.27	(f) 5.2	0.00	(h) 16.7	+0.25	24.2	+0.19265
EU/EEC supranational	(d) 2.5	+0.58	(g) 4.5	+0.41	(i) 26.4	+0.54	33.4	+0.52
All	17.5	+0.40	12.8	+0.24	69.7	+0.38	100.0	+0.36
Number of cases (N)	85		62		338		485	

(e), we find this 'bottom-up' linking of the EU into public debate three times more prevalent than the top-down type (d) in Britain (15.5 per cent), and ten times more so in France (26.6 per cent). This shows that the EU is brought into debate as an addressee much more than it puts itself forward. Another observation is the striking cross-national difference. This bottom-up vertical claims-making is significantly less present in Britain where it is strongly Euro-sceptical (−0.24). By contrast, it is the most prominent form of claims-making in the French public sphere, and European integration is evaluated more positively than in Britain (+0.29). This demonstrates that French actors have built an 'open' channel of communication through their political engagement that directly addresses European institutions, more so than the British. Such relationships mobilised upwards to the EU polity are also made significantly visible and accessible to the French public, allowing for processes of deliberation on the EU's political role. Compared to Britain, communication in the French public sphere exhibits at least some features that move in the direction of the federal model.

Regarding the emergence of 'horizontal' claims-making across borders between EU member states (b) and (c), we find relatively small amounts in both countries (taken together: Britain 5.8 per cent, France 5.4 per cent). So far, it appears that there is relatively little evidence for this type of transnational political communication that would be indicative of inter-acting member states. This is perhaps surprising, especially given the intergovernmental nature of much EU politics, and the increasing trans-national pooling and interweaving of policies of EU member states.

Lastly, the 'closed' claims-making that remains internalised within the nation state (a) is almost three times as visible in Britain (35.2 per cent), where it is the most prominent type overall, compared to France (12.6 per cent). This nationally internalised claims-making is also significantly more Euro-sceptical in the British public sphere (+0.12) than it is in the French (+0.39). Internalised debate and competition between national actors appear to be the defining characteristics of Britain's political communica-tion (Statham and Gray 2005). When mobilising over European integra-tion, British actors are twice as likely to address their demands to other British actors as they are to EU actors ((a) 35.2 per cent, (e) 15.5 per cent). The reverse holds for France, where national actors are twice as likely to address demands to the EU as they are to French actors ((a) 12.6 per cent, (e) 26.6 per cent). This shows an important difference in the way that political actors in the two countries have responded to the institu-tional emergence of multi-level European politics. British actors view the European project primarily as an issue *within national politics*. The sceptical position of such debates, ((a) +0.12 compared to the overall British mean +0.20, and the French (a) +0.39), also indicates a high level of criticism for European integration within national politics.

Regarding the 'passive' claims-making, which is 'external' to the domestic public sphere and does not engage national actors ((f)–(i)), of particular interest is the strong presence that we find for claims-making by supranational European actors, which also addresses supranational EU institutions and actors (i) (France 26.4 per cent, Britain 13.6 per cent). Here we see that claims made by EU supranational actors tend to remain 'enclosed' at the supranational level. This means that national publics get to see EU political affairs to a significant extent as 'externalised', rather than as directly engaging national actors. Thus the EU appears in national public spheres as a self-contained and separate supranational political entity. This EU self-referential component – coupled with weak vertical links – suggests that the federal public sphere model is weakly entrenched.

Thus, France is a country which is a driver of European integration and therefore witnesses a greater transformation of political communication in a way that allows meaningful political engagement with Europe. The more limited institutional engagement in European integration by the British produces a less substantively Europeanised public sphere. For the British public, European politics is made visible as a national issue, mobilised primarily by British actors addressing British actors. To a certain extent this precludes opportunities for citizens to see themselves having a direct relationship to EU institutions, and reproduces Europe as an epiphenomenon of national politics. Our comparison demonstrates that in France, processes of Europeanisation are most likely to occur through vertical claims-making by national domestic actors at the supranational level, whereas in Britain the 'closed' form of European debate through internalised national communications is most prominent. What this suggests in relation to the two models is that France has some limited but perhaps emergent traits of the federal model, whereas Britain has retained much of the national public sphere model. In Britain, even the regulatory model appears weakly entrenched.

Political claims-making over European integration: participatory?

In this second part, we address the relationships between national collective actors who mobilise political claims over Europe. In addition to cross-national variations, we aim to examine the extent to which Europeanised communication is participatory. Specifically, we inquire into the extent to which collective actors from civil society are engaged, and then, consider the nature of political party competition over Europe. Hence, we address two paths for linking citizens to institutional politics: civil society engagement and political party representation.

State and civil society

Tables 6.3a and 6.3b show the shares and positions of different national domestic actors in the 'Europeanised' communication of Britain and

Table 6.3a Britain: share and position of national collective actors in claims-making over European integration (1990, 1995, 2000)

	Share in claims-making (%)	Position over European integration (−1 to +1)
National domestic state and political party actors	**72.2**	**−0.02**
National domestic civil society actors	**27.8**	**+0.06**
Employers and private companies	6.0	+0.27
National central bank	2.2	+0.25
Other national state actors	1.4	+0.20
Unions and employees	1.6	+0.17
Scientific and research experts	3.3	+0.17
Economic experts	4.1	+0.07
Other national civil society organisations and groups	3.8	+0.07
National government and executive actors	42.5	+0.06
Pro/anti-European campaign organisations	9.0	−0.15
National legislative actors, political parties and politicians	26.2	−0.16
All domestic national actors	**100.0**	**+0.01**
Number of cases (N)	367	

Notes
Pro/anti-European campaign organisations (0.4 per cent) and other national state actors (1.5 per cent) are excluded from the subcategories, as the number of cases to calculate a position is too small (*n*<5).

Table 6.3b France: share and position of rational collective actors in claims-making over European integration (1990, 1995, 2000)

	Share in claims-making (%)	Position over European integration (−1 to +1)
National domestic state and political party actors	**74.8**	**+0.47**
National domestic civil society actors	**25.2**	**+0.13**
National government and executive actors	42.2	+0.54
National legislative actors, political parties and politicians	29.3	+0.37
Scientific and research experts	5.2	+0.36
Employers and private companies	2.6	+0.29
National central bank	1.9	+0.20
Other national civil society organisations and groups	6.7	+0.17
Economic experts	7.8	+0.14
Unions and employees	2.6	−0.43
All domestic national actors	**100.0**	**+0.38**
Number of cases (N)	270	

France.[5] In addition to showing the overall categories for state/political party versus civil society actors, the specific subcategories for actors are ordered according to their positions, with the pro-Europeans at the top and Euro-sceptics at the bottom. This visually presents the discursive distance between collective actors over European integration, based on their expressed claims, and identifies who are likely allies and opponents, as well as the public stances of different state institutions, relative to one another.

First, we see once more that French political debates over Europe are constructed around an axis that is significantly more pro-European (+0.38) than the British (+0.01). Regarding collective actors, we find overall similarity in shares of claims-making: state actors make three times more claims than civil society actors in both countries (Britain: state 72.2 per cent, civil society 27.8 per cent; France: state 74.8 per cent, civil society 25.2 per cent). This is indicative of a highly institutionalised field of politics and an especially elite-dominated debate. Previous research on Britain using the same method reveals that state actors account for a smaller share of claims-making in racism and discrimination (46.0 per cent) and unemployment (39.8 per cent) (Koopmans and Statham 2000; Statham 2003). Regarding participation, it seems that those collective actors who are already powerful within national politics are the ones who benefit most and are even more able to voice their demands within Europeanised communication.

Second, there is a striking cross-national difference: British state and civil society actors hold similar sceptical positions on Europe (state and political party –0.02, civil society +0.06), whereas in France, civil society actors (+0.13) challenge their state's strongly favourable stance to European integration (+0.47), by mobilising more sceptical claims. Thus, British conflicts over European integration appear to cross-cut political elites and civil society. In France, by contrast, the conflict line over Europe is between pro-European political elites and a more Euro-sceptical civil society.

Turning to specific collective actors, the nature of these differences becomes clearer. In Britain, the legislature and the political parties (26.2 per cent, –0.16) are the most Euro-sceptical actors, and also the government and executive (42.5 per cent, +0.06) appear at the Euro-sceptical end of the scale. This contrasts completely to the French situation, where the government and executive (42.2 per cent, +0.54) are the most pro-European actors, followed by the legislature and political party actors (29.3 per cent, +0.37). The stances over European integration which are advanced by the national political elites and institutions are diametrically opposed in Britain and France. In Britain, Euro-scepticism appears to be deeply entrenched, three decades after joining the EU, and governments and Parliament remain critical of the value of European integration. An elite consensus has not been reached over the benefits of European integration. In contrast, the French state, supported by its legislature, appears as a committed advocate for European integration. There is a clear consensus over Europe in the French political institutional arena. Political debate exists but is premised on the benefits of European integration, not questioning its value. French Socialist Minister of Justice Elisabeth Guigou's claim, on 26 May 2000, that the EU Charter of Fundamental Rights was a sign that the 'European Union is a matter of common values and identity' contrasts with the statement of Keith Vaz, British Labour Minister for Europe, on 7 December 2000, after signing the Charter: 'Get this clear. It is not a constitution. It is not legally binding. Nobody talked about it being legally binding.'

This has consequences because national elites and institutions importantly shape the opportunities for civil society actors to engage in politics as well as have a decisive influence on the country's relationship to the EU. British civil society actors exist in a situation of elite divisions and overall scepticism over Europe, which opens the issue to the public arena for challengers. In contrast, the French elite's pro-European consensus means that civil society actors mobilise in relation to this engaged stance over European integration.

In Britain, it is striking that we find no actors expressing more than a cautious pro-European stance, with employers and private companies being the most pro-European (+0.27), a position that in France (mean +0.38) would rank as relatively sceptical. To the cautious and limited extent that it is advanced at all in Britain, pro-Europeanism is mobilised by market actors, whereas in France it is promoted as a political concern by elites. This indicates that commitment to advancing European integration is part of a mainstream and institutionally-backed French political identity, which would be more in line with a federal public sphere model, whereas in Britain it is viewed more as a limited sectoral interest and economic concern which is negotiable and ad hoc, and is at most reflective of a narrow, particular public sphere in Europe.

Turning to the composition of civil society claims makers, for the most part these are economists, private firms, bankers and academics in both countries. These are hardly the types of actors who would be indicative of a participatory active 'demos' over European integration. Although undoubtedly important, the issues of European integration appear to have inspired little response in the form of citizen initiatives mobilising demands for political engagement. In fact, the exception is a dedicated European protest movement sector in Britain. This accounts for one-tenth of claims-making with an overall Euro-sceptical impact (9 per cent, −0.15). Elite divisions mean that competition over European integration spills over from the institutional arena into the public domain. In Britain, we find 13 organisations that exist specifically to campaign over Europe: *Britain in Europe* is the most prominent pro-European, and *Business for Sterling*, the most visible Euro-sceptical. However, public campaigns over

European integration are mostly from the Euro-sceptical camp (−0.15), which goes against the idea that civic participation necessarily leads to pro-European engagement. Such a public campaign sector was virtually absent in France accounting for a miniscule 0.4 per cent of claims. France has only one case: the *Alliance pour la souveraineté de la France*, which cooperates with British Euro-sceptics. This rare example of transnational bottom-up public mobilisation (again Euro-sceptical) is a protest event, which mobilised a 'Sovereignty European Charter' as an 'alternative' to the official Nice Summit.

In general, few French civil society actors find the resources to mobilise against European integration. The only consistent opponents, which are actually barely visible, are the trade unions and employees (2.6 per cent, −0.43), who mostly defend the French social model and criticise the neo-liberal project of the EU. Thus, Marc Blondel, general secretary of the trade union federation *Force Ouvrière*, declared on 7 December 2000 that 'it is not because bosses are more Europeanist that they are less bosses' and criticised the President of the European Confederation of Unions 'for being not very involved in defending employees'.

In sum, European politics mobilised in the public sphere is elite dominated and institutionalised. Europeanisation seems to empower the public voices of the already powerful. Regardless of cross-national differences, there is only very limited evidence for civil society activism and engagement of the participatory kind. When it does occur, it is mostly from the Euro-sceptic camp. An important explanatory factor for cross-national variations is the stance of national political elites. 'Fence-sitting' and 'foot-dragging' by national elites lead to political uncertainty over Britain's relationship with the EU. Elite divisions and ambivalence over European integration provide opportunities for single-issue campaign organisations to emerge over Europe in the public domain. By contrast, French elites are unequivocal 'pace-setters' in advocating European integration. This leads to a limited conflict between state and civil society, but one where civil society actors generally accept the values of European integration, but mobilise to defend their sectoral interests within that project.

Political parties

Given that for nation states, political parties are the classic form of intermediation between institutional politics and citizens, it is also important to examine party politics and European integration. A salient thesis is the inverted 'U' pattern: that parties' positions over Europe cross-cut left/right divisions, so that centre parties (left and right) are pro-European, with Euro-sceptical parties confined to the marginal poles of 'left' and 'right' (Hix and Lord 1997; Taggart 1998). The basic idea (often descriptive rather than explanatory) is that centre parties compete on a left/right axis and restrain themselves from competing over European issues, allowing a political space for parties at the margins of the political system to challenge them through Euro-sceptical mobilisation. So far, this thesis has been studied through analyses of experts' assessments of parties (Hooghe *et al.* 2004), party programmes (Gabel and Hix 2004) and parties' positions imputed by voters (Van der Eijk and Franklin 2004). Claims-making is arguably a more relevant form of data to address such issues[6] because it retrieves a party's actual intervention in the public domain, drawn from the medium by which parties communicate with citizens as an ongoing process, and in a way that is continuous over time. It is not based on their one-off strategic attempts to woo citizens at election times, or expert or public perceptions. Tables 6.4a and 6.4b show the shares and positions of actors with a party political identity, across the three same years.

A first important difference concerns the overall positions of the dominant centre parties: in France there is a pro-European consensus, whereas in Britain, the parties of left and right compete over Europe.

In France, the pro-European centrist consensus is formed by the centre-left, *Parti Socialiste* (PS) (+0.48), centre-right *Rassemblement pour la République* (RPR) (+0.56) and liberal/centre-right *Union pour la Démocratie Française* (UDF) (+0.68). Against this pro-European centre which dominates, accounting for four-fifths of party political claims-making (79.9 per cent), there is opposition to Europe from small parties on the left, such as the left-wing *Parti Communiste Français* (PC) (−0.14), and Jean-Pierre Chevènement's *Mouvement des Citoyens* (socialist nationalist) (−0.60) are prominent, and others, minimally present, include the Trotskyist left, *Lutte Ouvrière* (workers' struggle) and the *Ligue Communiste révolutionnaire* (LCR). There are also a very small number of Euro-sceptical cases from marginalised right-wing parties, usually in defence of national sovereignty, by the *Mouvement pour la France, Rassemblement pour la France* (RPF) and *Front National.*

Thus we find dissent against the dominant pro-European centre-party consensus from the radical left and right poles of the party system. In general, French parties' positions over European integration largely cross-cut the left/right distinction, following an inverted 'U' pattern between pro-European centre and Euro-sceptical periphery. However, in our time period, this inverted 'U' is not pure. Euro-scepticism comes more from the left than from the right pole. As in the case of unions and employees, this leftist Euro-scepticism is based mostly on a perceived defence of the French social model against a neo-liberal Europe. It is also worth noting that our data indicate that this opposition has become more prominent over time.

In Britain, Europe is an issue for party political competition between the two major parties. Overall, *Labour* (+0.33) has taken a more pro-European position compared to the *Conservatives* who have been strongly Euro-sceptical (−0.29). Conservatives were Euro-sceptics both as a

Table 6.4a Britain: share and position of political party actors in claims-making over European integration (1990, 1995, 2000)

	All		1990		1995		2000	
	Share	*Position*	*Share*	*Position*	*Share*	*Position*	*Share*	*Position*
Conservative	**53.3**	**−0.29**	**67.2**	**+0.02**	**95.5**	**−0.30**	33.0	−0.50
Labour	**41.9**	**+0.33**	25.4	0.00	4.5	NA	**61.5**	**+0.38**
Liberal democrat	2.5	+0.75	7.5	+0.80	–	–	1.6	NA
All political party actors[a]	**100.0**	**+0.01**	100.0	+0.07	100.0	−0.29	100.0	+0.09
Number of cases (*N*)	**315**		67		66		182	

Notes

Parties of Government are included in ***bold italics*** for the three years. Position score only given if *n*>5, otherwise not applicable (NA).

a Includes also political party actors that are not subcategorised in the table.

Table 6.4b France: share and position of political party actors in claims-making over European integration (1990, 1995, 2000)

	All		1990		1995		2000	
	Share	Position	Share	Position	Share	Position	Share	Position
Rassemblement pour la République	30.7	+0.56	31.1	+0.14	51.2	+0.64	23.3	+0.70
Parti Socialiste	38.5	+0.48	44.4	+0.40	14.0	+0.67	45.7	+0.49
Union pour la Démocratie Française	10.7	+0.68	15.6	+1.00	9.3	N/A	9.5	+0.45
Parti Communiste Français	3.9	-0.14	—	—	2.3	N/A	6.0	-0.14
Mouvement des Citoyens	2.4	-0.60	—	—	—	—	4.3	-0.60
All political party actors[a]	100.0	+0.40	100.0	+0.47	100.0	+0.47	100.0	+0.36
Number of cases (N)	204		45		43		116	

Notes
Parties of Government are included in **bold italics** for the three years. Position score only given if $n > 5$, otherwise not applicable (NA).
a Includes also political party actors that are not subcategorised in the table.

government party (1990, 1995) and as an opposition party (2000). However, this Conservative Euro-scepticism was relatively unchallenged by the Labour opposition in 1990 and 1995. At those times it appeared as if an elite consensus existed among the main parties that were against, or ambivalent towards, European integration. Nicholas Ridley, whilst Trade and Industry Secretary in the Conservative Government, claimed, on 14 July 1990, that handing over sovereignty to the EC was 'tantamount to giving it to Adolf Hitler' and that European monetary union was a German racket designed to take over Europe. In France, such extreme views would be inconceivable from a major party of government. To be fair, Ridley's xenophobia is a minority view. In France, however, such stances can only exist at the party political margins. Thus, the leader of the *Mouvement des Citoyens* on 21 May 2000 claimed that German Minister Fischer's proposals for a federal institutional reform of the EU 'were a sign that Germany was not cured of its Nazi past'.

Labour's lack of enthusiasm for Europe was also evident, for example, when Peter Shore, Labour Member of Parliament, on 11 June 1990 stated in a Commons debate that a European monetary union would deliver Britain, bound hand and foot, to the European decision-makers. After entering office, Labour's position became pro-European (+0.38), whilst in opposition the Conservatives became strongly Euro-sceptical (–0.50). Thus Britain does not conform to the inverted 'U' model with Euro-scepticism located at the mainstream centre-right. Britain's most consistently pro-European party are the *Liberal Democrats*, though they are barely visible in public debates over Europe (2.5 per cent, +0.75).

Competition is partly facilitated by the British party system, which produces single-party governments with strong executive power that have less need to moderate their stances to win support from other parties. The British electoral system is also much less favourable to smaller parties than the French. However, these general differences between political systems do not sufficiently explain the cross-national differences over Europe. Instead, there is an embedded and institutionalised difference between the ideological stances of British and French political elites over Europe that appears to reproduce itself over time. As a result, Labour's relatively recent conversion to pro-Europeanism is likely to lack the embedding and depth of the French centre parties. It will be able to shift more easily back to ambivalence or opposition in the future. This is partly because the British elites' pro-Europeanism tends to be based on ad hoc arguments about national gains, rather than the ideological commitment voiced by the French. In Britain, the Conservatives' Euro-scepticism is ideological, opposing the EU's possible social regulation of free markets and its threat to national political sovereignty, and claiming that market deregulation should not stop at European borders. For example, the opposition leader William Hague called the Nice Treaty, 'major steps towards a European Superstate'. Indeed Labour's new pro-Europeanism is perhaps more accurately depicted as anti-Euro-scepticism, since it opposes Euro-sceptics more than it builds the case for European integration.

In sum, British political elites view European integration as open to criticism and compete over it in the attempt to gain public support, whereas in France, the national commitment to European integration is largely unquestioned by the main parties and the Euro-sceptical impact of smaller parties has been very limited.

Conclusion

This chapter presents an empirically based 'snapshot' of the Europeanised communication patterns that are emerging in two national public spheres in response to advancing European integration. It captures how national actors publicly mobilise over European affairs, and the national images of European politics that are subsequently made visible to citizens of Britain and France. This allows us to describe two national experiences of transformations towards a European public sphere, to account for variations and to raise questions of 'performance' with regard to public participation in, and public representations of, European politics.

We find mostly striking cross-national differences in the countries' emergent patterns of Europeanised political communication, although one notable similarity is the very limited development of horizontal links between European member states, which is perhaps surprising given the intergovernmental nature of much EU institutional politics and underlines that patterns of political communication do not 'automatically' follow institutional developments.

The French public sphere has been transformed in such a way that political debates exhibit stronger linkages to the European supranational polity, a relationship that is mobilised 'bottom-up' by French national actors addressing EU supranational actors. This opens up and broadens the scope of the public sphere for political engagement by including the supranational European level above the nation state. However, EU actors' communications penetrate the French public sphere only very marginally, and EU supranational politics is largely self-referential and 'externalised' to national actors. This demonstrates the limited and one-sided nature of this development towards a 'vertically' linked Europeanised national public sphere. Closer examination shows that this relationship to the EU is driven largely by a pro-European consensus of French political elites. Political elites are the most pro-European actors, strongly promoting European integration and dominating the field of European politics. The values of European integration are largely unquestioned in public debates. Dissent is mostly about protecting one sectoral interest: labour. Trade unions, employees and far-left political parties defend the French social model against the perceived threat of the EU's neo-liberalism. In sum, the general impression with regard to the French case is that it exhibits some limited traits of the federal model of a public sphere, through the strength of its vertical linkages, although it falls well short of this.

The British public sphere is strongly characterised by a type of Europeanised communication that indicates inward-looking national relationships. British debates over Europe are nationally 'internalised', self-referential and significantly more opposed to European integration. The British address the EU supranational level less often than France, and European integration is strongly criticised. Subsequently, British Europeanised communication does little to open up spaces for meaningful exchanges with the EU as a powerful supranational actor. Also, as in the French case, EU actors largely fail to make themselves visible in the British public sphere. Thus, EU politics is made visible to British citizens primarily as a national affair. Again, this specific relationship to the EU is strongly driven by national political elites. British elites remain sceptical of European integration. At times, governments and the dominant centrist political parties have strongly questioned the values of European integration. Conservative Euro-scepticism ideologically opposes the EU as a regulatory threat to free markets, and as a threat to national political sovereignty. This has led to strong elite divisions and competition within national institutional politics over Europe. Such contention spills over into civil society, where issue-specific European campaign groups add their own voices to the debate over the value of national involvement in Europe (with an aggregate Euro-sceptical impetus). Labour's recent pro-Europeanism thus lacks the embedding of its French counterpart and is made on a basis of ad hoc national benefits, rather than an ideological commitment to the values of European integration. To conclude, the British case shows virtually no traits of the federal model, nor even the regulatory one, and it remains far closer to a national model of the public sphere.

This analysis emphasises the importance of national elites' positions on Europe, which shape the institutional and discursive political environment in which other collective actors mobilise demands. In France and Britain, Europeanised politics is an elite-dominated affair. There are only very limited signs of civil society actors mobilising to demand participation with regard to the politics of European integration. In sum, this underlines that Europeanised politics tends to disproportionately empower the participation of the already powerful. Such a finding is further supported by the Europub.com study and research on litigation in environmental politics (Koopmans 2007; Börzel 2006). It is precisely those sections of civil society depicted by normative theories as the source of a 'demos' that turn out to have most difficulty in making themselves visible in Europeanised debates. Furthermore, the few public campaigners for integration often come from the Euro-sceptical camp. The dominance of elite and institutional actors in Europeanised politics raises important questions about the democratic performance of a European public sphere.

Similar dilemmas occur with regard to political parties' representation of European politics to their national and EU citizens. The French people's rejection of the European CT in the 2005 referendum, despite overwhelming mainstream party support, arguably demonstrates that consensual party politics has provided insufficient representation of opposition to European integration, leading to a Euro-sceptical backlash. One could argue that the vociferous party political competition over Europe in Britain has also been 'unrepresentative', by resonating disproportionately highly, and conflictually, compared to the public's lower rating of Europe's importance. Perhaps the key innovation of the French referendum is that it provided a specific one-off 'political opportunity' for the public to make a political statement on Europe. It took away management and control of the European issue from national elites and party politics for a decisive moment. The long-term legacy is that national elites will find it even harder to advance European integration without including mechanisms for public consent and legitimation in the future. French public debates over Europe may even move in the direction of the British. What is clear, however, is that Europeanised politics requires new participatory and representative mechanisms when compared to those of the nation state, if it is to become a multi-levelled, transnational, open and legitimate form of politics. In contrast to the old days of Jean Monnet, Europe now needs 'to build in the presence of Europeans'.

This finding resonates with the main conclusion of this book, namely that the EU does not represent a case of gradual development towards the federal model but represents a more complex case of several models co-existing simultaneously. How resilient each model is depends on institutionalised patterns of communication; it also hinges on the character of the values the Union espouses and whether these can be given adequate institutional and constitutional shape. The eventual outcomes and interpretations of the constitutional process will shed important light on possible future outcomes.

Notes

This research is from the Europub.com (europub.wz-berlin.de) project (The Transformation of Political Mobilisation and Communication in European Public Spheres) funded by the EU's Framework programme (HPSE-CT2000–00046), and the British case, by the ESRC (RES-000-23-0886) (ics.leeds.ac.uk/eurpolcom/). The author gratefully acknowledges the inputs of Europub.com colleagues and, in particular, John Erik Fossum's work on this chapter in line with the interpretative framework of this book.

1 We code all acts in the field of European integration, and all acts with a European issue-scope in six strategically selected policy fields: two where EU competences have extended furthest (monetary policy, agriculture), two intermediary (immigration, troop deployment) and two where nation states retain most autonomous control (retirement/pensions, education). See the project website for further details (europub.wz-berlin.de).
2 In total, our sample covers 52 days for 1990 and 1995, and 104 days for 2000.

3 Reliability was high; see the Europub.com website for results. Coders participate in regular discussions about difficult cases.
4 Cases without an addressee and by (or on) non-EU foreign and supranational actors are excluded from this analysis.
5 These samples include cases where no addressee was specified.
6 See a criticism of other approaches in Mair 2006.

7 The European void
The democratic deficit as a cultural deficiency

Abram de Swaan

On croit souvent que la vie intellectuelle est spontanément internationale. Rien n'est plus faux.

(Bourdieu 2002: 3)

A Europeanization of perspectives is occurring (at least the first signs of it).
(Beck 2005: 109)

In the past half century, a peculiar political construct has emerged from the combination of European states: the European Union is more than a confederation but less than a federation; more than just a free-trade zone but not quite an economic whole (Therborn 2002);[1] almost a world power but one without an army or an effective foreign policy of its own; with a common currency, the euro, but with coins that reserve a different verso for each member state. And yet, taken together, in less than a lifetime, these are major achievements. The ambitions are even more grandiose: ever eastward. The Union, after expanding to Central and Eastern Europe, and the Baltic, one day may well come to include all of the Balkans, Turkey and, in the end, who knows, Ukraine, Georgia and even Russia. This geographic expansion is to be managed by further political integration. The Constitutional Treaty would have elevated the Union above a mere regulatory apparatus and closer towards a federal entity, to adopt the terms proposed in the introduction to this book.[2]

For the time being, however, the recent referenda in France and the Netherlands have put a damper on these designs, while the Austrian EU presidency during the first semester of 2006 set itself the objective of preventing the accession of Turkey.

An uneasy mood reigned among the Europeans even before the negative French and Dutch votes brought about an acute crisis, which in turn much acerbated the existing malaise. The institutions of the EU, elected directly or indirectly, have failed to capture the imagination of the electorate.

There is a Council of Ministers, in which the governments of the member states are represented, each supported by a freely elected parliamentary majority at home. There is a European Parliament (EP), directly elected by the citizens of each country. There is a European Commission (EC), which must take into account the Parliament's majority. Yet, no doubt, much of the widespread unease among the citizens of Europe is connected to the notorious 'democratic deficit' of the Union.[3] But the very plebiscites that had been staged to make up for this shortcoming elicited a resounding rejection.

The fragmentation of European public space

Europeans do not speak the same language and hence do not understand each other well enough to differ or agree. But quite apart from the confusion of tongues, opinions everywhere are shaped within separate national frameworks. What is passionately debated in one country is often not even an issue in adjacent countries where a different agenda prevails. In many respects, however, the debate on the European Constitution, and especially the referendum campaigns waged in France and the Netherlands, represented a turning point in the formation of a European public space. Not only did the proposed constitution evoke intense exchanges in each member state, it also elicited a vivid interest in the discussions going on in the other member states. Equally, the bomb attacks in Madrid and London on 11 March 2004 and 7 July 2005, respectively, were not reported as threats to the affected countries exclusively but rather as a menace to all of Europe. The riots in the French *banlieue* in October and November 2005 again prompted discussions elsewhere in Europe about the odds of similar troubles there. At an earlier stage, events such as mad cow disease or the introduction of the euro inspired synchronous discussion of identical issues across the EU (cf. Grundmann 1999). This also created an interest in the debates that went on in adjacent countries and in the European institutions.[4]

Yet, such common European debates are still the exception rather than the rule, and it is a rare event that prompts a discussion allowing voices from all member states to agree or disagree on the same issues, according to a common agenda. Even today, the political and cultural debate mainly proceeds in relative isolation within each national society. Abroad, it hardly meets any response. In short, there is no such thing as a European public space, as yet. As stated by Philip Schlesinger:

> The mediated public sphere in the EU remains first, overwhelmingly national; second, where it is not national it is transnational and anglophone but elitist in class terms; third, where it is ostensibly transnational, but not anglophone, it still decants principally into national modes of address.
>
> (Schlesinger 2003: 18)

In discussing Europe as a communicative space, much attention has been paid to the distribution of news and information, the professional task of journalists. Schlesinger (2000) and others have shown that news about the EU is perceived by reporters through national filters, edited according to a domestic agenda, and only sparsely absorbed by the home audience. Transnational media are almost without exception in English and aimed at a select public of financial, corporate and political elites.

The remarkable lack of interest in the culture and politics of other European states, even in neighbouring countries with an identical language, a similar culture and a shared past, is hard to explain. It registers as a sleepiness, a sudden onset of boredom whenever the other country comes within one's circle of perception. And underneath there often may linger disdain, or resentment, or both, reflecting past and enduring relations between more powerful and less powerful neighbours, or between centre and periphery. All this is part of a lasting national habitus which incorporates the relations of cultural capital that prevail within and between national societies. In fact, this pervasive habitus of disinterest is a result of the lack of debate and exchange that transcends borders. This, in turn, is due to the absence of a cultural opportunity structure that would allow public intellectuals, authors, artists and scientists to manifest themselves throughout Europe. It sometimes seems as if any intellectual who attempts to overcome this national closure is pulled back by the invisible gravity of the domestic institutional structure.[5]

So far, on the one hand, the paucity of resources and opportunities has discouraged intellectual entrepreneurs from seeking a transnational, European audience. First of all they have had to look for resources in their home society. On the other hand, the relatively laggard nature of European cultural elite formation has done little to prompt politicians or private sponsors to provide opportunities and resources at the European level.[6]

In the meantime, and in the absence of a single European public space, there are myriads of European niches, each providing a distinct meeting place for participants from all member states with shared interests. And the more circumscribed the agenda, the more smoothly the all-European exchange proceeds: experts, technicians and specialists have no trouble finding one another, nor do entrepreneurs from the same branch, believers from the same church, athletes from the same sport or scientists from the same discipline find it hard to congregate and communicate.

But these multifarious niches, neatly separated as they are, do not add up to a European space. On the contrary, as the agenda widens and comes to encompass broader cultural, social and political issues, communication becomes much more difficult. There are literally thousands of specialised journals that carry the epithet 'European' or an equivalent in their title.[7] But when it comes to general cultural and political reviews, there may be no more than a dozen that achieve a genuine European distribution, and almost all of these are in English.

It is unlikely that these specialised networks of exchange will coalesce into broader structures of communication. They do not at the national level. The mutual isolation between academic disciplines, or between technological specialities, is notorious (and once again, the opportunity structure, or rather the reward distribution, prevailing in these fields discourages adventurous, transdisciplinary initiatives). It is all the more unlikely that this vertical fragmentation would be overcome at the transnational level. Nor is it very likely that the elite publics that are each connected with a prestigious transnational medium, such as the *Financial Times*, the *International Herald Tribune* or *Le Monde Diplomatique*, will in due time be 'knitted together'. There is not much that connects the subscribers to different media, and their owners will be the last to encourage such promiscuity.

The impasse in the development of border-transcending media or associations is characteristic of general cultural and political communication in Europe but not for specific scientific, technological or commercial exchange. The more specific the theme of the network or the periodical, the more easy it is to put it together and keep it going. There is no dearth of associations, conferences or journals dedicated to a scientific or technological discipline, sub- or even sub-sub-discipline. Researchers and experts are very well informed about their peers throughout Europe and the rest of the world and keep in continual contact. On the other hand, the broader the scope of the intellectual encounter, the harder it is to create and maintain a shared agenda, to define common ground, across borders and across languages. But the vocation of the public intellectual is precisely to engage in debate on the broad issues of the day, and many in the audience want to hear a voice that is familiar from earlier discussions express its opinion on ongoing issues. One function of the much maligned celebrity intellectuals (cf. Bourdieu 1996) is to function as beacons that shed their light on the many and diverse issues that pop up in the sea of current events from a steady and familiar vantage point (much as familiar critics can help readers situate a work of art in the context of the art world, whether or not readers share their tastes). Another function of media intellectuals is to define new issues and introduce them into public debate. This is usually a shared endeavour, most often accomplished in mutual antagonism, by the debaters on both sides. Vital public opinion exists in a public of divided opinion. Intellectual debaters need a theatrical quality to command attention, to impose themselves upon a public that is constituted in the very course of the spectacle: assisting at a dramatic *choc des opinions* that may not always yield the truth, but is certain to inspire passion about public issues and thereby create a public.

The role of intellectuals in Europe

The deficient communication between the nations that make up the EU is not due to lack of political culture, or a scarcity of debate and polemics in each of the member states. On the contrary, every national society boasts the full gamut of newspapers, from the popular press to the most prestigious dailies. Each country is served by an array of TV channels, and a few of those provide some space for the discussion of public issues. In all member states, there are politicians and intellectuals galore who are perfectly capable and quite eager to discuss questions of politics, culture and morality. But time and again, the gravitational force of the national culture pulls back those intellectuals who might aspire to transcend the borders of their nation and the barriers of their language.

After all, it was the emergence, during the Modern Era, of the nation state in tandem with a national society that spawned a public space where people could exchange their opinions. Yet the history of the origins and evolution of a public sphere in European national societies offers a precedent, but it does not provide a blueprint to emulate on a European scale.[8] After all, most of these nations have been under the rule of a more or less autonomous, more or less effective regime for centuries. In each country, the various regional languages were gradually pushed aside by the language of the court and the capital city, which set the tone for the entire society. Hence, a coherent, literate public that shared a language and an agenda could emerge. A new kind of entrepreneur found its audience: independent authors who wrote for a clientele that bought and read books and newspapers. They were mostly small, self-employed operators trading in sentiments and opinions, in brief, intellectuals: people who speak and write professionally in public about concepts and ideas.

Intellectuals still exist today; there are even many more of them, although nowadays there are very few who still work on their own account, as 'freelancers'. By far, most are employed by universities, publishers and the media. All these institutions are very much oriented towards their domestic environment when recruiting students, seeking a readership or addressing an audience.[9] Moreover, they are bound to the soil of their national language. They also depend on the national government for legal protection and as the case may be, for financial support. As a consequence, academics, editors and journalists find almost all of their connections within nationally defined networks and build up their reputation within the confines of their home society. Thus, there are German intellectuals, and French, Greek, Portuguese and also Dutch intellectuals, each addressing their particular domestic public. But on the whole, the intellectuals *in* Europe are not the intellectuals *of* Europe.[10]

Intellectuals very rarely find a European audience or manifest themselves at the all-European level. Only a very small number have achieved a reputation that goes beyond the borders of their own society, allowing them to publish, in translation, in the other countries of the Union. The few who have achieved international renown as intellectuals have done so mostly on the strength of a literary or an academic oeuvre that was translated and published abroad, or because they have made a name for themselves as commentators on international affairs and in due time have been reprinted in other countries. Literary fame especially has allowed a select company of authors to make themselves heard throughout the Union, such as Günter Grass, Milan Kundera and Umberto Eco. Their observations on political and cultural issues are published and read throughout the Union after their novels have already provided them with an audience that recognises their voice. There are other remarkable exceptions, such as Jürgen Habermas and the late Pierre Bourdieu, both philosophers and sociologists, whose comments on the predicaments of contemporary society have resonated far beyond their home countries. But almost all the others among the handful of authors who have succeeded in building a transnationally valid reputational capital started out in the UK or the US, writing in English, before they acquired a name across the EU (even if they were born elsewhere in the former British empire and started life with a different mother tongue). Transnational reputational capital remains very scarce for intellectuals (and even more so for almost everyone else). The vast majority of reputations does not reach across the borders of language and culture.

Very few politicians have succeeded in extending their reputation beyond the confines of their home society, except through incidental news items. For example, Tony Blair, Silvio Berlusconi and Jacques Chirac are certainly well known all over Europe, but it is doubtful whether they can conquer an audience abroad beyond the eight-o'clock TV news. Winston Churchill and Charles de Gaulle are the shining exceptions as the great heroes of the Second World War, who were both authors in their own right. Surprisingly, the European commissioners have not achieved much transnational capital either, even though they appear exceptionally well positioned to do so. These admittedly haphazard examples seem to suggest that lasting, border-transcending reputations, surprisingly, are built more on a written oeuvre than on political capital or celebrity media exposure. At least among an elite public, literary and academic prestige seem to command more lasting attention from audiences than simple fame. The scarcity of border-crossing intellectual reputations seems to be a consequence of language barriers, but also of the 'cultural opportunity structure' of the Union and its constituent states. The concept is a variation of the notion of a 'political opportunity structure', current in the study of social movements, where it denotes the totality of 'signals to the social and political actor which either encourage or discourage them to use their internal resources to form social movements' (Kriesi *et al.* 1995: xiii).[11] Likewise, the structure of cultural opportunities determines the chances and incentives for academics, artists, authors and other intellectuals to reach an audience and earn an income through cultural pursuits.

What makes the concept interesting is the shift away from individual motivation and competence towards the broader social context in which people operate. Thus, the prevailing constellation of universities, newspapers, reviews and foundations granting subsidies or awards may much influence the career moves that intellectuals make.

Further, the networks that academics and authors form with their peers, and the way these ties are structured, may also shape their choices. Such networks may connect close colleagues but also members of an editorial board or an organising committee, comprising ties to departments in other universities, to translators and publishers. Citation networks chart another aspect of this opportunity structure. There is little doubt that invitations to conferences or acceptance for publication in reviews are more likely to be forthcoming for scholars or authors already connected with the organizers or the editors, and also in other respects well situated within the network.

To outsiders this may smack of favouritism, but from the inside it seems a simple matter of affinity of style and opinion, and of predictable performance. And finally, there is the overriding structural fact of the prevailing language. Most often, its impact remains largely unnoticed in the domestic context, where the single national language is shared as a matter of course. The European constellation of languages is the topic of the final section of this chapter.

The existing cultural opportunity structures in the national societies of Europe operate strongly against the emergence of border-transcending intellectual reputations. First of all, in order to cross borders, more often than not authors must switch languages. This compels them either to invest heavily in the cost of mastering a language to such a degree of perfection as to be able to write and publish in it, or it imposes the considerable costs of translation (and how to get editors and publishers interested in a text that has not been translated yet?). More fundamentally, language differences delimit the scope of attention and delineate networks of affinity among intellectuals. People 'naturally' (i.e. 'structurally') prefer to read texts in their own language.

Institutions provide very few career opportunities for intellectuals, writers, journalists and scholars outside their national societies. Language requirements severely restrict employment for academics at foreign universities (even for those who speak English) and they entirely rule out editorial or publishing jobs abroad. Equally scarce at the all-European level are the other ingredients of a successful career and a major reputation: awards, subsidies, commissions, committee or jury memberships and so on. Almost all these resources are proffered by national institutions rather than by European agencies. Moreover, as argued above, the odds of obtaining such prizes and positions are much improved by mutual acquaintance, while acquaintanceship networks rarely extend beyond the borders of nationality and language. There are, admittedly, a few very prestigious prizes intended for laureates from all over Europe, such as the Amalfi, the Erasmus or the Charles the Fifth awards. Further, there are the European University Institute near Florence, the College of Europe in Bruges and in Warsaw, and some 'Jean Monnet' and 'European Union' university chairs here and there. But even the rare intellectuals who qualify for such privileges must first build their reputation and win laurels within their own national societies.

Granted, things are changing in the direction of increasing European exchange, also among scholars and authors. A finely branched circuit of conferences and workshops has taken shape by now and continually brings together intellectuals, scholars, writers or artists from all over Europe. Moreover, a small number of periodicals already appear in several languages, such as *Liber*, now defunct, directed by the late Pierre Bourdieu, or *Le Monde Diplomatique*. But with the exception of the latter, the most widely read transnational publications in Europe are all British or American: from *The New York Review of Books*, the *London Review of Books*, *The Times Literary Supplement* and *The Economist*, to the *International Herald Tribune* and the *Financial Times*.[12]

The role of elite media

In 1990 the British newspaper tycoon Robert Maxwell decided to launch 'Europe's first national newspaper', aiming for an all-European readership. A few years later the daily was defunct and survived a few years more as a weekly publication. Losses have been reported at £70 million.[13] This debacle may have functioned as a warning for anyone attempting to try and embark on a similar enterprise again. There are, however, as mentioned, media that have succeeded in crossing borders.

In fact, the weekly British *The Economist* produces a special 'continental edition' for mainland Europe, with a circulation of 200,000 (as compared with the 150,000 of the UK edition and an overall global circulation of more than one million).[14] The London-based *Financial Times*, with a total circulation of 426,000, reaches 119,000 readers in mainland Europe and participates in 'partner' editions in German, French and Chinese.[15] Both publications cater mainly to the business elite throughout the EU, but they devote considerable space to general political and cultural issues, making them significant media of intellectual debate on the continent. The same applies to another worldwide publication, the *International Herald Tribune* (owned by the *New York Times*, which provides much of its editorial content). It mainly addresses American expatriates and the foreign business community with an overall circulation of almost 250,000 and a European readership of 145,000 (most other readers live in East Asia).[16] The largest intellectual, even 'high-brow' medium, is the bi-weekly *New York Review of Books*, with an impressive worldwide circulation of over 1.4 million, mostly American readers. In Europe, its combined subscription, news-stand and bookshop readership numbers about 13,000.[17] The bi-weekly *London Review of Books*, with a much smaller total circulation of 43,000, distributes a few thousand copies in continental Europe.[18]

These English language publications are mostly read in the Western part of Europe. Central and Eastern European countries may yet have to catch up, since foreign media became accessible only after 1989. The one exception to the predominance of the English language media that are based in London or New York is the astonishingly successful *Le Monde Diplomatique*, a political and cultural bi-monthly with a global printed circulation of 1.5 million in 21 languages. Its editorial position is clearly to the left, or rather *altermondialiste*. Outside France, *Le Monde Diplomatique* is usually published as a monthly supplement to a local newspaper or review, in the Middle East, Latin America and also the EU, where it has a combined foreign readership of almost 600,000. In the EU, it is the most widely distributed transnational medium for intellectual debate and the only one of some importance that is not based in the US or the UK.[19]

The impact of the electronic media is much harder to assess, since viewers and listeners tend to tune in whenever it suits them, and their habits must be assessed through periodical survey questionnaires of contested validity. Thus, Radio France Internationale (RFI), the French international radio and TV network, claims 44 million 'regular listeners' all over the world (the majority in Francophone Africa) and more than two million in Europe, 'West and East', for its broadcasts.[20] The French international TV channel TV5 Monde reports 72 million weekly viewers, 29 million in Europe alone.[21] These figures cover the audience for sports and news as well as more intellectual items such as documentaries and political or cultural features. The same applies to Deutsche Welle, which broadcasts mainly in German and English, mostly to a European audience, estimated to number some 65 million 'weekly' listeners and 28 million viewers. In the EU, it reaches roughly five million viewers and six million listeners on a weekly basis (especially in Central and Eastern Europe).[22]

BBC World, the British international TV network, provides programming in English for 4.5 million viewers every week, over the entire range of genres, with very frequent news broadcasts and a sizeable share of general cultural and political items.[23] The Franco-German channel Arte broadcasts its 'high-brow' programmes simultaneously in French and German throughout Europe for a rather small audience (e.g. 0.4 per cent of the market in Germany, corresponding to some 240,000 adult viewers).[24]

The Dutch Radio Netherlands (*Wereldomroep*) broadcasts in nine languages and reaches about 50 million weekly listeners, making it the fourth largest global network (the Voice of America is still the world's largest global broadcaster).[25] Many other countries support an international TV or radio station, broadcasting in several languages, but with rather small audiences. The smaller international stations increasingly rely on global news agencies, thus increasing the similarity of news broadcast across the globe, while at the same time increasing the variation of available items in any single location.[26]

A number of TV and radio stations limit themselves to news or sports broadcasts, such as CNN, in English (with a reported weekly audience of 7.5 million in Europe),[27] or CNBC, with 2.7 million European viewers on a weekly basis.[28] Most interesting for the present purposes is EuroNews, an editorially independent station under contract to the EU, which broadcasts in seven languages to 6.7 million European viewers every week.[29] Further, Eurosport is a highly successful channel, broadcasting in eighteen languages for a pan-European audience and devoted exclusively to sports coverage.[30]

Most printed periodicals as well as radio and TV stations have by now created websites that present published editorial material, usually with added comments, arguments, supporting documentation, audience reactions, etc. Increasingly, multilingual international websites that cater to a political and cultural elite appear on the World Wide Web, the most notable instances being Eurozine (edited in Vienna), with articles from some 100 cultural magazines in Europe, quite often in translation.[31] A site hosted by the European Cultural Foundation in Amsterdam will soon present a daily digest of major European newspapers in several languages.[32]

Sports and entertainment coverage crosses the barriers of language and nation with much greater ease than political and cultural items. Many of the programmes are initially produced by American media enterprises. But some are indeed of European origin and scope: the Eurovision Song Contest and the European Football Championship are among the most notable examples of shows that capture a vast audience throughout the Union (Martin 1999).

The emerging European public sphere

The national framework shapes opinion within each country, the national past determines shared memories, and the cultural opportunity structure in each society controls the intellectuals. It sometimes seems as if some kind of national gravity holds them back from even trying to transcend borders. It also reveals structures of national sentiment and practice that usually remain unnoticed, because they are so 'banal' (Billig 1995). This apt expression conveys the unreflective, unremarked upon, even unconscious implications of opinions, sentiments and practices that make up nationality in the course of everyday life.

And yet, some kind of European public space is bound to take shape in the not too distant future. It will certainly not be as coherent and homogenous as the term suggests in the singular. Like the public sphere in national societies, it will be fragmented, with the fragments hanging more or less together: 'a sphere of publics' (Schlesinger and Kevin 2000). In normal times, that is. There are moments in a given society when everyone's attention is drawn by one and the same topic. Fleeting moments of unanimous interest are achieved by the tragic death of a young celebrity, the exciting marriage of a royal couple, or the triumphant victory of a major football team. Other events have a more lasting impact on the attention economy of the nation, and they usually have to do with disaster, rebellion, crisis and war. Medrano (2003) speaks of a '*thematische Synchronizität*' ('thematic synchronicity') in the news coverage of the EU, and an increasing similarity of themes and political options in the separate member states. But the absence of debate across borders and the limited participation in national debate on the EU point to a public sphere that will remain fragmented, or 'pillarized' (*versäult*), into separate but congruent national spheres.

The recent debate on the European Constitution proceeded as a series of parallel national discussions, albeit in the awareness that the neighbours were talking about the same things at the same time (Medrano 2003). Clearly, no politicians or intellectuals managed to express what was at stake in terms that could have captured audiences across borders and beyond language barriers. This may have been due to the highly technical and rarified nature of the laws being proposed. Actually, during the debate that preceded the referendums in France and the Netherlands, rather strong feelings about the alleged impact of 'Brussels' on domestic politics and about the competition the enlargement of the Union would bring for workers at home became manifest. But such resistance is no less 'European' than a wholehearted acceptance of further integration. What was 'unEuropean' in these campaigns was the predominance of national politics, a symbolic use of the vote against the governments of Jacques Chirac and Jan Peter Balkenende, regardless of the European issues at stake.

Barring major disasters and wars, the most probable way for a European sphere of publics to take shape would be in the course of a fundamental conflict throughout the EU, not only similar and synchronous, but also this time interconnected across borders. The simultaneous rise of an anti-immigrant radical right and a fundamentalist immigrant movement in Europe might provide the fuel for a conflict that can command the attention of audiences across the EU and begin to connect the discussions in the individual member states. Under such conditions, journalists will provide the accounts that draw the public's interest, and intellectuals will coin the ideas and concepts that shape opinion and sentiment. The murder of the Dutch filmmaker Theo van Gogh by a young Dutch Islamist, the train bombings in Madrid and London and the widespread unrest evoked by the rioting youth in the French suburbs all elicited reactions throughout the EU, at times reacting upon the reactions in other member states in the manner of an incipient all-European debate. Another case in point: the commotion in Islamic countries about the cartoons in a Danish newspaper portraying Mohammed, and the concern that this in turn caused among European publics, provoking discussion throughout the Union, statements by national leaders and even a formal declaration by the EC. As might be expected, this communicative integration was brought about by an exterior reaction that was perceived as hostile to the Union in its entirety. But interior developments, such as low-wage competition from the new member states, or the takeovers of major national industries by competitors from other countries within or outside the Union also inspired spirited, synchronous, parallel debates, at times even interacting with those in other member states.

The inadequate cultural opportunity structure is coupled with a most persistent cultural obstacle structure: the coexistence of two dozen languages within the EU. This multiplicity, of course, also greatly hampers the emergence of a public debate at the European level, and hence prevents the formation of a public space.

The European language constellation and public space

The EU boasts a common currency, but so far lacks a common language. It continues to speak officially in all the languages of the member states, initially four, at present twenty-three and in the not too distant future possibly even twenty-five or more. This prospect has prompted much alarm but so far rarely any serious debate beyond the circle of specialists. French turned out to be stronger than the franc, Dutch more stubborn than the guilder and German even harder than the deutsche mark.

In fact, there is hardly a language policy for the EP, or for the Commission's bureaucracy, let alone for *l'Europe des citoyens*, for civil society in the EU. At the time, the six founding members contributed Dutch, French, German and Italian, an almost manageable number. The official languages of the member states were admitted as the languages of the Community. Without much discussion, French was accepted as the working language of the Community's budding bureaucracy, as it had been the language of diplomacy until then and the sole language of the European Coal and Steel Community (ECSC) that preceded the European Economic Community (EEC). In those post-war years, the Germans and Italians kept a low profile, and the Dutch (even when counting in the Dutch-speaking Flemish of Belgium) were not numerous enough to impose their linguistic interests.

The first great expansion of the European Community, in 1973, brought in the British, the Irish (almost all of them native English speakers)[33] and the Danes, of whom the vast majority had learned English in school. As soon as the UK joined the EC, English became the second working language in the corridors and meeting rooms of the Commission and the Parliament (cf. Schlossmacher 1994; Bellier 1995; see also Mamadouh 1995). As new members joined the Community, the number of languages grew accordingly.

In the meantime, from the 1960s on, secondary education had been rapidly expanding throughout Europe. Quite independently, the member states realized sweeping reforms of their secondary school systems. In the process, most of them reduced the number of compulsory foreign languages taught but kept English, either making it compulsory or leaving the choice to the students, who tended to opt for English anyway, since it seems to hold the best job prospects and radiates the glory of global mass culture. Due to the expansion of secondary education, there are now more citizens in the Union who speak French, German, Spanish or Italian as a foreign language than ever before, but many more, still, have learned English: almost 90 per cent of all high-school students in the Union. French scores half this percentage, German a quarter and Spanish one eighth.

This makes English, in fact, the vehicular language of Europe; however, not by right. First, the Union happens to be a combination of states which all hold on to their own official languages; second, numerous decisions taken by the Union directly affect the citizens in the member states and therefore must be couched in their own legal language. The Union's multilingualism is therefore a matter of democratic principle and fundamental treaty law. The current 20 languages are prescribed in the public meetings of the Council and the Parliament and for all decisions that immediately bear upon the citizens. Behind closed doors, however, the languages of choice are French, increasingly English and, far behind, in third place, German.

There can be no doubt that Germany, as the most populous nation and a founding member of the Union, is entitled to have its language treated on an equal footing with English and French. However this would compel Spain to insist on equal treatment for Spanish, which among the languages of the EU is second as a world language only to English. This would force Italy as a founding member of the Union to demand the same position for its language, and then unavoidably, the turn would come for another founding member, the Netherlands and so on, until all members would have formally secured the position of their language in the EU and everything would be exactly where it is now: all official languages are also formally working languages but only two are actually used on a day-to-day basis (De Swaan 2001: 169–71).

In border-crossing encounters, the Europeans speak English; in the East, they use German at times and in the South sometimes French. Within each national society (except Ireland and the UK) English presses on as the principal foreign language, the language of business, science and technology, international sports, transport and tourism, and of the worldwide mass media. As long as each state continues to support its own language in schools and courts, in national politics and administration, English, even though widely used, does not represent an acute threat. A condition of 'diglossia' prevails in all these countries: a rather precarious equilibrium between the domestic language and English, in which each one predominates in a different series of domains.

Since English is so visibly, so audibly present and so much more than before, one hardly notices the domains where it has not penetrated. In the private sphere, at home and among friends or close colleagues, people speak their mother tongue with abandon, eagerly adorned with anglicisms, but they use no English there. Many people read English books, but very few read newspapers in English. English is often spoken on TV, but it either comes with a 'dubbed' soundtrack or with subtitles in the home language. Quite a few people can follow a discussion, even at a high level, in English, very few can stand their ground in a debate in that language, unless it has been acquired as a native tongue. Almost no one who had to learn the language at a later age can write publishable English.

Within the prevailing cultural opportunity structure, English is the paramount medium of international exchange. Yet, reflection and debate in English are not encouraged at the European level, since the Commission does not want to appear to favour one language above other languages of the Union. Apparently, the British government does not consider its task to be active promotion of exchanges of opinion in English on the European continent, as this might even evoke contrary reactions from the other countries of the EU.[34]

The governments of the member states do not want to privilege a foreign language, out of 'language envy', even if their own language does not stand a chance abroad. The pattern is familiar from postcolonial societies where, notwithstanding strong anti-colonial sentiments and a new nationalistic fervour, the debate about a national language ultimately ground down into a stalemate: at independence, each indigenous language group supported the idea of a single indigenous language of country-wide communication for the new nation, but they all agreed that it was not to be the language of the other group. Since both the colonial bureaucratic elite and the liberation movement had used the colonial language as the unifying means of communication, only a very strong consensus and radical educational policies could have overcome the predominance of the colonial language at the time. Indonesia indeed succeeded in imposing Bahasa Indonesia (Malay) to replace Dutch and Javanese. Tanzania successfully introduced Swahili instead of (and next to) English.

Swahili and Malay were indigenous languages, but neither was strongly identified with a single, dominant ethnic group. Hindi in India, Afrikaans in South Africa, Wolof in Senegal, on the other hand, evoked language envy among the other groups. As a result, in many formerly colonised countries, English, or French, remained in place as the languages of government and administration, of business, science and technology, and nationwide elite media (cf. De Swaan 2001).

Another mechanism operated in the same direction: parents opposed the initiatives by well-meaning reformers to introduce indigenous languages as the medium of instruction in the schools. In public they would support the introduction of an indigenous language as the national medium, but in private they preferred their children to learn the language that promised the best opportunities in the labour market, the world language introduced by the former colonisers. This is a clear case of 'public virtue and private vice', as David Laitin (2000) astutely observed.

Likewise, the EU, in its campaigns for language learning and in its initiatives to support the smaller languages, officially and publicly continues to profess its unwavering commitment to full multilingualism. For their part, the envious member states will not allow any other language to take precedence over their own. In the meantime, European youngsters overwhelmingly (almost 90 per cent) choose or accept to learn English as a foreign language. In doing so, they privately undermine the collective, public commitment to the promotion of a variety of foreign languages. Such diversity, however, while favouring no single language, would leave all these new multilingual citizens with their different foreign languages still unable to communicate across the Union.

The EU is bound by treaty to leave matters of culture to the separate member states: this follows from the founding treaties and from the principle of subsidiarity which reserves all issues that can be dealt with separately by the individual member states for the national governments. However, the member states are in no position to introduce a common language for all-European communication, let alone to create a European public space. No intellectual networks can emerge in Europe; no all-European journals with a broad political or cultural orientation will appear, as long as intellectual exchange is hampered by the barriers of language and by the constraints of national frameworks. Given the cultural opportunity structure in the countries of Europe, there can be no substantive democratisation, no exchange of opinion that will affect Europe's citizens in sizable numbers. This is the principal democratic deficit of Europe.

There may be remedies. At the institutional level, the EC and the EP, faced with a Babylonian plethora of almost two dozen different languages, are currently experimenting with pragmatic arrangements in the hope of reducing the avalanche of translation and interpretation to manageable proportions.[35] Thus, committee meetings may proceed in English, French and, as the case may be, German or Spanish. Instead of translation from and into each EU language, facilities are gradually limited to interpretation from all languages into only two or three 'relay' languages and from those into all languages that participants may request. The Commission's officials use English and French in their oral communication and for the internal preparatory documents. Semi-official publications appear in English or French only. But the principle of full multilingualism continues to receive unabated lip service and a full public debate on the issue is strenuously avoided.

Clearly, the European language predicament is very similar to that prevailing in India and South Africa: both are highly multicultural and very multilingual polities, the former having succeeded in maintaining a degree of democratic rule for more than half a century and the latter having achieved a transition towards democracy in the past ten years. In this case, rather than the primeval model of the nation state – France – or the prime instance of a democratic federation – the United States – India and South Africa may provide the most relevant instances of comparison for the evolving EU. Both must cope with a multiplicity of languages and a great variety of ethnic and religious groups. Nevertheless, a democracy with a shared and lively public space has emerged in each country. Institutions and concepts that originated in Europe play a major role in both India and South Africa, in combination with Asian and African political traditions and practices. In one respect, the EU has a major advantage: the level of education is high and almost every child has an opportunity to learn at least one foreign language. But which one? As in the EU, so in South Africa and India, hypocrisy is the tribute that vice pays to virtue. Piously protesting the ideal of full equality for all languages, in fact both governments allow English to continue in its privileged position, thus permitting the educated elites to reap the benefits of their competence in that language.

As in the EU, the prevalence of English is a foregone but tacit conclusion. At this point, in the argument, Pierre Bourdieu once exclaimed (in French) '*Il faut désangliciser l'Anglais*'. But how to expropriate English from its native speakers? It is after all the first second language on a continent where it is nobody's first. A Euro-English dialect with its own generally accepted standards will not emerge, just as no Afro-English or Asian-English standard has appeared. The English-speaking elites have a vested interest in maintaining full intelligibility between their version of English and 'world-English' and the same applies to Europeans using the language for continental and global communication.

Thus, for a long time to come, 'transatlantic' English will remain the standard in Europe and in the rest of the world. In Chapter 8, Lars Blichner proposes to adopt a European 'meta-lingual language' that would systematise and unify the political concepts circulating in the Union's many different languages. But, whatever 'meta-lingual' may mean in this context, this proposal refers only to the lexical and semantic aspects of European usage; it has nothing to do with the morphological properties of current, natural languages in the EU. What is indeed needed is a good lexicon of 'Eurospeak' in 25 languages, a formidable task in itself.

The only promising interpretation of Bourdieu's exclamation would be to adopt English tooth and claw, but to 'de-anglicize' the institutional means of communication and distribution: create European journals, owned by European companies and run by European editors, found European distribution agencies for films and books that select productions from one member state to present in the others and initiate European scientific and cultural associations as an alternative to organizations under American tutelage.

English is not the problem; it is the solution. The problem is that British and American organisations control the distribution and exchange of cultural expression and scientific findings. That is what makes it hard for authors, artists and scientists in one European country to get access to the public in another country, unless they have first been selected by an editor, publisher or distributor in New York or London.

It appears that in the individual member states, in the long run, democracy cannot work if the major decisions are taken at a higher, European, level, without intellectual exchange and political debate taking place on a corresponding European scale. If that is indeed the case, then a European public space will in the end turn out to be a necessary condition for the survival of national democracies as well. That is why the individual member states and the Union as a whole should improve the cultural opportunity structure at the European level. That requires European journals, websites and newspapers, European universities and academies, and European cultural meeting points and intellectual networks.[36] In this manner the material conditions may be realised for a public debate, not delimited for the greater part by language and nation, but shaped by a joint, European agenda of dissent and consensus.

Notes

1 As Therborn points out, by dint of its heritage and present global position, it is also the most important force towards 'transnational normativity' in the contemporary world.

2 For a different perspective on a possible European future, see Axford and Huggins (1999) who perceive the EU as an emergent, highly differentiated network of networks, where spaces matter, not borders.

3 'Though the EU dresses itself up in the rhetoric of democracy – a fundamental requisite for Member States – it is covered at best by the scantiest of fig leaves.' (Bellamy and Castiglione 2000: 65). But this does beg the question of what democratic institutions would fit 'the mixed character of the European polity' (p. 83).

4 Christophe Meyer (2000) shows that since 1987 the number of journalists accredited in Brussels has grown steadily and that, as a corollary, coverage of EU news grew at a pace. Leonard Novy also stresses the national perspective of news reports on the EU. The EP, however, he qualifies as '*beinah öffentlichkeitsabstinent*' (almost entirely abstemious from any publicity); see his article 'Vom Schweigen der Union', *Eurozine*, 21 July 2004, www.eurozine.com/articles/2004-07-21-novy-de.html (accessed 13 September 2006).

5 This may be the structural basis of the sociological mentality that Ulrich Beck (2005) has aptly called 'methodological nationalism': an incapacity to grasp the emerging realities of the EU.

6 I have convincing experimental proof of my thesis. Some years ago, I intended to submit to the Brussels authorities a research proposal on the emergence, or rather the non-emergence, of European cultural elites. I was strongly discouraged by the research consultants in Brussels. The EU, I was told, avoids cultural topics and eschews anything to do with elites. Sadly, my assumptions were confirmed even before the research began.

7 Just typing 'European' in the periodicals catalogue of a large library yields thousands of hits: at the latest count 4,020 for the University of Amsterdam library. Many of those may, however, lead to the same publications or point to items other than reviews and journals.

8 Of course, there exists a spontaneous tendency to define an idealised version of the nation state as the final objective of European integration. Against it, a more sophisticated view considers the nation state completely irrelevant in conceptualising the integration process. Quite interestingly, Dennis Smith (1999: 246) argues in terms inspired by Norbert Elias, 'that the sociogenesis of the EU is a process that has a similar structure to the sociogenesis of the state, except that this process operates at a higher level of integration.' According to the author: 'At the centre of Europe-formation is a shift from national states that mainly *impose* discipline on those subject to their domination to national states which are themselves to a very considerable extent *subject* to continuing discipline from "above" ' (ibid.: 249–50).

9 See Craig Calhoun, 'The Democratic Integration of Europe: Interests, Identity, and the Public Sphere', *Eurozine*, 21 June 2004, www.eurozine.com/articles/2004-06-21-calhoun-en.html (accessed 13 September 2006).

10 Thus, in May 2003, when seven European newspapers decided to publish the reactions by seven of the most celebrated intellectuals in Europe (Jacques Derrida, Umberto Eco, Jürgen Habermas, Adolf Muschg, Richard Rorty, Fernando Savater and Gianni Vattimo), to the question 'What is Europe?' commentators in each member state concentrated almost exclusively on the contribution from their countryman: 'Despite its grandiose pretensions, the Habermas initiative has become a striking example of the difficulties confronting the modern Babylon that goes by the name of Europe in establishing a transnational discursive and deliberative space worth its salt.' See Carl Henrik Frederiksson, 'Energizing the European Public Space', *Eurozine*, 13 May 2004, www.eurozine.com/articles/2004-05-13-fredriksson-en.html (accessed 13 September 2006). Frederiksson is editor of *Eurozine* (www.eurozine.com), which is among the most successful of pan-European cultural and intellectual websites.

11 The formula cited here has been adopted from Sidney Tarrow. The concept has been around at least since the early 1970s.

12 'Although [...] the press remains almost exclusively a national medium, there are, nevertheless, newspapers and magazines that self-consciously address a European (as well as global) elite audience' (Schlesinger 1999: 271).

13 Cf. Frederiksson, supra note 10.

14 Audit Bureau of Circulations, www.abc.org.uk (accessed 25 November 2005). The author wishes to express his gratitude to Christine Lohmeier for her research into the circulation figures quoted here; to Isabelle Steenbergen, who made an initial inventory of border-transcending printed and electronic media in the EU; and to Marianne Bernard, who revised it for publication on a website of the European Cultural Foundation.

15 Audit Bureau of Circulations, www.abc.org.uk (accessed 25 November 2005).

16 Information from *International Herald Tribune* marketing department and www.iht.com (accessed 25 November 2005).
17 Information from *The New York Review of Books* marketing department, 27 November 2005.
18 See the *London Review of Books* media information, www.lrb.co.uk/advertising/media.php (accessed 27 November 2005).
19 Oral communication by Dominique Vidal; see also www.monde-diplomatique.fr/int (accessed 9 December 2005).
20 RFI, Direction des Études et des Relations Auditeurs; see also www.rfi.fr/pressefr/articles/072/article_30.asp (accessed 12 March 2006).
21 See TV5 Monde at www.tv5.org/TV5Site/tv5monde/publicite.php (accessed 10 February 2006).
22 Communication from Dr. Roland Schürhoff; see also *Deutsche Welle,* 'Weltweite Schätzung der täglichen und wöchentlichen Reichweiten für das DW-Programangebot' (14 January 2005).
23 In addition, BBC World Service broadcasts news and features in some forty different languages all over the world for 146 million listeners across the globe as of June 2004; see www.bbc.co.uk/pressoffice/pressreleases/stories/2004/06_june/21/ws_figures.shtml (accessed 28 November 2005).
24 Communication from 'Arbeitsgemeinschaft Fernsehforschung', see www.agf.de/daten/zuschauermarkt/marktanteile (accessed 23 November 2005).
25 See 'Facts and figures about Radio Netherlands', 28 October 2004, www.radionetherlands.nl/aboutus/aboutrnw_facts (accessed 6 July 2006).
26 This, in a generalised version, is of course an apt definition of globalisation in general; see De Swaan 2002.
27 Written communication from CNN.
28 Ibid.
29 Ibid.
30 No overall viewer ratings are available, only those for the highly educated audience.
31 See www.eurozine.com.
32 See www.eurocult.org for recent developments of the site under construction.
33 Although Ireland joined the Union in 1973, Irish was not adopted as an official and working language of the Union until 2005. In a population of 5.5 million (including Northern Ireland), there are about one million speakers of Irish, and some 50,000 citizens who speak the language on a daily basis (*Gaeltacht*); the others speak no Irish at all. Cf. Price 1998, also Kloss and McConnell 1989.
34 British publishers, and especially the providers of language courses do, however, actively promote English abroad; see Graddol 1997.
35 Chris Longman (2007) relates how during the plenary meetings of the Convention on the Future of Europe (2002–2003) all official languages (11 at the time) were used, while in the Praesidium and the working groups English and French were predominant in written and spoken communication, for practical considerations, obviously.
36 See the challenging diagnosis and remedies in Klaic 2005.

8 Political integration in Europe and the need for a common political language

Lars Chr. Blichner

Introduction

Two beliefs are often expressed more or less explicitly in connection with discussions of European political integration. The first holds that it is possible to continue the process of economic integration without a parallel process of political integration. This belief can be seen as grounded in a long-established technocratic economic doctrine within the European Union. It holds that cooperation among European states, as long as it is beneficial to all in economic terms, would also get public support. The second holds that political integration in Europe is unlikely, if not impossible, because of the existing cultural heterogeneity, language being the most important obstacle. Any effort at political integration implies an impossible or unwanted policy of cultural homogenisation: 'Put simply, democratic politics is politics in the vernacular' (Kymlicka 2001: 213). Peaceful coexistence and stability through political integration can be best achieved when 'ethnos' and 'demos' overlap with the boundaries of the nation state.

Contrary to these two sceptical views on political integration, I conclude that increased economic integration and increased cultural diversification in effect set the stage for European political integration. If continued, these tendencies would make political integration both more likely and more necessary. The question is whether political integration will be democratic in the sense that it is supported by Europe-wide public spheres. My basic argument is that this, at least in part, may be realised by the development of what I call a common political language, a language that parallels what I take to be the existing economic language that has emerged in Europe over at least the last 30–40 years.

These languages can be seen as examples of what I shall call meta-lingual languages, in contrast to vernacular languages. Meta-lingual languages are languages in the sense that the meaning communicated relating to a particular subject matter is roughly similar and reflects a common conceptualisation across different vernacular languages. The speculation is that, for example, football enthusiasts in different countries, even though they speak different vernacular languages, may use roughly similar terms of discourse when discussing football, or that Catholics throughout the world may use roughly similar terms of discourse on matters important to their faith, or that the large subsection of Spanish-speaking people in the US may speak about politics in Spanish in ways roughly similar to how the rest of the population speaks about it in English. What all three examples have in common is that there exists an authoritatively established set of concepts, established by the rules of the game, fair play and so on in football, by the church in Catholicism, and, at least in part, by the constitution in the US. If groups of people that speak similar meta-lingual languages, but different vernacular languages, suddenly were able to speak to each other in the same vernacular language (and sometimes they can of course) they would find that they could communicate their differences in a much more efficient way than people that do not master the meta-lingual language.

An economic language and a political language are two examples of what may be called meta-lingual languages.[1] I argue that European political integration, fostered by public consent, is dependent on the development of a common meta-lingual language that speaks not only of change in terms of efficiency – an economic language – but also in terms of change in more basic goals and values – a political language. A common political language at the European level may make a common European political discourse possible. In the following pages, I first explain what I mean by an economic language and why this has been the dominant language in the EU. Second, I discuss why a political language has been poorly developed thus far and also why such a language may develop.

Why the EU has been dominated by an economic language

An economic language is derived from one particular conception of the word 'political', and is in line with the basic properties of the regulatory model, as outlined in the introduction to this book. When the word political is used, it usually refers to a situation where different actors have different goals; where the pursuit of these goals produces conflict; and where some kind of collective agreement is called for. The participants' goals may be seen as stable or as open to change. An economic conception of politics is based on the premise that goals are stable. If goals are seen as stable, or at least as exogenous to a particular political process, agreement can be reached only through some sort of aggregation process. In a democracy it is assumed that the aggregation process builds on established procedures which, at least ideally, ensure that all relevant interests are represented, where there is room for negotiation, but where a final decision, in principle, is reached through majority voting. This is sometimes referred to as an economic model of politics. According to Elster (1989: 61), it has dominated western political thought since the Second World War.

When viewed from this perspective, politics is seen as a struggle between different interests which will use all legitimate means at their disposal in order to reach a favourable outcome for themselves. The final agreement will reflect the relative power and bargaining skills of the different participants involved. Goals are stable in the sense that the participants' preference-ordering is not affected by the political process itself, although participants may decide to use their resources to pursue a less important goal if this is seen as the most realistic alternative given the particular situation they are in. The language used is economic in the sense that it relates to concepts that speak of societal efficiency and a just and relatively stable organisation of the economy. It is premised on the assumption that individual action is driven by self-interest, only constrained by institutionally defined rules of conduct (a regulated market). It is a language dominated by concepts related to bargaining, compromise and exchange, on the one hand, and parametric instrumental reasoning, on the other.

With an increasing number of exceptions, in scholarly accounts the EU is often portrayed in line with this basic model of politics,[2] a tendency that is not too surprising. The story of European integration from the late 1950s to the mid 1980s is foremost a story of economic integration (Diez 1997: 292). If peace and economic interests have been the two main legitimising factors in the transfer of power from the constituent states to the EU, the balance has shifted to the latter over time for practical purposes (Calhoun 2002). This development may, in part, be seen as a continuation of what has been called a technocratic strategy in the EU. This builds on a belief 'that the creation of effective administrative government in discrete policy areas would provide the economic welfare which would in turn generate public support' (Wallace and Smith 1995: 144).[3] The technocratic strategy can also be made understandable from a domestic point of view. Domestically, the need for international cooperation is often, at least implicitly, legitimated in instrumental economic terms. In its simplest form, cooperation is seen as necessary in order to safeguard the security and economic prosperity of national citizens. Nation states have a common interest in cooperation. Thus, economic cooperation is legitimised as a means to secure ends shared by all citizens.

However, due to differences in economic, structural and institutional arrangements between nation states, cooperation affects nation states differently. Group interests as well as long-term and short-term interests, within each nation state, will have to be balanced. This activates a bargaining process at the national as well as the international level, which involves threats, warnings, compromises, coalition building and exchange. Sometimes this process may result in the establishment of new principles; sometimes it results in ad hoc solutions. The argument here is that, over time, a common understanding related to some basic economic principles has been arrived at.

At the European level, this understanding is reflected in concepts such as a common market involving fair and free competition and a reference to the inherently international character of economic development. This also involves an idealised vision of the market as a level-playing field and a negative attitude towards all forms of protectionism. The claim has been that an open- and free-market economy would eventually increase the well being of all. More generally, as Calhoun somewhat pointedly puts it:

> an economistic imaginary has been basic to arguments for European integration. The notion that 'we must compete' has been recurrent, framing the interests of Europeans as producers and marketers of goods. At the same time, consumers have been encouraged to think of European integration as a program for the improvement of restaurants and supermarkets.
>
> (Calhoun 2002: 296)

One traditional role of the state has been to secure the functioning of the market. Most of what has been written by economists, in line with Adam Smith, centres on this one issue: when do markets fail and how can we make them perform better? Another traditional role of the state has been to correct various problems created by the market or to take care of problems that the market cannot deal with adequately. These problems are linked to inequalities among citizens that challenge basic human and democratic values. The solution has been the creation of democratic institutions and the welfare state. The role of economists in this has been to assess how different policies affect the economic efficiency of the market. In free-market terms, this role of the state will not create problems as long as the rules are applied equally throughout the market; as long as the most effective solution is chosen once democratic and human considerations are taken into account; and as long as these values and the institutional solutions are relatively stable in order to protect the expectations of the participants in the market. The main role of economists has been to point out when and how these criteria are met, but they have no way of evaluating the validity of the existing norms other than by reference to efficiency.

The development of a common economic language in the EU has made it easier to discuss such problems across state boundaries. Gradually, agreement has been reached on a set of basic principles that are relevant to economic cooperation. Discussions taking place in different countries, in widely different institutional settings, at different levels of government as well as in the private sphere have, through a cumulative process, gradually produced a common understanding. The free market does not actually exist anywhere, but the idealisation does. Whenever state intervention into the market is proposed, this serves as a common evaluative standard against which any new proposal may be judged. A new direction may only be taken by questioning the basic principles or adding new ones that fit in with the old ones.

My hypothesis is that this system of common economic principles is agreed on at the elite level internationally, and made understandable to national publics by national debates. In the process, a common economic language is created. People know what is meant by a 'level playing field', a 'free market', 'fair competition' and so on, because these concepts have the same meaning in different countries.[4] This common language makes communication easier both at an elite level and between the elite and national citizens, as long as the issues under consideration are economic in nature. This language, however, is ill-equipped to deal with what I term genuinely political issues, issues that do not relate to questions of efficiency and bargained distribution alone, but also include conflicts over norms and values. The economic language does speak of justice when referring to a free and fair market, but in economic terms the justification for this is societal efficiency, not justice in itself. To borrow a term from Elster (1983: 92), one may say that struggles for justice in the marketplace, from a societal point of view, are an essential by-product of efficiency aspirations, meaning that one may do without the moral argument.

Through an economic language it is only possible to communicate within one value system, where the basic values are efficiency and equal access to the market. This is a value system that transcends national borders, but is indifferent to cultural diversity. It may be argued that this value system threatens the cultural integrity of nation states in a much more fundamental way than does political integration. To summarise, my claim is that cooperation in Europe through the EU has been dominated by weak evaluations,[5] and that this is reflected in the development of what I call an economic language. This language has made it easier to communicate across language barriers in Europe on a whole range of important issues, but is limited by its inability to foster discursive agreement or disagreement on the goals to be pursued in common.[6] That the EU is dominated by choices based on weak evaluations implies that a strongly evaluative language – a political language – has been poorly developed as compared to the economic language.

A political language in the making?

An alternative to the economic model of politics, more in line with the federal model presented in the introduction to this book, sees participants' goals as open to change through discussion. A change of goals is fundamental in the sense that it is based on new insights gained through communication with others; thus it is not linked to pragmatic efficiency considerations alone. Through discussion, agreement on common norms and values may be reached, which in turn allows for agreement on which goals to pursue in common. A political language, then, is a language that makes communication across apparently different value and norm systems possible through the creation or discovery of common values and norms,[7] but such a language has not developed very far within the EU. One reason why EU members can relate to a conception of economic cooperation based on a free and fair market is that it has been, in different forms, an important part of how their societies have been organised. But these countries are also democracies, sharing a democratic tradition. Why is it that a common language based on this common tradition has not emerged?

The most simple and obvious answer is that genuine political issues have been avoided in order to prevent too much time-consuming conflict and complexity. Derek Urwin (1995), for example, describes how one EU commissioner, Lord Cockfield, responsible for drawing up a timetable for measures to be implemented by 1992 relating to the internal market, avoided measures that would have had potential political implications. The measures were economic and practical. If genuine political issues that evoke ethical or moral disagreement have been avoided, this again makes discussion of political issues more difficult, and the development of a political language has to go hand in hand with the discussion of specific and genuinely political issues. Within the nation state, political and economic languages have developed in parallel. In contrast, the EU has been dominated by an economic language and this has hampered political integration.

If anyone challenging EU policies on moral or ethical grounds is met by the invocation of 'It's the economy stupid', and there is no way to make a convincing argument to the contrary across borders, public spheres will not develop, at least not very far. For a public sphere to develop at the European level, real and widespread discursive disagreement is needed. One may disagree discursively on pragmatic matters, of course, as proposed by the regulatory model, but it would be a limited disagreement, more appealing to the expert than to people in general. The more you know about the means-end relationship, the better equipped you are to take part in the discussion. When moral and ethical questions are involved, the role of the expert dwindles. Anyone can legitimately discuss the moral and ethical concerns linked to abortion and reach a conclusion (for themselves at least), while in order to make a judgment as to whether one policy or another will lead to more or fewer abortions or more or less physical harm to pregnant women, expert knowledge is needed. The same goes for policies on drugs, culture, social policies and so on. Most political issues may be cast both in pragmatic and in moral or ethical terms. Still, it is in the latter case that people in general get involved and more basic changes may be possible.

For various reasons, disagreement at the EU level has been framed in instrumental terms. However, regulatory policies alone are not the stuff that basic political conflicts are made of. They are political in the sense that they address collective problems and are decided on by elected representatives, or at least by someone who has the competencies to act in the place of the people. National representatives, for instance, may decide on the level of integration according to national interest. However, as long as the basic goals are taken for granted and what is left to decide is which measures to take, it is hardly politics proper.

It is beyond doubt that a process of establishing politics proper at the EU level has been under way for some time, but the EU still seems to be hampered by its technocratic roots. The EU's response when a democratic deficit was 'discovered' and linked to the lack of a European civil society was, typically, 'Let's make one'. Even if one is able to foster cooperation between national civil-society organisations across borders, with the help of financial support and privileged access to decision makers, there is no way one can force people to listen and make a stand. Moreover, if we presume that in a truly *public* sphere everyone, at least in principle, will get the chance to speak from time to time while at least someone is listening, the EU-made alternative is a non-starter (see Eriksen 2001).

Another reason why a common political language has not developed may be that political languages are tied up with the conception of the nation state. Contrary to the debates on economic issues which refer to basic economic principles, the debate on democracy is, surprisingly, more often linked to the democratic institutions of the member states, or as David Judge (1995: 96) puts it: 'European institutions still seem remote to many citizens of the EU and European issues still tend to be seen through national lenses'. As regularly noted, we lack common words and ideas relating to the EU's political institutions as well as democratic criteria for evaluating this new construction. What should we call it? A state, a federation, an international organisation, multilevel governance? There is as yet no proper agreed-upon word. However, it is possible to call it a 'common market', given that a common conception of what this entails has emerged over time. Common idealised democratic principles that all agree upon have not developed very far. Solutions considered to be democratic may differ substantially. Thus, there is no common standard by which to judge the political institutions of the EU. Each member state tends to evaluate the EU as a political entity on the basis of the words and ideas that are used to discuss, describe and legitimise the democratic institutions of that country.

A third reason may be that the proper institutions necessary to develop such a language are either weak or missing. The EU lacks truly integrative institutions that make the development of common meaning and understanding possible. It may also be the case that the EU lacks the authority or legitimacy necessary to establish conceptualisations that people in general will accept and use. One may argue that anyone who wants to influence EU politics will have to adapt to conceptualisations established by the EU, in particular relating to the Treaties and the way these have been interpreted. If you do not know how the EU is conceptually framed, you will be less likely to succeed. This gives the EU a fair amount of power to impose its own political language on those affected by EU policies. Still, the question is whether this language will spread beyond the more or less professional lobbyists and diehard integrationists.

Faced with these problems, how can we envision the development of political language in Europe? The institutions that make up the EU may be seen as an arena where representatives from different member states come together and develop an agreement on how to conceptualise a common world. In this process, they also create this world, but it is a world limited by the range of concepts used, how these are linked, and the extent to which agreement is reached on the meaning of the concepts used. There will probably never be complete agreement. Key concepts in any language will normally be contested concepts that change their meanings over time. It may even be argued that a defining characteristic of a political concept is that it is contested. Still, there has to be some agreement at the core, or at least some agreement about the range of possible meanings, even if the denotation of each concept is somewhat imprecise at the boundaries.

From a democratic point of view, debate is necessary not only at an elite level, even if this elite is made up of elected representatives, but also among citizens, and between citizens and their representatives. If it is impossible for citizens throughout Europe to speak to each other directly because of language barriers, the second-best thing would be if citizens could debate political issues within national or more local settings, but in relation to some emerging common conceptualisations that they share with citizens elsewhere. This would mean that there is a common understanding as to the core meaning of the concepts. Such common concepts would then be the building blocks in the development of a political language.

At the national level, increased Europeanisation forces elected representatives, more often than before, to ask: 'What is this or that institutionalised practice a case of?' They must be able to explain to a European audience the existence of a certain national practice, if in some way it is seen as affecting the interests of non-citizens. The challenge facing the national representatives is, on the one hand, to explain or justify a given practice to representatives of other member states, and on the other hand, to explain or justify changes in a given practice to a national audience. One way of doing this is to effect a 'translation' between the national and the European contexts by linking the practice to more general and abstract concepts or principles that are understood or can be made understandable to all EU members.

The quality of such a language will depend on a rather complicated process, where the content of a concept and its relation to other concepts are discussed continuously at different levels and in different types of communities, both nationally and internationally, and where the discussions at one level help inform those at another level. Thus, if a concept such as 'transparency' is presented in the European Parliament (EP), as something wanting in the EU, the national delegates may go home and try to make sense of this concept in a national context, e.g. by introducing the content of this concept into their own language in private discussions, public debate or national parliament. They may then go back to the EP for new discussions, better prepared to explain to other delegates what the concept means in a national context and how it accords with the meaning it is given at the European level. Each time the concept is evoked in practical politics, the content of the concept will be reaffirmed, changed or further refined. One also has to assume that it is possible to reach some kind of understanding on the core meaning of the concept. Insofar as the discussions taking place include and are informed by different publics throughout Europe, we would expect that the emerging language makes it easier for national representatives to inform and deliberate with national publics on European matters, within a common frame of reference.

In the last few years, there has been intense debate over the sharing of responsibilities within the EU. This has been linked to questions concerning the appropriate balance of power between different levels of government and the democratic deficit as well as the general lack of legitimacy of the Union. Concepts such as transparency – actualised by the complexity and lack of openness of European institutions – and subsidiarity – which addresses the claim that too much power or the wrong powers have been concentrated at the European level – have played a major role in these discussions. These may be seen as genuine political concepts – concepts with a normative content that goes beyond economic efficiency considerations.[8] The concepts may be seen to question the idea that legitimacy can be achieved by establishing a system of cooperation that enhances the wellbeing of citizens in economic terms. Many doubts may be raised about the degree to which such concepts really will develop into workable European concepts with roughly the same meaning in different countries, concepts which can serve to focus the debate on democracy at the European level (Blichner and Sangolt 1994). However, there are also good reasons to believe that these or similar concepts will.

One reason is the possibility that economic integration has reached a level where problems can no longer legitimately be dealt with in economic terms; regulatory policies create disagreement that challenge the more fundamental premises of EU policies. Another possible reason is that cultural diversification creates problems that have to be solved at the political level. It is unlikely that the EU will be able to contain inherent disagreements through a process of bargaining alone. In open and free societies, it is not possible to bargain about social justice, forms of democracy or cultural identity purely by reference to efficiency.

Within the economic sphere, a process of 'translation' has been going on since the very start of the EU, and this has led to the development of a common economic language. However, at some point, economic integration creates a need for solutions that involve genuinely political issues, where agreement based on compromise is not possible. Agreement cannot be reached without some kind of change in the goals involved or at least a change in the ordering of these goals. This happens when decisions taken at a supranational level fundamentally affect the national political institutions, when conflicts of interest due to increased economic integration can no longer be solved only through bargaining between different national interests and with reference to principles of economic efficiency.

For example, EU citizens are now free to work in any member state they wish. Still, the many different national pension laws make it difficult for them to plan their retirement. The choice of a national policy based on private pensions as compared to state pensions is a genuine political question. Agreement cannot be reached through reference to efficiency considerations alone. Other examples are linked to the different national policies on drugs and alcohol, which are based on different traditions and conceptions throughout Europe about the relationship between state and civil society. The Dutch policy on drugs, for example, is not only based on pragmatic concerns where efficiency criteria apply, but has a more basic liberal foundation. When border controls between European countries are relaxed, this, at least to a certain extent, implies that the liberal Dutch policy becomes the European policy. This creates a need for discussion where agreement would be difficult to reach with reference to efficiency criteria alone.

These differences come into view in ways different from matters such as the free movement of people, goods, capital and services. The EU can no longer simply decide not to discuss these issues. The choice will be between continued economic integration and a debate on basic political principles, both at the national and at the European level, or it means facing a halt in economic integration.[9] The suggestion is rather that continued economic integration, if it is to be accepted by people throughout Europe, creates the need for solutions that cannot be achieved through conceptualising the world in economic terms.

Meaning, culture and political institutions

The view that cultural diversification creates problems and that these may be solved at the political level, implies a distinction between shared meanings emanating from a shared culture and those deriving from common political institutions which transcend cultural borders (March and Olsen 1995: 34).

Increased cultural pluralism may increase potentially destructive conflicts, making it difficult to reach collective agreement. This is likely to be the case at the level of the nation state as well as at the European level. The choice is no longer between a multicultural European political union and culturally homogeneous nation states. Thus, the challenge linked to increased cultural diversity at the European level is similar to the challenge faced by nation states throughout Europe, even though in different countries the challenge may be more or less acute. This makes it more likely that a common political language might develop at a European level as lines of conflict will tend to cross borders, with the EU as a possible common point of reference for solutions to such conflicts.

The answer to these challenges from a traditional state-building point of view is a renewed effort at cultural homogenisation or different forms of border control, between cultures within, or between, nation states. The relatively strong mobilisation in many European states by political movements arguing along these lines is indicative of some of the difficulties involved in further political integration. It is not surprising that this reaction has gathered support. Multiculturalism is perceived by many as a grave threat to their distinct way of life.

One may ask how much cultural heterogeneity a political unit can possibly include without undermining the stability that is essential to any democratic system of governance. This depends on the strength of the political institutions and to what degree they are acceptable to the people they are supposed to serve. If increased cultural diversification challenges this acceptance, a more realistic alternative than cultural homogenisation may be a change in the existing political institutions. Such change can only be accepted if it is able to coexist with and protect the autonomy of different national cultures.

Political integration across cultural borders does not imply or necessitate cultural homogenization. Any deliberate effort at the European level to achieve linguistic, ethnic or religious homogenization, or any cultural homogenisation directed at forcing groups of citizens to abandon their preferred way of life, would probably decrease rather than increase the prospects for further European political integration. A distinction between culture in this sense and political culture has to be made. A common political culture, based on common principles relating to formal equality, tolerance, freedom of speech and freedom of association, is needed for political integration to take place.

Still, to develop a political language, more than a declaration of principles is needed. A political language develops from the practical application of principles. A universalised philosopher-king kind of language will probably have as little chance to succeed as Esperanto. The practical experience of immigration across Europe is rich and varied. As long as problems associated with this are defined in national terms, as a French or a Danish problem, little will be gained from the point of view of a common political language. However, this has hardly been the case. In

2006, both the French suburban disorder and even more so the furore over the Danish cartoons of Mohammed were at least discussed in each and every country throughout Europe. Fundamental issues were raised on the balance between respect for cultural diversity and the exercise of free speech and between personal responsibility and freedom. The debate over the wearing of headscarves by Muslim girls in French schools certainly made headlines around the world and informed public debate in the most unlikely places, the language barrier seemingly a lesser obstacle than that of understanding the French political culture. Arguments travel all over the world, and a functioning national democratic civil society only assures their domestication. As basic political issues are confronted in practical politics at the European level and proper institutions develop, the EU may go a step further and establish a truly European-wide political language on democratic grounds.

There are obviously many reasons why such a language might not develop. It may be that each member state, even though inspired by conceptualisations brought in from the outside, will use its own cultural codes to develop its own language in dealing with the EU. If subsidiarity has different meanings in different countries, depending on cultural background, little is gained in terms of a common political language. Likewise, such a language will have to be able to penetrate not only EU institutions, but also public discourse at different levels and in different settings, in such a way as to inspire debate. A common language existing only as a top-down description of the current state of EU affairs holds out no prospects for the development of common European public spheres.

New conceptualisations need not only, or even mainly, emerge at the EU level. The 'democratic deficit', with its economic connotations, sounds like a concept invented by the EU. However, the invention was triggered by widespread discontent, expressed at a different level and in other words. Furthermore, everyone may not recognise the term 'democratic deficit', but may nevertheless recognise the core meaning of the concept expressed in different words: it is a problem that the EU is not democratic – this has been recognized by the EU itself and there is an ongoing debate on how to deal with it. All this may not seem like much, and public spheres do not develop overnight, however, compared to a situation where discussions on democracy are considered to be a no-go area due to fear of insoluble conflict, it is a decided step forward.

Conclusion

It is argued here that the EU has been dominated by an economic language. The reason for this is that the EU, from the very start, has concentrated on economic cooperation. It was conceived of as having a 'technocratic' rather than a political role. Political issues that challenged national sovereignty or threatened agreement were deliberately kept out or downplayed. To the degree that such a strategy succeeds, it makes the development of Europe-wide public spheres unlikely, since public spheres thrive on disagreement. However, as the EU has become more integrated, the distinction between more practical economic cooperation, on the one hand, and cooperation challenging basic political principles – including principles of democratic governance, on the other, has been more and more difficult to sustain.

The development of a common political language does not necessarily mean agreement but only that one is able to speak about roughly the same issues and phenomena within a common frame of reference. In the same way that people speaking the same language understand each other while disagreeing, people speaking the same political language may also understand each other while disagreeing. Disagreement is constitutive of a public sphere, and complete agreement, whether discursive or non-discursive, would undermine any public sphere. When conceptualisations from different political cultures meet, disagreement and discussion about meaning may be facilitated by the fact that such disagreement and discussion are normal within each of these political cultures.[10]

A political language, therefore, may be seen as an institutionalisation of meaning, a storage device for shared understandings. For such a language to emerge, there has to be contact between representatives from different communities on a continuous basis. Institutions are needed, not only for this reason, but also to remind the participants of the meaning they have agreed on. Or, as Simone Chambers (1995: 245) puts it: 'Shared understandings are fluid and change over time. [...] The continuity of an understanding [...] does not depend on there *being* good grounds for such an understanding, but on those good grounds and that understanding being reproduced [...]'. Political institutions are important for this very reason. They may be seen as arenas where it is possible to develop and stabilise shared understandings. The expectation is that general agreement on the meaning of some common concepts in turn will affect how different practices are evaluated. In William Connolly's words (1983: 39): 'In convincing me to adopt your version of "democracy", "politics", or "legitimacy" you convince me to classify and appraise actions and practices in new ways; you encourage me to guide my own conduct by new considerations.'

In order to serve democratic integration, a common political language has to be based on ordinary language in use in each of the EU member states, by contrast to expert or systemic languages. The necessary process of translation may be seen more as an ever-present opportunity to clarify a common understanding than as an obstacle to such an understanding. The use of different national languages guarantees continuous discussion on how to constitute a common political interpretative grammar, nourished by alternative democratic traditions. Civil society, seen as the cradle of political ideas, may be enhanced not sidelined, in the process of making sense of the emerging political order in Europe. From this point of view, in a globalised world in need of political control, the danger lies more in the stubborn stability of political ideas than in the possible disorder brought on by the clash of ideas.

Notes

1 A meta-lingual language in this sense is not the same as a meta-lingual discourse; it is what makes a meta-lingual discourse possible. To discover if a common political discourse is possible throughout Europe by way of common meta-lingual languages, we have to start by looking for different key concepts that have similar meanings in different countries, and words or expressions that are developed as simplifying substitutes or specifications of such key concepts.

2 An illustration can be given by citing Fritz Scharpf (1994: 227): 'At the highest level of analytical abstraction, central government rules in a multi-level system may serve three functions: redistribution of resources among constituent units, co-ordination for the prevention of negative external effects and for the achievement of collective goods, and co-ordination for the better achievement of private goods.'

3 Stone Sweet and Brunell's (1998) study of Article 177 references (EEC Treaty 1958) illustrates the tendency nicely. This covers instances where EC law applies to cases brought before national courts and gives the judge an opportunity and sometimes a duty to ask the European Court of Justice for the correct interpretation of the law that the national court has to follow when settling the case. Between 1961 and 1992 there was a steady rise of such references. More importantly, there is a nearly perfect match between the average number of references per year and internal trade figures.

4 Notwithstanding the disagreement among scholars and others on what exactly the term 'market' means.

5 Charles Taylor (1989) makes a distinction between 'weak' and 'strong' evaluations. Weak evaluations are concerned with pragmatic issues, linked to instrumental reasoning, where the main interest is with the weighting of alternatives relative to some desired end. The desires themselves are not discussed and remain inarticulate. Strong evaluations, in Taylor's own words, involve 'discriminations of right or wrong, better or worse, higher or lower, which are not rendered valid by our own desires, inclinations, or choices, but rather stand independent of these and offer standards by which they can be judged' (p. 4). To engage in strong evaluations implies becoming more articulate about one's own preferences. Goals are not accepted merely as contingent desires, but are discussed relative to more fundamental concerns.

6 For a discussion on the distinction between discursive agreement and discursive disagreement, see Blichner 2000.

7 Such a language will be the medium through which it will be possible to come 'together on the basis of shared values, a shared understanding of rights and societal duties and shared rational, intellectual culture which transcend ethnonational difference' (Weiler *et al.* 1995: 19).

8 The efforts made to reduce the normative content of the concept of subsidiarity to efficiency criteria may be seen as a further indication of the dominance of an economic language in the EU.

9 See Stone Sweet and Brunell (1998) who predict that as the scope of EU rules

expand, the legal system will not simply be a vehicle for trading interests, but also for more diffuse 'public' interests. The 'diffuseness' is what I argue will be helped by a common political language.
10 For discussions, see Gallie 1956; Connolly 1983; Blichner and Sangolt 1994; Waldron 1994, 2002.

9 EU enlargement, identity and the public sphere

Maria Heller and Ágnes Rényi

Introduction

All the preconditions for a lively European communicative arena exist, but there are obstacles and barriers to its development and smooth functioning. In order to restructure the European Union to make it an effective institution capable of performing its role of uniting and governing 27 or more countries as a regional superstructure, several conditions have to be met. Political and institutional restructuring is vital, but cognitive aspects, attitudes and feelings have to be taken into account as well. Communication among decision-making bodies, representatives and general publics has to be reinforced because the millions of EU citizens need to forge some kind of common identity. This is an indispensable precondition to the elaboration of the social solidarity without which the Union will never be able to develop into a strong polity. The collaboration of citizens and their free associations as well as political forces and institutions requires mutual advantages, a common future, mutual responsibility and solidarity. For a vast social programme to be successfully implemented, objective and subjective conditions have to be ensured. This chapter concentrates on the relationship between nation states, identities, citizenship and the public sphere, with a particular emphasis on Central and Eastern Europe (CEE).

Identity constructions in public discourse

Europe and the world are presently witnessing the strengthening of diverging and exclusionist tendencies, whether around ethnic, religious or other cleavages. Divergent identities are expressed with increasing vitality and lead to civil unrest. The problem of identities is a core issue not only for European integration but also for global processes. Identities help individuals to feel involved and oriented in the world, acquire a cultural heritage, value systems, group belonging and patterns of behaviour. They are part of individuals' basic social knowledge.

Identities are constructed through discourses that speakers adapt to concrete communicative situations. They take into consideration the public or private character of the situation, relationships with partners, and the political, cultural, social, religious context. People use different strategies of self-expression, categorisation, classification, justification and argumentation, as well as discursive methods of exclusion and inclusion because they calculate differently in concrete situations. The notion of identity is closely related to that of citizenship and for the formation of common European solidarity, diverse processes and patterns of identity formation (whether national, ethnic, religious, gender or other) have to be analytically examined.

Identities are strongly influenced by collective cultural, historical, religious and social traditions and also by individual cognitive and emotional elements, driven by personal experience, family memories, habits and local traditions. In everyday situations, people tend to harmonise different roles that involve different layers of their identities. Public debates on identity occur where conflicts among divergent identities become salient, when participants sharpen their definitions, distinctions and criteria. Public debates radicalise conceptions of group membership, and make expressions of identity more thoroughly elaborated. One of the preconditions for EU integration is that citizens of various nation states should consider having common causes and interests. Common belonging will strongly influence the legal-political structure the Union will be able to achieve. Although decisions are taken by powerfully-strong publics and institutions, the adherence of the general public to these decisions is crucial. Therefore, identity debates and public debates on diverse community issues have to be taken into consideration.

Liberal theory acknowledges morally autonomous individuals as acting and reacting freely in a society where universalistic traditions constitute the governing principle, while communitarian social theory, placing its emphasis on collective action and solidarity, subordinates individuals to collective goals and traditions. Individual and collective identities are constructions. They are flexible, changing and unstable. Their social role is to define and represent the 'self' and its place among others. Moreover, identities are not free from inner instability and incoherence. Each person's identity is multiple, involving different layers. Depending on the situation, different elements of this incoherent concoction are in focus and govern acts and feelings. Moreover, identities are communicative constructions elaborated in discourse (Ricoeur 1992; Bauman 1996; Benhabib 1996). Identity discourse is directed both inwards and outwards and is subject to change with the communicative characteristics of each situation.

Groups and societies face the necessity of self-definition. Any group – however large – needs to tackle questions of belonging, hence the need to define its members and differentiate them from the rest of the world, the non-members. Thus, groups of any size are confronted with the problem of definition and categorisation. But different traditions make use of totally different theoretical and procedural means. These definitions play a crucial role in the definition of Europeanness, and national identities are the most important constructions that may influence European development.

Identity and categorisation

The central stake in national identity debates is the delimitation and stabilisation of the category 'we', the in-group, as opposed to the category of the 'other', the out-group (Wodak 1998).

According to one position, the 'we' category may be constructed through discourse as a notion of community (*Gemeinschaft*), which includes ascriptive traits like kinship, blood relationships, affiliation and collective membership in ethnic groups, or religious or cultural collectivities. This organic determinist discourse of identity strengthens the borderlines and considers them insurmountable. The construction of the twin categories of 'us' and 'them' is strong and often regarded as self-evident. The individual, in this view, is the embodiment of all these essential traits. He/she is forever defined by membership of the group and has no choice or freedom to change or leave the group and abandon his/her identity. Culture is considered as the transmission of tradition and is a compulsory part of the heritage of the individual member. The individual has practically no choice in constructing his/her identity. He/she is not a free, autonomous, sovereign being and carries the burdens of the collectivity and is subordinated to it. At the same time he/she is a token of this collectivity, carrying its essence in his/her own body. Topics related to the individual are considered, in this approach, as belonging to the public sphere. Organic determinism attempts to categorise individuals into homogeneous groups according to primordial criteria, like gender or ethnic affiliation. Group affiliation is not subject to individual choice; individual trajectories or cultural achievement cannot modify affiliation, which is based on ascriptive criteria.

The opposed view in identity debates speaks a universalistic discourse. It postulates that individuals are equal and free. In this approach, the very fact of diversity in human life is a value, regardless of group membership. Individuals have the right to define their own identity. Classification does not depend on ascriptive but on achieved qualities and traits, and its principles are subject to choice. Liberal ideology cannot help defining borderlines but does not restrain individual movement. Borderlines between groups are not sharp or given. The individual has the right to control the domains of his/her individual life. The category of the public is conceived of as a network of groups of freely associated individuals. Membership in groups can be achieved. According to universalist individualism, cultural and linguistic forms of behaviour become more and more universalised as part of a long process of evolution and refinement. Participation and belonging are subject to individual choice; culture and civilisation can be achieved through individual learning, assimilation, cultural experience, individual decisions and performance. In the course of development, nature-bound forms of identity give way to more abstract and universal forms of identity. The history of evolution is constituted by a long process of liberalisation of the individual, by the universalisation of forms of communication between individuals, and by the elaboration of liberty of choice for the individual between different identities. In this view, the only legitimate system of inequalities is meritocratic, based on achievement; but social solidarity, for humanitarian reasons, can correct or ease the system of inequalities. These solutions then become public issues and have to be discussed in public.

The conception of the nation and national identities

National ideology and national identities are a special kind of historic compromise between local and global society. The nation state is an attempt to combine local, ethnic, historical and cultural particularities with certain universal norms (such as human and citizen rights). The modern notion of the nation has for centuries combined a form of collectivism on the one hand (organic, territorial or ethnic membership), and an abstract universalistic concept of citizenship, on the other. This is an ambivalent and fragile construction where national identity is a compromise between two different value structures. It is based on exclusion, since it has to define who the members are, thus excluding others, but at the same time it gives universal equality to all members.

National sovereignty, as a universal legitimising principle (a notion that is put into question by EU integration), is only meaningful if there is an underlying particularistic legitimising principle, which delimits a given nation within geographic boundaries. The nation as a construction is universal in its inclusiveness: it comprises the whole society vertically and horizontally, emancipating all its members legally, expanding equal rights to all participating members. But the notion of the nation also presupposes a principle of exclusion, based on particularist categories, of all non-members, which justifies geographic, horizontal delimitations. The notion of the nation, as a historic invention and construction, is based on the ethnic group, developed from an archaic community of language and culture (Smith 1986).

An essentialist view of the nation affirms the existence of a particular essence, held by the core of the ethnic group, and perceives this as a finite, delimited set, ignoring any common elements with other groups having a common historical experience. It petrifies the content and form of identity and thus eliminates individuals' right to multiple identities or chosen groups.

The development of societies in Western Europe, the process of civilization, which involved secularisation, the elaboration of civic rights and the emancipation of individuals resulted in the construction of sovereign nation states where membership is a legal category. In Central Europe, and even more so in Eastern Europe, historical and political constraints held back this evolution and contributed to the construction of 'state nations' or 'culture nations', which have had difficulty, throughout their history, in accepting and handling minority identities. The main reason for this failure is that their legitimacy is based on a cultural-linguistic community, which itself is thought to result from direct affiliation (based on ethnic, cultural or linguistic traits) (Elias 1982; Szücs 1988). The lack of flexibility in terms of identity leads to continuous problems of loyalty in culture nations. Loyalty is considered a result of common ascriptive values and a matter of irrational feelings of belonging but not as a rationally elaborated notion of citizenship and common interest related to the public good, liberty, solidarity and equality. Here the notions of citizenship (a legal category) and nationality (ascriptive membership) are assigned on different bases.

For example, essentialist Hungarian discourse uses words like '*Hungarianness*' or '*Hungaritude*' and considers that there is an eternal substance that cannot be modified by non-members. It should be preserved unaltered, protected from dangerous incursions and deterioration as it is the most highly valued heritage ever. Hungarian nationalist ideology considers the peasantry to be that traditional centre of Hungarianness.[1]

The struggle between the two identity constructions identified above has direct relevance for representations of and expectations about the EU. Either protagonists of an essentialist conception are in an anti-EU position, considering that their country has no interest in becoming a member and should preserve its 'national sovereignty', or they consider that the EU framework should be restricted to transnational governance, where specialised agencies are appointed to problem-solving tasks. This conception of the Union is congruent with a loosely structured European public sphere, which tackles only administrative problems. Universalist protagonists expect a more tightly constructed political, cultural and economic community, a federal or supranational Union based on citizens' equality and solidarity, and a mutual acknowledgement of rights and duties. This conception involves conscious elaboration of common governance, institutions and alternatives of development in all fields of life as well as a rich web of interacting groups and individuals constantly reflecting on common topics, choices, problems and solutions. Such cooperation among individuals, civil society groups and institutions, general and strong publics, necessitates a multifold public arena, where differently shaped and sized public spheres coexist, interrelate and enhance public discourse. The European public sphere, according to this orientation, has to be structured as a mosaic of overlapping and related public spheres, which facilitate discussion at all levels.

CEE: the problem of accession

While the Eastern enlargement of the EU is a logical and salutary decision because it erases (at least symbolically) a century-old historical cleavage and restores a certain European community and unity (Schlesinger 2000; Eder and Trenz 2003; Fossum 2003; Eder 2004), this move, however, introduces not only new problems concerning economic and welfare questions but also problems in the domains of culture and communication, which will affect the emergence of a European public arena.

The end of the twentieth century witnessed the reawakening of collective communitarian identities (religious, ethnic, national). After a period of development in the opposite direction, with the spread of universal principles of solidarity and brotherhood – especially in the 1960s – the late 1980s and 1990s saw the re-emergence of collective identities based on small-group belonging, ascriptive categories and the exclusion of out-groups, leading to social unrest, ranging from limited clashes to regional warfare.

Since the 1980s, as part of a process of widely growing instability and loss of confidence in institutions provided by state-run policies, large numbers of people searched for their roots. The construction of communitarian groups must be interpreted as a sign of individuals seeking protection, stability and less alienated institutions. It is clearly motivated by the growing need for institutions and communities that are close to peoples' everyday life-world and knowledge. The need to find one's own roots, reinforced the attempts at self-definition and shifted the focus of interest to the problem of identities, both individual and collective.

Constructions of political, ethnic, national or religious identities became central issues of political mobilisation and topics of public and private discourse. Such constructions serve as a basis of self-definition for persons and groups and can foster the constitution of deep dividing lines between groups inside societies.

Central and Eastern (or East-Central) Europe[2] constitutes a special case. While there has always been a strong wish to belong to the West in a certain section of the population, others have always been strongly against a Western affiliation, preaching national or ethnic difference and isolationism. This deep internal cleavage meant that the dilemma of accession had important stakes and that both referenda concerning accession to the North Atlantic Treaty Organisation (NATO) and the EU provoked strong public debates in the region. The political changes at the end of the 1980s stirred up the region's many unsolved problems, some centuries-old, others more recent.

Identity problems play an important role in recent development in CEE. In the political vacuum that the collapsing state-socialist system left behind, violent debates emerged on topics of ethnic, religious and national identity. In most places, these were accompanied by acts of hatred, distrust and exclusion, but were contained in communicative and symbolic forms. The symbolically elaborated topics of out-groups and scapegoats were used by opposing political forces in their fight for power and symbolic domination and even led to fratricidal civil war.

Public speakers (writers, intellectuals, élite groups, professional communicators) are the most active participants in public debates. Their role involves the elaboration of public representations and the construction of the symbolic stockpile of a society. Constructions of national identity are part of the symbolic representations over which different factions of the symbolic élite keep on fighting.

Problems of nationhood and national identity are, and have been, at the centre of debates in CEE for centuries. The most central problem in the region is a dilemma of models of development. CEE is, and has been, in an equivocal, intermediate position between divergent models of power structure and social development, and at the crossroads of different structural, economic, religious and cultural paradigms. These countries, with more or less determination throughout their history since the Middle Ages, have been trying to catch up with Western European development. There have been attempts to adopt European patterns of modernisation. But some forces have tried to elaborate their own models of development, differing from Western Europe and based on each nation's presumed particular characteristics and resources. The long-lasting structural shortfall resulted in constraints on catching up and inferiority complexes mixed with compensatory superiority (Bibó 1986). For centuries, alternative patterns of development were in competition. Competing models involved a Western-type model of development and modernisation relying on universal and liberal values, backed by a traditionally strong faction of urban liberal intellectuals. The strongest opposing model was a search for intrinsic national models of development, based on particularistic traditions presumed to have preserved the original national and ethnic values. This orientation emphasises a traditional collective consciousness. A third model was introduced in the twentieth century, constituted by socialist modernisation, also based on universal and egalitarian values. This was a hasty attempt at forced acceleration for catching up with the West.

Different élite groups promulgated different responses to the problem of model choice thus creating deep cleavages in the political, cultural and ideological field. The difference in value structure, in style, in discourse and in role-consciousness between 'populists' (*narodniks*) and 'westernisers/ urbanists' (*zapadniks*) has been the most important cleavage for the last 150 years in the region.

A feeling of belonging to the West is rather strong in the region. Hungarian public discourse often thematises the country's Western orientation throughout history. The underlying argument takes into consideration the religious affiliation of the country, its sacrificial role during the Tartar and Turkish occupations, strong cultural ties with the

West (Latin alphabet, common scientific and artistic heritage), economic ties and similar social and political development.

Although most countries of the region have had the same fate and the same problem of belatedness, a long history of ethnic conflicts, rivalry and continuous grievances against each other has hampered collaboration between them. The well-known policy of the Austrian rulers – *divide et impera!* – profited from and reinforced the existing conflicts. Later developments did not efface them.[3] Geopolitical tensions still exist in the region, after 45 years of 'socialist internationalism'.

There were, however, attempts to find common solutions. The idea of the 'Danubian Confederation' already present in the nineteenth century was later re-elaborated by Hungarian liberal intellectuals at the beginning of the twentieth century. But such plans for future common development were never realised.[4]

The dilemma of retarded development and model choice has been burdened by other problems: the long historical period of defeat, lost wars and territories, foreign occupation and ethnic conflicts and rivalry. The accumulating problems and the ever-growing delay brought about a complicated mixture of pride and inferiority, shared by large masses in the region. Social historians (Bibó 1986; Hanák 1992), in analysing Central and Eastern European nations, described 'distorted national characters', a complicated concoction of collective superiority mixed with a deep inferiority complex. Local populations had to elaborate cunning techniques of concealment, strong separation between their private and public lives, doubletalk, reading between the lines, etc. in order to survive. Rival social, ethnic or religious groups have regularly been pointed to as scapegoats in public discourse, and long-lasting historical constructions of blame and innocence became common constructions instigating different groups against each other.[5]

Research on public debates in the region[6] shows that the most important topic is still the problem of the nation and national identity, and this is closely connected with the construction of supranational loyalty and the interpretation of European integration. The cleavages and animosities might hamper the construction of an enlarged European space.

Although the question of the nation and of national identity is the most vivid unsettled problem in the region, it was a taboo topic during state socialism. In Hungary, between the 1956 revolution and the 1990 political changeover, a certain 'restricted public sphere' functioned (Heller *et al.* 1994), which was subordinated to and governed by the political centre. The most important 'innovation' of the new leadership after 1956 to create political consolidation and to ensure social stability was a tacit compromise with the population which involved the withdrawal of politics from the private sphere, renouncing political mobilisation, a slow but steady liberalisation of the spheres of private life (freedom of religious activity, the introduction of different genres of popular culture) and a slowly growing consumerism ('frigidaire-socialism' or 'goulash-communism'). The division between public and private life, topics and issues became even stronger than before, creating a considerable difference compared to Western Europe, which may still play a role in the construction of today's European public sphere.

The existence of the restricted public sphere in Hungary was a result of the political changes after 1956. The new non-Stalinist leadership needed legitimation that could only be ensured by the discursive activity of the intelligentsia, of public speakers. Thus the cultural leadership elaborated a series of compromises with different Hungarian intellectual groups, giving them a certain liberty of expression and hoping for loyal discursive activity in return. The bargains were non-public and the compromises also intended to divide the intellectual field alongside the already existing dividing lines (populists and westernisers). Intellectuals accepted the compromise, expecting to be able to push back the barriers of the restricted public sphere. The compromise offered them the possibility to appear and speak in public. It also reinforced the traditional importance of intellectuals, their historic role to speak for the nation, for the voiceless people.[7]

The notion of a 'restricted public sphere' attempts to grasp the particular nature of a public arena where, in spite of restrictions on the public sphere, a certain freedom of expression existed: public matters were discussed, public debates were not totally defined by the political authorities. Restrictions operated on certain values, political or ideological alternatives. The pluralistic character of the public sphere was also restricted but the public sphere was still able to function, mainly due to special discursive techniques of veiling, of conveying hidden meanings and the competence of the public of reading between the lines. There were ideological and cultural debates and censorship operated mainly after publication, and was more often substituted for by mild self-censorship. From the mid-1970s, a 'second public sphere' was created by dissenters of the democratic opposition and the 'restricted' character of the special Hungarian public sphere became more and more visible. In fact, a restricted public sphere can only function temporarily. It is either a sphere clearly dominated by propaganda which loses its legitimating effect, or it pretends to function as an unlimited public sphere while the restrictions, taboos and other limitations become more and more visible, as was the case in Hungary.

The systemic changes in 1989/90 found the societies of the region unprepared, and brought to the surface all previous unsettled problems. The political changeover radically changed the whole public sphere. Suddenly, all former constraints on the 'restricted public sphere' were removed, giving place to an extremely liberated domain of public discourse where the rules of public communication were swept away. This resulted in a sudden explosion of rather violent debates, where all former taboo questions burst into the public arena and fierce struggles for positions invaded the public sphere. The political arena witnessed divergent development and radicalisation of the different orientations, fighting fiercely for public recognition. The public debates became highly ideological and symbolic and restructured stylistic and discursive differences into deep political differences. Symbolic politics became a major battlefield, thematising inner contradictions: the 'small state' problem, and clashes between citizenship based on criteria of ethno-national belonging and that based on administrative–legal criteria.[8]

Presently, the Hungarian public sphere is deeply divided and the situation is similar in neighbouring countries. Most debates do not seek consensus, they function like zero-sum games in a politically over-exposed situation where the goal of the participants is to defeat the opposing side. The most important cleavage remains the opposition among populists and westernisers. Most of the divergent positions are based not only on ideological and political differences but also on cultural and intellectual differences regarding the choice of political and ideological models and value structure. This also affects the stances taken concerning European integration. The NATO and EU accession debates took place amidst these conditions.

After the collapse of state socialism, the fiercest debates immediately addressed national identity. The main narrative stake was the struggle to monopolise definitions of categorisation: 'Who is a true Hungarian?'. Irrational, romantic or even jingoistic notions of an ethnically defined state nation and its emotionally bound subjects have been opposed to the notion of a rational nation state and its legal definitions of inclusive citizenship. This is a relevant problem for the EU: in CEE, even the nation state is not a fixed and settled category. Transcending the nation state in this region calls for arguments that are different from those in the West.

The central problem of national identity has become a structuring trait not only of the Hungarian political public sphere but also in the rest of the region. It involves the most important dividing line between intellectual groups of different cultural traditions and has constituted an ideological battlefield in the debates over NATO and EU accession. These debates clearly show that conceptions of identity and citizenship are closely connected with attitudes towards enlargement.

The accession debates

The debates preceding the 1997 referendum on Hungary's NATO entry and the 2003 referendum concerning EU accession were also closely related to the problem of belated development, the dilemma of model choice and the problem of national self-definition. In both cases the cleavage was between the country's Western alignment and a particularistic national pattern of development. The questions at stake included a choice between economic and political development in the wider European context or closing up the country under populist, nationalist rule.

Analyses of the accession debates show that a Western orientation was popular among Hungarian voters (Heller and Rényi 2003a, 2003b). All parliamentary parties agreed on the proposed membership, and only a few non-parliamentary parties and scattered civic groups were against.

The referendum, however, was not without risks. Since its creation, and especially during the Cold War, NATO had enjoyed a rather negative image in the Hungarian public sphere. There were justifiable fears in political and military circles that the public might not back the decision because of the population's traditional aspiration for neutrality. The example of the western neighbour, Austria, also had its effect.[9] Nationalist discourse used arguments about losing sovereignty and the glorious national past and reminded the audience that hopes for Western military help in 1956 were never satisfied.

Because of the uncertainty concerning public opinion, a rather strong pro-NATO campaign was orchestrated by the authorities. While nearly no important details about costs, future military obligations, necessary modernisation, etc. were made public, the whole topic was widely constructed as a diplomatic event, as an issue of foreign affairs. Particular narratives were introduced to present the whole accession process as a glorious march to success and as already decided. Similar narrative strategies preceded the EU accession debates six years later.

Topic constructions

In public discourse, there were several competing topic constructions dealing with the two accessions. The question was most often treated as a pragmatic one, based on a calculation of advantages and disadvantages, necessary investments and expected benefits, and rarely tackled from the point of view of abstract values and ideological alternatives.

The success of the NATO referendum was mainly due to the way the topic was publicly constructed. Because of NATO's ambiguous evaluation in public opinion, mainstream discourse concerning the NATO alliance accentuated its relatedness to Hungary's planned and widely expected entry into the EU. Public discourse focused on this relationship. It was generally presumed that NATO accession would help legally and symbolically to reconstruct the once existing ties between Hungary and the West and to contribute to joining the EU. NATO accession was most often presented as an initial phase in a well planned series of actions: the first step in Hungary's 'return to the West'.

In mainstream pro-NATO discourses, NATO appeared as a highly active organisation engaging in activities of large-scale international significance (summits, negotiations, diplomatic events and peace talks). It was represented by high-ranking officials and internationally renowned

personalities. Such pro-NATO discourses clearly tried to demonstrate
NATO's great international prestige. Pro-EU discourse used similar patterns, projecting the Union both as an efficient transnational problem-
solving entity and as a value-based supranational alliance, representing the
most fruitful project of future development towards a superstate without
inner borders, including peacefully evolving wealthy regions. As proof of
the country's acceptance, this topic construction often showed Hungarian
politicians, diplomats and army officials successfully negotiating with EU
officials.

In some discourses, NATO and the EU were shown as value-based
organisations, just and democratic institutions, a part of the 'Western'
civilisation 'we' also belong to. Discourses treating the democratic qualities, the consensus-seeking decision-making processes within NATO, the
decrease of its military character and the peace-keeping role given to
NATO by the UN were all meant to support NATO's qualification as a
value community. In the EU, the values of civilisation, culture, social
justice and security, welfare, political stability and scientific and technological development were accentuated.

But the EU, and more often NATO, were also depicted as interest-
based organisations. There were two different positions concerning the
interests these alliances were supposed to observe. In pro-integration discourses, these interests were shown to suit 'our' own interests. The main
stake of such discourses was to show a community of interests between
existing members and candidates. Common interests were referred to in
order to explain the act of candidature of Central and Eastern European
countries and also to underline the two alliances' willingness to negotiate
their admission. Positive discourses thus reinforced the idea of a community between Eastern and Western Europe, and depicted a basically homogeneous European landscape with compatible aims and interests.
Interest-based discourses, however, represented all partners as basically
following their own ends, and thus conceived of them as loosely integrated communities, made up of autonomous self-interested nation states.

Anti-integration discourses denied common interests between the
alliances and the accession countries. A 'scenario of denunciation' is
generally characteristic of these discourses. NATO and the EU are
represented as alien, interest-based organisations seeking to exploit 'us',
observing their own interests that are antagonistic to 'ours'.

For Hungary's western affiliation, historical ties, cultural and religious
arguments were often advanced. The western way of life and standard of
living also holds strong appeal to the public. It was, therefore, important
for anti-NATO speakers to try and deconstruct the link between NATO
and the EU by stressing a presumed American dominance inside NATO.

The NATO and EU accession debates testify to a strong desire in the
population to join the most fortunate, most wealthy and most peaceful
part of the continent. Public speakers favouring a western affiliation

attempted in both debates to symbolically deconstruct an 'old we' category of identity, where Hungary was on the bad side, always a loser, just envying the more fortunate 'others'. In opposition to the 'old we' category, a 'new we' notion was elaborated, characterised by a more universalistic discursive mode, built on open, inclusive categories and values and on universal principles. The 'new we' notion constituted a common participatory category, in which 'we', 'new Europeans' were full-time members. Hungary's membership in Europe was based on a common past, culture and shared values and presented as a perennial quality. Constructions of Hungary as a macro-subject were found frequently in the accession debates, thematising accession as a macro-subject's collective wish, preponderant if not unanimous. Thus the problem of the underlying decision was not thematised as a political choice, having several alternatives; it was presented as evidence.

There was, however, another pro-accession discursive strategy: in some discourses a strategy of threat was used, stating that a negative or invalid referendum would generate a bad image of the country in the West. Such a result was described as totally illogical, contradicting the long efforts made by the whole country, the government and the diplomatic institutions for the sake of integration. This discursive strategy constituted a kind of coercion, a moral and cognitive obligation to produce a positive referendum.

Narrative scenarios

The analysis of the two debates found the existence of several distinct discursive scenarios. The different scenarios or narrative structures often overlapped in the discourses. Their role was to represent the decision to accede to NATO and the EU as self-evident and unquestionable.

One of the most frequent narrative constructions for accession was 'the good student' narrative, which used a school metaphor, with traditional competition among students. According to this, Central and Eastern European countries are in competition for acknowledgement from the West. Hungary is personalised as 'the pre-eminent student', complying with all the requirements, fulfilling all the conditions set by the severe examiners. Hungary acts like an overzealous student, trying to anticipate the requirements of and obediently agreeing to all new conditions. This scenario constructs a meritocratic frame, where competitors are continually evaluated according to their achievements. A strong asymmetry can clearly be detected in this scenario between the 'students' and the 'examiners', between those 'inside' and those 'outside'.

Another narrative structure contains as its central topos a contest or a trial, where among all the different contestants 'we' did well, stood the trial, and thus got the expected prize. The contest-frame signifies that the goal that all those engaged in the race want to attain is positive. The outcome of this narrative script is that the focus of the problem is shifted: the question is not whether 'we' want to join, but whether 'they' want to admit us. Other narrative structures use similar frames, such as a typical folk-tale narrative, Hungary, like the cunning youngest son, wins the contest and the fabulous prize. In the enlargement debates, narrative constructions of contests allow 'us' to boost 'our' achievements in comparison to the neighbours. Hungary appears in these scenarios as more skilful than the other contestants. Other narratives represent Hungary as a defenceless child that needs the protection of strong 'adults'. Hungary is a 'small' actor compared to the others (the West), who are represented as strong and resourceful.

All these scenarios depict a paternalistic relationship between the 'small' and the 'great', the 'candidates' and the 'judges'. The relationships among the countries are always hierarchical. Hungary is often represented as outpacing the other candidate states, but is in a subordinate position compared to NATO and EU member states. The discourses clearly show that the accession countries are also in competition with each other, and the main stake is which country is 'allowed in' first. There are no common plans or actions; thus such discourses predict a Union with member states of different strengths and authority and contrasting interests.

The debates also clearly show where the speakers situate Hungary in European space. In most of the discourses, the main issue at stake is making it clear that Hungary is not on the periphery, not in the 'East' and especially not in the Balkans. For many speakers, the main concern about EU integration is whether 'we' can be considered to be part of 'the West'.

Representatives of the essentialist conception of the nation were against enlargement. Approaching the West means giving up national sovereignty, losing specifically Hungarian characteristics, melting into an alien culture and giving up national interests to serve foreign ones. For leftist anti-integration activists, a future stronger alliance with the West means leaving behind former fellow countries, breaking former solidarities and giving up humanistic egalitarian values and engagements.

East–West and North–South oppositions, which divide geographical space horizontally, also signify a vertical, hierarchical value distribution in the discourses. Different dimensions are set to define the borderlines between the two regions. Their former common fate, cultural and historical relations, and past solidarity were mentioned, but the long-standing historical tensions and competition between countries of the region make the relationships among them rather fragile. Relations with the West and competition among accession countries receive more prominence in the discourses than solidarity or collaboration in problem-solving. On the other hand, Hungary was often defined as being able to play a role in bridging the two parts of Europe.

The EU and globalisation

Political affiliation, attitudes towards the problem of national identity and developmental models played a role in the choice of the standpoints taken in the accession debates. Positions taken with respect to essentialist or pluralist conceptions of the nation predetermined discursive strategies. The accession debates reinforced former cleavages over the most relevant problems of development models but at the same time caused the appearance of new dividing lines defined by diverging conceptions of the role of the nation. New cleavages have also appeared and blurred the lines. At certain points in the debates, actors of radically different orientations found themselves – rather embarrassedly – in the same camps, using similar discourse and argumentation. Activists of anti-militarist peace movements, former communist leaders and new communist activists, extreme-right politicians and populist writers argued against integration using arguments of solidarity, anti-capitalism, anti-globalisation, national identity and sovereignty.

The vast topic of European integration includes many interrelated problems: the relationship between the state and the citizen, the definition of in-group and out-group membership and the conception of globalisation. Views and standpoints concerning global development frame conceptions of the EU as a transnational or supranational institution. The development of the Union is often treated in the discourses as an answer to globalisation. Many public speakers consider the EU itself as the result of a globalising tendency and evaluate it positively or negatively depending on their view on globalisation. Others consider the EU to be a defence cooperative, a counter-tendency to the American-driven process of globalisation. The topic of national identity is also characteristically redefined in this context. Radical anti-globalisation discourses are based either on universalistic principles of solidarity and equality (left wing) or on an exclusionist and segregationist definition of nationhood (right wing). The standpoints regarding globalisation and the future structure of the EU show isomorphic characteristics. Those accentuating equality among citizens based on universal rights and duties back the construction of a 'new' EU with tight links and common governance, mutual recognition of freedom and the expression of common values. Contrariwise, those who cling to traditional particularistic values and communities do not want to give up their 'restricted' sovereignty.

A common European public sphere?

EU institutions and decision-making bodies define the agenda and the necessary legal framework for the existence of a common arena. The functioning of EU institutions necessitates public control, different political and economic decisions constitute issues for debate, and the very process of the construction of a new and large community raises many problems that have to be tackled by different institutions and publics. These topics concern all citizens of the member states as European citizens. Common European public matters embrace political, cultural, economic and social problems. Besides, issues produced by a globalising world also have relevance for the EU and its citizens. Although the EU aims to preserve its members' divergent national cultures, languages and traditions, the construction of a 'community' of European citizens needs public reflection on a common public arena. Although the existence of different cultures and languages (which in a sense is an advantage and a source of symbolic wealth) causes some technical problems, there are successful attempts to overcome these difficulties and create European fora for discussions available for general publics.[10] This proves that various European media could constitute the arena for European public debates even if linguistic barriers and national boundaries hamper the establishment of a unique European public field of communication.

The elaboration of a European public sphere, however, faces several challenges. There are competing public spheres of diverse sizes. Globalising tendencies both in the economy and in culture and politics, the appearance of multinational companies and of transnational political formations, as well as the emergence of new information and communication technologies have led to the emergence of overlapping public spheres (Keane 1995), a new structural development which has broken up the privileged status of the public spheres of the nation states. In fact, with the nation state gradually losing its primacy (relegating territorial bonds to the background) and new transnational power structures appearing on the global scene, the structure of the public sphere has become severely modified: publics of a different size have appeared in differently sized public arenas.

Different topics necessitate different kinds of accessibility. Digital net communication makes it possible to create communicative events on a global scale and also facilitates reaching small local or regional groups. And although people's free time has not increased significantly, digital and computer-mediated communication and the economic use of fragmented timespots through mobile devices have already greatly increased people's communicative activities. In fact, people's various relationships through either weak or strong ties have already been enhanced through new Information and Communications Technologies (ICT)s; public and private topics are discussed and debated through quickly growing channels of communication.

As opposed to the period of electronic mass media, the period of digital net communication increases people's active participation in communicative actions. The easy reach of different communicative channels and increasing interactivity may lead to citizens' more active participation in discussions in the public sphere (also in the transnational public sphere), thus enlarging democratic participation. The increasing choice of ICTs and the parallel increase in people's communicative activities reinforce possibilities for the emergence of a richly structured European public arena, where different topics generated by a gradually more complex integration can be discussed on different levels by the publics concerned. The EU, in the course of its restructuring, needs to rely more effectively on the new possibilities of communication. Issues have to be debated across nations, countries, languages, social groups and weak and strong publics in order to achieve not only good structural solutions but also public consent, support and participation. Not only the structure of the Union has to be invented and implemented, but so does that of the new European public sphere. The emerging European public sphere will be a complex structure of different layers, incorporating a colourful mosaic of differently sized overlapping public spheres, which foster the accessibility of all topics for all participants.

The changing structure of the public sphere, however, is not the only problem touching the emergence of a European public arena. The analyses of the hierarchy among accession countries and the extended Union do not predict a smooth development towards a supranational structure where nation states would give up their national sovereignty, their popular self-representation and narcissistic attitudes in order to construct a new entity with new institutions, tasks and solutions. Old animosities, identity problems and defeatism are still strong in the region. Boundaries and barriers that hamper the creation of a complex European public sphere are created not only by differing languages. Language barriers are just obvious symbolic signs of inner cleavages, among which the most deeply rooted are geographically defined and often ethnically conceived nation states and the strong feelings of identity and belonging that bind their citizens to these 'imagined communities' (Anderson 1991). Ethnic, religious and national affiliations, struggles over definitions of belonging and over criteria of group membership, categorisations into in-groups and out-groups ('us' versus 'them') exist in different regions of the continent even if age-long animosities have been contained in other regions. Old loyalties, exclusionist definitions of membership, old wounds and grievances counteract the creation of a common European public sphere and these cleavages are harder to erase than sheer language differences.

The problem is whether and to what extent EU citizens feel not only national but 'European' and are concerned about common problems. The question arises at the level of identity and a sense of belonging, which are necessary conditions for participating in public discussion on common matters. For a European public sphere to exist, European identity has to be reinforced and European citizens have to take responsibility for common public matters without only observing the interests of their own local, regional or national community. The diversity of forms and notions of the nation and its role in the enlarged EU, the different conceptions of identities and citizenship, the divergent criteria of exclusion and inclusion and loyalty, have to be tackled in the near future with careful, tolerant and empathetic means.

A European public sphere or a complex structure of overlapping public spheres will exist and play its role if, and only if, all citizens of the member states are concerned about common issues and if they also feel that their problems are considered by the rest of the community. For this to happen, the institutions of the Union have to come closer to the population and have to address the citizens. A community should be constructed in which all traditions, differences, languages and cultures are considered equally important and the heritage of all. A European public sphere will not only be the result of the dissolution of present cleavages, but also be the result of the very space in which communicative action can reinforce their dissolution.

Notes

1 They are called 'deep-Hungarian', while the deprecated category of cosmopolitan others is called 'diluted Hungarian'.
2 Such differences in denomination are topics of ideological debates in the countries of the region. Denominations, expressions and discursive modes often indicate political and ideological affiliations to the competent interlocutor.
3 For example, the 1920 Treaty of Trianon, dismembering Hungary after the First World War, caused a deep shock in the Hungarian population and led to the country taking the side of Nazi Germany – a fatal move sanctioned by the reaffirmation of the Trianon Treaty after the Second World War.
4 It is important to note that 100 years before the idea of the EU, the liberal, universalistic option of collaborating nation states and populations was already present in the region.
5 The tendency to doubletalk and concealment can be traced in the discrepancy between collective memories, official remembrances and family memories, between public and private narratives of the same historic events or personal life trajectories, openly asserted or secretly related (Heller and Rényi 1996).
6 The research has been conducted in several countries of the region using methods of critical discourse analysis on various public discourses (Van Dijk 1985; Wodak 1991). In Hungary, it is based on several analyses on public debates in newspapers, television programmes, presidential speeches, letters to the editor and related materials conducted by the research team Maria Heller, Dénes Némedi and Ágnes Rényi during the last decade. For other research on Hungary and other East European countries, see e.g. Mänicke-Gyöngyösi 1996 and Kovács and Wodak 2003.
7 This role conception has recently become rather antiquated with the emergence of parliamentary democracy and a pluralist public sphere.
8 There were, e.g. 15 million ethnic Hungarians versus 10 million Hungarian citizens.
9 See detailed analyses of the situation in Hungary and Austria in Kovács and Wodak 2003.
10 Such initiatives are, for example, the French- and German-speaking TV channel ARTE, the intellectual periodical *Liber*, initiated by the late Professor Pierre Bourdieu, and previously the journal *Lettres Internationales*.

10 Religion and the European public sphere

François Foret and Philip Schlesinger

Introduction

The European Union is at a liminal stage. It is poised uncertainly between two major development paths, each of which has major implications for the prospects of a European public sphere. The alternative models may be identified as the *regulatory* and the *federal*.

The regulatory model entails, at best, the weak development of transnational institutions and the continuing pull of the public sphere at a national level: political communicative space is principally located within the boundaries of member states, reinforced by well-entrenched patterns of communication. Debate in the EU (and this applies to religious questions as it does to other fields) is mainly conducted in the national public spheres of member states.

To the extent that a *European* public exists, it is likely to remain the stamping ground of the Euro-epistemic communities preponderantly populated by highly knowledgeable and expert actors involved in lobbying and otherwise influencing the working of the EU's institutions (Schlesinger 2002, 2003).

A decisive shift towards a federal model, as has been argued in the introduction to this book, is more likely to foster the development of a general (i.e. a broadly based supranational) public sphere, with its centre of gravity significantly situated at the EU level. Although this kind of public sphere will necessarily be highly complex in how it is articulated across the EU's continuing diversity, it might stand a chance of mobilising citizens to address the EU in terms of their *European* political identity.

Our premise is that the nature and workings of the public sphere are best revealed by concrete analysis of given fields of operation. The EU's constitutional debate has offered an excellent occasion to analyse how religious actors have used the present opportunity structure in the EU to pursue their interests in the context of increasing challenges to a secular order. European states have been constructed by way of a progressive enlargement of claims to rights that have simultaneously accompanied, channelled and shaped the development of national political institutions.

The rise of a new, supranational entity such as the EU has provoked the reshaping of systems of deliberation, decision-making and of political action. This has brought about, however indirectly, a redefinition of the relations between the holders of public power and religious bodies, notably the churches.

In this chapter, we shall focus principally on how the pursuit of religious interests relates to questions of EU governance, with only passing attention paid to the question of identity.[1] The project of European governance rests on a partnership between political institutions and civil society in which – certainly in the view of the European Commission – the public sphere is supposed to be a major engine of integration.

Religion – despite having undergone profound changes and despite its supposed decline – still has a noteworthy place in social, political and private life in Europe. The European constitutional process relaunched the debate over the legitimation – and indeed the nature – of the EU (Eriksen et al. 2004). That is because it has posed questions about the very foundations of the political community, mobilising lobbying activity in some sectors and a plethora of communications about EU matters. The religious dimension has warranted attention on two grounds. First, the controversy about whether or not to make reference to Europe's Christian heritage in the Preamble to the Constitutional Treaty; and second, whether or not the churches should enjoy particular recognition as interlocutors with the EU institutions in virtue of their specific contribution to governance – an issue eventually addressed in the provisions of Article 52 of the Constitutional Treaty (Schlesinger and Foret 2006: 69).

Acting as members of a potentially transnational epistemic community of believers, religious organisations deliberate and lobby to shape public policy. As purveyors of faith and a sense of belonging, these organisations and their followers bring religious discourse into wider political debate. We therefore address religions first, as constituting a particular public sphere, and second, as a component part of a general European public sphere.

We focus on the organisation of the religious field at the European level in response to the opportunity for intervention opened up by the debate over the Constitutional Treaty, from the declaration of Nice on the future of the EU to the French and Dutch referenda and their aftermaths (2000–2006). We treat this as an exemplary moment that revealed the balance of forces in play. Our approach to religion is to ask how it works rather than what it is (Wallis and Bruce 1992: 10–11). Our principal focus – for reasons that will become obvious – has been the churches, and among them, the Roman Catholic church, by far the best organised and most prominent force in the religious field.

Religions as a particular public sphere

Religions may be analysed as constituting a particular public sphere in the EU. This involves focusing on a set of actors, institutional structures, networks and systems of representation which, taken together, constitute a space of deliberation about, interaction with, and means of addressing the holders of political power.

Christian influences have been one of the original elements of the founding ideology of the European project. Guy Hermet (2004: 164) has noted that the notion of 'civil society' was exhumed from Hegelian thought and reactivated in John Paul II's Poland during the 1980s to designate the Catholic 'counter-public sphere' that opposed the Communist regime. This mobilisation of social forces under the banner of liberty was rapidly emulated and frequently referred to.

Rather more directly, social Catholicism was an inspiration to a number of the founding fathers of the European Community, providing them with intellectual and organisational resources that can be traced in the evolving structures and concepts of European integration. As Holmes (2000: 47–8) has shown, social Catholicism offered a certain conception of federalism, articulated around the pivotal notion of 'subsidiarity'. From this perspective, man can only perfect himself *within society*. The state is there to help him live and to accomplish his social task. However, the help provided by the state needs to remain indirect: above all, it needs to create conditions that allow individuals to fulfil their needs. To create suitable conditions for the full flowering of the person is to pursue the mission of the 'common good'. Social Catholicism doubly defines the state's action: it both legitimises it and at the same time strictly limits it. The state's aim should be to sustain the interdependence of individuals and social groups so that mutual assistance and services might be supplied without obstacle. Social Catholicism implies the active, autonomous engagement of all, without impediment by the state. That is the meaning of subsidiarity: it acts as a barrier to state action, with the state limiting itself to undertaking only what is necessary.

Although religion, especially Roman Catholicism, has been a major source of inspiration for the European project, the involvement of religious actors often resulted from requests made by the political institutions themselves. It is actually those in political power – those on whom limitations are supposed to be imposed – who have instigated the involvement of the churches and other religious bodies, sometimes needing to overcome their unwillingness to be involved, as the former President of the European Commission, Jacques Delors, reported in his *Mémoires* (2004). Here he recounted how difficult it was for him to establish a dialogue with the churches in Brussels. Some had no representation, and this therefore had to be established. Others – for diplomatic reasons – were very circumspect. The Roman Catholic church, represented by the Papal Nuncio, was already located in an intergovernmental framework. Delors, however, preferred to work with the Catholic body, the Commission of the Bishops' Conferences of the European Community (COMECE), which he considered to be somewhat better informed about how Brussels operated. It took almost a decade for resistance to be overcome and for a form of dual representation by COMECE and the Nuncio to be installed and the first exchanges to begin (Delors 2004: 330–2).

Other factors propelled the initially timorous religious actors into taking on an active role inside the Union. According to Massignon (2005), Christian institutions have become progressively aware of the issues involved in European integration. Initially, the Council of Europe seemed to be the institution favoured by the churches as it was more in tune with their concerns (human rights, education, bio-ethics, social questions and so forth). By contrast, European integration referred much more to economic and technological matters. For the Protestant churches, the European Community also smacked of being a 'Vatican Europe', with a strong suspicion of Catholic manipulation behind the scenes. Furthermore, beyond the 'little' Europe of the European Economic Community (EEC) was the 'greater' Europe, and the aim was also to transcend the existing pattern of the Cold War by working at east–west reconciliation. Nor may we ignore the importance of initiatives taken by individuals and groups, either outside the Church hierarchies or at middle-ranking levels. The first Christian organisations of European scope were developed by European civil servants on the Protestant side and by religious orders on the Catholic. In the Roman Catholic camp, the Vatican exercised primacy over matters of representation. However, changes in doctrine after Vatican II promoted more collegiality inside the Church and opened the door to greater autonomy for COMECE, which set up an 'antenna' in Brussels at the start of the 1980s and began to have a growing role. This went hand in hand with the evolving perception that European construction, now an increasingly ramifying political enterprise, was raising questions not only about inter-state relations (the Vatican's domain) but also about relations between different societies (Massignon 2005). So far as the debate over European integration was concerned, Christian strategies were influenced by confessional interests, by internal change inside the churches and by the political calendar. On the whole, the role of the churches was more reactive than proactive.

The growth of religious lobbying has been an outcome of the growing opportunities for participation offered by the European institutions. It is also a result of the diversification of the interests represented in Brussels, differentiation on a national and confessional basis and distinctive strategies and goals. This is part of a general trend towards the specialisation and institutionalisation of interest groups.

The really decisive step in the recognition of the churches came with the Delors presidency. The creation of the organisation 'A Soul for Europe' in 1994 demonstrated this. Its origins lay in an initiative launched by Jacques Delors to 'give Europe a soul' by conferring a spiritual dimension on the integration process, without which – according to the then President of the European Commission – the EU would be condemned to fail.[2] The project took off just as the Single Market project and the mobilising effects of '1992' were losing momentum. The faith communities (which included humanism) were invited to reinforce their dialogue with the European institutions and to suggest various projects such as seminars and meetings financed by the Commission to emphasise the ethical and spiritual dimensions of European construction.

While it was Delors' personal initiative, A Soul for Europe was obliged to fit in with the vagaries of subsequent Commission presidents. The Santer Commission kept the same set-up, but it worked less vigorously. The Prodi Commission wanted to engage in modest reform. The initiative, A Soul for Europe – now, significantly, at the request of the Commission transformed into an Association with its own autonomous articles – was still recognised as a partner of the Commission and benefited from financial support. However, its relationship had become more distant than in Delors' time.[3] There was an increased focus on meeting the short-term demands of the political agenda, it would appear, at the expense of seeking to enhance the EU's spiritual dimension. Ultimately, A Soul for Europe went into a slow decline because of its inability to extricate itself from what proved to be two contradictory goals – pursuing political dialogue between actors on the Brussels scene and engaging in communication with the general public, a classic dilemma in the EU's attempts at legitimation (Foret 2001). It was the requirement to separate these two tasks from one another, under the pressure of the European Parliament, which led to the Association's dissolution in early 2005.[4]

A Soul for Europe's decade or so of life (1994–2005) demonstrates the extent to which a particular European public sphere can be structured by establishing a distinct public linked to the centre of the political system. While the organisation itself changed, the range of practices and actors it gathered together was there for the long term. The new Association was defined in its statutes as an ecumenical space where religions could meet one another. Syncretism and proselytising were off the agenda. This was one way for religious interest groups – as the Commission's interlocutors – to benefit from an initial level of institutionalisation.

Such an opening was in keeping with a longstanding claim to recognition by the Roman Catholic church. Vatican diplomacy sought to advance further the institutionalisation of a partnership between the churches and the European institutions at the start of the negotiations over the Amsterdam Treaty (1997); however, France and Belgium opposed this. In his post-synodal apostolic exhortation, *Ecclesia in Europa* (2003), Pope John Paul II reaffirmed a position worked out throughout his pontificate. The intention was to gain specific recognition for the church by having religious representatives present at the heart of the institutions.

> The presence of Christians, properly trained and competent, is needed in the various levels of European agencies and institutions in order to contribute – with due respect for the correct dynamics of democracy and through an exchange of proposals – to the shaping of a European order which is increasingly respectful of every man and woman, and thus in accordance with the common good.
>
> (John Paul II 2003: 46)

The late Pope held back from fundamentally challenging the relations between religion and politics, but he did agitate for a flexible definition of the respective domains of the spiritual and the temporal: 'In her relations with the public authorities, the Church is not calling for a return to the confessional state. She likewise deplores every type of ideological secularism or a hostile separation between civil institutions and religious confessions' (ibid.). Since his enthronement in April 2005, Pope Benedict XVI has taken positions in line with those of his predecessor.

The Roman Catholic church's lobbying, supported by the Protestant churches of the Conference of European Churches (CEC), had already resulted in the recognition of the 'specific contribution' of the Churches and other religious communities in the White Paper on European Governance (European Commission 2001a: 17). The issue was a topic of lively debate inside the Convention on the Future of Europe (2002–2003). Many *conventionnels* questioned the idea of a particular dialogue with the churches, suggesting that instead it should be handled within the framework of a general dialogue with civil society. Article 52 of the Constitutional Treaty addressed the churches' claims (De Poncins 2003: 218–20). But precisely which bodies were to benefit from the 'open, transparent and regular dialogue' foreseen in the text? A clause stipulating that to be selected for such dialogue it was necessary to respect the EU's common values was set aside on the grounds that the Union had no competence to determine the status of churches and religions (ibid.: 220). Religious recognition is based on national criteria, with the grounds for eligibility differing from state to state. The list of Commission's interlocutors is published on the web. All organisations recognised as churches, religious communities or communities of belief in member states are considered to be potential partners. This includes the Church of Scientology, whose status as a religion is widely questioned in many member states.

The recognition of religious interests as constituting a particular public and the entry into the European public sphere by religious actors have been largely conditioned by the EU's institutional demands. The function of the churches is deliberative. If there is an exchange relation between the Commission and the religious lobbies, that exchange is highly asymmetrical. Churches and other faith communities have been approached by the Commission in the course of consultation procedures aimed at sharing information between the parties. Religious bodies benefit from

EU finances while, in return, being required to participate in the legitimation of European construction. The formalisation of dialogue under the terms of the Constitutional Treaty – should this ever come into effect – will, at the margins, reinforce continuous deliberation. However, this would not mean that the churches thereby become actors directly accountable for decision-making.

No level-playing field

Although the religious lobbies are numerous and diverse, having unequal resources at their disposal, they do not have equality of access to key decision makers. Sixty-seven groups are listed as the Commission's official 'dialogue partners'.[5] A political adviser to the President of the Commission said that he had been in contact with some 150 faith communities, of which around 50 had some kind of representation in Brussels.[6]

The Roman Catholic church is by far the most highly geared actor with the greatest investment in European affairs. The Papal Nuncio and the Order of Malta are the only offices accorded legal recognition in virtue of an international treaty with the Commission. As at the United Nations (UN), the Vatican's status as a state gives it a strategic advantage over other religions because, uniquely, it has diplomatic relations. There is also other Roman Catholic representation. For instance, the Jesuits alone have four separate offices. The linchpin of Catholic relations with the European institutions is COMECE, which is the voice of the national church hierarchies acting in liaison with Rome.

The Protestant churches' link with the Commission is mainly through the Church and Society Committee of the CEC. Although the Protestants are in the majority in this body, they take account of others' views, such as the Orthodox churches. This means that their lobbying is always constrained by the need to consult. The third major force is that of the humanists. The European Humanist Federation (EHF) brings together a wide range of lay organisations. Its heterogeneity, however, does not prevent it from taking strongly articulated positions in European debates, its unity deriving above all from its opposition to the churches.

Other interlocutors of the Commission are less structured and proactive. The Orthodox churches are split between the CEC and the Office of the Orthodox Church, and often air their divisions. The Jewish community makes its voice heard mainly through the Conference of European Rabbis (CER). However, this body was relatively uninvolved in A Soul for Europe and appears more concerned with its own internal debates than those outside.[7] The rabbis did not make a submission to the Constitutional Convention. Nor indeed did the Muslim Council for Cooperation in Europe, whose seat is in Strasbourg rather than Brussels, and which has not taken on the role of representing a religion so far little engaged in politics at the EU level.

The field of religious interests in Brussels, therefore, is one in which Roman Catholics predominate, with – to a significantly lesser extent – a Protestant presence. Humanists make their presence felt in opposition to the churches and the other faith communities are still very much on the margins. This was basically the scenario during the debates on whether or not reference should be made to the Christian heritage of Europe in the Preamble to the Constitutional Treaty and also regarding Article 52 of the Treaty, which focused on the participation of the churches in the EU institutions. An alliance between COMECE and CEC confronted the EHF. This is not an open pluralistic setting: positions once secured in a field of political struggle tend to be enduring.[8]

Talking to the institutions

Although there are diverse relations with all the institutions, those with the Commission predominate. Inside the Commission, the political adviser in charge of relations with the faith communities – a post openly described as a 'one-man show' – plays a pivotal role.[9] The Directorate-General for Education and Culture is the other point of contact with religious actors, making efforts to develop dialogue by financing conferences that bring together different components of civil society.

The European Parliament has a traditional role as a source of information and an access point for interest groups, even if it has for long been considered less powerful than the Commission. The European People's Party (EPP) is active in the pursuit of Christian interests, as shown by its efforts to secure a reference to the European Christian heritage in the Constitutional Treaty.[10] However, for religions with fewer resources, the outcome of lobbying the Parliament is full of uncertainties. In a multi-centred institution, they might find a representative ready to be their spokesperson if the Commission is not accessible or responsive; but the result of making representations is open to question, considering that the assembly is diffuse and has relatively little formal competence in the field of religious interests.

By contrast, the European Council, the Council of Ministers and, above all, the member states that compose the EU remain prime targets for the faith communities. The principle of subsidiarity keeps the regulation of religious affairs at the national level. Most interest representation is by national actors at the national rather than at the European level. Religions have won the right to meet each new EU presidency when it takes office to discuss its programme and to make their positions heard. Moreover, the Vatican still pursues its own separate intergovernmental policy. Finally, the Economic and Social Committee (ESC) is restricted to its habitual role as a source of information and of anticipating the Commission's attitudes. The churches do not see the ESC as a way of influencing the EU's decision-making process. It is, nonetheless, identified by some in the humanist camp as a potential alternative space for consultation and specifically for institutionalising dialogue with the churches. For the humanists, the issue is one of treating religious bodies in the same way as the generality of civil society organisations, thereby denying their claim to special treatment. The ESC is regarded as potentially useful to that end.[11]

The religious lobbies in Brussels therefore operate within an imperfectly pluralistic system. They reflect the overall logic of the EU's political framework, pluralism (in its various guises) being the most relevant model for interpreting interest representation in Brussels in most areas of public activity (Ayberk and Schenker 1998; Grossman and Saurugger 2006: 215). In this regard, there is nothing peculiar to the workings of the religious field. The need to be represented in Brussels tends to homogenise organisational structures because playing the European game implies adopting similar strategies of professionalisation, specialisation and acquiring a reactive capability, all of which require a certain measure of autonomy in dealing both with national and international centres of decision-making. Nevertheless, lobbying generally originates at the national level, is then coordinated at the European level, and in some cases it might involve an interfaith dimension.

The churches operate in Brussels in part because they are concerned to ensure that the positions achieved at a national level are not prejudiced by political developments at the supranational level. This can be interpreted as defensive lobbying that favours the status quo. Transnational alliances may occur on a case-by-case basis. The mobilisation over the reference to Christianity in the Constitutional Treaty was a particularly good illustration of this, as is the more general issue of the status of the churches in the EU. Such alliances are flexible and do not guarantee the development of either solidarity or a lasting modus vivendi between those concerned. For the most part, interfaith initiatives have been undertaken at the behest of the Commission and their social impact is open to question.

The construction of representative religious bodies at the European level remains incomplete. In many respects, this is because of the incomplete nature of the European public sphere itself.[12] The religious field is rather weakly institutionalised at the European level, because the EU does not have an executive that can exercise authority in the religious field. While the Union may have developed its relations with churches and other faith bodies because of their competence in social and ethical matters, that does not mean there can be an overall policy on religion. The competence to regulate spiritual affairs remains subsidiary and lies in the hands of the member states. However, European legal requirements cannot be ignored. In fact, the development of European norms lies in part outside the EU itself, with the European Court of Human Rights. In 1993, for instance, Greece was condemned for a breach of the European Convention on Human Rights. The case concerned a Jehovah's Witness who had been convicted for proselytising, an activity forbidden by the

Greek Constitution. Furthermore, before the provision was abolished in 1997, the European Parliament had reminded the Greek authorities that their requirement to state one's religion on the Greek identity card was unacceptable in Community law (Willaime 2004: 109). On delicate matters like the regulation of religious symbols in schools, the European Court of Human Rights is also to be taken into account, even if its jurisprudence is very cautious and case-driven in the absence of a shared basis in legal norms (Bribosia and Rorive 2004).

To summarise, as a particular public sphere in the EU, the religious field remains rather weakly institutionalised, unequally structured in terms of the resources available to different actors, and does not as yet constitute a major space for deliberation.

Religions in the general European public sphere

Above, we have considered whether or not a *particular* public sphere, focused on religious interests, has emerged. In what follows, we deal with the question of whether religions are able to insert themselves into a *general* European public sphere in terms of the audiences addressed, the discourses offered, the roles played and the legitimacy claimed.

First, our analysis shows how the debate on spiritual issues primarily takes place in national discursive spaces rather than in a unified European public sphere. Next, we illustrate how churches define their mission in the framework of European integration, their conception of their social and political role and its compatibility with the rules of representative democracy. Finally, the study of the principles enunciated by religious actors to justify their claims – here, we take the Roman Catholic church as our case – casts light on the workings of a potential European public sphere, above all concerning the questions of the rationality and universality of exchanges.

Weak Europeanisation: national publics and debates

The relations between state and church depend greatly on how these have evolved historically in each national context (Madeley and Enyedi 2003). The contemporary place of religion often remains a matter of controversy. Two key issues are the relations between spiritual and political power on the one hand, and the inter-relations between different faiths on the other.

France, the traditional terrain for battles between convinced lay interests and the Catholic 'counter-state', has experienced recurrent controversies in the field of schooling (Deloye and Ihl 2000). The role of religion during François Mitterand's funeral in 1996 (Julliard 1999) and the haste with which the authorities decided to fly the flag at half-mast when Pope John Paul II died in April 2005 caused a certain stir. Other European countries, in their different ways, have held the same kinds of debate. In Spain, following the national funerals of victims of the 11 March 2004 bombings, representatives of the Protestant, Jewish, Muslim and Adventist communities expressed their concern at the exclusively Roman Catholic ceremony. They proposed holding an ecumenical ceremony in a civic space that would also take account of the sensibilities of atheists and agnostics. The stances taken by the Spanish Catholic Church and the Vatican against the Zapatero government on subjects such as homosexual marriage and religious education have also caused serious waves. Fierce debates occurred in Italy over abortion, in vitro fertilisation and the recognition of homosexual partnerships during the run-up to the 2006 general elections. In the UK, well before the 7 July 2005 bombings, which sharpened debate about who does and who does not belong to British society, a former Archbishop of Canterbury (the leading cleric in the Church of England) characterised Islam as a religion that had long and ubiquitous associations with violence and also remarked that no major inventions had come from the Muslim world for several centuries. For the British Muslim community, this denunciation showed a lack of respect for its beliefs and raised questions about its place in British society. Subsequent events – notably the alleged plot to blow up transatlantic passenger flights in August 2006 – have kept the relation between sections of the Muslim community and terrorism a matter of heated debate. In Germany, at the start of 2006, the Land of Baden-Würtemberg introduced a controversial questionnaire that aimed to evaluate the attachment to democratic values of Muslim candidates for German citizenship. In Denmark, the publication in September 2005 of cartoons of the prophet Mohammed by the country's largest-selling daily newspaper *Jyllands-Posten* eventually provoked a huge wave of reaction in January and February 2006 by Muslims throughout Europe and in the Muslim world. The furore over the cartoons achieved the status of a trans-European agenda item, although political reactions in the different states were not uniform. More generally, the wearing of various kinds of head cover by women and the place of other signifiers of religious orientation in the public domain was also widely debated (Lorcerie 2005).

However, while the issues might well be common, the construction of agendas and how these are handled is mostly governed by the particular rules of the game in each national polity. The picture is one of a constellation of national public spheres that occasionally interconnect when some major event is taken up and news crosses the boundaries and seizes widespread attention. The election of Pope Benedict XVI in April 2005 was such an instance.

The same national framing comes into play where religious matters directly connected to European integration are at stake, as was clearly demonstrated during the constitutional process, which did not alter the routine ways in which the debate was publicised. The question of including a reference to the Christian heritage of Europe in the Preamble to the Constitutional Treaty did gain at least some media attention but in ways closely linked to domestic politics. The issue did not become a major campaigning matter during the European Parliament elections in June 2004, except in Poland.

Initiatives were taken to try and build a movement at the level of the EU, but without great success. A group of Members of the European Parliament (MEPs), with Elizabeth Montfort, a French member of the EPP to the fore, launched a petition that aimed to collect one million citizens' signatures in support of recognising the Christian heritage of Europe (*Le Monde*, 13 December 2003). In February 2004, Montfort claimed to have gathered some 700,000 signatures, without counting the support of organisations allegedly representing some 40 million citizens.[13] She maintained that her action contributed to keeping the issue on the political agenda against the wishes of several member states, and that this constituted a kind of victory. The promoters said they were convinced they had raised awareness of the spiritual dimension of integration, establishing a basis for future mobilisation. However, according to our research, key actors in the debate on religion in Brussels (civil servants, politicians and church representatives) were often unaware of the petition's existence. Media coverage was minimal. And in the end, the political decision taken did not go in the desired direction. The case of the petition illustrates rather well the limitations on Europe-wide communicative strategies, whether concerning religious or other matters, and the difficulty of attracting widespread attention for a 'European' cause.

Between mediator and guardian

If religion as a topic has had little impact on the development of a Europe-wide debate, what then is the role of the churches? They lay claim to a mission that gives them a special political status and is not limited to organising the daily round of worship, pastoral care and the like. Of all the churches, the Roman Catholic has the most ambitious and fully worked-out discourse on the matter and is therefore the focus of our discussion. It aims to exercise a mediating role between the private and the public; between the social and the political; between different social forces; between Europe and the rest of the world.

The way in which the Roman Catholic Church's mission has been developed by COMECE in Brussels illustrates the positioning strategy involved. Its discourse synthesises long-term reflection by the national religious communities, both independently of the Vatican and at the same time in interaction with it, reacting to developments in the constitutional process and to the day-to-day workings of the EU. By means of this discourse, the Roman Catholic church has demonstrated that it wishes to be a wide-ranging actor, offering views on subjects as varied as the Lisbon strategy or family policy.[14] Properly understood, this is a political approach, albeit a somewhat indirect one.[15] Faith is there to illuminate and nourish individual and collective Christian political engagement, be it that of believers or of those simply concerned to recognise themselves as the inheritors of a tradition. This gives the church a justification for intervening in public debate, without entering the ungodly territory of political power; at the same time, it is not constrained from intervening in whatever domain may be required, thus laying claim to the full gamut of its liberties, its specific role in relation to individuals, to the faith community and to society.[16]

In this way, the Roman Catholic church has assumed the role of a medium between the private sphere – claimed as territory beyond the reach of political power – and the public domain. This articulation between the public and the private, the individual and the collective, locates it as the linchpin of social and political life. Although a major interlocutor inside the EU, the Church also wants to be a partner in Europe's external relations. COMECE underlines its role in interceding with the rest of the world. For instance, it took part in the stabilisation of the Balkans by working for reconciliation, the strengthening of civil society and the primacy of legality. It also intervened over the creation of development policies to favour the needs of the south.[17]

By its self-definition of what should be the church's role in public and political space, the Roman Catholic lobby demonstrates what motivates its claim to special status in the constitutional framework in the name of offering a 'specific contribution' to governance. This is part of a developing strategy for making use of participatory democracy and action within civil society to impose some limits on the scope of political power. A special status is claimed within the general public sphere by calling for an institutionalised place for the churches in the decision-making process. So while the ideal of a European public sphere is being promoted, it derives from the pursuit of a specific interest.

Conflicts of legitimacy and regulation of a European public sphere

The churches' participation in the practice of good governance proposed by the European institutions is challenged by their detractors, who criticise them for damaging the universalistic and rationalistic principles that are supposed to underpin the EU's model of procedural democracy.

The religious organisations offer three main grounds for their legitimacy: their expertise, their place in a representative democracy and their normative authority. The churches, first and foremost the Roman Catholics, invoke their 'expertise in humanity', according to Pope Paul VI's famous phrase, uttered at the UN in 1965 (Kalinowski 2002). COMECE follows the same line when it makes reference to the churches' unique contribution which underpins their claim to 'co-manage the social': 'religions propose an orientation towards, and answers to, the fundamental question of the meaning of life. They therefore have the potential to innovate in society and in governance'.[18] Accordingly, to be deprived of the unequalled knowledge of the churches would be a 'technical error'. Even worse, it would cause a democratic deficit because the religious institutions are – in their own eyes – guarantors of liberty as *intermediary bodies* positioned between the authorities and the citizen. COMECE has underlined the importance of having respect for such groups, to which the citizen may freely choose to belong. It is seen as a corrective to what is seen as the excessively individualistic approach taken in the Charter of Fundamental Rights (2000). Ignoring the churches would also be a loss to democracy because – in their view – they are highly *representative* non-governmental organisations (NGOs). This is what John Paul II propounded in *Ecclesia in Europa*:

> Churches and Ecclesial Communities and other religious organizations [...] where these already existed before the foundation of European nations, they cannot be reduced to merely private entities but act with a specific institutional import which merits being given serious consideration. In carrying out their functions the various national and European institutions should act in the awareness that their juridical systems will be fully respectful of democracy if they provide for *forms of 'healthy collaboration'* with Churches and religious organizations.
>
> (John Paul II 2003: 45)

In its contribution to the Convention, COMECE pursued the same logic:

> For citizens to identify with the values of the European Union and to show that political power is not absolute, the secretariat of COMECE suggests that a constitutional text recognise the openness and the ultimate otherness that is linked to the name of God. An inclusive reference to transcendence is at the same time a guarantee for the liberty of the human person.[19]

This strategy conforms closely to analyses of the window of opportunity opened up to religions by the present crisis of the major political ideologies. In this connection, Jean-Pierre Willaime (2004) has argued that the crumbling away of the myth of scientific reason has tended to undermine the mobilising utopianism of ideas of economic and technological progress. Religions, therefore, constitute a resource against the emptying-out of a democratic order that is undermining its own foundations. 'Ultra-modernity' – to use his term – pushes the primacy of the individual to an extreme, eventually leaving him isolated, powerless and defenceless in the face of an overbearing state. Ultramodernity signifies the apogee of reflexivity, the generalisation of doubt in all institutions and beliefs, a scepticism that ends by eroding all worldviews and thus by effacing the cleavages that produce the very debates that are indispensable to the good functioning of democracy. From this relativism emerge human rights, which are treated as the ultimate in sacredness. However, Willaime argues that the normative content of human rights has become so consensual, routine and bureaucratic that it has lost its substance. The state, which has to manage the human-rights agenda, is assailed by demands and claims coming from particular interests, and does not have the necessary authority to arbitrate between them. This is what leads those in political power to seek the support of the overarching ethical visions provided by religions, as these may help to entrench the state's legitimacy and support its decisions.

According to this analysis, the churches are gaining a new position in the public sphere, alongside the state, in the management of the collective imaginary in a pluralistic society. They are charged with contributing to shaping the ethical content of political debate and with encouraging engagement in deliberation. This is precisely the approach taken by COMECE in appealing to Roman Catholics to exercise fully their responsibility as citizens, in ways complementary to their identities as believers.[20]

The Roman Catholic church's rhetoric, therefore, draws a fine distinction between a full and complete acceptance of the democratic rules and an affirmation that not everything can be subordinated to the politico-legal domain; there are superior norms that may simultaneously both guarantee and relativise politics. There is but a tenuous boundary between simply being part of the public sphere while, in principle, respecting the idea of a neutral exchange and the equality of other participants, and that of making a claim based in the specificity of one's religious tradition or in a transcendent view of reality.

The perceived propensity of religious actors to set themselves apart from common norms has drawn criticisms. These derive from defenders of a lay worldview that rejects any special status for religions; it also comes from some movements of believers disenchanted with what they see as the overbearing role of religious hierarchies. The counter-arguments are focused on the churches' diverse articulations of their legitimacy and, in particular, reject any special claim to 'expertise in humanity', seeing the normative authority of the church as standing in contradiction to democratic values.

The arguments developed by the EHF are a good instance of such criticism. This organisation, at the head of movements defending a strictly lay approach, was very active during the constitutional process, taking part in the consultations organised by the Constitutional Convention and the European Commission as well as giving its views to the media. The churches were held not to be socially representative, given the fall in church attendance. Moreover, it was argued that their claim to address their message of transcendent values to the generality was, in reality, based on their address to limited groups of believers.[21] Thus, according to the EHF's secretary-general, they should not be considered to be more than 'sectoral NGOs' and ought not to be distinguished from the rest of civil society in consultations.[22] Criticism also came from within the Christian world, from believers protesting against the usurpation of a wider Christian representation by the traditional church hierarchies.[23]

Such debates about whose authority and whose word should prevail inside the religious world reflects an often virulent debate over values. The legitimacy of the Roman Catholic church in setting norms has been particularly subject to attack. On issues such as abortion, euthanasia, sexual freedom, women's rights and so forth, Catholic doctrine has been presented as contrary to the values behind European integration. For those such as the EHF, who believe that the system of deliberation should be neutral, the very presence of religious bodies in the public sphere is deemed to be unacceptable. The establishment of a privileged partnership between the political institutions and the churches is seen as an instance of the 'danger of the political will to give a meaning to things and to define a collective spirituality'.[24] From this point of view, the artificial restoration of an obsolete moral authority would contradict the emancipatory vision of civil society carried forward by the European project of a participatory democracy. Moreover, so it has been argued, there is a danger in ignoring the rifts produced in the past by the idea of a religious identity, an idea that it would be sensible to renounce and whose use the churches should themselves be asked to proscribe.[25]

Conclusion

National and confessional divisions still dominate the world of religious actors in Europe. At the same time, there is now a significant tendency to reinforce their communicative activities and strategies at the European level. If we think of the religious field as constituting an emergent *particular* European public sphere, it is one in which deliberation and lobbying rather than actual decision-making are the order of the day. In seeking to influence decisions about their own influence and the spiritual dimension of the EU, Christian bodies – and notably the Roman Catholic church – are increasingly linked into the EU's institutional world. However, this is a fissiparous institutionalisation and religious bodies constitute a relatively *weak* public.

Nonetheless, religious discourse does remain controversial because of its potential challenge to a conception of a general public sphere rooted in universality and rationality. The churches' activities to date have not greatly enlarged the social basis of the debate on European integration or indeed its media audience. To the extent that they are present in such debate, this is still largely governed by the constraints of national political systems. While the churches' conversion from transcendent authorities into bodies exercising a traditional and moral influence has been quite effective inside the EU framework, it does continue to arouse fierce resistance in some quarters.

In the field of conflict over values at the European level, the opposition between secular and religious positions is akin to that which has shaped national debates and histories. A key difference, however, is that now the divisions are no longer between church and state but rather traverse civil society.

Indeed, the EU and the religious institutions are in a relationship that is more cooperative than antagonistic. But the present expedient solidarity may be read in a variety of ways. First of all, at least in part, it is an outcome of Roman Catholic influence on the EU's institutional design and policies, exemplified by the doctrine of subsidiarity and support for civil society. Next, it arises from the respective weaknesses of each party. The EU is hard-pressed by the issue of a 'democratic deficit' whereas the churches and other religions are challenged by changes in the nature of belief. Both, therefore, have to cope with the need to build up their social constituencies. The ideology and practice of good governance tend to circumscribe the scope of the political, in effect creating reduced spaces of pluralism and publicness, underplaying normative debate to avoid fundamental conflicts of purpose.

This strategy is particularly well adapted for both EU and religious institutions whose legitimacy rests on shaky ground and whose acceptance by the generality of citizens remains far from settled. It is an alternative to mobilising general publics – which could destabilise the precarious balance of the EU's political architecture.

The question of religion, then, offers a particularly instructive insight into the as-yet-incomplete nature of the European public sphere. Ulrich Beck (1992) has pertinently noted how – having swept aside other systems of belief – science is now subject to its own crisis of legitimacy, once again opening the door to the irrational. It is clear that reason alone is not enough to secure legitimacy for the emergent European polity, whose regulatory model lacks the capacity to produce solidarity and cohesion. A touch of faith alongside technocratic reason therefore comes in handy. But can religious influences help bring coherence to the European space? This is doubtful, even in a closed pluralistic contest for attention, since – whatever its practice and professions of interfaith goodwill – in the end, each faith makes claims to have access to an absolute truth. Religious mobilisation in Europe is by no means limited to Christianity alone.

Notes

1 That is not because we minimise its importance. We have already dealt with the issue elsewhere (Schlesinger and Foret 2006).
2 *Rapport d'Activite d'Une Ame pour l'Europe*, 2003. The name is drawn from a speech by Jacques Delors to the churches in Brussels, 14 April 1992.

3 Its position worsened by degrees, with increasing distance being taken by the Commission, according to our sources.

4 Interview with Johannes Laitenberger, member of President Barroso's cabinet, Brussels, 14 June 2005.

5 The list is available at ec.europa.eu/dgs/policy_advisers/activities/dialogues _religions/docs/list_of_dialogue_partners_fr.pdf (accessed 31 August 2006).

6 Interview with Michael Weninger, Brussels, 30 March 2005.

7 Interview with Win Burton, coordinator of the A Soul for Europe Association, Brussels, 19 November 2003. The political shortcomings have been increasingly recognised by the European Jewish Congress (EJC), which is particularly concerned about mounting anti-Semitism in Europe, as well as anti-Israel policies and sentiments, and has increased its lobbying and monitoring. Information from Pierre Besnainou, EJC President, Glasgow, 16 March 2006. The emergence of other Jewish bodies may be noted. For example, the European Rabbinic Center, a representative body of the Lubavitch movement, is increasingly challenging the CER and the EJC.

8 Having reached similar conclusions, Massignon (2002: 30–1) refers to a closed pluralism, which makes reference to the preferential relations that exist between European states and particular religions, notably the national churches. This is by contrast to the open pluralism of the USA where all religions are formally equal before the law.

9 Interview with Michael Weninger, Brussels, 18 November 2003.

10 The president of the EPP, Wilfried Martens, revived the debate in March 2006 by calling on his political allies 'to re-launch the efforts to get God back into the constitution'. Lucia Kubosova, 'Centre-right EPP revives EU Constitution God debate', *EUobserver*, 29 March 2006.

11 Interview with Georges Liénard, General Secretary of the European Humanist Federation, Brussels, 20 November 2003.

12 For pertinent discussions, see Dacheux 2003; Foret and Soulez 2004; Mercier 2003.

13 Telephone interview with Elizabeth Montfort, Member of the EPP in the European Parliament, 10 February 2004.

14 See the publications 'Strengthening the European Social Model – Ideas for a Renewed Lisbon Strategy of the European Union', 11 March 2005, and 'A Plea for a European Strategy in favour of families', Autumn Plenary, Brussels, 16–18 November 2005, both available at COMECE's website www.comece.org (accessed 31 August 2006).

15 'The Evolution of the European Union and the Responsibility of Catholics', Brussels, 9 May 2005, p. 14, available at www.comece.org/upload/pdf/ evo_cath_EN_050509.pdf (accessed 31 August 2006).

16 Ibid., pp. 41–7.

17 See COMECE's press release 'President Barroso and COMECE Bishops Committed to Unity in Diversity in the European Union', Brussels, 11 March 2005, available at www.comece.org/comece.taf?_function=news_archive&_sub=&id= 25&language=en (accessed 31 August 2006).

18 COMECE, 'Contribution de la COMECE au débat sur l'Avenir de l'union européenne dans la Convention européenne', 21 May 2002, paragraphs 12–15, available at www.comece.org/upload/pdf/secr_conv1_020521_fr.pdf (accessed 31 August 2006). (Authors' translation.)

19 Ibid.

20 COMECE, supra note 15, at p. 41.

21 'Valeurs, Etat de droite – Société civile – Science et société – Rôle du secteur public', submission by the EHF to the White Paper on European Governance, March 2002, pp. 4–5, available at www.humanism.be/in/doc/pdfs/ whitepaper-fr.pdf (accessed 31 August 2006).

22 Liénard, supra note 11.
23 See the report by Catholics for a Free Choice, 'Preserving Power and Privilege – the Vatican's Agenda at the European Union', Washington, DC, 2003, available at www.catholicsforchoice.org/topics/reform/documents/2003 preservingpowerandprivilege.pdf (accessed 31 August 2006).
24 Liénard, supra note 11.
25 EHF, supra note 21, at p. 5. The same line was argued in 'Les Communautés de foi et de conviction et l'Union européenne', a submission to the European Convention, 5 June 2002, available at www.humanism.be/fr/doc/pdfs/conv07-fr-comm%20convict.pdf (accessed 31 August 2006).

11 The public sphere in European constitution-making

John Erik Fossum and Hans-Jörg Trenz

Introduction

When in October 2004 the heads of state and government gathered to put their signature on the treaty establishing a constitution for Europe, often touted as the first constitution for a united Europe, this event was held up as a major milestone in European history. It took place amidst considerable political support. All major political parties had been behind the constitutional project, and major non-governmental organisations (NGOs) and representatives from civil society had expressed their overall satisfaction by acknowledging that the Constitutional Treaty (CT) would improve the social and political rights of European citizens and would enhance civic participation in EU decision-making.[1] Confidence in the success of the constitutional adventure was backed by Eurobarometer opinion polls, which indicated that a substantial majority of the populations of all the member states (with the exception of the UK) was in favour of the Constitutional Treaty.[2]

Nevertheless, subsequent popular responses brought to light what is now referred to as a deep gap between citizens and elites. In their respective national referenda, French and Dutch citizens some seven months later rejected the CT by wide margins and impressed upon their leaders that the CT should effectively be consigned to the proverbial dustbin of history.

Why was the Constitutional Treaty rejected? In some quarters, it was taken for granted that people should approve of a constitutional text whose presumed effect would be to expand their rights and enable them to participate more effectively in decision-making processes at the supranational level. These participants and analysts were perplexed when they found that large portions of the peoples of Europe – maybe even a majority – did not take up the offer or simply did not care. One important way to improve our understanding of the reasons behind people's reactions is to look at the structural determinants of mediation and public communication between European constitution-makers and their diversified constituencies.

In this chapter, we discuss the ratification failure in relation to the

'European public sphere deficit'. Two possible explanations can be discerned from the state of the art of European public sphere research; both relate to the two models of the EU that animate this book. The first explanation posits that constitution-making, in order to be successful, must rely on pre-existing resources of common trust, solidarity and understanding, which are *constitutive* of a shared public sphere. The Union, as a mere regulatory-type structure, does not have it nor can it foster it; hence the requisite trust and solidarity to sustain a constitutional arrangement is absent. The second explanation takes as its point of departure the view that a process of constitution-making which unfolds through public reasoning and debates can have a catalytic function that in turn can *constitute* a shared public sphere, which makes it possible for people across Europe to accept the CT. For the Union to develop into a federal-type entity, such a catalytic spark is necessary (Habermas 2004). From this perspective, the CT was rejected because the process was *not* sufficiently catalytic.

In the following pages, we develop these two state-of-the-art explanations in further detail and briefly assess their adequacy. As explanations of ratification failure, we argue that the first is inaccurate and the second needs supplementing. In response to this, we propose a third possible explanation, which is based on a configuration of the public sphere that better speaks to the distinctive character of the EU. It attributes ratification failure to the manner in which mediatisation affects public communication in the EU. The contingent character of mediatisation carries with it three risks for EU constitution-making: the European constitutional message could be misunderstood; it might not reach its addressees; and it could be openly rejected by the electorate. This third explanation helps underline that the basic question pertaining to the public sphere in Europe is not whether there is a European public sphere, but rather what kind of public sphere there is. The prospect of any future European constitutional endeavour will hinge on how this is navigated through the murky waters of Europe's mediatised spaces of communication.

Constitution-making through stealth?

The first explanation for ratification failure stems from the widely cited notion that the EU has no general public sphere. Instead, in line with the regulatory model outlined in Chapter 1, it is only made up of *particular* or *partial* publics, which cannot effectively establish European popular opinions or forge any reliable process of European will formation. This shortcoming becomes particularly acute during instances of treaty-making and change. The closed nature of treaty-making through the Intergovernmental Conference (IGC) method has given treaty change a strong *self-referential* component (Fossum and Menéndez 2005), which is to be expected from a particular public much of which is located in Brussels and sustained by networks and working groups made up of experts and executives.

Each instance of EU treaty change takes as its point of departure the unresolved problems from the previous instance(s), and seeks to grapple with these in a manner the representatives of the institutions see fit, rather than undertake treaty change in response to popular demands.

This explanation posits that the system organised around IGCs, with roots in interstate diplomacy, has fostered a gradual process of constitutionalisation 'through stealth'. If we look closer at the process of treaty change, we find that much of the work to prepare the treaty is done by officials (Beach 2003). The General Affairs Council, which is made up of the member states' foreign ministers, is politically responsible for the IGC. This body is assisted in its work by the Committee of Permanent Representatives (COREPER), which undertakes the preparatory work. It consists of the member states' permanent representatives in Brussels. The General Secretariat of the Council assists these bodies in their work. The relative weight of experts and national representatives has varied with each IGC, so that in some cases the European Council has merely rubber-stamped the work of the preparatory bodies, while in other cases extensive negotiations have taken place.

These bodies are *not* strong publics. They are closed bodies that deliberate in secret. Their members are institutional participants, and they do not include representatives from civil society. The drafting phase is based on the work of the expert groups and formalised in the European Council, which produces the official text that is submitted for ratification. At such meetings, the heads of government and their supporting staffs meet at various intervals to negotiate the new treaty or treaty changes. This might take one to two years and up to six meetings.

The actual drafting process is also closed. The Council presidency draws up drafts of the treaty amendments, when the process permits. The actual drafting work is undertaken by the Council Secretariat. Beach (2003: 9) notes that 'the Council Secretariat's Legal Services provided sole legal advice to the IGC in the past four IGCs, giving it a monopoly of authoritative legal advice to the IGC'. The final text of the treaty is negotiated at the final European Council meeting, often in marathon sessions. The format of the meeting is such as to permit the heads of state and government to speak freely. But the limited time available, the high political stakes, the expectation of results, the lack of detailed expertise at hand during meetings and the often very comprehensive agenda inject the process with a strong bargaining impetus.

The argument is that the many instances of treaty reform since the early 1980s (Single European Act, Maastricht, Amsterdam and Nice) have unfolded with a similar organisational logic. This system has the European Council as its core body and draws on a much larger system of executives and experts that together undertake treaty reform. This system helps sustain a regulatory-type Union, and one whose undertakings have limited prospects for fostering general European debates and publics. Instead, in this model, the public basically enters the process at the ratification stage, and then as a collection of national publics relating to their respective national officials and positions.

The net effect of this system is to foster juridification largely bereft of democratic control and oversight. This system does little to ameliorate the heterogeneity of the EU multilevel system, and instead helps to sustain cultural pluralism and institutional heterogeneity. The ensuing Byzantine structure is seen to place strong de facto constraints on citizens' participation and involvement. This helps spur opposition, frustration and disenchantment, which are vented on any possible occasion, and notably during national popular referenda. The Union's structure, this argument runs, sustains a strong national imprint on the debate also on issues and questions that concern the European level.

This explanation is problematic on two grounds. For one, it implicitly denies the important *European* dimension to the ratification debate and, importantly, how this dimension helped prompt the rejection of the CT.[3] Further, it understates how the IGC method has gradually become more open and transparent, with stronger inputs by parliaments, both the European Parliament (EP) and national ones.

A depoliticised union with weak catalytic functions?

The second explanation takes as its point of departure that the Union has gradually revised the procedures for constitution-making over time, the single most important indicator of which is the European Convention (2002–2003). To this is added a second component, namely that the Laeken constitution-making process was the first occasion on which the Union's institutions officially declared that the Union was involved in a process of constitution-making. The heightened expectation was that this open and participative process would itself greatly contribute to the forging of a European general public sphere.

The explanation for ratification failure thus refers to the insufficient institutional and procedural design of the Laeken process, which had not been sufficiently developed to launch the public disputes and debates that were needed to promote citizens' involvement and understanding. In short, the pattern of deliberation that the process spurred did not have the presumed public-sphere-generating catalytic effects that some analysts have attributed to democratic constitution-making.[4] In contrast to the first explanation, which conceives of a Union with partial and particular publics only capable of producing treaty changes through stealth, the notion of the public sphere that the constitution-as-catalyst is based on is that of a political community of active citizens, who challenge the legitimacy of existing institutions and styles of policy-making; thus it is akin to the federal model of the Union outlined in Chapter 1. The key to understanding the catalytic function of the public sphere is thus *politicisation* in the sense of mobilising citizens' support or resistance. Habermas notes that:

> this convergence [of Europeans] in turn depends on the catalytic effect of a constitution. This would have to begin with a referendum, arousing a Europe-wide debate – the making of such a constitution representing in itself a unique opportunity of transnational communication, with the potential for a self-fulfilling prophecy.
>
> (Habermas 2004: 27–8)

In these terms, the European public sphere deficit has been linked to the under-politicisation of the EU with the expectation that public mobilisation would follow, once extensive opportunities for the articulation of voice by affected citizens had been created. The predicted end of the permissive consensus after the Maastricht Treaty could be assumed to have helped bring about a situation wherein public silence would be slowly replaced by voice through the official and unofficial channels of the EU.

The EU's post-Maastricht development has had democratic effects: this includes an EU-based institutional arrangement with certain representative qualities; a *material* constitution with basic rights protection; transparency provisions and popular consultative mechanisms; and a kind of intermediary structure of civil and political organisations at the EU level. The Union has also experimented with new modes of participative and consultative governance where citizens and their representatives have been included. Together, these arrangements have increasingly come to bind further steps of integration to the direct or indirect approval of the public.

Nevertheless, some 15 years after the proclaimed 'end of the permissive consensus', Peter Mair (2005) still speaks of the 'remarkable under-politicization' of the EU, which is surprising in light of the high potential for conflict over its reach, its form and its *finalité*. Low turnouts in European parliamentary elections illustrate that there is limited public enthusiasm and probably even a declining interest among European citizens to make use of the European channels for voicing their concerns. Patterns of public opinion and will formation are still very narrow, national media formats treat European issues and debates with marginal and shifting attention, and only a limited number of debates take place in fora that are able to reach ordinary citizens.

But given the strengthened commitment to democracy and the fact that the Laeken constitution-making process was far more open and accessible to the public than any previous constitution-making event in the EU (Fossum and Menéndez 2005), are the *recent* constitutional referenda the beginning of the long expected politicisation of the EU with political parties, general publics and electorates finally turning their attention to Europe? The largely unforeseen protests against the EU and the referenda results in the Netherlands and France are certainly examples of politicisation, albeit belated ones, as they were expressed after the constitutional proposal had been forged, that is, at a point when voice was disconnected from the substantive contents of the decision. But can this be properly considered as *catalytic*?

There was no common European referendum to set off the catalytic spark, which Habermas' notion presupposes. But there were ten national referenda planned. We could modify Habermas' position so as to allow for the catalytic thrust either to emanate from the combined impact of the referenda or from the process preceding this. The point is that when part of a properly set up deliberative constitutional process, referenda are far more than simple 'approval-machines'. The process can be catalytic when referenda follow *after* a comprehensive process that has helped to establish a common focus and common attention to constitutional debates, that is, where the same issues are debated and the same normative arguments are put forward and negotiated throughout the polity. This assumption derives from the rationalising potential of a well-functioning public sphere that mediates vertically and horizontally across different levels and arenas, and promotes a common understanding among European constitution-makers, the national political arenas and the general publics. Such a public sphere must provide opportunities for the proponents and opponents of a European constitution to unfold their arguments that have been previously tested out in policy debates and are now proposed to the general public. It further presupposes a media system as the carrier of rational discourse and a general audience that develops critical capacities to make their choice on the basis of their best knowledge and information. This conception of a catalytic constitution includes structural-institutional components, so that the catalytic impetus is seen as related to the character of the *overall process*, that is, as involving both strong and general publics rather than simply the activation of general publics at the referendum stage.

Why was the process not catalytic?

The Laeken process of constitution-making was structured so as to lend little systemic impetus to polity-wide politicisation. Instead, the process was highly fragmented – with quite diversified national ratification procedures – which encouraged a greatly fragmented process of voice. The wide range of different ratification procedures ended up paying tribute to the fragmented nature of a Union still made up of largely national public spheres. The ideal that there should be a common focus and a shared relevance to the process was undercut by the reality of uneven attention in fragmented constitutional debates in the member states which varied widely in intensity and content. Within this context, the referendum became a singular and quite unique opportunity structure, which helped spark a lively debate in France and the Netherlands in April and May 2005. But this was not automatically carried on to other countries (there had also been far less debate in the Spanish referendum in February 2005). Many of the countries had decided to ratify the constitution by parliamentary vote, which resulted in extraordinary approval rates (between 90 and 99 per cent). Here, all-partisan consensuses in the respective countries[5] emerged, but without larger publics taking much notice. German newspapers, for instance, debated the possible choices of the French people quite intensely, but few debates were launched on what choices the representatives of the German people should make. When it came to the vote in the German Bundestag, the *Süddeutsche Zeitung* was claiming with some plausibility that even many Members of Parliament had limited knowledge of what exactly they voted for.

Long-term catalytic learning processes are dependent on the consistency, the overall resonance and the persistence of the ongoing debates. For the constitutional dimension to figure systematically, the process also has to be framed in explicit constitutional terms. At Laeken, the catalytic spark failed to ignite because of the basic ambiguities that inhere in the EU constitution-making itself. The title of the final product – 'Treaty establishing a Constitution for Europe' – is quite telling. Taken literally, the title suggests that the evocative power of the term 'constitution' cannot be properly unleashed unless and until the present treaty is converted into a constitution. The CT was framed as a constitution by the Convention and the IGC, although it was also frequently noted that this was a distinctive type of constitution, a *constitutional treaty*. The Laeken process, although not at the outset set up to be an explicit constitution-making process, ended up in dressing up the present-day EU in constitutional garb. Beyond this, the process was framed and organised in basically the same way as previous IGCs, with the exception of one innovation: the Convention. The Convention was initially intended as a preparatory body for the IGC, and the latter would take the decisions that had to be ratified by each member state.

The Convention, once established, portrayed itself as a constitution-making body.[6] This attempt at a more open and deliberative approach to constitution-making took place in the absence of an initial constitutional signal. The 'shadow of the IGC' (Magnette 2004; Magnette and Nicolaïdis 2004: 382) was hanging over the whole process; it constrained the process of deliberation and prevented a proper mediation between strong 'deliberative' publics and general (or 'weak') publics[7] at the European level. Assessments of the entire Laeken process have found that the degree of interconnection of strong and general publics was low, while inclusiveness and transparency were insufficient to characterise the process as a properly constitutional one, from a deliberative-democratic perspective (Shaw 2003; Closa 2004; Fossum and Menéndez 2005). Part of the reason for ratification failure is found in the ambiguous signals and the fragmented character of the process that preceded the referenda.

The ratification debates testify to the irregular and episodic character of the citizens' voice.[8] In the absence of a prior process of mobilisation, politicisation through referenda is restricted to a short moment in time. Only a couple of weeks prior to the referenda, the European constitution had no particular meaning to the overwhelming majority of voters. The negative referenda in France and in the Netherlands are better seen as the endpoints of short electoral campaigns, than as staging events for further politicisation.

Within a fragmented process, the reality of mass-mediated communication in highly commercialised national public spheres makes referenda into launching pads for de-contextualised public debates that are partly outside of the control of constitution-makers and which may torpedo the whole process of constitution-making. To the logics of arguing and bargaining that dominated the drafting phase, a referendum adds a different logic of symbolic politics and populism. Ratification then becomes a matter of presenting a *text* for approval in a new *context*. The *text* that is the outcome of arguing and bargaining has to pass the test of the public in the new *context* of broadened debate. This results unavoidably in a process of *re-contextualisation*, in which the original input changes.

Such de-contextualising of debates is nourished by the belated ratification-driven politicisation of the EU with a transnational dynamic. The negative voice of the people could also draw on a certain common transnational focus on issues other than those in the constitutional text. Claes de Vreese predicted as early as 2004 that the Dutch people's vote would be deeply affected by anti-immigration sentiments, pessimistic economic outlooks and the flagging popularity of national governments, making 'no' the most likely outcome of the referendum. The turn from permissive consensus to resistance has apparently affected broad strata of European societies. This movement is not simply nationalistic, but can be grouped along ideological cleavages with a new 'left' fighting the perceived undesired effects of globalisation – of which the EU is seen to be integral – and a new 'right' using the European setting as a vehicle for promoting a neo-liberal agenda. What is seemingly a national cleavage – such as the notorious confrontation between continental Europe and the UK – can easily be turned into an ideological cleavage entrenched, on the one hand, in concerns with economic protection and social welfare and, on the other, in market liberalisation and individual responsibility. This can feed resistance both to further integration and to the present-day EU, which is seen as inadequately supranational.

Similar ideological cleavages can be found in foreign and security policy with the emphasis on 'normative power Europe' (Manners 2002),[9] dividing actors on their relationship to the USA. These broad ideological debates on the shape of the EU polity are also found in those countries where no referenda took place. The politicisation of Europe can thus be partly explained as a collective European experience, where ratification provided an opening for citizens' engagement, not simply in the acceptance or rejection of the constitutional text but as a part of ongoing struggles over the restructuring of European welfare states; the balancing of supranational versus national democracy; the entrenchment of human rights in a state-dominated system; security; global justice and solidarity; international crime and terrorism; and global environmental degradation.

Referenda that are not properly connected to an explicit constitutional signal and a process of constitutional decision-making wherein the people have been explicitly acknowledged as vital proprietors and where national votes take place at distinct instances over a lengthy period of time, can best be seen as a collection of garbage-can processes. Voting takes place under conditions of ambiguity and as a result of the partially random coupling of independent streams of politics that are only loosely coupled to the constitutional text (Cohen *et al.* 1972; Kingdon 1984). Different actors use the referenda as 'windows of opportunity' to come forward with very different problems and their perceived solutions. In such a situation of deep ambiguity, the constitution is a means to different ends and can signify quite different things, as illustrated by the French debate. Within the conservative camp the constitution was conceived of as a bulwark against Anglo-Saxon market ideology (Jacques Chirac) or, quite the opposite, as a tool against the French trust in the state (Nicolas Sarkozy); and within the socialist camp as a weapon against the existing liberal market jungle (François Hollande) or as the first step into the jungle (Laurent Fabius).

In a democratic setting, it is difficult for other actors to control access and to close down this 'window' for the 'de-contextualised' participants. This leads to an inevitable crowding of the open democratic arena: rational debate risks being turned into noise. Ratification can thus be marked by a deep rupture in constitution-making, where the results of the previous phases have only a very limited bearing on the actual outcome. Independent of the quality and contents of the constitutional text, it is now the context that determines the fate of constitution-making. The re-contextualisation of the constitutional text in different national settings increases the garbage-can effects with incalculable and often purely casual outcomes. It is then no wonder that ratification seems to resemble more of a lottery than a rational process.

Ratification failure as failure of communication?

The third explanation takes as its point of departure that there is a pattern of European communication, albeit one with several distinctive features of direct relevance to explain ratification failure. This pattern does not qualify as a European public sphere in the conventional sense. It is distinctively mediatised and notably is more media dependent than are national publics. It is a relatively thin veneer on top of a system of largely segmented national publics, and where the respective contributors are not well joined together (institutionally or conversationally) or synchronised. The effect is to highlight the vertical top-down thrust of communication over that of the horizontal one, so that media and institutions talk *to* people more than they talk *with* them, and where the mechanisms for ensuring that people talk with each other across boundaries are still weak. Such a public sphere is marked by a great element of contingency, with a greater propensity for the re-contextualisation of debates, as well as for communication to fail.

The core component of this explanation is that mediatisation affects the scope for deliberation and shapes the character of debate. Media apply their own rules in selecting and framing political news. They turn inputs from the political system into critique; they de- or reconstruct 'the facts'; they frame events along distinctive worldviews and lifeworld expectations; and they reshape the legal-normative context by means of expressive and identitarian mechanisms. Such processes take place not only through direct discursive exchange but also through other mechanisms such as diffusion, frame alignment and transnational resonance that provide for horizontal and vertical processes of intermediation within the multilevel polity of the EU (Snow and Benford 1999; Trenz 2005a). Mediated communication functions here, therefore, not simply through interaction structures constituted by communicating actors but also by way of the structure of issues and of rhetorical elements which create resonance in distant arenas, without speakers necessarily referring to each other. One obvious effect is for mediatised debate to make the *context* more important than the constitutional text. In this sense, opening public debates entails re-contextualising the text that has been finalised by the IGC. It is clear that the contents and the framing of news coverage in relation to the EU's overall constitutionalisation process are increasingly determined by European patterns and commonly defined agendas. Nevertheless, the more intense and nationally organised ratification debates still retain strong national foci, so that *national patterns of media framing* continue to shape the concrete ratification debates. What, therefore, from the perspective of the Union takes the shape of a fragmented and garbage-can type of ratification debate, is from a mediatised perspective also to a considerable extent the way in which established media frames are encountered and mobilised in relation to European constitution-making.[10]

Debates can also fragment due to more general developments, such as the fact that issue-attention cycles have become short, as too many issues compete for attention in the media. This restricts the potential for the unfolding of long-term debates or even of learning processes linked to the common experience of discursive interchange. Research on the unfolding of debates in the EU has shown that there are common peaks in the attention cycle of European issues and that the same issues are discussed at the same time but such debates are very short-lived (Trenz 2005a). These findings are not unique to the EU. We also see national public debates unfold within ever-shorter issue cycles and with high risks of various public attention distractions.[11]

The transformation of the European media landscape in the direction of *infotainment*, a process mainly driven by private television and the tabloids (whereas the input of European news delivered by European institutional actors is still mainly framed for quality newspapers) may produce a systematic bias towards misunderstanding, once European politics enters the national power play.

Mediatisation can reduce public discourse to a *struggle for attention* with frequent recourse to 'illicit' measures. This might explain the success of marginal groups in the French and Dutch constitutional referenda in carrying on their struggle for recognition, primarily as a struggle for attention through expressive means and symbolic action. In contrast to the 'rational commitment' of European actors and institutions, the highly mediatised national power play is deeply affected by such 'de-contextualised' logics of political debate, which all too often find easy access into the media.

When taking proper account of the contingent character of the mediatised public sphere, in particular within such complex and composite settings as the EU, we recognise that the very launching of public communication is imbued with risks. The senders of political messages in the EU cannot rely on a routine kind of public understanding, precisely because they encounter such a multitude of nationally framed settings. There is a high likelihood that someone out there will *not* catch the intended message or may not even be willing to pay attention.

The particularity of communication failures is that they result in follow-up communication and not in the cessation of it (otherwise we would not be able to realise that communication has failed). Failed communication must be communicated. It typically results from the observation that particular communicative efforts have not produced understanding. This perceived rupture in the communicative process then shapes subsequent steps of communication. Failed communication therefore does not, as is generally assumed, indicate the lack of a public sphere, but points to different, contingent and unpredictable ways of connecting communicative events. In this sense, failures of communication can be seen as the basis for reflection, which does not restore understanding as it was originally meant, but instead allows for a second-order observation of communication. Such a conception of the public sphere can explain how failures are detected and what comes after failure.

With this conception of communication failure in mind, two aspects of the European case stand out. One is that by now there is a rather lengthy history of European constitution-making, the unfolding of which serves to shape actors' expectations and media frames. This helps to underline that Laeken was *not* a starting point but was itself a case of follow-up communication: from the Union's perspective, it was set up as an explicit effort to remedy past failures of communication. Part of the reason for the Laeken failure was that the process was too fragmented to remedy the problem. To this could be added the mediatisation effect, i.e. how its entering into national frames generated additional distortions.

The second aspect is that the Union's effort at public communication is more fact oriented and less explicitly tailored to distinctive media frames than is the case in most national settings. Whereas this should ameliorate the effects of mediatisation, there are several factors that prevent such a mitigating process from occurring. Crucial is the discrepancy between how European political actors consider the role of media and how media work. European political actors with limited experience in dealing with the media tend to assume that media should work as the mirror of the EU political system so as to amplify its normative debates and to ensure that compelling arguments are visible to everyone. When finding discrepancies they respond with disdain. Consider the following statement by the French Commissioner, Jacques Barrot, in *Le Monde* on 29 May 2005: 'We are facing a disinformation campaign which means that lies sometimes prevail, simply because it's good form to say no. It's snobbish to say no.'

The effect is for these political elites to conclude that they cannot trust in the public's ability to comprehend the constitutional message. Statements to that effect by political elites may in turn foster public mistrust in their elected or self-appointed political representatives. The EU may have weaker means of countering such a dynamic than most national systems because of its great size; its limited scope for access and participation; and because the multifaceted European publics have limited capacity and ability to attend to and understand each other. In a polity that is marked by deep heterogeneity and poly-contextuality, constitutional debates are almost inevitably context bound and pluri-contextual. The expected decontextualisation of normative debates turns the empowerment of the people, through referenda, into a risky undertaking. Europe faces the problem of pluri-decontextualisation: one text, but quite different contexts.

Much of European public communication proceeds in the form of messages not received. The efforts to go public remain unresponded to. This points to a general dilemma of constitution-making, which addresses the public as a social constituency, i.e. as a totality, but which still cannot guarantee the full attention of the public and only gets disparate responses. The nation state was based on the assumption of a high congruence between the publics addressed and the attentive publics. In the EU, the gap between those who are addressed as a social constituency and those who pay attention or respond has widened.

Ratification failure can also be explained by reference to the instrument of the referendum itself. A referendum as a decision-making moment regulates communication through yes or no options. This stands in some contrast to the modus operandi of epistemic choice that marked the rounds of constitutional deliberation preceding ratification. Such previous rounds can be characterised by expanding the modus from 'either/or' to 'as well as' (Beck 1993: 9). Process deliberation recognises the ambivalence of the *yes* and the *no*, whereas ratification requires a clear choice. In Laeken, the process was de-linked so that the referenda as choice situations were overloaded: the rather short periods of ratification debate had to carry both the exploratory *and* the decision-framing dimensions of deliberation – within mediatised settings wherein infotainment flourished. The problem here is that in the absence of a previous process wherein 'symbolic cleansing', issue offloading, and epistemic exploration might take place and are harmonised, the referendum as a decisive moment is overloaded and privy to all kinds of other dynamics.

After failure – from rupture to reflection

The simple lesson to be drawn from the history of ratification failure is that the expansion of public and media communication about the EU as a project of democracy does not necessarily enhance a common understanding and agreement on a set of specific institutional choices for the process of democratisation. The effects of mediatisation and processes of democratisation run in parallel but without necessarily converging into a common European will. To capture this, we have broadened our conception of what European public sphere might entail, so as to conceive the public sphere not simply as the necessary infrastructure of a European democracy, but also as the realm of commercialisation, entertainment or lies.

After the negative referenda in France and in the Netherlands, these effects of the mediatisation of the EU and their impact on the project of EU constitutionalisation and democratisation have become apparent. The diagnosis of ratification failure as a failure of communication and the ensuing 'crisis' of the European integration process ask for rectifying measures. After a failure, three possibilities emerge: (a) a disregard of such a failure by those who have launched the constitutional project (business as usual); (b) resignation by the constitution-makers and a subsequent cessation of communication; and (c) reflection that leads to efforts to increase the chances of understanding, public engagement and agreement about the EU constitutional project.

In the current debate, proponents of all three solutions can be found. The first *pragmatic option* has been promoted by some of the governments and has also become the majority position of the EP, which in its plenary of 14 December 2005 criticised the present 'ratification blockade' and called upon the member states to continue the ratification process with practical solutions to be found for France and the Netherlands, once all the other member states had ratified the Treaty. This was also to be understood as a message against the Commission whose President, José Manuel Barroso, admitted several times that the constitution was on ice and that the EU should not be nostalgic for it, but instead should make the most of the existing treaty framework.

The second *regressive solution* is an attempt to reintroduce the intergovernmental model of a Europe of nation states as the only feasible option after the failure of European constitution-making. Such a position is still minoritarian in the old member states but is prominently promoted by some governments in the new member states, giving a new renationalising twist to European integration. For the Polish President Lech Kaczyński, the EU has to be considered an 'artificial construct', held together by some directives but not by legal norms, and therefore it should not allocate further competences. There also can be no potential for further integration, since 'there is no European public sphere but only national ones'.[12]

The third *progressive option* has become the kind of official position of former constitution-makers, including the Commission and the governments of the so-called core member states. It has materialised in new communicative efforts to open a period of dialogue and reflection between European institutions and the people of Europe. The forward-looking aim of such initiatives is to prepare the ground for the re-launching of the constitutional project that should be made more accessible and comprehensible for everybody. Ongoing constitution-making is still bound to a project of deepened integration with an inevitable allocation of competences at the supranational level and a redefinition of the role of citizens therein. Such efforts contain the risk of ignoring the will of the people to fit in with the presumed good reasons of the constitution-makers. It also opens the chance to broaden reflection and learning towards a new constitutional endeavour. How can we account for reflexive mechanisms after communication failures and how likely is it that this third option will be able to overcome the present impasse?

Reflection is commonly conceived of as a rescue mechanism of understanding, a corrective measure for communication failure. From this perspective, the EU's resolve to institute a reflection period is perfectly comprehensible. However, our analysis of ratification failure underlines the need to consider reflection not only through the lenses of reflexivity as a self-correcting process of learning but also through the lenses of collective identity formation. This latter notion posits the public sphere not simply as a mechanism for influencing the state or for controlling state policies; it is also a critical component in the shaping of the social imagination of a political society, the kind of reflexivity that informs not only the state but also the self-conception of the public as a political entity. It assumes the role of an 'arena of cultural creativity and reproduction in which society is imagined and thereby made real and shaped by the ways in which it is understood' (Calhoun 2003: 249). 'To see the public sphere entirely as a realm of rational–critical discourse is to lose sight of the importance of forming culture in public life, and of the production and reworking of a common social imaginary' (ibid.: 257).

To what extent constitutional debates have triggered off such processes of 'reflexive integration' beyond the evidence of ratification failure remains open to empirical analysis. The 2006 'Year of Citizens' dialogue will very likely not bring about the long-aspired breakthrough and promote a shared sphere of public opinion and will formation – not least because the targeted publics are again the citizens of the member states, i.e. the national publics.[13] In the absence of an explicitly declared will on the part of the system to channel arguments into binding actions, which includes structuring the process in such a manner as to enable citizens properly to *imagine themselves as Europeans*, citizens may be appeased by symbolic politics or may react with disdain or not feel affected at all. The alleged European public sphere will then resort to mere reflection on its own structural deficits and normative shortcomings. Such a form of institutional self-reflexivity about the difficulties of citizens' dialogue might trigger off institutional learning processes, but it is still largely (and involuntarily) excluding European citizens.

Notes

1 See the assessment of the Convention's outcome by the NGO members of the Civil Society Contact Group, 17 June 2003, available at www.act4europe.org/code/en/civi.asp?Page=94 (accessed 27 July 2006).

2 See Special Eurobarometer 214 'The Future Constitutional Treaty', March 2005, available at ec.europa.eu/public_opinion/archives/ebs/ebs_214_en.pdf (accessed 27 July 2006).

3 Consider the French case where the 'No' was principally motivated by alternative conceptions of the European public good and the shortcomings of European constitution-making identified in the debate.

4 That such a catalytic function for the emergence of a European public sphere would come to bear in the context of European constitution-making was most prominently predicted by Jürgen Habermas (2004) in his debate with Dieter Grimm (1995, 2004).

5 For details on the national ratification procedures, see the documentation provided by Carlos Closa and collaborators at the University of Zaragoza, available at 'The European Union Constitution' website www.unizar.es/euroconstitucion/Home.htm.

6 This was clearly expressed by its President, Valéry Giscard d'Estaing: see his 'Introductory speech to the Convention on the Future of Europe', SN 1565/02, 26 February 2002, available at european-convention.eu.int/docs/speeches/1.pdf (accessed 27 July 2006).

7 See Eriksen and Fossum 2002 for this model of mediation from strong to general publics.

8 Mair (2005) might therefore be premature in announcing that the EU is now 'ripe for politicization' and in expecting that policy entrepreneurs would soon seize the opportunity to mobilise on EU issues.

9 For a discussion of the merits of this notion, see Sjursen 2006.
10 How much the concrete Laeken process relied on established frames as opposed to being reconfigured in relation to the distinctive traits of Laeken is a matter for empirical analysis.
11 See Kepplinger 1998 for Germany and McNair 2000 for the UK.
12 Lech Kaczyński, speech at Humboldt University on 9 March 2006 and interview with the German newspaper *Die Welt* on 9 March 2006.
13 The Commission speaks of the organisation of 'broad ranging national debates on the future of Europe' through the involvement of national, regional and local Parliaments and through the national media (European Commission 2005: 4).

Part III

Institutional conditions and the European context

John Erik Fossum and Philip Schlesinger

This Part addresses the workings of specific EU institutions, offering a critical take on the prospects for a European public sphere. What are the institutional conditions for a public sphere within the EU? And how do these conditions relate to contemporary European realities – not least the EU's development as a polity?

The conception of the public sphere outlined in the introduction includes institutions as vital components. This is reflected in the 'circulation of power model', which assumes a close link and interplay between a general public based in civil society and institutionalised will-formation in parliament (a strong public). To address the first question, that of institutional conditions, the literature contains various sets of criteria for evaluating the EU's strong publics, including how these relate to general publics. The role and salience of strong publics in the EU can be assessed in relation to the following criteria: the existence of institutionalised fora for discussion of common concerns and for joint decision-making; deliberation, i.e. that decision-making is preceded by deliberation and that decisions are justified through giving reasons; and accountability, i.e. that all those potentially affected by decisions have their say and/or can dismiss incompetent leaders (see Eriksen and Fossum 2002).

Parliaments – whether European, national or regional – are the quintessential strong publics in the multi-level EU. The European Parliament is modelled on national parliaments and linked to these by various means. To establish the salience of strong publics in the EU we need to assess the impact of representative bodies at all levels of governance. In addition, we also need to consider the role played by other strong publics such as conventions (the Charter Convention and the Laeken Convention). Ulrike Liebert's chapter focuses on the European Parliament, and there are references in other chapters (for instance, in Eriksen and in Fossum and

Trenz) to other fairly strong publics, such as the Charter and Laeken Conventions.

But to establish the prospects for a European public sphere, we cannot confine the analysis *solely* to those institutions that qualify as strong publics. That is because deliberative theory sees public opinion not only as a constraint on power but also as a medium potentially able to rationalise power (Habermas 1992a: 441). Thus, a viable public sphere places demands on institutions, in respect of publicity, transparency, accountability and even predictability. As public sphere theorists have recognised, even those institutions associated with the 'system-world' must conduce to a flourishing public sphere. For instance, as Gutmann and Thompson (1996) make clear, a viable democracy presupposes a central role for the publicity principle. Public policies need to be justifiable to the citizens whom the policies bind. A critical issue here is to what extent public opinion frames and shapes the operations of the political system as opposed to simply responding to the system's actions. The chapters by Deirdre Curtin and Andy Smith address these matters.

Regarding the EU, its own development has brought the question of a public sphere to the forefront as an intrinsic part of the Union's democratic deficit, an issue that came to a head at Maastricht in 1991. After the initial Danish 'no' to the Maastricht Treaty, Pascal Lamy, Delors' *chef de cabinet*, said that: 'Europe was built in a St Simonian way from the beginning, this was Monnet's approach. The people weren't ready to agree to integration, so you had to get on without telling them too much about what was happening' (Lamy in Ross 1995: 194). Integration presupposed the setting up of institutions that could foster further integration. Up until Maastricht, the process had been orchestrated from above. After Maastricht, Lamy also noted, 'St Simonianism is finished. It can't work when you have to face democratic opinion'. This also demonstrates that the EU has come under heightened pressure to explain *why* integration is justified, a point which the recent ratification debates have helped to amplify.

The EU has also set up a large number of institutions and procedures that are consistent with the basic tenets of the constitutional state pertaining to provisions for reason-giving and justification. There are also in place mechanisms of critical scrutiny, judicial review and openness. These are intended to ensure the inclusion of interests and hearing of grievances (Majone 1996; Risse-Kappen 1996; Joerges and Vos 1999). As argued elsewhere, not only has the EU set up central polity-like political and legal institutions, but there are also provisions in place to ensure that justificatory claims can be made and met in policy networks, committees and conventions.

Nevertheless, it should be noted that with regard to the dynamic and still open-ended EU, in polity terms the challenge is not simply to establish what its present institutions have done to produce reasons and justifications. The EU's unique and dynamic character raises a further issue, namely how best to develop a proper understanding of *how* and *under what conditions* institutions can actually help to foster the development of a public sphere. If we are to take the EU seriously in this regard, we have to ask *which institutions* are the critical mainstays of a public sphere, and which are merely supportive to the core ones. We also need to ask which institutions may obstruct or impede the very emergence of a public sphere. And do the dividing lines run between institutions or within them?

12 European Commissioners and the prospects of a European public sphere

Information, representation and legitimacy

Andy Smith

Introduction

As part of its formal duties to represent 'the European interest' and propose means of deepening European integration, the Commission produces and disseminates a wealth of information about itself, its activities and those of the European Union as a whole. Contrary to popular perceptions and the omnipresent political discourse about the Union's 'democratic deficit', it is therefore difficult to argue that this organisation lacks transparency. Rather the central challenge facing the Commission concerns how its agents render the information released 'legible' for journalists and a general public still largely unused to the specificities of Europe-wide politics. In more analytical terms, studying the communication activities carried out by Commission staff from the angle of political representation – defined as both 'speaking for' and 'symbolically incarnating' (Abélès 1997: 247) – sheds light upon a number of traits of the EU which constantly sap its legitimacy as a source of political discourse. More precisely, the puzzle for empirical research then becomes how practioners within the Commission strive – sometimes successfully, often unsuccessfully – to legitimate themselves. By legitimation is meant the transformation of public acceptance of their self-organisation from one based upon an unstable consensus of interest-based calculations into one based upon a durable 'belief in the social value of institutions' (Lagroye 1985: 399).

Drawing on former research on European Commissioners in general and eight in particular in the period 1989–99 (Joana and Smith 2002; Smith 2003),[1] the central claim made in this chapter is that the EU possesses both an embryonic single European public sphere and a series of overlapping national and subnational spaces for public deliberation and debate. The legitimacy and social meaning of all these spaces do not, however, simply stem from the length of their respective pasts or the existence of formal bodies. Instead, they are shaped by the manner through which a range of identifiable and 'studiable' actors interact and render public this activity. Although most of these have built the existence of the EU as a space for political negotiation into their daily political work, the vast majority still do not see it as a space for political representation.

From this angle, three aspects of the representational activities of the Commissioners studied are analysed in order to explain why they are so often presented as 'technocratic' that is, distanced from political competition, deciding upon the basis of expertise rather than upon values and, more generally, behaving in a discreet or 'non-public' manner (Radaelli 1999).

First, it is argued that Commissioners frequently find themselves at a disadvantage when competing for media attention with Members of the European Parliament (MEPs) and national ministers. Part of this asymmetry is due to their non-elective positions. More deeply, however, the relative weakness of Commissioners is due to deep-rooted expectations regarding their behaviour in public fora. In short, presenting oneself as dutifully respectful to ministers and MEPs is a key component of the institutionalised role of a Commissioner.

Second, the capacity of these actors to communicate publicly is often hamstrung by the Commission's inability to 'speak with one voice'. On one level, this trait is due to competition between individual Commissioners and various administrative services. However, the underlying cause of this fragmentation lies in the multiple roles of the Commission. Torn between acting as an initiator of law and policy, a deliberator, a mediator between national and sectoral interests, a negotiator and a watchdog over implementation in the member states, the organisation's claims to represent 'the European interest' are constantly undermined by the daily behaviour of its own agents. In other words, not only are public expectations about the Commission unclear, but the professional identity of those who work for this body is also frequently confused and confusing.

Finally, details of the relationship built up between Commissioners and the media need to be elucidated. The relatively low level of coverage given to EU politics by national media cannot simply be explained away by general arguments about cultural difference and socialisation. If these issues have great importance, they are mediated in very concrete terms around the precise relationships built up between public actors on the one hand and journalists on the other.

In presenting these arguments and our data, it is recognised that a certain number of Commissioners have occasionally managed to overcome constraints upon their representational activity and thereby reach certain parts of Europe's general public. Nevertheless, the central message of this chapter is that the legitimacy of such political representation is constantly undermined by the specific set of rules and expectations that lie at the heart of the institutionalised role of a European Commissioner. It is this role, rather than the personality of each incumbent, that almost invariably leads Commissioners to engage in political representation from the perspective of a technocratic or diplomatic broker rather than from that of a fully legitimate political participant in Europe's public spheres.

The publicisation of institutional competition: Commissioners, the Council and the Parliament

The Commission as a whole is stuck between a rock and a hard place: regularly chastised by national actors for 'engaging in propaganda' when it provides information and for 'acting technocratically' when it does not. Most Commissioners, however, are not prepared to admit that they are in a 'no-win' situation. Instead, their daily work leads them to compete with MEPs and national ministers for media attention, and more fundamentally for legitimacy. Although they and the Commission did possess some potent arms of their own, the Commissioners we studied often found themselves battling from a position of structural weakness. In order to elucidate the institutional source of this situation, our research seeks to answer the following questions: (i) to what extent does competition for public attention impact upon the dominant forms of political communication in the EU? and (ii) does competition contribute to the building of a single European public sphere or simply further consolidate a set of overlapping national spheres?

Commissioners versus MEPs

Orthodox commentary on the EU has frequently underlined how the formal legitimacy of MEPs – their democratic election – contrasts with the influence of agents of the Commission, which stems from their organisation's agenda-setting function and its privileged access to decision-shaping arenas. Prior to the mid-1990s, the resulting institutional competition was heavily focused upon attempts by MEPs to use their authority over the EU budget in order to obtain isolated concessions and grudging recognition from staff in the Commission. However, two sets of changes introduced with the Maastricht Treaty have led Commission officials in general to take the Parliament more seriously. Indeed, they have obliged Commissioners to engage in processes that have had an impact upon their own practices of political representation.

The first of these innovations concerns the introduction of an investiture procedure for the College.[2] Prior to 1995, Commissioners were simply nominated by national governments and began work as if hired by any private company. The Maastricht Treaty did not change the nomination process but it did introduce a requirement for Commissioners to present themselves and their respective portfolios to sessions of parliamentary committees open to journalists and other interested members of the public. Although we did not conduct systematic research on the impact of this form of investiture upon the College,[3] it considerably shaped the subsequent priorities and behaviour of at least two of the Commissioners studied in detail: Yves-Thibault de Silguy and Edith Cresson. More precisely, both were given a particularly rough ride by MEPs but reacted to this experience in ways that provide insights into how they envisaged the role of a Commissioner and the shape of public space in Europe.

As Commissioner responsible for economic policy in general and monetary union in particular, during the investiture hearings, de Silguy came under attack from a number of left-leaning German MEPs who criticised his faith in the European Monetary Union (EMU), his political inexperience and, implicitly, his right-of-centre party affiliation. Having opened the proceedings with what he and his cabinet considered to be an effective and technically impressive presentation of his policy priorities, de Silguy was clearly unprepared for the politicised nature of the MEPs' comments. This 'breaking of the frame' (Goffman 1974: 347) is highly revealing in two ways. First, it exemplifies the extent of change in the relationship between the Parliament and the Commission because de Silguy, once a senior member of Commission president Gaston Thorn's cabinet, clearly expected the MEPs to stick to a more policy-centred line of questioning. Second, the incident led this Commissioner to decide actively to seek the support of the parliamentary committee for the relaunch of the EMU. This was done in particular by choosing to make the initial presentation of many decisions and policy initiatives before the committee rather than in the press room of the Commission. In summing up the relationship developed with this committee, a member of de Silguy's cabinet considered that 'Yves behaved as a minister would within a national Parliament'.[4] More generally, this stroking of MEPs' vanity through recognising the legitimacy of their institution contributed to de Silguy rapidly developing a 'European credit', which benefited him throughout his mandate as Commissioner.[5]

Like her French colleague, Edith Cresson also began her life as a Commissioner with a difficult parliamentary hearing. Criticised for not appearing to master the technical detail of training policy, unlike de Silguy, she reacted by considering the European Parliament (EP) an arena to be avoided. Instead, Cresson consistently presented new policy initiatives directly to conferences of economic and social actors concerned with her portfolio. History informs us that this neglect of, or even disdain for, MEPs was to prove costly when charges of financial mismanagement were brought against her at the end of 1998 and early 1999. By then, and despite a concerted but desperate last-minute attempt to recapture lost ground,[6] it had become too late to recognise the legitimacy of MEPs and, hence through a process of reciprocation, to bolster that of Cresson, the office of Commissioner in general and that of the Commission.

The second change in EP–Commission relations brought about by the

Maastricht Treaty concerns the knock-on effects of the introduction of 'co-decision'. By increasing the EP's capacity to amend draft legislation, this treaty change upgraded the importance of parliamentary committees and obliged many Commissioners to include them in their respective negotiating strategies (Fouilleux *et al.* forthcoming). Indeed, from the point of view of policy-making, all the Commissioners we studied considered it necessary to bear in mind constantly the political equilibria of these committees and endeavoured to seek allies or neutralise probable opponents. However, and notwithstanding the example of de Silguy, it is not clear that Commissioners in general have come to see the EP as an effective means of support for communicating about their activities and aspirations. On the contrary, as Olivier Baisnée (2003b, 2004) has shown so effectively in his sociology of the Brussels press corps, Commissioners are very much aware that most journalists specialised in coverage of the EU are far more interested in the discourse of the Commission than that of MEPs.[7] In short, European parliamentarians are certainly now taken more seriously by Commissioners as policy experts and negotiators, but not as political representatives of the EU.

The implications of this are far-reaching. Although many Commissioners clearly see MEPs as fellow politicians with whom they have much in common, the inter-institutional competition at the heart of the EU's decision-making process strongly discourages overtly political discourse and opposition between members of each institution. If avoiding such conflict is seen as facilitating the production of EU law and policies, it also contributes to technicised practices of political representation, depoliticised media coverage and, ultimately, limited legitimacy of both the EP and the Commission. In other words, it contributes neither to the construction of a single European public sphere nor to the widespread recognition of an overlap between such a sphere and its national counterparts.

Commissioners versus national ministers

Paradoxically, if Commissioners compete even more intensely with national ministers than they do with MEPs, their battles are much less open to observation by journalists and other EU watchers. This characteristic can be explained on one level by noting that much of this interaction goes on within meetings of the Council of Ministers from which external observers are specifically excluded. But the institutionalised processes at the heart of Council proceedings also frequently lead Commission representatives to downplay their own contribution to Council debates in order to position themselves as potential brokers of compromise agreements between the member states. More specifically, in encouraging Commissioners to technicise their arguments during negotiations and in discouraging them from presenting themselves as the equals of ministers, a number of the Council's rituals and implicit rules contribute strongly to weakening Commissioners' political legitimacy. More fundamentally, by doing so they also reduce the likely emergence of a single European public sphere.

The tendency of Commission representatives to depoliticise or technicise their discourse and action has been recently highlighted by some astute EU policy analysis (Radaelli 1999; Robert 2004). In our case studies of European Commissioners, we also came across a number of negotiations where these actors deliberately chose to accentuate arguments based upon economic or legal expertise in order to further their respective policy objectives. In the case of research policy, for example, Edith Cresson based much of her attempt to reform the Framework Programme for Research upon 'the requirements of scientists and industrialists' rather than upon an ideological commitment to research as part of industrial policy. Similarly, once the EMU was firmly back on the EU's agenda, de Silguy and his team concentrated upon the detail of producing a single currency and preparing different economic sectors for this innovation. However, many of our other policy studies showed quite the opposite: Commissioners striving to set the EU agenda by politicising issues ranging from Common Agricultural Policy (CAP) reform (Ray MacSharry) to the harmonisation of VAT levels (Christiane Scrivener). A range of standard political tools, notably public speeches and press releases, were used to stress that the issue at hand was not just about policy efficiency, but also entailed questions of equity and even morality. In short, far from being avoided, the question of the values underlying the policy was deliberately made public. It is important, therefore, to underline that Commissioners are by no means condemned to act technocratically. However, they appear most free to act politically during the phase of European problem definition and agenda formation. Once negotiations in the Council begin in earnest, most Commissioners consider that their legitimacy is under threat and therefore rely much more heavily upon the legal and economic expertise they are able to muster in order to back up their arguments. In a word, the phase in the policy cycle symbolised by Council meetings sharpens the definition of the hierarchy between Commissioners and ministers, which until that stage, most often remains fuzzy and ambiguous.

The question of hierarchy is particularly evident at the end of Council meetings when press conferences are held and the proceedings are relayed to the media. On such occasions, the official spokesperson for the meeting is the minister from the member state that currently holds the presidency of the EU. Commissioners usually attend such conferences but are generally confined, and confine themselves, to the role of providing additional, and often detailed, information. One such example concerns Yves-Thibault de Silguy and the posture he adopted after monthly meetings of the ECOFIN council. Despite the work he did to prepare, structure and run such meetings, at each press conference he had to take on a demeanour that clearly showed he was not even a member of the 'club'[8] of Finance ministers, let alone one of their equals. Faced with the symbolic authority of national ministers, other Commissioners adopted strategies that were either openly combative (e.g. Sir Leon Brittan and his use of the media, see below) or based upon 'the logic of the by-pass' (e.g. Ray MacSharry and his use of a captive specialised agricultural press). Most Commissioners, however, appear fatalistic and frustrated by living in the shadow of national ministers for whom, for a number of ideological and career-driven reasons, they often have little respect.[9]

In summary, the Council 'brings out the technocrat' in European Commissioners for reasons beyond pure negotiating strategy. Instead, over the course of the EU's history, perceptions of the legitimate role of a Commissioner have hardened into a set of institutionalised expectations and rules. These largely determine both how holders of this office see themselves and are seen by their political allies and adversaries. Once again, these expectations and rules militate against publicisation within a genuine European public sphere, or even against greater overlap between and amongst European and national spaces of deliberation and debate.

The limited publicness of competition between Commissioners: discretion or denial?

Of course, a Commissioner's political friends and enemies exist not only outside the Commission. Indeed, in quantitative terms, the interlocutors they most frequently come into contact with work inside the College itself or in one of the Commission's Directorates General (DG). Fragmentation at this level has been documented by books about this organisation as a whole and, in passing, by a wealth of EU policy analysis which uses the theory of 'bureaucratic politics' to explain the Commission's incoherent or lowest common denominator outputs. Such an explanation is often fruitful but tends to neglect the role of Commissioners and the College. In the case of the Commission's communication activities, this omission is particularly glaring and leaves one unable to explain why the organisation has never been able to construct public information on the EU as a legitimate 'European problem'. In order to grasp the effects of competition between Commissioners over the Commission's communication practices and on public spheres in Europe, a shift of focus is needed. Instead of conceptualising competition between Commissioners as mere power struggles, one needs to see that battles within the College are played out within an institutionalised order which consistently favours 'technocratic' forms of representation over 'political' ones.

The mirage of unified information

From at least 1958 to 1999, responsibility for information within the College was a task that no Commissioner wanted.[10] Almost invariably, this

234   *A. Smith*

portfolio was attributed either to a Commissioner from a small member state or to the 'second' Commissioner from a larger country. One of the reasons for this was that the corresponding administrative unit, DG X, was always weak in terms of personnel and legitimacy as compared to other DGs. In charge of 'general' publications, the officials from DG X could do little to counter the proliferation of information units in other DGs and the resulting cacophony of publications emanating from the Commission. But merely describing this characteristic begs the question of why the College as a whole, and the Commissioner in charge of information in particular, almost never even broached the issue of how the Commission should be communicating. Through our analysis of the activities of two holders of this portfolio (Jean Dondelinger and Marcelino Oreja) and indirect information on a third (João de Deus Pinheiro), light can be shed both on the fragmentation of Commission information policy and some important unwritten rules governing the College.

During the nine years which span Dondelinger's (1989–92) and Oreja's (1995–9) terms of office, Commission archives reveal only one public speech on the subject of how the organisation should be communicating.[11] Just as tellingly, neither engaged in launching any initiative within the Commission in order to provoke internal debate and decision-making about how information policy should be framed and implemented. In interviews, the personal staff of both these Commissioners excused this low level of investment in information policy by underlining how busy their respective 'masters' had been in more legislation-based policy areas (in particular the audiovisual sector and, for Oreja, preparing the Amsterdam Treaty). However, since use of an actor's time depends a great deal on what they consider important, this explanation merely serves to highlight how, for these Commissioners, information policy was not only a low priority, but one which they had great difficulty in tackling.

Pinheiro's two-year term (1993–4) provides both an interesting contrast with those of Dondelinger and Oreja as well as more insights into the intrinsic 'slipperiness' of the information portfolio. In the aftermath of referendums on the Maastricht Treaty, lack of public support for European integration suddenly became an issue that was pushed up (or even onto) the agenda of the College. Pinheiro and his cabinet reacted by creating a strategy unit on information,[12] which was given the task of producing papers for the College as a whole. They also established a 'users council' and commissioned a report from a 'Committee of wise men' chaired by a Belgian MEP, Willy de Clerq (1993). This report was supposed to 'propose a mid-term communication and information strategy which would enable the European Institutions and the Member States to take into account the needs, the concerns and the hopes of citizens at a decisive moment for the process of European integration' (De Clerq 1993: preface, author's translation). However, Pinheiro considered some of the report's recommendations too audacious, an opinion confirmed as soon as the *Financial Times* labelled them 'the fantasy of advertisers' (Tumber 1995: 517; Shore 2000: 54–6). More generally, the College as a whole distanced itself from these issues and instead participated in producing a general discourse upon 'transparency' and 'openness'.[13]

The vacuity of this discourse merits study in its own right. What our own research shows is that for agents of the Commission, 'elevating' the problem of information to such a level of abstraction had the advantage of side-stepping the thorny issue of who should be responsible for making information policy and what powers they should have over other actors engaged in communicating about the EU. This lament by an official from DG X reveals some of the causes and effects of a fundamental characteristic of the College:

> The Commissioners have never worked upon their own image. Such work would involve building a communication strategy, revisiting what they do in their respective countries, spending more time outside Brussels (as Bonino and de Silguy do), using media other than the *Financial Times*. But all that is taboo. DG X has no mandate to give advice to Commissioners about how they communicate. Some cabinets sometimes think about information strategies. However, at the end of the day, each Commissioner is an autodidact who improvises his or her own practices [...]. In short, there is no longer any debate at the level of the College about how we communicate. Worse, we don't even give ourselves the means to analyse this question. Consequently, any discussion there is on this subject is like a chat in a pub.[14]

In other words, behind the myth of the unity and the collective responsibility of the College lies the mirage of a unified Commission information policy reaching out to 'the European citizen'. In reality, the College is an arena for political competition within which practices of information and communication are jealously guarded resources for advancing ideological preferences, national or sectoral interests and personal careers. Consequently, these practices are not for pooling as part of a Commission-wide strategy for building either a single European public sphere or encouraging overlap between nationally or sectorally segmented spheres.

The myth of a single press office

The impact of the myth of collegial unity upon the Commission's relationship to 'the public sphere' also needs examination from the angle of its press office. Since the beginning of the 1960s, a Service des porte-parole (SPP, spokesperson's service) has constituted the official interface between Commissioners and journalists. Formally, each spokesperson does not work for a Commissioner but for the SPP as a whole in order to ensure that the Commission 'speaks with one voice'. In reality, two further characteristics of the role of Commissioner largely explain both why each occupant of this post has a great deal of control over his or her spokesperson and why the latter are used in such different ways.

The first concerns the selection of spokespersons. Although the Secretariat General goes to great lengths to establish short-lists of candidates for these positions, ultimately each Commissioner decides whom they want as their media representative. This is usually determined through a process of interviews where personal commitment to the Commissioner is clearly an important criterion. A Commission official who was interviewed unsuccessfully for the job of Leon Brittan's spokesperson provides a telling insight: 'I made the mistake of saying, "Of course, I would be working for the Service des porte-parole". To which Brittan replied, "Of course, if you wish to work for another Commissioner, you are quite free to do so".'[15]

Those that are nominated generally have their allegiance to 'their' Commissioner reinforced by being treated as an additional cabinet member.[16] Once incorporated into the Commissioner's 'political enterprise',[17] most spokespersons consider themselves part of a team in competition with those of other members of the College.

At least until the reform of the press office in 1999, a second trait of the College also had considerable impact upon the unity of the SPP. This concerns the liberty given to Commissioners to hire spokesmen or women from inside or outside the Commission. Many Commissioners (e.g. Oreja, Brittan) used this leeway to hire journalists from their own country in order to deal with the press. Others (MacSharry, de Silguy) preferred to take on an 'ordinary'[18] official from the DG to be responsible for their portfolio. This practice clearly sapped the internal cohesion of the SPP by injecting it with a mixture of professional identities. More fundamentally still, it provides yet another indicator of how little each Commissioner feels bound to act according to an institutionalised set of rules, rituals and expectations. Consequently, it is no coincidence that Commissioners who considered their portfolio as the centre of their activity selected Commission officials, whereas their counterparts who saw themselves as generalist politicians were more likely to hire journalists.

The fragmentation of the College and the SPP constituted an important ingredient in the fall of the Santer Commission, which cannot be analysed here.[19] What does need stressing is that this episode precipitated a reform of the Commission's press services, the disappearance of DG X and a rather desperate attempt by Romano Prodi to centralise communication around the Commission Presidency (Baisnée 2004). At the same time, however, Prodi put an end to the physical grouping together of Commissioners in one building and sent them and their cabinets out to work alongside their respective DGs. In-depth research has yet to be conducted upon the effects of this decision. At least in terms of the Commission's communicative practices, however, it appears to have accentuated rather than attenuated the individualistic behaviour of Commissioners. Contrary to what even many social scientists appear to believe, this individualism is not the effect of personality or 'cultural difference'. Instead, as has been argued here, it stems directly from the nature of the College as a political arena within which a Commissioner's commitment to his or her colleagues is constantly cross-cut by their engagement in a form of ideological, inter-sectoral, international and personal competition which discourages public debate both 'in Brussels' and in the member states.

Commissioners and the media: getting heard or being forgotten

If the position of Commissioner per se is not an obstacle to an active approach to communication, clearly there are constraints that affect how successful an occupant of this post can be in reaching the eyes and ears of Europe's citizens. Over and above the resistance of national actors, the most powerful of these is the sociology and structure of the European media. Contrary to a large number of policy sectors, these media have not undergone a significant process of 'Europeanisation'. For this reason, Commissioners are condemned to working with two quite different sets of journalists: the Brussels press corps and reporters located in the member states. In both cases, but for different reasons, they cannot simply expect journalists to write or broadcast about their respective actions or public pronouncements. Instead, if a Commissioner seeks to remain or become a public figure, the media have to be worked on in ways that frequently differ from national political practice. In more analytical terms, the institutionalised role of Commissioner vaguely incites its incumbents to foster a single European public sphere and to encourage national public spheres to recognise their degree of mutual interdependence. However, it does not provide them with a ready-made road map for moving in both or either of these directions.

Commissioners and the Brussels press corps

The Commission's 800 accredited journalists based in Brussels make up what Olivier Baisnée (2000) has identified as the EU's 'first public'. Not only are these reporters paid to specialise in news about the EU, since the 1960s their standard method of collecting and processing information has led them into a relationship of deep dependence upon the staff of the Commission. This relationship is nurtured by the importance accorded to the Commission's midday press briefing both by journalists and civil servants. During this briefing, a sharing of values occurs and a set of implicit rules about what constitutes European news emerges. Although some investigative journalists have recently broken with this mould, the general expectation is that members of the press corps produce articles on the detailed outcome of College meetings, negotiations with the Parliament and the Council and third countries. However, they avoid in-depth analysis of the battles that precede the setting of a Commission decision, or those that continue to take place 'behind closed doors' once this decision becomes part of a formalised debate with national governments. Stigmatised as 'trivial' by civil servants and most journalists, this conflict is therefore almost systematically kept out of the public eye. However, one only needs to make a cursory examination of national press, radio or television to see that the 'trivia' of political jousting are the spice that interests a variety of publics. Moreover, analysis of the type of conflict papered over by the Brussels press corps shows that ideology and power are precisely what they leave out, thus paving the way for depiction of the Commission as a haven-of value-less 'technocrats'.

It would be erroneous to suggest that all Commissioners and their staff are aware of this context when they take up office. Indeed, many still seem unaware when they leave. However, as the following examples illustrate, they all soon learn either how to fit into the institutionalised relationship between the Commission and the media, or the risks and costs involved in trying to break with it.

A first, and probably most common, way of adapting to this relationship is to stick rigidly to one's portfolio and concentrate upon providing the press corps with detailed information about policy developments. This was the approach adopted by Franz Fischler, Commissioner responsible for agriculture between 1995 and 2004. A captive audience of specialised agricultural journalists based in Brussels was used as a platform for a highly sectoral form of communication. For the first three years of her mandate, Edith Cresson also dealt with the press using a similar logic. In contrast to Fischler, however, she did not court the Brussels press corps, apparently believing that she could reach the national media more directly using the sectoral route or her own personal reputation.

A second type of Commissioner attempts to make more strategic use of journalists based in Brussels in order to further his or her respective policy aims. As Commissioner for agriculture from 1989 to 1992, Ray MacSharry used the agricultural press in order to set the agenda for reforming the CAP. Unlike his successor Fischler, however, MacSharry politicised his criticisms of this policy and did not attempt to downplay the fact that under his leadership the Commission was seeking to change the very foundations of farm subsidies. In this way, this Commissioner also attracted the attention of the more general media. Yves-Thibault de Silguy adopted a similar approach to his portfolio of economic and monetary affairs. Conscious of the importance of the *Financial Times* amongst political and economic elites, but also as a relay to other parts of the media, at the beginning of his mandate, de Silguy and his (British) spokesman made considerable efforts to win the respect of the *Financial Times*'s journalists in Brussels. Similar efforts were made with leading newspapers in all the large member states. Part of a wider strategy to make the euro 'credible', this approach to the Brussels press corps aimed to go beyond a highly specialised type of journalism and attract the attention of media generalists.

The interest of the general media is the objective of a third and final type of Commissioner for whom the Brussels press corps is essentially a stepping-stone with which to reach the national media in general, and that of their own country in particular. In our panel, only Sir Leon Brittan fitted this category. Considering that it was his role and right as a Commissioner to look after his own portfolio but also 'to cover the whole waterfront',[20] Brittan constantly sought media coverage of his actions and of himself. Like de Silguy, he and his cabinet were in daily touch with the *Financial Times* and other 'heavyweight' papers. Again, like his French colleague, he made public speeches throughout the EU. However, the specificity of Brittan was that he always explicitly voiced an ideologically driven set of opinions about what the EU was and what he thought it should be doing.

In summary, analysis of the different communication practices of Commissioners provides important insights into differing ways of working in and trying to deepen Europe's public sphere. For some holders of this office, the most effective way of doing so is to act technocratically in the hope that carefully controlled publicity about EU affairs will steadily increase the legitimacy of the EU. For others, however, it is precisely through engaging in overtly political conflicts that the Commission is best able to push EU matters onto the forefront of public debate within Europe.

Commissioners and their national public spheres

Brittan's ideological commitment may have made him interesting for the media to cover. But it is also important to highlight how this Commissioner, like many others, strove to remain part of his country's public sphere and not simply become a 'European without a homeland'. Over and above the particularities of the Brittan case, comparison with that of the Frenchwoman Christiane Scrivener provides a means of addressing a second aspect of the communication practised by Commissioners: their dealings with their own national media. In turn, this subject allows one to address empirically the question of the degree to which overlapping European and national public spheres have emerged and, more precisely, whether it is possible for Commissioners to operate effectively at both levels. The analytical pay-off of this approach lies in conceptualising 'overlap' in terms that are sufficiently precise to encourage better understanding of how political representation actually operates in contemporary Europe.

Brittan in Britain: Europe as ideology

In January 1989, Leon Brittan arrived rather reluctantly in Brussels for two reasons. First, his nomination was interpreted as a form of sidelining that would slow down or even end his political career.[21] Second, like many British Conservatives, at that time he was sceptical about the ideological content of many European policies. Over the next ten years, however, he not only became convinced that the EU could and should be a vector for extending neo-liberalism beyond the English Channel, but also undertook a personal campaign to attempt to convince his political party to trans-form this argument into a central plank of its political agenda. If, as Conservative policy on Europe in the 1990s illustrates, this sustained effort clearly failed, it is nevertheless highly instructive to examine both how and why Brittan committed so much energy and resources to what turned out to be a series of lost battles.

Brittan's British campaign was essentially waged in two ways. First, although only 21 per cent of his written speeches were delivered in the UK, he made numerous other public interventions and gave talks to a plethora of Conservative constituency parties. This activity was orches-trated partly by a member of Brittan's cabinet in Brussels, and also by a Conservative backbencher, Spencer Batiste, 'Brittan's de facto parliament-ary private secretary'.[22] This speechmaking was supplemented by a series of books written during and just after Brittan's mandate as Commissioner (Brittan 1992, 1994, 2000).

The second strand of Brittan's strategy consisted in giving a vast number of interviews to British radio and press reporters. Although rarely seen on television, BBC Radio 4's *Today* programme – the premier polit-ical morning talk slot in the UK – regularly used him as an all-purpose 'rent a quote' on European affairs. The press was used even more systematically in order to defend the EU, for example when calling on Conservatives to ratify the Amsterdam Treaty[23] or castigating Tory leaders for their Euro-scepticism.[24] Indeed, given the energy that was also expended by Brittan and his cabinet on policy-making and international negotiations, it is particularly important to note that dealings with the press were key parts of their daily routine. As one cabinet member laconi-cally recalled: 'In cabinet meetings the first point was the press. The second was "How do I get things (and me) into the press?" And only then would we move on to matters of substance.'[25]

Why this commitment and why this strategy? Our research reveals two answers to these questions. To pursue an idea introduced above, the first of Brittan's motivations was one of rapidly acquired political conviction:

> In general terms, Leon genuinely believed that European integration had been a boost to prosperity and to deregulation and economic reform in Britain, and therefore that it was compatible with Toryism

[Conservatism]. He could never understand why the Tories [Conservatives] were turning their backs on this achievement, and incidentally turning their backs on the role played by British Conservatives such as him in Europe. He believed Europe was going in the Conservatives' direction. He was therefore very upset that his own party was turning its back on this and on him. He was never reluctant to speak about this.[26]

A second explanation is that throughout his years in Brussels, Brittan continued to see himself not only as a political actor, but also as a leading politician who had a career to make and manage. Once again, members of his cabinet provide telling testimony of this self-image and its effects:

> The classic worry for all Commissioners is that they will go to Brussels and be forgotten because they don't get enough publicity. Brittan was probably worried that this was the end of his political career; that he was going to be sucked into the role of a technocrat.[27]

History tells us that despite all his efforts, Leon Brittan largely failed to convince his fellow Conservatives to support greater European integration or even to get his views disseminated beyond the British elite.[28] Constantly in the news in Brussels, and followed avidly by the Brussels press corps, our case study of Brittan in Britain highlights how difficult it is for even the most committed of Commissioners to penetrate national public spheres and begin to modify the representations of the EU which predominate there.

Scrivener in France: Europe as blind faith

In contrast to Brittan, Christiane Scrivener was already a committed pro-European activist well before becoming a Commissioner in 1989. A centre-right minister in the late 1970s, Scrivener became a MEP in 1984. Both from this position and as a Commissioner, she returned frequently to her native France in order to 'preach the gospel' of the need for deeper European integration. However, she received relatively little media coverage via the Brussels press corps and virtually none in France itself. In examining how and for what reasons, she continued to engage with journalists, the puzzle is why so much effort went so unrewarded.

Scrivener's media strategy towards France contained three components. The first was her own newsletter – *Lettre d'Europe-Avenir* – where, from 1984 to 1994, she signed editorials and 'wrote' other articles. The second was through speechmaking. Thirty-three per cent of her written speeches were made in France and 19 out of 29 general policy speeches made in six years were delivered there. Finally, she also gave interviews to the press but essentially on issues related to her tax and consumer affairs portfolio. Indeed, it is important to note that her spokesperson for much of her mandate was a legally trained European civil servant and that her head of cabinet, an *Enarque* (a graduate of the elite National Administration School) from the French Ministry of Finance, was clearly little disposed to dealing with the press.

In examining the content of Scrivener's communication activities, the most striking feature is the way she consistently argued for closer European union from postulates of faith in European ideals and the inevitability of deeper integration ('progressive Europeanism'). Indeed, throughout Scrivener's speeches two meta-narratives constantly appear: how the EU saved Europe from a third world war and the economic dangers of 'non-Europe'. In neither case are these arguments carefully illustrated or linked to an explicit political ideology. Instead, between the lines one can detect a centre-right sub-text about the benefits of bigger, more open markets and less bureaucratic red tape. Indeed, Scrivener regularly used vague references to her past as a private sector 'entrepreneur' in order to convince audiences of her credibility.

Not surprisingly, Scrivener was clearly shaken by the results of the French referendum on the Maastricht Treaty in September 1992. To her usual arguments in favour of European integration, she then began to add the theory of 'communication failure' for which the Commission was partly responsible: 'We have not sufficiently explained something which is difficult to explain.'[29] However, the perspectives set out for the future remained largely unchanged, clearly believing that in order to be heard in the member states the Commission simply needed to shout louder.

If Scrivener's approach to the media clearly contrasts with that of Brittan, this is partly because her own national debate in France on European integration was, at least until Maastricht, essentially consensual. Moreover, less personally ambitious, actively involved in a political party and committed to a combative ideology, she quite simply appeared less interesting to journalists outside a small circle of economic and financial specialists. Nevertheless, her case is of wider interest to social science because in many ways her approach to both public communication and relations with the media appears highly representative of that of many other Commissioners. For these actors, arguing for 'more Europe' from a postulate of faith in vague European ideals and the intrinsic worth of a unified economy provides a safe means of avoiding politicised conflict with the member states and the EP. This stance is also a means of convincing oneself that those who oppose deeper integration are incurable heretics who, having turned their backs upon the course of history, are not even worth debating with. In short, for such actors the EU already is a public sphere and the more one keeps politics and ideology out of it the better.

Conclusion

From several different angles, this chapter has sought to show how and why most European Commissioners find it so difficult to operate both in 'Brussels-centred' and national public spheres. Indeed, this trait goes to the heart of their weakness as political representatives. To paraphrase one of Marc Abélès's (1996: 61) conclusions on MEPs, Commissioners '*make* Europe through engaging in a continuous process of negotiation [...], but they *are* not Europe'. As François Foret (2003) also rightly concludes, a limited European public sphere can be said to exist wherein the participants share a number of codes and rituals which ensure a minimal level of homogeneity and mutual understanding. However, there is little sign that this sphere is extending because:

> it comes up against the fact that less specialized actors and the general public possess no particular motivation to engage in the required cognitive investment. More profoundly still, their reluctance to change is compounded by the fact that so few efficient symbolic mechanisms exist which might encourage a rearticulation of their habitual framework of references and the upheavals introduced by the emergence of a European level of government.
>
> (Foret 2003: 82, author's translation)

Indeed, although most public actors in Europe now tackle most of their political work as if one single government of Europe existed (Smith 2004a), the representative dimension of their activity singularly fails to reflect this transformation.

Shorn of many of the resources and rituals usually associated with political representation, Commissioners lack political legitimacy and these traits seem unlikely to change in the foreseeable future. Asked to do the impossible work of straddling the gulf between an embryonic European public sphere and its highly institutionalised national counterparts, little wonder that most holders of the office simply give up and take refuge in the role of technocrat or ambassador. Over and above what this tells us about Commissioners and the Commission, it provides important reasons for reflecting upon the specificity of politics as an activity within the EU as a whole (Smith 2004b). Such politics takes place within a single European public space that is far from complete, largely because most practitioners such as Commissioners consider it fruitless to invest heavily in their representational resources at this level. Less the result of careful calculation than an effect of institutionalised roles, this relative neglect of the EU as a sphere for public deliberation and debate leads such actors to attempt to remain present in national public spheres without necessarily giving them the resources to do so with much chance of success.

Notes

1 Part of our research entailed sociographical analysis of all the Commissioners who have held office since 1958. The bulk of our study, however, was centred upon eight Commissioners from two Colleges: Sir Leon Brittan, Ray Mac-Sharry, Christiane Scrivener and Jean Dondelinger of the second Delors Commission (1989–93); and Leon Brittan, Edith Cresson, Yves-Thibault de Silguy, Marcelino Oreja and Franz Fischler of the Santer Commission (1995–9). Although three of these persons were interviewed, most of our 70 interviews targeted the cabinet members of each Commissioner and their opposite numbers in the DG. In addition, the Commissioners' public speeches were systematically analysed. Of course, the College of Commissioners has evolved since 1999 and our study dealt only superficially with these changes. Nevertheless, unsystematic observation of recent events does not appear to invalidate analysis based upon previous periods.
2 For analysis of the investiture procedure per se, see Magnette 2001.
3 Given the controversies sparked by the investiture of the Prodi and Barrosso Commissions, the time is certainly ripe for an in-depth and comparative study of this question.
4 Interview, November 1999.
5 In particular, it facilitated the obtaining of an enhanced communication budget for the campaign for the euro.
6 Cresson spent much of January 1999 trying to persuade MEPs to lift the charges against her. Recalling this episode, a member of her cabinet stressed that 'there were journalists all over the place – the dramatisation of a large-scale trial. She had to respond to questions and in the cabinet we prepared her for this by doing simulations and writing "defensive points". But we were up against MEPs who mixed everything up and others who distributed tracts during our meetings.' Interview, November 2000.
7 On this point, Baisnée (2004: 231) recounts how during a press conference he attended in the EP in November 1999, most journalists only arrived in time to listen to Romano Prodi and Commissioner Barnier. As soon as these actors left, the press gallery emptied.
8 This term was used by one of de Silguy's cabinet members. Interview, October 1999.
9 Many of our interviewees criticised media coverage of the EU and sometimes even accused journalists of a form of 'European treason'. Interview, October 1999.
10 See the novel by Stanley Johnson, an ex-European civil servant (1987: 52–5).
11 This finding is based upon the Secretariat General's archives of written speeches and those placed on the Commission's website. The speech in question was by Oreja in Lisbon on 27 March 1995 during the opening of a European Information Centre.
12 This unit was made up of Pinheiro's head of cabinet, members of President Delors' cabinet, and officials from DG X and the Secretariat General.
13 This discourse was subsequently formalised in a communication from the European Commission (1996).
14 Interview, December 1998.
15 Interview, November 1998.
16 There are some exceptions to this rule. Revealingly, Edith Cresson kept two of her three spokespersons outside her cabinet.
17 First used by Max Weber (1971: 114), the concept of 'political enterprise' has been used by political scientists to denote 'all conscious attempts to conquer and exercise political power' (Gaxie 1993: 27). It encourages us to examine the

goals and strategies of Commissioners and their closest collaborators, not just what structures their activity (Joana and Smith 2002: 19).

18 That is, an official recruited by competition and who, therefore, would have been trained in law or economics but certainly not in journalism.

19 This is done in Joana and Smith (2002: 224–31). For a full analysis of this episode and its consequences, see Baisnée 2003b (Part 3).

20 The expression was used by one of his former cabinet members. Interview, November 1999.

21 Brittan himself recounts that, during a farewell meeting with activists from his constituency party in late 1988, 'Most people did not know what a Commissioner was and I found it hard to explain. The only people who understood were the farmers because of the CAP – they were the only ones to actually congratulate me!' Interview, January 2001.

22 Interview with cabinet member, January 2001 and confirmed by Brittan himself (2000: 185).

23 See 'Don't Oppose Blair Tonight', a personal opinion published in the *Daily Telegraph*, 12 November 1997.

24 See, e.g. 'Brittan lays into Hague's "dated" policy on Europe'; *Guardian*, 29 May 1998.

25 Interview, November 2000.

26 Interview with cabinet member, November 2000.

27 Interview, December 2000.

28 This also reflects a lack of attention given to the popular press. 'It worked for a while with the *Sun* because Leon is good with the soundbite and got on well with Trevor Kavanagh, the political editor. But as it became too Europhile, we dropped this angle. Ultimately, he had an instinctive desire to talk to "his" press – the *Telegraph* and *The Times* – because it was what his cronies read. He hardly ever cared about the *Independent* or the *Guardian*.' Interview with one of Brittan's spokesmen, May 2001.

29 Interview on a Belgian television channel, 29 September 1992. Also see her speech to the Kangaroo group of MEPs, London, 12 November 1992.

13 Transparency, audiences and the evolving role of the EU Council of Ministers

Deirdre Curtin

Introduction

The sphere we call public is an area of public space. This is well reflected in the manner in which Habermas uses the word '*Öffentlichkeit*' in the sense of 'openness' or 'publicity' to represent the notion of public space. In this public space, matters are *ipso facto* conducted 'in public'. Publics form themselves around visible and audible focuses of attention (Hannay 2005: 33). *Public* deliberation and/or debate can be considered the single most important element in the assessment of *democratic* quality. In an open public debate, decision-makers are forced to give *reasons*, and this enhances transparency and public accountability (Eriksen and Fossum 2000: 17). The term 'public' and the principle of publicity are often subsumed under the concept of 'transparency' in the context of debates in the European Union. *Brewer's Politics* even defines the term 'transparency' as 'the catch word for the openness of the operations of the European Community to the public gaze'.[1]

Transparency is in fact more often invoked than described, and it is more often described than defined. The term 'transparency' is quite simply the condition of being transparent. The origins of the term from the Latin '*transparere*' suggest something appearing as a result of light shining through; as a result, the composition of the space in question can be seen and understood. The aim of achieving more transparency in the functioning of public EU institutions is lauded by the European institutions themselves, the politicians and bureaucrats, Members of the European Parliament (MEPs), the judiciary and civil society. All these actors expect beneficial effects of EU transparency. In the short time frame of its emergence as a fundamental guiding principle of the EU political system, it has been presented as a type of holistic medicine designed to remedy many of the ailments the body of the EU is perceived to have. Thus, we are told, it will increase the legitimacy of the EU, increase the citizens' understanding of what the EU is about, stimulate deliberation about policy matters and enable participation by citizens and their representatives. A central ailment is the EU's limited legitimacy, and transparency (through the Internet) has been propagated as a means to boost its legitimacy. Most recently, in the text of the Constitutional Treaty, the Preamble informs us of the symbolic value of transparency since a 'reunited Europe' intends to 'deepen the democratic and transparent nature of its public life'.[2]

Although not always up-front, it seems that transparency in the sense of (voluntary) disclosure of information by public actors is generally closely connected to social legitimacy. It is often argued that transparency (and deliberation) will enhance public acceptance of institutional structures (see, however, Curtin and Meijer 2006). One of the fundamental assumptions underlying a more deliberative, participatory understanding of democracy – which is even enshrined in the text of the Constitutional Treaty – is that the requisite information is easily and publicly accessible. Hence, transparency can be considered an essential part of its operating system. Without transparency and readily available information on 'visible' actors and policies, no proper deliberation and participation is feasible.

One is accustomed to analysing the European Commission both as a nascent federal type of 'government' and as a regulator and facilitator of networks. At least as regards the former, its systemic role with regard to an evolving (supranational) public sphere is readily apparent. The discourse is quite different with regard to the Council of Ministers, however, which is traditionally analysed as the intergovernmental body *par excellence* in the EU, with its ministers tied to the national democratic and public spheres only. It is traditionally argued that opening up its meetings and documents would hamper the ability of the Council to reach decisions at all. It has gradually been recognised that as an arm of the legislative power at the EU level, the Council must open up quite significantly. Less well accepted is that with regard to its non-legislative role, especially in the newer policy areas of a Common Foreign and Security Policy (CFSP) and Justice and Home Affairs (JHA), the Council also needs to work actively on making its structures, committees and agencies much more 'visible' and open to the public and to other fora, including both the European Parliament (EP) and national parliaments. In this regard, the debate at the European level has tended to focus on the Commission and its various roles, with under-recognition of the fact that in some respects the Council of Ministers can be considered to be a parallel public administration, with significant non-legislative tasks and activities. The fact that much of this activity takes place away from the spotlights of publicity and openness lends support to the role of the Council in non-legislative problem-solving that fits within what has been termed a *regulatory model* of the EU, a term normally reserved for the Commission and its role inter alia as a facilitator of networks.

The evolving non-legislative role of the Council of Ministers

The Council of Ministers is traditionally perceived as the 'decision-making centre' of the EU (Wessels 1991: 133). Its legislative role has been consolidated in recent years, either in partnership with the EP or alone. Just as it has taken some time to realise that in the newer so-called 'intergovernmental' areas of 'cooperation' the Council effectively performs a legislative function, it is also taking some time to recognise that the Council of Ministers is also carrying out tasks that can only be described as being of a non-legislative and hence executive nature. Traditionally, in the Community system, lawyers recognised that the Council of Ministers possessed residual executive power – but power explicitly meant to be delegated to the Commission (Lenaerts and van Nuffel 2005).

In particular, the Council of Ministers largely assumed responsibility for the implementation of legislation and delegated rule-making in the newer policy fields (CFSP and JHA) in a manner which it never did in the traditional Community system (under the so-called 'Community method'), where the Council simply had some reserve powers of execution (in addition to control over the Commission for the manner of its execution of Community legislation). The Council of Ministers, as an institution, exercised its newly found powers in a manner that largely excluded the Commission, thereby ensuring the marginalisation of the Commission's position in these newer policy fields. While rarely expressed in these terms, the Council as an EU institution acquired and exercised a series of executive-type tasks which would normally have been entrusted to the Commission under the Community system, or hitherto to the member states themselves. In the newer policy areas, the Council has come to occupy a role very similar to that exercised by the Commission with regard to the older policy areas. For example, the Council plays a very important executive role in setting the overall JHA agenda, in a sense usurping the role that the Commission has traditionally played with regard to other policy areas. The same phenomenon can be noted with regard to external relations matters, with either the Council or its organs playing the leading role (e.g. the Director of Europol as regards agreements with third countries and other international organisations).

Moreover, the 'threat' to the institutional position of the Commission has not come simply from the fact that the Council, over the course of little more than a decade, has kept for itself tasks which it would normally have delegated to the Commission in the Community system, but also from the fact that it has effectively established an additional locus of executive power at the Union level, with its own 'satellites' alongside that of the Commission and its 'satellites'. This is a new phenomenon, which could not be said to exist prior to the entry into force of the Maastricht Treaty in 1993. It has come about mainly due to the fact that the exercise of the Council's original executive power is not only to be understood as the technical or other implementation of legislative-type measures (in parallel with what the Commission does under 'comitology') but also as the building up of decision-taking instances under the auspices of the Council, as well as the construction of an (increasingly elaborate) 'operational' strand to its activities across a wide variety of internal and external policy-making fields. In other words, such activities and tasks carried out under the auspices of the Council of Ministers accord more with the *regulatory* model of the EU than with the *federal* model, as outlined in Chapter 1.

The tendency across academic disciplines, but in particular in law and political science, has been to discuss the institutional position of the Council of Ministers vis-à-vis that of the Commission in the familiar, but ultimately not very helpful, language of intergovernmentalism versus supranationalism. Many authors have argued that the Council is to be understood as institutionalised intergovernmentalism by the member states acting collectively (Christiansen 2001). The Council provides for the formal representation of member states in the EU. Yet given that there is not one single member-state point of view on any given policy initiative, the Council is *ipso facto* the main forum for negotiation in the EU.

One of the defining features of the Council of Ministers is that, by diplomatic negotiations, it distils the bottom line in terms of the collective of national interests. In other words, the process of reaching a decision by negotiation and compromise – until very recently behind closed doors – gives the Council a distinct institutional status in the EU landscape. Such arguments have been advanced in recent years to substantiate the claim that the Council cannot be subject to the obligation to open up its proceedings, as letting in some sunshine would at the same time negate its ability to reach decisions at all (Bunyan 1999). However, what Christiansen (2001) refers to as 'institutionalised intergovernmentalism' may in fact need a further nuance, since in the exercise of both its legislative and executive role the rather autonomous nature of the Council of Ministers' activities as an institutional actor is becoming apparent. This is in spite of the strong governmental inputs fed into its decision-taking mechanisms, by means of the national civil servants sitting on the committees and working parties of its rotating Presidency system. It is precisely the 'actorness' of certain levels of the Council that has accelerated considerably in recent years with the General Secretariat and the Secretary-General, both assuming ever-greater responsibilities and tasks as the process of European integration progresses in intensity and scope. On this reading of both normative provisions and legal and institutional practices, it seems that some re-evaluation as to the nature of the Council of Ministers may well be called for.

What is often underestimated in considering the Council is the important role played by the permanent officials and by the national civil servants who staff the Council's gamut of working parties and co-ordinating committees – such as the Strategic Committee on Immigration, Frontiers and Asylum (SCIFA) – in driving forward specific measures, within the broad parameters of policy set by the member state holding the Presidency. The General Secretariat of the Council has evolved from having a passive notary or registrar role to a much more active one in assisting the Presidency:

> not only in the application of procedures, but also in preparing for substantive negotiations; at the same time, the role of the Legal Service has become established and has developed to encompass intergovernmental conferences; in general, the six-monthly rotating Presidency with its increased role has made it more and more necessary to call upon the General Secretariat's assistance in ensuring continuity and efficiency of work by giving successive Presidencies the benefit of the experience it has accumulated over the years.
>
> (Trumpf and Piris 1999: Chapter 12)

Some are beginning to recognise that the General Secretariat of the Council has a pivotal role to play in behind-the-scenes outcomes and even, on a number of occasions, has shifted outcomes closer to its own vision of the manner in which the EU should evolve (Christiansen 2003; Beach 2004). It plays a central role in the Presidency's gathering of information and works side by side with the Presidency throughout negotiations. Through long-term involvement in dossiers and informal communication with government representatives, the Secretariat gains an in-depth and horizontal knowledge of state preferences: 'Much like Commission officials gain intimate knowledge of a subject when preparing a proposal, the civil servants of the Secretariat develop an issue-specific expertise when tracing a dossier through the Council machinery' (Talberg 2004).

The evolution of transparency in the Council of Ministers

In 1998, the European Ombudsman, Jacob Söderman defined the term 'transparency', in a rather narrow fashion, as mandating that 'the process through which public authorities make decisions should be understandable and open; the decisions themselves should be reasoned; as far as possible, the information on which the decisions are based should be available to the public' (Söderman 1998). The emphasis in this definition clearly lies on the legal dimension – the formal manner in which decisions are reasoned – as well as on the issue of public access to information (Vesterdorf 1999: 903; Deckmyn 2002: 35). According to Lord Nolan (1995: 14), transparency is said to require that 'holders of public office should be as open as possible about all decisions and actions they take'. They should, in his view, give reasons for their decisions and restrict information only when the wider public interest clearly so demands. It can be argued, however, that transparency not only incorporates the rather passive right of every citizen to have access to information (if they activate that formal legal right) but also the much broader and more proactive duty of the administration itself to ensure that information about its policy and actions is accessible.

The evolution of the concept of transparency in the context of the EU can be divided into two periods. The first – initial – period was dominated by a legal understanding and, in particular, a focus on the principle of access to information. This built on existing legal case law on the right to be heard, the right to have reasoned decisions and to have access to a file (Bradley 1999; Ragnemalm 1999; Vesterdorf 1999). It gave further substance to the quite developed legal accountability mechanisms within the framework of the EU. It is based on the specific responsibilities of three decision-making institutions (the European Commission, the Council and the EP) that have now been laid down in increasingly 'hard' legal instruments and also the interpretation by the European Courts of legal standards laid down in such measures.

The focus in this first time period was on gradually constructing a right of access by the public to certain categories of document held by the three decision-making institutions. The European Courts played a crucial role. In a short period of time, they effectively built a body of case law that on the whole kept pressure on the institutions to behave fairly and to devise adequate systems of scrutiny. They tended rather generously to interpret the scope of the legal provisions so that, for example, specific institutional arrangements did not operate to reduce the reach of the access provisions. Thus, in the very first case to reach the European Courts, the *Guardian* journalist John Carvel successfully challenged the Council's refusal to grant him the agenda and minutes of various Council meetings, including those relating to policy-making in the new and sensitive area of Justice and Home Affairs. Later, the Swedish Union of Journalists challenged the refusal of the Council to reveal documents relating to the establishment of Europol, using the more generous Swedish Freedom of Information Law to highlight the unnecessary degree of secrecy that prevailed at the European level.

The technique of legal interpretation used by the Courts during this foundational period involved a type of teleological reasoning which placed the Code of Conduct adopted by the three decision-making institutions in the context of its broader democratic purpose. The Courts tended to emphasise the underlying purpose of access to information, namely to provide the 'public', the citizens, with a means of controlling the abuse of power and corruption, as well as resting on general notions of public control of the activities of public institutions. Thus, the Courts developed what can be termed a constitutional perspective on access to information provisions *avant la lettre*. Only later were these 'rights' given an explicitly constitutional foundation, first in the Charter on Fundamental rights and later in the Constitutional Treaty. This thinking is clearly based on ideas of a democratic-constitutional model, in line with the *federal* model outlined in Chapter 1.

The legal phase culminated with the adoption of a new and binding legal instrument, Regulation 1049/2001 that entered into force on 3 December 2001. This Regulation introduced more transparency into the work of the EU institutions (European Commission 2003). In conclusion, some ten years after its commencement, the legal-constitutional approach can be considered as solidly anchored in legal texts, including those at the most fundamental level of the Constitutional Treaty. The provisions on public access to documents clearly have caused changes by giving citizens a tool to obtain the documents they wish to obtain, albeit with a considerable and significant time lag.

The Internet played a limited role in this period since the EU did not actively create transparency. Documents were provided to citizens only when they specifically asked for them. It was, however, only the implementation in practice of the obligation on each of the three decision-making institutions to make available and maintain a register of documents that enabled the 'public' to know to what sorts of documents they might want to have access. In providing such a register, the Internet does play an important role.

During this first, more legal stage of transparency and access to information, the Council was adamant that it would not be appropriate to open up further its decision-making processes. In particular, it insisted in various court cases in the mid-to-late 1990s that its decision-making procedures could not be compared to those of a legislative body as, due to its composition by government ministers, it proceeded by *diplomatic negotiation* which depended on a large measure of secrecy and discretion. Moreover, at least during the 1990s, a majority of the member states rather persistently resisted attempts to open up further the Council proceedings, often voting against applications by individuals taken under the access-to-documents provisions in place at that time. Simultaneously, the same majority voted for changes to the Council's Rules of Procedure that only half-heartedly gave effect to the principle of public access to documents.

The legal approach was underpinned by the complementary work of the Ombudsman who also adopted a rather legal approach in his work, although his emphasis was more on the structural aspects of the manner in which certain institutions, mainly the Council and the Commission, made information available or not. Thus, the first Ombudsman tended to focus on substantiating what he termed 'good administrative behaviour', in a manner highly complementary to the more formal judicial interpretation of the Courts (Magnette 2003). Indeed, the work of the Ombudsman helped to move the understanding of transparency in the EU context away from an individual and passive focus on the legal right of every citizen to have access to certain documents to a much broader and proactive duty of the EU administration to ensure that information about its policies and actions would be made genuinely accessible. The work of the Ombudsman in this period facilitated the process of creating visible public spaces around which publics could form.

The best way of understanding the legal contribution to the transparency discourse is that it has made some of the institutions more aware of how they can proactively make their own information available to a broader public using information and communication technologies. The second phase in the debate on transparency has come from the institutions themselves albeit prompted, and at times pushed, by certain actors such as active members of the general public seeking to push back the frontiers of openness.

In the later, and more overtly political phase of the development of transparency in the EU, transparency is perceived not only as a goal in itself but also as a tool for a more democratic way of working and reaching decisions. The Commission's *White Paper on Governance* also suggests that more transparency will lead to a better involvement in the processes of EU policy-making (European Commission 2001a). The Commission also makes the link with increasing the citizen's sense of belonging in Europe:

> Democracy depends on people being able to take part in *public debate*. To do this, they must have access to reliable information on European issues and be able to scrutinise the policy process in various stages. [...] Providing more information and more effective communication are a pre-condition for generating a sense of belonging to Europe.
>
> (European Commission 2001a: 11, author's emphasis)

This argues that transparency will enhance public acceptance of the institutional structures of the EU. The White Paper also suggests that more transparency will lead to better involvement in the processes of EU policy-making.

The Council was initially not very forthcoming in ordering its information in a user-friendly fashion, perhaps because it has had more difficulty in being candid about the scope of its expanded executive-type tasks in recent years (Curtin 2004). In any event, the legislative role of the Council, both with regard to traditional EC policy matters as well as with regard to the new policy area of Justice and Home Affairs, gradually became more visible. For example, after the Council Framework Decision on the European Arrest Warrant was approved, few could deny that such measures, adopted in secret conclave by the Council with no drafts made available on time for either parliaments or individuals to make any input in the debate and decision-making process, were effectively binding legislation to be implemented by the member states. There are few who now argue that there should not be full openness and transparency as far as the legislative activity of the Council is concerned (Bauer 2004; Driessen 2005). Indeed, the text of the Constitutional Treaty confirmed this by defining in a much more distinct manner the definition of what constitutes a legislative act and requiring that the Council's legislative activity take place under the public gaze. The bone of contention concerns the Council's 'non-legislative' work, which as the Constitutional Treaty itself reveals, is made much more visible than was previously the case (Curtin 2004). The analogy is made by some between the need for the Council's non-legislative work to be afforded a comparable degree of confidentiality to any collective 'cabinet' type function in order to ensure an effectively functioning executive (Bauer 2004).

It has often been because of a process of pushing and pulling by certain more active members and organisations of civil society that EU institutions have made available whole categories of information in the public domain, thus increasing the visibility of particular questions. Thus, during the late 1990s the British civil liberties organisation Statewatch mounted a concerted strategy of challenging Council practices by reference to the Ombudsman about how they made their information available to the public. The result is that today the Council maintains an extensive and accessible register on the Internet of its documents pertaining both to its legislative and executive activities. Furthermore, information on the composition of committees and working parties and the like can be found on the website.

In this second period, the Internet has played a much more important role and is the main medium for the EU to create transparency for the widely dispersed population of Europe. European websites grant access to an enormous amount of information on European policy-making and policy execution. The increased development of Internet use and the growing transparency of the EU are indeed concurrent developments. Despite the Council's maintenance of an extensive register of documents that is more complete compared to that of the Commission, some structural problems remain. For those with the expertise, time and courage to wade through the masses of documents placed on the Internet, it is possible to engage in a process of some scrutiny of and deliberation about the multifarious activities of the Council in its diverse configurations. Those who use the access provisions have tended to be professionals (journalists, lawyers and academics) with some of the required expertise. The legal arena of rights and principles has only to a very limited extent empowered the 'public' in any meaningful sense.[3] For this reason, the exercise of the formal legal right of access to information has been dismissed as insignificant in the first ten years of its life (Cotino 2005). One can, however, argue that the early challengers were given the tools to peer into previously dark rooms and to force the institutions to justify and, more often than not, modify their behaviour.

From previous studies it is clear that as a matter of practice only those citizens with expert knowledge of the policy subject make use of the possibility to read information about a particular policy, the process and the actors involved (ibid.). It follows that increasing public access to documents will not automatically lead to a situation in which a majority of citizens feel sufficiently well informed on European matters to constitute an 'audience'. The Council, along with the other institutions of the EU, subscribes to the objective of a more active policy of making information available – but struggles to make it a reality. There are several other relevant factors in this context, such as professional capacities in dealing with the press, quality of the information, readability of documents, hierarchy of information criteria and selection of the news by the media (Deckmyn 2002: 120). Moreover, the sting in the tail with regard to the Council is that it is only now beginning to face the fact that it performs a range of executive-type activities that previously might have been carried out by the Commission and that it believes that many of these activities can be fenced off from the public and from the possibility of any meaningful public debate.

Understanding the Council as speaker and performer

Those who insist on a purely intergovernmental reading of the Council as composed of national ministers subject to national accountability, albeit indirectly in the national political system, underestimate the role of the Council as a 'performer' or a 'speaker' in the European arena. The Council has evolved as an institution and with tasks of public administration in its own right. First, it is not only the ministers who are the 'performers'; even more significant in recent years has been the accretion of tasks and the growth in the role of bureaucrats in the system. There are two strands: bureaucrats working in the Council's General Secretariat and those coming from national administrations that participate and take decisions in various Council committees. Second, the Council, like the Commission, increasingly needs to have recourse to 'experts'. These are both expert bureaucrats and autonomous scientific experts such as those in the comitology committees or independent agencies. Generally, however, scholars analyse and comment on the role of experts in relation to the Commission and not the Council, even though when looking at the type and complexity of issue areas that are being dealt with by the Council, this can be considered surprising and seems to be an unnecessarily myopic view.

The paradox is that expertise is a resource increasingly sought for policy-making and for social choice, but at the same time one also increasingly contested (European Commission 2001b: 4). In general, the lack of transparency in the way expertise is selected, used and diffused by governments is considered by many to undermine the legitimacy of the policy process. Efforts to restore the credibility of expertise, and trust in it, have been part of the Commission's thinking on the reform of EU governance, in particular in its White Paper. The trend is to open up the 'technocratic' process, formerly regarded as driven by an expert elite, to increase transparency and to broaden participation in decision-making. Making expertise more accessible is considered important by the Commission and progress has been made, but as the Commission itself has pointed out:

> [T]his has to go hand-in-hand with other more fundamental changes. Among these, [...] more accountability and procedures to provide a 'trace' of sources and uses of expertise; procedures to acknowledge minority views; involvement of 'stakeholders' at early stage; and better management of uncertainty.
>
> (European Commission 2001b: 14)

Why is it important for citizens to know which experts participate in policy-making and how they influence the process? First of all, it is vital for citizens to check the independence of experts. According to Guy Peters and Anthony Barker (1993: 189), it is essential for experts to be independent of the governmental process and for their advice to be entirely based on their expert knowledge and not on their personal interests. Only bodies with established competence and the ability to form their opinion independently can give advice on decision-making (Joerges and Vos 1999: 333). Interestingly, experts often present themselves as independent (Fischer 1990: 160). Through transparency mechanisms it is possible for citizens to check the backgrounds, opinions, interests and working procedures of experts and they can conclude for themselves whether an expert is independent or not. To control their independence, citizens are dependent on the public nature of the information in question (Welch and Wong 2001).

The Council and its various performers conduct a discourse among themselves but the issue of an audience with some distance from the performers is more problematic. The role of the public as an audience is emphasised by Jürgen Habermas (1989), and the distance between the performer(s) or speaker(s) and the audience must be accounted for. This brings an important conceptual clarification, namely that if it is only a question of speakers or performers appreciating each other's performances then, arguably, a requisite part of the public is missing – the audience. Only with publicity can discussions be conducted in front of an audience. As Elster (1998: 111) observes, the effect of publicity is 'to replace the language of interest by the language of reason'. If discussions are conducted in front of an audience, speakers not only have to try and persuade their opponents, they also have to show that they take impartial concerns seriously. Otherwise, their proposals will easily be rejected as contradicting the collective well-being (Neyer 2003: 694).

The audience may consist of the general public or of more specialised publics and the communication taking place is part of 'opinion formation' (as opposed to 'will formation'), which is the domain of the public sphere. One of the problems in the context of the EU is that the European public space is disjointed and fragmented, leading to the risk that different speakers talk to different audiences (often disconnected national publics) and serve different, and even mutually exclusive normative expectations. With the Council as an evolving executive power, it is thus important to differentiate more precisely what types of public it interacts with. Also, we must consider what mechanisms of transparency and communication exist in order to facilitate this discourse.

What often seems to happen in the interstices of Council decision-making is that the discussion only takes place between the performers themselves, as bureaucrats (both European and national) or as experts, or as both. As has been pointed out above, one can only refer to discussions, deliberation and decisions taking place in a public sphere when there are both performers and an audience with some distance between them.

Publics do not act; they do not take decisions – they merely deliberate and form opinions about what should be done. Informal arenas for public discussion and opinion formation provide what Erik O. Eriksen (2000: 54) refers to as a 'context of discovery'. In that context, problems are identified and solutions articulated, thematised and dramatised in such a way that potentially they become relevant for formal decision-making bodies. Moreover, it is important to recall that the public sphere is not entirely an entity in itself; rather, it is created and formed in opposition to decision-making agencies. In other words, there must be some sort of open and public interplay between institutionalised will formation ('strong publics') and informal opinion-formation processes ('weak publics') (Eriksen and Fossum 2000).

Conclusion

Transparency can be considered a necessary condition for broad public debate on policy-making processes. The criterion of public debate means that deliberation by policy makers has to be rendered public and debated in national and European media and through national and European parliaments (De la Porte and Nanz 2004). In Habermasian terms, it is crucial for opinion formation to lead to will formation in the political public sphere. There can only be public debate to the extent that information is made public. From the outset, the practice developed by the Commission was to send its annual reports not only to the parliaments (both national and the EP) but also to make them available to the public. The same line has been followed by the Council, which has adopted the practice of preparing and disseminating annual reports on the activities of the EU. The latter have tended to focus on developments in the newer policy areas of CFSP and JHA where the role of the Council has been primordial. All are distributed widely in the national and European contexts and are made public, most recently on the Internet.

Given the EU's bad reputation for secretive decision-taking behind closed doors, it seems particularly appropriate to focus on the issue of the *public* nature of decision-making. A crucial part of the executive and legislative structures in the EU, namely those involving the Council, are often set apart from debates on increasing public deliberation over various EU processes. In other words, not only is the Council not engaging with non-bureaucratic actors in a deliberative way prior to decision-taking, but there are also largely non-public conclaves nestling within its institutional structures. The newer policy areas of CFSP and JHA have certainly helped to bring the problem more to the fore. The hypothesis is that there is a mismatch between the rhetoric and practice on transparency and public access to documents on the one hand, and the Council's secretive structures and rule-making processes on the other, especially in the more executive sphere of activity. The Council still represents a bastion of bureaucratic decision-making both by European and national civil servants with a veneer of ministerial involvement. The 'audience' is still distant from the Council's performances and speech acts.

Notes

1 William Safire, 'On Language: Transparency Totally', *New York Times*, 4 January 1998, p. 4.
2 Treaty Establishing a Constitution for Europe, *Official Journal of the European Union*, C 310, Vol. 47, 16 December 2004.
3 See e.g. the review of the operation of the regulation (European Commission 2004) and the Council's annual report on access to documents (Council of the European Union 2005).

14 Transnationalising the public sphere?

The European Parliament, promises and anticipations

Ulrike Liebert

Introduction

It is conventional wisdom that the European Union is short of a truly
democratic transnational public sphere, conceived of as a 'space for the
communicative generation of public opinion, in ways that are supposed to
ensure (at least some degree of) moral-political validity' (Fraser 2005: 37).
Yet it remains controversial as to whether such a transnational communicative sphere is necessary, desirable and feasible for the EU, and what it
eventually should look like.

On the one hand, there are those who envisage a federal republic of
Europe understood, ultimately, as a community of citizens. From this
perspective, a European public sphere is transnational and a correlate of
authoritative decision-making by the Union. Especially in the context of
enhanced pluralism and deepened inequalities in the New Europe, it
matters who participates on what terms since transnational communication is supposed to enable the citizenry to exercise influence over European political elites as well as vis-à-vis private powers. On the other hand,
there are those advocating a Union of sovereign states sharing a common
market regime. In this view, the need for inclusive discursive arenas for citizens' public information, opinion formation and communicative empowerment vis-à-vis governments remains largely confined to member states,
but transnational communicative spaces might emerge, if triggered by
functional interests and depending on the logic of the market.

In both perspectives, whether a democratic political vision or a merely
functional finality of European integration, the ensuing processes of Europeanisation will affect the patterns and dynamics of nationally bounded
communications, albeit in different forms and with different outcomes. In
the first case, as a consequence of European political integration, the
politicisation of conflict will be a catalyst for transnationalising the mass
public spheres. By contrast, functional integration will promote sectoral
publics, leaving mass publics segmented by national boundaries, with little
synchronisation and limited convergence. To fulfil the norms of a democratic public sphere, each of these models of European public opinion

and will formation needs to connect to the circuits of authoritative decision-making. If modern democratic legislatures rely on the idea of an institutionalised space for public communications that is supposed to empower the citizenry vis-à-vis the state as well as with regard to private powers, the European Parliament (EP) takes centre stage.

However, surprisingly little is known about the EP's functions in relation to a European public sphere. Political scientists, due to their disciplinary fascination with power and attachment to the liberal democratic paradigm in parliamentary research, frequently privilege legislative activity, interest representation and negotiation; media sociologists, on the other hand, prefer studying the media and civil society communications instead of parliamentary deliberations.[1] This chapter aims to assess the promises and pitfalls regarding a truly democratic public sphere of European communications by focusing on the EP. Hence, it explores whether the EP can be conceived of as a 'strong public', constituting a central site for engendering European political communication. Given the current configuration of the EU polity, what are the limitations of the EP with respect to a democratic public sphere? Furthermore, which parliamentary mechanisms of representation account for the different patterns of communicative Europeanisation and their deficits? Finally, given the current practices of the EP, which model promises best to resolve both the EP's weaknesses of communication and its democratic deficit?

My argument is that the EP's shortcomings as a 'strong public' are rooted in its representative role, since the liberal democratic representative link with constituencies reduces the EP's potential for more deliberative forms of communication. Hence, liberal representation explains why the EP reproduces the segmented condition of the European communicative space. Strengthening deliberative representation will promote a transnational European sphere of publics.

My argument proceeds in three steps, analysing the pitfalls, prerequisites and promises regarding the EP as a central site of communicative Europeanisation. First, regarding its limits as a potentially 'strong public', I assess the EP's configuration within the EU polity. Second, by drawing on Jane Mansbridge's (2003) typology of representation I explore how 'promissory' and 'anticipatory' representation work as means of public communication and as prerequisites for the EP to evolve into a stronger public. Finally, I map out the vision of a 'federal Europe of citizens' which vis-à-vis that of a 'Europe of states' promises to best resolve the EU's communication gap and thus its democratic deficit.

A 'strong public' in the EU? Pitfalls of the EP

In view of the unprecedented structure of the EU as a new form of multi-level and pluri-national polity, the European public sphere cannot be conceived along national lines and should rather be depicted as a radically different, possibly 'postmodern' form. To capture the 'polyphonic and polymorphic European public spaces' that are deliberately forged or unintendedly provoked by the evolving European polity, Erik Oddvar Eriksen in Chapter 2 distinguishes between 'general publics', 'segmented publics' and 'strong publics', where the last is defined as 'legally institutionalised and regulated discourses specialised in collective will formation at the polity centre' (p. 32).

Given the configuration of the EU, to what extent can we classify the EP as a 'strong public'? Political scientists are sceptical about whether contemporary parliaments can provide democratic legitimacy for collective decisions. Over more than a millennium of parliamentary history, this institution has assumed multiple functions. These range from the oversight, selection and sometimes removal of political authority, public discussion, social representation, legislation and policy-making, to protecting transparency, accountability, and the openness of the political process, especially in European systems of parliamentary majority rule (Döring 1995; von Beyme 1999). Yet, the evolution of parliaments is portrayed as a history of crisis and decline. Democratic parliamentarism is seen as undermined by the advent of party government and interest group politics, constrained by globalisation, overburdened by new technological risks, the increased scientisation of politics and the use of experts by nonparliamentary systems of 'governance', all to the disadvantage of parliament (Burns 1999; Burns *et al.* 2000; cf. Maurer and Wessels 2001). Spanning at least a century and half, the controversy about parliamentary decline has not stopped short at the national level and has reached the EP as well.

The idea of modern democratic legislatures as institutionalised spaces for public communication that empower the citizenry vis-à-vis the state as well as with regard to private powers appears to contrast with the EP's practices. First of all, the EU is a conglomerate of varied organisational forms, including decision-making bodies such as the Commission, the Council and the European Court of Justice (ECJ); agencies and committees such as the Committee of Permanent Representatives (COREPER), Comitology and the Conference of Community and European Affairs Committees of Parliaments of the European Union (COSAC); and deliberative bodies such as the two European Conventions. Caught within this highly complex configuration, the EP cannot be regarded as a 'central complex' according to any model of national parliamentary government. Rather, although far removed from the public eye, the Council enjoys the unrivalled political authority of making binding decisions, while the EP offers only one point among many points of access. Most importantly, the EP's institutionalised space for negotiation and deliberation is only selectively linked to the loci of decision-making.

Hence, to assess to what extent the EP can be depicted as a strong public space for institutionalised deliberation we need to establish: (1) in the EU's semi-parliamentary system, how closely the EP is effectively linked to the centre(s) of European political decision-making; (2) whether legal requirements allow for parliamentary deliberation that can hold decision makers accountable and have them provide justifications; and (3) whether the EP has the capacity of transforming input from the public sphere – by social constituencies and civil society as well as market forces – into communicative power that 'in turn serves to legitimise political decisions in parliament' (Habermas 1996a: 371).

Regarding the powers of the EP compared to the standards of parliamentary government, the Green Paper on 'the future of parliamentary democracy' (Burns *et al.* 2000) showed little disagreement that globalisation and European integration have strengthened the executive, the judiciary and the private powers at the expense of parliaments. Yet in view of this recurring perception of parliamentary decline the EP is a contradictory case in point, in four respects.

1   The EP, as the only example worldwide of a supranational parliament that has been elected directly by citizens of the member states since 1979, has established itself as a driving force behind important EU policies and reforms, by adopting reports designed to steer EU policy in a particular direction (Corbett 1998; Corbett *et al.* 2003). Examples are the EP's major contribution to the Charter of Fundamental Rights of the EU and its support for the creation of a Convention as a new way of preparing treaty reform by the Intergovernmental Conference (IGC). The latter was aimed at responding to European citizens' desire 'that the policies and procedures adopted to determine the future course of the Union will make the Union more democratic, more effective, more transparent, more vigorous and more responsive to social issues' (European Parliament 2001).

2   The parliamentarisation of legislation proceeds, although with delays with respect to granting the EP co-decision powers, in all areas of EU competence where majority voting prevails in the Council (Maurer and Wessels 2003: 85ff.): The treaty reforms of the 1990s successively reinforced the EP, in competition with the Council of Ministers, but the gains in power for the EP have barely compensated for losses suffered by the national parliaments. Since then, the EP has continuously strengthened its formal and informal powers, starting with the Single European Act (1987) and with each successive treaty reform. Thus, the EP has become a more influential player in EU policy-making, in institutional and in constitutional reform (Maurer 2002; Corbett *et al.* 2003; Judge and Earnshaw 2003; Maurer and Wessels 2003). By using its powers – from appointment and censure, through monitoring and consultancy to legislation and budgetary power – the EP fosters publicity and transparency in a range of activity spheres of the Union that otherwise would go completely unnoticed by the public.

First, the Council Presidency presents its programme and biannual report to the EP and informs it of the preparation for and outcome of European Councils. The EP's President makes a number of recommendations to the European Council as it sets general political guidelines for the Union. After each summit meeting, the President of the European Council reports to Parliament. Second, the Council consults the EP on major foreign policy decisions. The EP's recommendations to the Commission in relation to the World Trade Organization (WTO) carry a great deal of weight, since the EP has to give its assent to the outcome of WTO negotiations. Third, the EP's co-decision competence – its shared powers with the Council as the standard procedure of legislation – has enhanced the EP's political clout, but has also made legislative processes more transparent. Fourth, the EP and the Council share the power of the purse, as they share budgetary authority. The EP not only adopts the annual budget or rejects it if it believes it does not meet the needs of the Union, it also monitors the way the budget is spent. Finally, the EP has increasingly engaged with issues close to citizens' concerns that member governments were less interested in, namely education, consumer protection and equal opportunities.

3   Furthermore, over the past two decades and half, the EP has experienced a process of institutionalisation, including a continuous expansion of its competencies, the consolidation of its party structures and its committee organisation. Thus, the EP has turned away rapidly from an 'arena type parliament' – where ideological debates without political impact prevailed, such as in the British House of Commons – into a pragmatic, cooperative and increasingly successful actor in the legislative process, comparable to the US House of Representatives (Kreppel 2002).

4   Finally, over time, the EP has achieved increasing leverage over fraud control. In its 1999 budget monitoring, the EP found members of the European Commission guilty of financial mismanagement, did not approve the budget, and forced the Santer Commission to resign. It was also pivotal in setting up OLAF, a body devoted to combating fraud and corruption. As the effectiveness of the EP's monitoring and control functions confirm – it also changed the composition of the Barroso Commission through the appointment hearings in October 2004 – it should be acknowledged that the emerging EU polity is based on a separation of powers, where the EP is gradually strengthening its position vis-à-vis the Council and the Commission. EP powers do not include the appointment of the Commission but the ratification of the appointment of the Commission President, including confirmation hearings of the nominee commissioners, as well as censure of the Commission, deciding whether or not to remove the Commission by a vote of confidence.

Thus, thanks to repeated intergovernmental treaty negotiations, the EP as the EU's only directly elected institution has continued to expand its powers, from a modest 'conditional agenda-setter' (Tsebelis 1994) to a more influential co-legislator (Rittberger 2000), sharing legislative authority with the Council of Ministers and the Commission in an expanding number of areas (Pinder 1999; Hix *et al.* 2003; Pollack 2003: 256ff.; Rittberger 2003; Maurer 2005). Given the substantial differences in parliamentary and Council prerogatives across the various policy domains, we cannot speak of a progressive parliamentarisation of the executive. The governmental system of the EU polity remains distinct from the parliamentary systems of government that are dominant in Europe, since the EP does not elect either the Commission or the Council. It is also different from a presidential system of government, since member governments represented in the Council nominate the Commission members and president, which the EP approves. Although equipped with a growing range of competences (Rittberger 2003), its range of powers is still much more limited than that of parliaments in consolidated or even in new democracies. Hence, the emerging system can best be described as one of 'semi-parliamentarism' (Magnette 1999; Peters 2003). Furthermore, strengthening the EP's competences vis-à-vis the Council and the Commission is not sufficient to turn the EU into a viable 'communicative community' capable of generating direct democratic legitimacy. As long as other prerequisites are lacking – such as viable European political parties, a European identity and effective accountability at the domestic level – the EP may become a more powerful legislator, without necessarily resolving the EU's alleged democratic deficit (Dehousse 1998).[2] These reservations notwithstanding, the evolving EP and the idea of European representative government are nevertheless acknowledged as appropriate foundations for democracy in the EU (Pinder 1999).

In contrast to liberal theorists of 'deliberative democracy' who position themselves close to constitutionalism and see the public realm for effective, rational and legitimate deliberation as confined to traditional government institutions – notably courts and legislatures – as John Dryzek (2000: 3, 12) points out, critical and pluralistic theorists of 'discursive democracy' emphasise communicative spaces to which larger publics can be admitted. These include parliamentary procedures of formal deliberation that open themselves up for social, intersubjective discourses and public discourses that extend beyond state boundaries into settings without any constitutional framework.

Theories of deliberative democracy and the public sphere posit high standards, since the only force should be that of the better argument, with the aim of clarifying and appropriately transforming individual and collective interests, in the direction of both congruence and conflict.[3] From a deliberative theoretical perspective, European parliamentary procedures yield democratic legitimacy to the extent they provide space for public deliberation. To what extent are important decisions taken by the EU, where the EP serves as a central site for holding decision makers accountable, linked to influential parliamentary deliberation that includes perspectives from across member publics?

The EP can be depicted as a quintessential and unique sphere for transnational deliberation in five respects:

1   The EP – as a nomadic parliament that commutes between three different countries – convenes in Strasbourg for its plenary debates, has Luxemburg providing the site for the parliament's administration and gathers in Brussels for committee and party meetings. Members of the European Parliament (MEPs) spend one week each month at a plenary session in Strasbourg, and additional two-day sittings are held in Brussels.

2   Respect for linguistic and cultural diversity is enshrined in the European Charter of Fundamental Rights adopted by the EU in 2000. Language being a key marker of national identity and cultural diversity, the EP plenary operates under the constraints of extreme multilingualism. No other multinational body at regional or global level speaks as many official languages as the EU.[4] The 2004 enlargement brought the number of EU members from 15 to 25 and nearly doubled the number of official languages, from 11 to 20.[5] But the use of approximately 150 non-official regional or minority languages spoken by up to 50 million people in the member countries is also recognised, preserved and promoted by specific policies, programmes and actions.[6] Prior to the 2004 enlargement, the main EU institutions employed approximately 12,000 translators, translating nearly three million pages of text a year. To manage multilingualism, approximately one third of the EP's staff – some 3,500 officials recruited from all the member states – work as translators or interpreters. This investment, in fact, is a function of the EU priding itself on its distinctive multicultural and multilingual identity.[7]

3   European political parties are recognised by the Treaty as 'a factor for integration within the EU which contributes to forming a European awareness and to expressing the political will of the citizens', yet they do so without necessarily mobilising public opinion. Since the 1999 elections, the EP has had seven political groups that draw on more than 100 national parties as well as 'non-attached' members. One week of every month is reserved for meetings of parliamentary groups in Brussels. A parliamentary committee, a political group or a given number of MEPs can put oral questions to the Council and Commission on topics of public interest that usually lead to a debate. During plenary sessions, 'Question Time' with the Council and Commission provides a forum for such debates on topics of public interest. The mode of consensus-based decision-making is frequently seen as an

impediment to mobilising public opinion and structuring political conflict about European issues along ideological or programmatic party divisions. Yet analyses of voting patterns by the major parties in the EP since 1979 indicate that despite growing internal national and ideological diversity within the European party groups, the increased power of the EP has meant increased power for the transnational parties, and due to increased internal party cohesion and inter-party competition, the party system in the EP has become less collusive and more competitive as the powers of the EP have increased (Hix *et al.* 2003, 2005).

4   MEPs also sit on 17 parliamentary standing committees which do the preparatory work for the plenary sessions, draw up and adopt reports on legislative proposals and own-initiative reports and prepare opinions for other standing committees. In addition, the EP can set up temporary committees and committees of inquiry. Two weeks of every month are set aside for meetings of committees in Brussels.

5   Finally, a joint EP and Council regulation stipulates rules for transparency and openness regarding public access to EP, Council and Commission documents.[8] The translation of all final documents in all official community languages is legally required.[9]

These important preconditions of public deliberation notwithstanding, the EP's practices do not easily constitute a truly democratic site of public opinion formation because of several constraints. First, EP plenary debates are hardly ever transmitted by the national mass media. Second, MEP–constituency communications are structured by an electoral system that privileges national and not European political parties, thus fostering the 'segmented Europeanisation' of political communications within the boundaries of the member states. Third, institutional efforts have not been sufficient to secure the vital nexus between parliamentary deliberation and national public opinion formation. For instance, the mass communication deficit of the EP's press directorate on the occasion of the poor turnout in the 1999 elections has prompted two researchers to dub it a 'Great Non-communicator': MEPs failed to address key causes of electoral decline in the mass media, although these are a 'crucial means of communicating images of the Parliament to the electorate' (Anderson and McLeod 2004: 897). Finally, the established practices of broad cross-party consensual decision-making, and in the cases of the Commission and the Council, the lack of incentives for majority voting, make party-political controversy the exception rather than the rule, with detrimental effects for mobilising and structuring public opinion.

For the EP to reach out to the public, it must overcome the lack of certain preconditions that are normally taken for granted (although questionable) at the national level: a common language, a media and educational system, a 'demos' and a civil society. Given nationally fragmented media and the diversity of civil society in Europe, in view of the multi-plicity of languages, educational systems and 'demoi', it needs to be explained why the construction of European public spheres does never-theless occur and to what extent the EP takes part in it.

To generate democratic legitimacy on the input side, the EU builds on two sources. In a 'Europe of States', the European Council constitutes a source of indirect legitimacy derived from governments that are democra-tically elected in member states; from the perspective of 'Federal Europe' the EP is a carrier of authority delegated by the citizens through the act of voting. Regarding the latter, the right to vote in European parliamentary elections is considered to be the best developed, most visible and – relat-ively speaking – most effective of all rights that Union citizenship provides for. Regular elections guarantee a level of voter mobilisation that exceeds other forms of participation, with the exception of some member states where EU referenda are held (Hix *et al.* 2003).

On the other hand, critics point to plummeting participation rates in European parliamentary elections over the past 25 years.[10] It is doubtful that abstention is primarily motivated by the perceived powerlessness of the EP and whether strengthening its competences would reduce absten-tion since the communicative link between MEPs and member states' cit-izens might indicate structural weaknesses. To account for the declining attachment of citizens to the EP, a number of flaws have been explored (Blondel *et al.* 1998).

1   Successive enlargements and treaty reforms have structurally reduced citizens' voter power over their representatives, with mounting inequalities between the voting weight of large and small member states' constituencies.
2   As Blondel and others suggest, institutional changes such as that from non-proportional to proportional electoral systems, as has occurred in France, have helped to depress turnout by distancing the candidates from the voters and have given rise to dissatisfaction with the electoral process (Blondel *et al.* 1997: 265); yet, apparently in the UK it did not have this effect.
3   Attitudes do matter in shaping turnout. 'Lack of interest' was the primary reason given by two out of every five abstainers (ibid.), but also 'political distrust', 'dissatisfaction' and 'lack of knowledge' were frequently mentioned as accounting for abstention. Among abstain-ers, knowledge of European affairs generally and the lack of a 'more widespread positive image of the European Parliament' were conspic-uously absent.
4   Experience of European electoral campaigns was found to affect turnout positively. While intensive campaigning has an effect, the striking variations in election campaign penetration between coun-tries were not found to account for differences in levels of turnout.

But 'over and above campaign exposure people are motivated to vote by their attitude to Europe and to European questions and to the Parliament' (ibid.: 268).

5   There are deficiencies regarding media coverage of the EP, as it fails to transmit the information necessary for citizens to assess their representatives' performance and whether they have kept their promises. The Europeanisation of news remains weak and is mainly limited to events selected through the 'national filter', namely conflicts between states in the Council. By contrast, media interest in the EP is feeble, especially since its proceedings are consensus oriented, frequently involve large party-group coalitions and, hence, offer a low level of politicisation and polarisation. Anderson and McLeod (2004: 897ff.) find that 'the problems experienced by the European Parliament as a communicator with the citizens of Europe exist on every level of its political and bureaucratic structures.' They argue that:

> the press and information service contains a mixture of highly competent and less able personnel and is handicapped severely by being led by senior officials who have no professional background in press and public relations matters. It is woefully under-resourced as a result of MEPs', and more specifically the relevant budget committee's failure to appreciate adequately the importance of, and the need for, their own information service.
>
> (Anderson and McLeod 2004: 915)

More is possible: for instance, in the US Congress, both parties in each chamber dispose of an impressive range of procedures employed for winning constituency support for their positions during the policy process (Oleszek 2001: 302–3).

6   For maximising problem-solving effectiveness, aimed at making up for the declining problem-solving ability of the member states, the EU has turned from unanimity to majority decision-making in an expanding range of policy fields. In areas with unanimity decision rules, national parliaments can act as 'needle's eyes' and use veto powers. In the other fields of majority voting, the EP's powers of co-decision-making match those of the Council of Ministers. Hence, the more regulatory powers the EU attains that are premised on Council majorities, the more the EP is called on to become co-legislator in a widening range of policy fields. Yet, since EP decision-making is most frequently based on cross-party consensus, this does not necessarily translate into strengthening a transnational public sphere.

With regard to its current preconditions and constraints the EP can be conceived of as an incipient transnational public sphere. However, it stands at a crossroads between a regulatory and a federal model of the

European polity. Its impressive empowerments notwithstanding, the EP has not been capable yet of turning its effective powers into political capital. If electoral participation rates are in continuous decline, the expansion of parliamentary powers is necessary, but obviously not sufficient for mobilising citizens and conferring a democratic quality on transnational deliberation beyond the nation state. But what is the missing link? Assuming that the EP's legitimacy is a function of citizens' support and electoral participation and that these, in turn, depend on the strength of the EP's public sphere, in what follows I examine parliamentary representation as a key to the Europeanisation and transnationalisation of the public sphere.

Deliberative parliamentary representation as a venue for a European public sphere

The traditional liberal democratic model of parliamentary representation relies on the dyadic 'delegation and aggregation' relationship where voters induce preferences in representatives (Blondel *et al.* 1997). The citizens, by the act of voting, delegate power to a representative who appears trustworthy, promising to stick to his (party's) electoral agenda. I suggest that linking parliamentary research to deliberative democratic theory will be greatly beneficial for both, allowing for 'rethinking representation' (Mansbridge 2003) through the lenses of the deliberative and discursive turn, while inducing us to assess the question of the European public sphere in the framework of traditional and new forms of deliberative parliamentary representation. The EP gains its potential neither by generating 'input legitimacy' (preference inducements from citizens to representatives and decision makers) nor from turnout rates in the electoral act. Rather it is the processes of mutual learning between elections as well as multilingual deliberation in plenary debates and committee meetings that earn the EP a pivotal role (Lord 2002: 225).

It is argued that the 'prerequisite thesis' – that European parliamentary governance depends on previously resolving the EU's alleged *Öffentlichkeitsdefizit* – misses relevant developments, in two respects. On the one hand, European public sphere research provides a growing body of empirical evidence to confirm that there is always public communication about European issues within member states (Peters *et al.* 2005). Although the literature on the transnationalisation of the public sphere diverges on the normative conceptions and empirical criteria for measurement, in practice a consensus has emerged that the Europeanisation of the public sphere is unfolding, placing new empirical questions on the research agenda, such as the patterns of constitutional claims-making in the quality press (Statham and Gray 2005; Jentges *et al.* 2006); the dynamics of transnationalisation in constitutional discourses (Liebert *et al.* 2006); and the impact of media voices in the ratification process (Trenz *et al.* 2006).

Regarding the role of the EP and MEPs in these public debates, one should reverse the 'prerequisite' theory of 'No Public Sphere – No Parliamentary Democratic Legitimacy' and ask different questions. How do parliamentary procedures and processes contribute to forging a European public sphere, and what are its conditions for providing the EU with democratic legitimacy?

Adopting a deliberative democratic perspective, Mansbridge (2003: 515ff.) argues that 'good deliberation' should work through the electoral process as well as through other processes of mutual education. She suggests we assess parliamentary representation by the norms of public deliberation as a mechanism for generating democratic legitimacy. Her criteria include 'access to deliberation'; 'transparency and access to information'; 'responsiveness to stakeholder concerns'; and 'inclusion of all voices'.[11] Mansbridge draws on the – party-political – notion of 'substantive policy representation' and the feminist conception of 'descriptive' representation to distinguish four forms of representation. Representation is conceived of as communicative interaction between the representative and the represented. I shall briefly introduce each of the four types of representation, by describing its potential for promoting a strong parliamentary public sphere.

Promissory representation is premised on the assumption of 'coercive power' that the citizen delegates to the representative by the act of voting, and also of a moral obligation of the latter to conform. Normatively, this traditional model of aggregative democracy mandates that each voter's preferences should have equal coercive power over the outcome of decision-making. Legislative studies often reduce the democratic norms underlying this type of representation to a criterion of morality, namely whether the elected legislator pursues policies that conform to the preferences of voters in the legislator's constituency. For checking the MEPs' 'morality' in keeping 'electoral promises', voters need to rely on information and public relations policy, on accountability procedures in local electoral districts and on full transparency and the public's access to EP documents. Arguably, such procedures can be expected to help foster top-down processes of communicative Europeanisation that are segmented along the lines of general national and subnational publics.

Anticipatory representation requires good communication between citizens and representatives in the period between elections and presumes that voters are educable (or manipulable), although not only by the representative who seeks to 'explain' his position, but also in democratic practice by parties, interest groups, media, opposition candidates and other citizens (Mansbridge 2003: 518). Here, the quality of deliberation and EP–citizen communication during the legislative term depends on parliamentary procedures regulating the accountability not only of MEPs but also of EU decision makers, and having them explain their reasons to constituencies. Mutual education and learning can also be enhanced by institutions such as the Ombudsman; by Union citizens' rights such as petitions (or the popular legislative initiative); as well as by hearings and the use of polling and focus groups. Arguably, this pluralist deliberative model of representation could be expected to promote a two-way vertical process of communicative Europeanisation between the EP – as a strong public – and the publics constituted by the various social constituencies.

In *gyroscopic representation*, voters affect political outcomes 'by selecting and placing in the political system representatives whose behaviour is to some degree predictable in advance based on their observable characteristics' (Mansbridge 2003: 521). They choose a representative whom 'they expect to pursue a certain vision of the public interest' and select individuals likely to deliberate well, leaving them free to choose the means to pursue the goals. As an example, Mansbridge (2003: 521) refers to the 'party discipline' model that is characteristic of much of Europe.

Here the quality of deliberation depends crucially but not only on constituency–representative communication during election campaigns. In addition, the ritual presentation twice a year by EU-presidencies of their programme in the EP provides for transnational debates in the EP plenary and their translation into the realm of the mass media and thus, the general public. More than other forms of representation, gyroscopic representation can be expected to foster the transnationalisation of the public sphere, generated by the EP as a strong public, but firmly rooted within and across member-state publics.

Surrogate representation contributes to good legislation 'by making it more likely that varied and important perspectives will be included' in deliberation (Mansbridge 2003: 522ff.). Here, legislators represent constituencies that did not elect them, and hence cannot be held accountable in traditional ways, but act to promote their surrogate constituencies' perspectives and interests for 'reasons internal to their own convictions, consciences, and identities' (ibid.: 524). Normative criteria to judge the degree to which surrogate representation meets democratic standards include, first, that the legislature as a whole should represent the interests and perspectives of the citizenry roughly in proportion to their numbers in the population; and second, that the deliberative aims of democracy require the perspectives most relevant to a key decision to be represented. The goal is to produce the best insights and the most relevant information, through mutual influence, which in deliberation may legitimately be unequal, provided there is a certain 'threshold' presence of each perspective to contribute to the larger understanding (ibid.). The quality of EP constituent–representative communications is defined by the quality of deliberative supranationalism, not confined to expert committees, but does include parliamentary committees. In order to balance the Council's majority-decision bias, the EP will tend to make consensus decisions: parliamentary hearings and devices for conflict intermediation help secure the representation of all conflicting interests as well as the representation of all relevant perspectives. Hypothetically, we would expect 'surrogate representatives' to be experts and part of sectoral networks, leaving domestic publics largely unaffected.

As outlined in Table 14.1, liberal aggregative democracy, pluralist national and transnational variants of deliberative democracy, as well as deliberative supranationalism, will rely on variable modes of parliamentary representation. Furthermore, these will be likely to promote different patterns and dynamics of communicative Europeanisation, with implications for the potential and limits of the kind of European public sphere emerging.

From a 'Europe of states' to a 'union of citizens and states': EP devices for promoting a deliberative European public sphere

Bearing the pitfalls of the current configuration of the EP in mind, but situating it in the framework of deliberative representation, what are, in parliamentary practice, its conditions for overcoming segmented Europeanisation and forging a transnational democratic public sphere? In the preceding section, I have suggested that the EP's shortcomings as a 'strong public' are a matter of liberal democratic representation. The 'promissory' link with its constituencies reduces the EP's potential for more effective forms of communication. In other words, I claim that the dominant mode of liberal representation in the EP will inevitably reproduce the segmented condition of the European communicative space that is characteristic of the 'Union of states', whereas strengthening deliberative forms of parliamentary representation promises to benefit the emerging transnational European sphere of publics, a prerequisite for a Union of citizens and states.

In the remainder of this chapter, I shall situate these theoretical expectations in the framework of the constitutional debate on the future of the EU: whether the EP is to be configured as a sovereign power and central site in an emerging federal democratic EU polity, or whether it is to be constructed as a peripheral correlate of a European regulatory regime controlled by democratic member states. The question is which EP devices are best suited to redress the deep divisions between the country-based citizenries and the transnational private and supranational public powers that hamper the emerging EU polity.

Conceiving the EP as a correlate to a federalising union of citizens and states requires the EP to define itself as a democratically constituted, institutionalised strong public where key EU decision makers can be effectively held accountable for their actions by citizens, acting indirectly through the competition and cooperation of their representatives.[12] In this view, crucially, the EP promotes European public communications by holding Commission and Council representatives to account. The more prominent

Table 14.1 Representation, public sphere and democratic legitimacy

Form of representation	Promissory	Anticipatory	Gyroscopic	Surrogate
Focus	Moment of election	Between elections	Election campaign	In legislature
Voter power	Delegated to representatives: – forward-looking – inducing preferences – little trust required	Through representatives: – backward-looking	Through party system: – uncrystallised interests – changing context and issues	Delegated to member-state governments, economic and civil-society organisations
Public sphere	Top-down segmented Europeanisation of general national publics	Two-way vertical Europeanisation by strong public(s)	Transnational strong public(s)	Domestic publics; sectoral expert networks
Norms for assessing EP representation and deliberation	MEPs' 'morality', keeping promises: – information and public relations – MEP mandate and accountability – full transparency and public access to EP documents	Quality of deliberation and EP–citizen communication during term: – accountability of EU decision makers, explaining reasons to constituencies – mutual education and learning – Ombudsman – petitions – hearings – polling, focus groups	Quality of deliberation during election campaigns: – articulating European values, identities, visions in party manifesto – EU programmatic election campaigns on EU presidency – transnational debates translated into general publics (reflected by mass media)	Quality of EP deliberation: – balancing Council majority decisions – consensus decision-making – proportional representation of conflicting interests – representation of all important perspectives (participation of stakeholders in parliamentary hearings)
Problems	Works badly under conditions of rapid change	Requires citizens to want to learn and representatives to teach the EU	Requires trust of constituencies in political parties	Requires trust of constituencies in national and organisation leaders
Democratic legitimacy	Liberal aggregative democracy	Pluralist national deliberative democracy	Pluralist transnational deliberative democracy	Deliberative supranationalism

Source: Adapted from Mansbridge 2003.

the federal model of the EU polity becomes, the stronger EP control competences will need to be, and the more public scrutiny and monitoring will benefit the European public sphere. By expanding co-decision-making by the EP across more policy sectors, the transparency of EU legislation will increase. The model of an asymmetrical 'Federal Republic of Europe', where decision-making is dominated by the Council of Ministers and controlled by an EP that provides democratic legitimacy to the EU, would rest on a division of labour between three kinds of arena: national parliaments, where national executives are held accountable; Council deliberations held in public; and EU parliamentary procedures for the public scrutiny of EP and Council legislation. But even if the EP defines itself as the 'citizens' chamber' in a – hypothetically symmetrical – bicameral system where the Council is conceived of as the representative of member states, it is still a system of representation that needs to improve its quality of representation and participation.

By contrast, in the model labelled a 'regulatory regime', the EP's legislative competences and control powers will be weaker. A link between European institutionalised decision-making and the general public debate is not required. Although this model does not rely as strongly on direct sources of legitimacy through European elections but rather on democratic (input) legitimacy in member states and participatory modes of EU governance, it still requires legitimacy derived from effective problem-solving. Yet, if output legitimacy is to translate into empirical legitimation, public support and citizens' loyalty also depend on public communications where the themes and topics, problems and solutions advanced by the Union are aired in the general public, with reactions eventually filtering back into decision-making circuits.

The link between voters and MEPs focuses on the voting act but places little weight on the quality of the process of communication. To ascertain whether elected legislators pursue policies that conform to the preferences of voters in the legislators' constituency, even promissory representation requires good deliberation, namely about whether or not representatives have fulfilled their promises or have persuasive reasons for not doing so (Mansbridge 2003). Anticipatory representation, as a step towards a mutually educational public sphere, requires mutual learning by citizens as well as representatives. This means not only transparency but an explicit 'education function', namely expecting the EP to teach citizens why to change preferences. There is some empirical evidence to illustrate this claim.

In preparing citizens for the euro, the EP contributed to supranational 'discourse management' (Shaw 2000: 406ff.) in the EU's most extensive and costly information and mass communication campaign since the inception of the European Community (Liebert 2001).

Mutual teaching and education may also occur through non-governmental and economic interest organisations using the lobby registration procedure. Due to its openness, the EP has become a mediator between organised interests in the Union: more than 3,000 lobbies are accredited with the EP, few with representation at the European level, and the majority coming from member states. Depending on interest groups' expertise for improving the effectiveness of legislation, the EP's lobbying regime (Liebert 1995) with its privileging of well-organised interests, nevertheless raises questions of democratic legitimacy.

Furthermore, the EP has built channels for communication with individual citizens who can bring complaints of maladministration by a European institution before the Ombudsman appointed by the EP. Furthermore, anyone residing in a member state has the right to submit a petition to the EP, individually or as part of a group, on matters concerning him or her directly, which fall within the EU's remit. Members of the public can also obtain information from the EP's information offices in the member states or via a Citizens' Mailbox. Taking the petition procedure into account, the EP profiles itself as an addressee for the wishes of European citizens by responding to which it can educate itself.

There is also the matter of digital resources for European Communication: ICT knowledge, media competence, resolving the digital divide between different constituencies (age, gender, education, etc.), between East and West and between language communities. In 2003, the EP overhauled its Internet presentation and tools for interaction with citizens.

Regarding its involvement in constructing a global transnational public sphere, the EP has attained the status of an international forum, being addressed by major heads of international organisations and of state. It is firmly entrenched in a global network of interparliamentary communication, including transatlantic cooperation and a strategic partnership with Russia.[13]

Not only the media but also political parties are key 'messengers' in linking the circuits of power and decision-making in the EU to the citizenry. Both are blamed most for not contributing sufficiently to public information, opinion and will formation on European issues (Norris 2000). Only a few parties take interest and initiatives in 'truly European electoral campaigns' that, beyond any national aspects, 'would enhance both the visibility of the party and the transnational themes it represents' (Grunberg and Moschonas 2002: 97).

In EP proceedings, grand coalitions generally outweigh simple majority coalitions, a possible impediment to gyroscopic representation by political parties and developments towards a self-inducing European sphere of publics. In explanation, it has been argued in the case of enlargement negotiations that the EP has had substantial influence, although it does not enjoy formal agenda-setting power and does not have the means to change the position of the European Council. Nevertheless, it can try reversing the status quo by using its informal bargaining power, the effectiveness of this strategy being largely dependent on its ability to reach a unified position. Key mechanisms to that end are party-group pressure, overriding national preferences. The activities of MEPs are not structured by national delegations but by transnational organisational forms. However, a system of representation that is primarily based on political parties requires high amounts of trust. Despite its record as a strongly institutionalised public sphere, and although trust in the EP is higher than in any other EU institution, scarcely more than 50 per cent of citizens would trust the EP.[14]

As the Green Paper on 'the future of parliamentary democracy' (Burns *et al.* 2000: 6) pointed out, 'parliamentary territorial representation entails the involvement of a select few in law- and policy-making, and provides a reliable basis for well-organized deliberation and decision-making. Such arrangements risk a de-coupling between Parliament and "the people".' Although regular parliamentary elections and a free press had been expected to redress this problem by re-coupling the citizenry and elites, more is needed.

The EP is a parliament *sui generis* which reflects its diverse social constituency, with a unique combination of characteristics. It represents states and people, operating in an intergovernmental as well as in a supranational framework. Currently, the EP's 732 members have a high turnover rate of 50–60 per cent. Furthermore, its membership shows a steadily rising level of feminisation, with the share of female MEPs after the 1999 elections at 29.7 per cent rising to 30 per cent after the 2004 elections. Yet while the EP apparently ranks high on pluri-national representation, given its multinational and multilingual composition and procedures respecting them, the EP's capacity for social representation appears relatively weak (Marsh and Norris 1997). Ethnic minorities – for instance, Russian non-citizens in the Baltic countries or Muslim long-term residents – and socially marginal groups – such as the long-term unemployed or people with low levels of education – are underrepresented or not represented. To redress its social bias, 'surrogate representation' can work, for instance, by institutionalising parliamentary hearings on a regular basis for diverse social constituencies as an opportunity for voicing their concerns directly or indirectly.

Conclusion

In the New Europe, the public has become ever more polymorphic and polyphonic. The EU therefore features traits of transnational communicative spaces that not all the citizens of EU can take part in or have access to, but where sectoral publics evolving around policy networks and legally institutionalised discourses are specialised in collective will formation. From the perspective of a transformation of democratic institutions aimed at expanding citizens' political opportunities (Cain *et al.* 2003), I have explored the prospects for deliberation in the EP's practices of representation. This account, I argue, is more realistic than the 'prerequisite theory of parliamentary legitimacy' for the EU, which stipulates a pre-existing European public sphere. The framework of 'rethinking representation in the EP in terms of deliberation' maps a renewed research as well as an institutional reform agenda, critically assessing traditional forms of representation and devising novel forms through deliberative communication inside and outside the EP.

In view of the shortcomings of the EU's current condition, five propositions can be summarised that designate the EP as key to the construction of a transnational 'European sphere of publics' (Schlesinger and Kevin 2000). First, the European public sphere is constructed as the result of mechanisms of parliamentary representation and communication among constituencies and representatives. Second, a deliberative theory of democracy provides normative criteria for assessing the communicative quality of different kinds of parliamentary representation beyond the liberal-aggregative promissory model, namely (1) communication between citizens and representatives during the legislative term and (2) during electoral campaigns; and (3) deliberation in plenary debates and in specialised committees. Third, to evolve as a 'strong public' the EP cannot count on making majority voting the norm nor rely on a stable transnational political party system; rather it will proceed by semi-consociational multi-party coalitions and deliberation, structured by flexible, cross-national and cross-party discourse coalitions. Fourth, the parliamentary sphere will be the stronger the more it operates as a mechanism for overcoming segmented Europeanisation and linking the general public to sectoral publics. And finally, the EP has created a European digital communication network, using the Internet as a mechanism of information, communication, control, interest articulation and interaction that is – in principle at least – accessible to every interested and knowledgeable citizen as an opportunity structure for Europeanising national and regional public spheres. But to make use of knowledge-based resources, citizens as well as MEPs must be taught to learn mutually from each other, all the more so in a world where the EU is engaged in global, transatlantic and 'neighbouring' projects that need correlative spaces of public communication.

Notes

1 Qualitative studies on parliamentary discourses are rare, so far. See, among others, Dubiel 1999; Wodak and Van Dijk 2000.
2 See Dieter Grimm, 'Mit einer Aufwertung des Europa-Parlaments ist es nicht getan. Das Demokratiedefizit der EG hat strukturelle Ursachen', *Der Spiegel*, 18 October 1992, and 'Die größte Erfindung unserer Zeit. Als weltweit anerkanntes Vorbild braucht Europa keine eigene Verfassung', *Frankfurter Allgemeine Zeitung*, 16 June 2003.

3 For a discussion of the criteria for good deliberation that are linked to a theory of democratic legitimacy, see Mansbridge 2003, p. 526.
4 Although the United Nations has more than 190 members, it uses only six languages. The Council of Europe and NATO, each with more members than the EU, publish official documents only in English and French.
5 On a daily basis, 500 meetings are calculated to require the skills of 12,000 translators and interpreters.
6 Three categories of minority language are accepted: regional languages (Catalan, Sardinian, Welsh, etc.); languages spoken by a minority in one state but which are official languages of another member state (German in southern Denmark, French in northern Italy, Hungarian in Slovakia, etc.); and non-territorial languages (Romani, Yiddish, Armenian, etc.). However, the wide variety of languages from other parts of the world spoken by immigrant communities in EU countries, such as Turkish, Arabic, Hindi, Balkan languages or Russian, are not given formal status or recognition or covered by EU language-teaching programmes.
7 See European Commission, Directorate General for Interpretation: ec.europa.eu/comm/scic/thescic/multilingualism_en.htm#2 (accessed 10 July 2006).
8 Regulation (EC) No 1049/2001 of the European Parliament and of the Council of 30 May 2001 regarding public access to European Parliament, Council and Commission documents (OJ L145).
9 A register open to the public in each institution and accessible via the Internet has been set up since 3 June 2002 to make access and the search for documents easier.
10 From the first to the fifth direct election to the EP, electoral turnout has steadily fallen, from 63 per cent in 1979 to a historical low of 45.5 per cent in 2004. Exceptions to this trend are Belgium and Luxemburg (due to compulsory voting), the UK (turnout has increased from 32 to 39 per cent in this period) and Denmark (where it has remained at about the same level, 48 per cent). See Blondel *et al.* 1998.
11 Following John Dryzek (2000: 134), 'deliberative virtues' such as 'respect' and 'reciprocity' and 'equality in the ability to raise and question points' should also be taken into account.
12 I expand Philippe Schmitter's (2000: 3) proposal that a 'Euro-democracy' should fulfil all the characteristics of a modern political democracy to include citizens' direct control of their representatives.
13 MEPs take part in 34 interparliamentary delegations to non-EU parliaments and countries.
14 See 'Trust in EU institutions' (Eurobarometer 61, April 2004).

15 Conclusion

Philip Schlesinger and John Erik Fossum

This book has shown that it is against both present achievement and future uncertainty that we need to discuss the arguments about a European public sphere. Linguistic, political, economic and cultural diversity is the essential background to a discussion of the prospects of a European public sphere, not to speak of the continuing importance of diverse histories and how these continue to shape collective identities. Such deep diversity (Fossum 2003) is still profoundly linked to the continuing vitality of Europe's dominant political framework: what we (not always felicitously) call the nation state. It is the nation state that has been the locus classicus of thinking about a public sphere – often conceived as a space of critical discourse about public matters. The actions of civil society, coupled with mediated communication, have commonly played a key role both in articulating and disseminating opinions and arguments. The European Union of course, is not a nation state, and the theoretical challenge has been – and continues to be – how to think about the public domain in relation to an entity that is in a process of continual transformation. Thinking of nations as publics bounded by a state has been the starting point for much theorisation (Splichal 1999: 16). And to the extent that the EU has some of the characteristics of a polity, it therefore becomes obvious – at least in part – to think about a public sphere in relation to its core institutions. In short, the model of the national public sphere exerts its influence on how we conceptualise a framework, which is actually quite different from, but at the same time linked to – and based upon – a union of European nation states. We have sought to address this ambiguity by working with three de facto polity models, each of which has a distinct vision of the public sphere. The first model is that of the nation state, which serves as a critical reference point for subsequent discussion. We have labelled the two other, respectively, the regulatory and federal models. In what follows, we highlight the main findings of this book in relation to the three main questions posed at the outset.

At a *theoretical* level, our contributors highlight what has become widely accepted, namely that the EU has helped to foster or to make more explicit new conceptions of the public sphere and new ways of configuring it. Any assessment of the prospects for a European public sphere has to take this properly into account. But this book also demonstrates the resilience of nation-state-based public sphere thinking, whether conceived as a normative regulatory ideal, as a basic research framing device or as a contested ontology. Cognisant of these tensions, we have sought to navigate the still murky waters between what organisational theorists label 'exploitation' and 'exploration'.[1] The EU has been built on the template of the member state and many of its reforms are based on this. In other words, by adopting already known procedural and institutional arrangements in the states, the EU *exploits* these. But the EU is also based on an *exploration* of new arrangements and solutions. The perceived need for this is probably heightened by the greatly altered international (and national) context in which the EU is being forged, a setting in which the member states themselves are also being transformed.

Our contributors offer different takes here. For Erik O. Eriksen, the prospects of an EU public sphere remain tied to greater public participation at the EU level, facilitated by transnational media and based in new modes of collective identification. Klaus Eder, for his part, considers that the very process of questioning the present lack of democratic credentials of the EU has set in train a learning process that could result in greater democratisation, even though there may be various kinds of blockage along the way. Philip Schlesinger perceives contradictory tendencies in the EU's communicative spaces: on the one hand there are transnational networks and communicative flows and the steady rise of a lingua franca. On the other hand, mediated communication is still predominantly framed in national terms. If there is an emergent cosmopolitanism, this is in tension with the national principle and still quite fragile. These contributions relate to both of the EU models outlined in the introductory chapter.

Turning now to the EU's *political institutions*, this volume testifies to the salience of one of the most widely held assumptions in EU research, namely that institutions are critical vehicles in the fostering of a European public sphere. We have provided an assessment of their role in fostering strong and general publics. Clearly, not all of these institutions are themselves strong publics. But it matters greatly to the emergence of a European public sphere whether institutions propagate the basic norms and essential features of a public sphere or whether they act as blockages. Every viable public sphere depends on a workable institutional infrastructure. We have demonstrated that the EU's institutional framework has significant deficits, in particular when assessed in relation to the federal model.

With regard to more specific institutional arrangements, both Andy Smith and Deirdre Curtin agree on the relative failure of the Commission to communicate effectively, either with its key mediators (the Brussels press corps) or with the key national publics whose support it so much requires. Within the Commission, as Smith shows, there are warring tendencies about how best to relate to publics, and the role of an information strategy is given low priority. Curtin supplements this analysis by emphasising the inadequacies of the Commission's commitment to a transparent information regime, which is shared – to an even greater extent – by the Council. Curtin further notes that the Council's two main roles – those of legislature and executive – operate with very different norms concerning transparency. This problem is given added credence by the fact that the Council's executive functions have increased considerably over time.

So far as the European Parliament (EP) is concerned, however, Ulrike Liebert's analysis suggests a rather different picture. She argues that its communicative practices, not least the focus it provides for networking across the different levels of the EU, have indeed allowed it to function as a strong public that is now in the process of building a wider general public. But even this process takes place within an institutional setting with important constraints.

While we have demonstrated the significance of institutionalised communication, we now turn from communication that is highly institutionalised to the general public sphere. Hans-Jörg Trenz highlights the role of the quality press in articulating its own understanding of public opinion through editorials. He identifies the quality press as an engine of integration and, broadly speaking, as giving most space and attention to a federal model of the EU. Elite newspapers are, he contends, for the most part, collectively involved in creating a transnational political community, even though they are operating at a national level.

Press coverage in France and the UK, according to Paul Statham's comparative analysis of 'claims-making', suggests a more complex picture. There are distinct divergences between the structure of national public spheres, given their different histories of integration and quite different approaches among political elites. While 'Europeanised' claims-making is present in each of the public spheres, this does not produce identical results. This analysis questions whether the elite press as a whole can be seen as kind of cross-national cheerleader for the EU, since the contexts of reception differ so greatly.

John Erik Fossum and Hans-Jörg Trenz discuss public-sphere-related explanations for what is evidently a ratification failure (but not a constitutional failure). They identify how the constitution-making process failed to ignite a 'catalytic spark' and was not set up so as to foster Europe-wide communication. This links to the role of media, since the issue is not *whether* there is transnational communication in Europe, but rather what its consequences are.

In this regard, Abram de Swaan has argued that we do not so far have a European intelligentsia with its own common means of communication. Moreover, as he notes, linguistic (and cultural) diversity are still underpinned by the policies of member states whereas the cultural 'opportunity structure' of the EU militates against the formation of an overarching public sphere.

Lars Blichner substantiates the view that there is transnational communication; however, as he also points out, this is dominated by an economic discourse rather than a common European political discourse. How this extends to the new member states is explored by Maria Heller and Ágnes Rényi, who show in the case of Hungary that European discourse is refracted by national conditions.

Finally, François Foret and Philip Schlesinger's analysis demonstrates that the picture of the integration process is more complicated than one of pursuing a single line of development to greater democratisation and a common 'community of fate'. The *démarche* of the churches during the recent constitutional debate has promoted a particular version of Europe's religious history and therefore has had the capacity to divide and exclude in terms of identity and community – both inside and outside the EU – rather than to promote a federal vision. The above chapters, once again, all relate to both of the models outlined in the introduction.

Taken in the round, what do these contributions say about the prospects for a European public sphere? Whereas all our contributors take the view that increased democratic deliberation is a desirable normative goal, there are some key differences as to how they evaluate the present state of the EU. For instance, De Swaan, Eriksen and Schlesinger consider that a common European public sphere is needed for an effective deliberative democracy to operate and that the present segmentation of the EU into national publics weakens its overall deliberative potential. Overlapping flows of information do not in themselves ensure that overlapping publics come into existence outside the most institutionalised areas of expertise. For their part, Heller and Rényi point to possible future problems related to the integration of current members and new accessions.

Eder and Trenz note the magnitude of communicative activity already present at a national level. They maintain that this can serve the wider European purpose and carry forward a learning process that will ultimately result in wider democratisation. However, this need not result in further integration. Relatedly, Statham tends to emphasise the continuing importance of the national public sphere as a way of mediating European political action. He discounts the view that some overarching EU public sphere will emerge and sees the linkage between the national and the EU levels – via the mediation of political elites – as key to political communication. Foret and Schlesinger are also sensitive to the role of elites seeking the role of privileged interlocutor with the EU institutions as opposed to civil society entering the stage. In this case, the churches – on the model of political elites – have secured their status as brokers between the institutions and general publics.

The evidence from our other contributors takes two forms. Smith and Curtin underline the present shortcomings of the Commission and

Council and point to the need, if not to create an overarching European public sphere, certainly to attend to how general publics might be fostered by the core political institutions. Liebert takes the view that partly through the EP a 'sphere of publics' is in the process of formation, underpinned by the communication strategies of the EP, and that this is at least beginning to address the question of the democratic deficit and failings of legitimacy. Finally, Fossum and Trenz point to the missed opportunity to foster a more explicit Europe-wide debate within the framework of the constitution-making process.

Closing reflections

Our book has sought to demonstrate that institutional factors warrant more systematic attention in public sphere research than they usually receive. Consequently, we have included chapters that cover the EU-based institutions. A more comprehensive study, however, would require that attention be paid to the *multilevel configuration that makes up the EU* (at local, regional, national and European levels).

A theme for future attention is the nature and workings of intellectual fields. This is an important entrée into the study of European communication, and a way of analysing the preconditions for a viable European public sphere. While De Swaan has noted that we do not so far have a European intelligentsia with its own common means of communication, the problem-oriented theorising and empirical research that has accompanied the growth of the European institutions, nevertheless, has created a common transnational object of study. The horizontal research networks that have grown up in the European social sciences and humanities do not enjoy a public presence equivalent to that of a national intelligentsia. But they are a resource whose potential for shaping debate over policy has yet to be fully explored.

A final important theme that this book has broached is that of organised religion, which constitutes an important part of civil society. The relation between the political conception of a European identity and Christianity is both close and antagonistic. Both have been in constant interaction but also in competition. In the same way, at the level of the nation state, church and state have both continuously opposed and aped one another in the construction of their institutional apparatuses and the worldviews that these have embodied. National identities have been partly constituted by a religious dimension, however attenuated that has now become in much of Europe (Madeley 2003; Willaime 2004: 26–7). Apart from providing an administrative model, the churches have also provided states with theories of legal legitimation and rituals to copy (Kantorowicz 1957). Political power has been defined both by, and in opposition to, religious institutions. Churches may therefore occupy quite an ambiguous status. On the one hand, they may operate as strong publics, as in the case of some national churches, having special access to political power. At the same time, they may also function as managers of morality and mediators of the sacred, pitching their tents in civil society, and mobilising general publics. Foret and Schlesinger argue that through sparking debate over the place of Christianity in European politics and society, the churches have made an important comeback. The Convention on the Future of Europe's deliberations over the EU constitution threw into relief the role of religion in defining 'Europeanness'. In the context of a secularised Europe, Christianity has been fighting for its institutional recognition and space in the public sphere. Religion may offer a cultural identity to many Europeans and work simultaneously both to resist and to accommodate change. However, Foret and Schlesinger point out, the Christian mobilisation has been challenged by those who defend the secular order. Because of this far-reaching discursive struggle, the debate over whether Christianity should be seen as constitutive of a European identity has been framed by wider concerns about collective identities and memories in Europe.

Religion's ambiguous public sphere status raises a conceptual issue. Our book has shown that the distinction between strong and general publics is a useful heuristic device to improve our understanding of the institutional contribution to the public sphere. However, as we suggested in the introduction, this is not a simple dichotomy but has two dimensions: strong–weak and general–particular. Our accounts have shown that these terms (strong and general) may be understood as distinct points or values on a larger continuum of degrees of institutionalised communication: from communication that is highly institutionalised to the wide-open and anarchic character of the (very weakly institutionalised or completely non-institutionalised) general public sphere. Further, the institutional dimension operates within a territorial space. A general public is one where the communicative community covers the entire territorial space, whereas a particular public is a territorially or functionally narrow communicative setting. Our two-dimensional grid (see Figure 1.3 on p. 18) helps us to distinguish integration from democratisation. Integration – as reflected in our first regulatory model – may stimulate institutional development but this need not activate more than particular publics.

Our findings underline the well-known fact that the EU is a highly complex formation, which it is presently difficult to characterise in any settled way. Its intergovernmentalism means that it operates as a key *regulator* of the political European space, based in treaties that have accreted the *acquis communautaire*, a unique constitutional construct, best thought of as a *material constitution*. The brusque check to the constitutional process that resulted from the French and Dutch refusals to ratify the Constitutional Treaty in May and June 2005 has meant that – at least temporarily – the drive towards a federal model has been stalled. In overall terms, the EU remains poised somewhere between being a *regulator* and a *federation*, with its future course quite undecided and unpredictable. Perhaps too little has been made, to date, of how such uncertainty complicates our thinking about what a public sphere at the EU level might actually look like.

This question requires us to pay adequate attention to the character of the emerging EU polity. The development of the EU might actually challenge the widely held, yet often unspoken, assumption of a linear development or transition *from* regulator *to* federation. Rather than giving rise to one constellation, what appears to be emerging, and is hinted at in several contributions here, is the gradual emergence of a system marked by *both* models. There is no unambiguous evidence that one model is replacing the other. Consequently, what we see is presently better considered as a difficult case of co-existence.

From a normative standpoint, the EU's trajectory underlines the need to insist on the publicness of the constitutive multitude of publics. It is certainly more appropriate to imagine the EU as constituted by a multiplicity of communicative spaces than to think of it as having one overarching public sphere. In empirical terms, the Union is still composed of a wide range of diverse publics which, however, still fall well short of the federal model. Of course, that does not mean that we should rule out the prospects of their moving towards greater overlap, convergence and mutuality. That said, a future Union of multiple, overlapping publics evidently still remains a distant prospect.

Note

1 'Exploitation' refers to 'such things as refinement, choice, production, efficiency, selection, implementation, and execution.' 'Exploration' refers to 'search, variation, risk taking, experimentation, play, flexibility, discovery, and innovation' (March 1994: 237). See also March and Olsen 1995 (Chapter 6).

Bibliography

Abélès, M. (1996) *En attente d'Europe*, Paris: Hachette.

—— (1997) 'La mise en représentation du politique', in M. Abélès and H.-P. Jeudy (eds) *Anthropologie du politique*, Paris: Armand Colin.

Anderson, B. (1991) *Imagined Communities: Reflections on the Origin and Spread of Nationalism*, 2nd edn, London: Verso.

Anderson, P. J. and McLeod, A. (2004) 'The Great Non-Communicator? The Mass Communication Deficit of the European Parliament and its Press Directorate', *Journal of Common Market Studies*, 42(5): 897–917.

Arendt, H. (1958) *The Human Condition*, Chicago, IL: The University of Chicago Press.

Axford, B. and Huggins, R. (1999) 'Towards a Post-national Polity: The Emergence of the Network Society in Europe', in D. Smith and S. Wright (eds) *Whose Europe? The Turn Towards Democracy*, Oxford: Blackwell.

Ayberk, U. and Schenker, F.-P. (1998) 'Des lobbies européens entre pluralisme et clientélisme', *Revue Française de Science Politique*, 48(6): 725–55.

Baisnée, O. (2000) 'Commissioners and Their First Public: Journalists in Brussels', presentation at the UACES workshop 'European Commissioners and the Political Representation of "Europe" ', Loughborough University, 22–23 June 2000.

—— (2002) 'Can Political Journalism Exist at the European Level?', in R. Kuhn and E. Neveu (eds) *Political Journalism*, London: Routledge.

—— (2003a) 'Une actualité "invendable": Les rédactions françaises et britanniques face à l'actualité communautaire', in G. Garcia and V. Le Torrec (eds) *L'Union européenne et les médias*, Paris: L'Harmattan.

—— (2003b) 'La production de l'actualité communautaire: Eléments d'une sociologie comparée du corps de presse accrédité auprès de l'Union européenne', PhD thesis, University of Rennes I.

—— (2004) 'The Politics of the Commission as an Information Source', in A. Smith (ed.) *Politics and the European Commission*, London: Routledge.

Balme, R., Chabanet, D. and Wright, V. (2002) *L'action collective en Europe*, Paris: Presses des Sciences Po.

Barber, B. R. (1984) *Strong Democracy: Participatory Politics for a New Age*, Berkeley, CA: University of California Press.

Bastin, G. (2003) 'L'Europe saisi par l'information (1952–2001): Des professionnels du journalisme engagé aux content coordinators', in G. Garcia and V. Le Torrec (eds) *L'Union europeenne et les médias*, Paris: L'Harmattan.

Bauer, M. (2004) 'Transparency in the Council', in M. Westlake and D. Galloway (eds) *The Council of the European Union*, London: John Harper.

Bauer, O. (2000) *The Question of Nationalities and Social Democracy*, trans. J. O'Donnell, Minneapolis, MN: University of Minnesota Press.

Bauman, Z. (1996) 'From Pilgrim to Tourist – or a Short History of Identity', in S. Hall and P. du Gay (eds) *Questions of Cultural Identity*, London: Sage.

Beach, D. (2003) 'Towards a New Method of Constitutional Bargaining?', The Federal Trust Online Paper 13/03, London: The Federal Trust. Available at: www.fedtrust.co.uk/uploads/constitution/13_03.pdf.

—— (2004) 'The Unseen Hand in Treaty Reform Negotiations: The Role and Influence of the Council Secretariat', *Journal of European Public Policy*, 11(3): 408–39.

Beck, U. (1992) *Risk Society: Towards a New Modernity*, London: Sage.

—— (1993) *Die Erfindung des Politischen*, Frankfurt am Main: Suhrkamp.

—— (2003) 'Toward a New Critical Theory with a Cosmopolitan Intent', *Constellations*, 10(4): 453–68.

—— (2005) 'An Empire of Law and Consensus: A Call for a Europe – and Europeans – Beyond the Nation-state', *Internationale Politikk*, Special Issue, Transatlantic Edition, 4: 105–11.

—— (2006) *Cosmopolitan Vision*, Cambridge: Polity Press.

Bellamy, R. and Castiglione, D. (2000) 'The Uses of Democracy: Reflections on the European Democratic Deficit', in E. O. Eriksen and J. E. Fossum (eds) *Democracy in the European Union: Integration Through Deliberation?*, London: Routledge.

Bellier, I. (1995) 'Moralité, langue et pouvoirs dans les institutions européennes', *Social Anthropology*, 3(3): 235–50.

Bendix, R. (1978) *Kings or People: Power and the Mandate to Rule*, Berkeley, CA: University of California Press.

Benhabib, S. (1992) *Situating the Self: Gender, Community and Postmodernism in Contemporary Ethics*, New York, NY: Routledge.

—— (1996) 'Toward a Deliberative Model of Democratic Legitimacy', in S. Benhabib (ed.) *Democracy and Difference: Contesting the Boundaries of the Political*, Princeton, NJ: Princeton University Press.

Bibó, I. (1986) *Misère des petits États d'Europe de l'Est*, Paris: L'Harmattan.

Billig, M. (1995) *Banal Nationalism*, London: Sage.

Blichner, L. (2000) 'The Anonymous Hand of Public Reason: Interparliamentary Discourse and the Quest for Legitimacy', in E. O. Eriksen and J. E. Fossum (eds) *Democracy in the European Union: Integration Through Deliberation?*, London: Routledge.

Blichner, L. and Sangolt, L. (1994) 'The Concept of Subsidiarity and the Debate on European Cooperation: Pitfalls and Possibilities', *Governance*, 7(3): 284–306.

Blondel, J., Sinnott, R. and Svensson, P. (1997) 'Representation and Voter Participation', *European Journal of Political Research*, 32: 243–72.

—— (1998) *People and Parliament in the European Union: Participation, Democracy and Legitimacy*, Oxford: Clarendon Press.

Blumler, J. G. and Gurevitch, M. (1995) *The Crisis of Public Communication*, London: Routledge.

Bohman, J. (2004) 'Constitution Making and Democratic Innovation: The European Union and Transnational Governance', *European Journal of Political Theory*, 3(3): 315–37.

—— (2005) 'Reflexive Constitution-making and Transnational Governance', in E. O. Eriksen (ed.) *Making the European Polity: Reflexive Integration in the EU*, London: Routledge.

Bohman, J. and Rehg, W. (eds) (1998) *Deliberative Democracy*, Cambridge, MA: MIT Press.

Boisot, M. (1999) *Knowledge Assets: Securing Competitive Advantage in the Knowledge Economy*, Oxford: Oxford University Press.

Börzel, T. A. (2006) 'Participation through Law Enforcement', *Comparative Political Studies*, 39(1): 128–52.

Bourdieu, P. (1993) *The Field of Cultural Production*, Cambridge: Polity Press.

—— (1996) *Sur la télévision*, Paris: Éditions Raisons d'agir.

—— (2002) 'Les conditons sociales de la circulation internationale des idées', *Actes de la Rercherche en Sciences Sociales*, 145: 3–8.

Bradley, K. (1999) 'La transparence de l'Union européenne: Une évidence ou un trompe l'oeil?', *Cahiers de Droit Europeen*, 35(3–4): 283–362.

Bribosia, E. and Rorive, I. (2004) 'Le voile à l'école: Une Europe divisée', *Revue trimestrielle des droits de l'homme*, 60: 941–73.

Brittan, L. (1992) *European Competition Policy: Towards a Level Playing Field*, London: Brasseys.

—— (1994) *L'Europe qu'il nous faut*, Paris: Plon.

—— (2000) *A Diet of Brussels*, London: Little Brown and Company.

Brubaker, R. (1996) *Nationalism Reframed: Nationhood and the National Question in the New Europe*, Cambridge, MA: Cambridge University Press.

Brunkhorst, H. (ed.) (1998) *Demokratischer Experimentalismus*, Frankfurt: Suhrkamp.

—— (2002) 'Globalising Democracy without a State: Weak Public, Strong Public, Global Constitutionalism', *Millennium*, 31(3): 675–90.

Bunyan, T. (1999) *Secrecy and Openness in the EU*, London: Kogan Page.

Burkard, E. and Grande, E. (2003) 'Die Europäische Union als Regulierungsstaat: Transnationale Regulierungsnetzwerke und die Informalisierung des Regierens in Europa', in M. Jachtenfuchs and B. Kohler-Koch (eds) *Europäische Integration*, Opladen: Leske und Budrich.

Burns, T. R. (1999) 'The Evolution of Parliaments and Societies in Europe: Challenges and Prospects', *European Journal of Social Theory*, 2(2): 167–94.

Burns, T. R., Jaeger, C., Liberatore, A., Mény, Y. and Nanz, P. (2000) 'The Future of Parliamentary Democracy: Transition and Challenge in European Governance', Green Paper prepared for the Conference of the Speakers of EU Parliaments, Rome, 22–24 September 2000. Available at: www.camera.it/_cppueg/ing/conferenza_odg_Conclusioni_gruppoesperti.asp.

Cain, B. E., Dalton, R. J. and Scarrow, S. E. (eds) (2003) *Democracy Transformed? Expanding Political Opportunities in Advanced Industrial Democracies*, Oxford: Oxford University Press.

Calhoun, C. (1992) 'Introduction', in C. Calhoun (ed.) *Habermas and the Public Sphere*, Cambridge, MA: MIT Press.

—— (2002) 'Constitutional Patriotism and the Public Sphere: Interests, Identity, and Solidarity in the Integration of Europe', in P. De Greiff and C. Cronin (eds) *Global Justice and Transnational Politics*, Cambridge, MA: MIT Press.

—— (2003) 'The Democratic Integration of Europe: Interests, Identity, and the Public Sphere', in M. Berezin and M. Schain (eds) *Europe Without Borders: Re-*

mapping Territory, Citizenship and Identity in a Transnational Age, Baltimore: Johns Hopkins University Press.

Castells, M. (1996) *The Rise of the Network Society*, Malden, MA: Blackwell.

—— (1997) *The Power of Identity*, Malden, MA: Blackwell.

—— (1998) *End of Millennium*, Malden, MA: Blackwell.

—— (2001) *The Internet Galaxy: Reflections on the Internet, Business and Society*, Oxford: Oxford University Press.

Chambers, S. (1995) 'Discourse and Democratic Practices', in S. K. White (ed.) *The Cambridge Companion to Habermas*, Cambridge, MA: Cambridge University Press.

Christiansen, T. (2001) 'The Council of Ministers: The Politics of Institutionalised Intergovernmentalism', in J. Richardson (ed.) *European Union: Power and Policy-making*, London: Routledge.

—— (2003) 'Out of the Shadows: The General Secretariat of the Council of Ministers', in R. M. van Schendelen and R. Scully (eds) *The Unseen Hand: Unelected Legislators in the EU*, London: Frank Cass.

Closa, C. (2004) 'The Convention Method and the Transformation of EU Constitutional Politics', in E. O. Eriksen, J. E. Fossum and A. J. Menéndez (eds) *Developing a Constitution for Europe*, London: Routledge.

Cohen, J. and Sabel, C. F. (1997) 'Directly-Deliberative Polyarchy', *European Law Journal*, 3(4): 313–42.

—— (2003) 'Sovereignty and Solidarity: EU and US', in J. Zeitlin and D. M. Trubek (eds) *Governing Work and Welfare in the New Economy: European and American Experiments*, Oxford: Oxford University Press.

Cohen, M. D., March, J. G. and Olsen, J. P. (1972) 'A Garbage Can Model of Organizational Choice', *Administrative Science Quarterly*, 17: 1–25.

Connolly, W. E. (1983) *The Terms of Political Discourse*, Oxford: Martin Robertson.

Corbett, R. (1998) *The European Parliament's Role in Closer EU Integration*, New York: NY: Palgrave.

Corbett, R., Jacobs, F. and Shackleton, M. (2003) *The European Parliament*, London: John Harper.

Cormack, M. (2000) 'Minority Languages, Nationalism and Broadcasting: The British and Irish Examples', *Nations and Nationalism*, 6(3): 383–98.

Cotino, L. (2005) 'Theory and Reality of Public Access to EU Information', in D. Curtin, A. Kellermann and S. Blockmans (eds) *The EU Constitution: The Best Way Forward?*, The Hague: Kluwer.

Council of the European Union (2005) Council Annual Report on Access to Documents – 2004, Luxembourg: Office for Official Publications of the European Communities. Available at: ue.eu.int/uedocs/cmsUpload/new08896. en05INT.pdf.

Curtin, D. (2004) 'Mind the Gap? Democratic Accountability and the Evolving EU Executive', Third Walter van Gerven Lecture, Groningen: European Law Publishing. Available at: www.law.kuleuven.ac.be/ccle.

Curtin, D. and Meijer, A. (2006) 'Does Transparency Strengthen Legitimacy? A Critical Analysis of European Union Policy Documents', *Information Polity*, 11(2): 109–22.

Dacheux, E. (ed.) (2003) *Construire l'Union européenne. L'espace public européen en question*, Saint-Etienne: Presses Universitaires de Saint-Etienne.

—— (ed.) (2005) *Comprendre le débat sur la constitution de l'Union européenne*, Paris: Publibook.

290 *Bibliography*

Dahl, R. A. (1994) 'A Democratic Dilemma: System Effectiveness versus Citizen Participation', *Political Science Quarterly*, 109: 23–34.

—— (1999) 'Can International Organizations be Democratic? A Skeptic's View', in I. Shapiro and C. Hacker-Cordón (eds) *Democracy's Edges*, Cambridge: Cambridge University Press.

Dalton, R. J. and Kuechler, M. (eds) (1990) *Challenging the Political Order: New Social and Political Movements in Western Democracies*, Cambridge: Polity Press.

Dayan, D. (2005) 'Mothers, Midwives and Abortionists: Genealogy, Obstetrics, Audiences and Publics', in S. Livingstone (ed.) *Audiences and Publics: When Cultural Engagement Matters for the Public Sphere*, Bristol: Intellect.

De Clerq, W. (1993) 'Réflexion sur la politique d'information et de communication de la Communauté européenne', Report to the European Commission, Brussels.

De la Porte, C. and Nanz, P. (2004) 'The OMC – A Deliberative-Democratic Mode of Governance? The Cases of Employment and Pensions', *Journal of European Public Policy*, 11(2): 267–88.

De Poncins, E. (2003) *Vers une constitution européenne: Texte commenté du projet de traité constitutionnel établi par la Convention européenne*, Paris: Edition 10/18.

De Schutter, O. (2003) 'Civil Society in the Constitution for Europe', in E. O. Eriksen, J. E. Fossum and A. J. Menéndez (eds) *The Chartering of Europe: The European Charter of Fundamental Rights and its Constitutional Implications*, Baden-Baden: Nomos.

De Swaan, A. (2001) *Words of the World: The Global Language System*, Cambridge: Polity Press.

—— (2002) 'The Sociological Study of Transnational Society', in D. Kooiman, A. Koster, P. Smeets and B. Venema (eds) *Conflict in a Globalising World: Studies in Honour of Peter Kloos*, Assen: Royal Van Gorcum.

De Vreese, C. H. (2004) 'Why European Citizens will Reject the EU-Constitution', Center for European Studies Working Paper 116, Cambridge, MA: Harvard University.

Deckmyn, V. (ed.) (2002) *Increasing Transparency in the European Union*, Maastricht: European Institute of Public Administration.

Dehousse, R. (1998) 'European Institutional Architecture after Amsterdam: Parliamentary System or Regulatory Structure?', *Common Market Law Review*, 35(3): 598–619.

Delanty, G. and Rumford, C. (2005) *Rethinking Europe: Social Theory and the Implications of Europeanization*, London: Routledge.

Delors, J. (2004) *Mémoires*, Paris: Plon.

Deloye, Y., and Ihl, O. (2000) 'Deux figures singulières de l'universel: la république et le sacré', in M. Sadoun (ed.) *La démocratie en France: Idéologies*, Vol. 1, Paris: Gallimard.

Deutsch, K. W. (1966) *Nationalism and Social Communication: An Inquiry into the Foundations of Nationality*, 2nd edn, Cambridge, MA: MIT Press.

Dewey, J. (1927) *The Public and its Problems*, Chicago, IL: Gateways Books.

Díez Medrano, J. (2003) *Framing Europe: Attitudes to European Integration in Germany, Spain, and the United Kingdom*, Princeton, NJ: Princeton University Press.

Diez, T. (1997) 'International Ethics and European Integration: Federal State or Network Horizon', *Alternatives*, 22: 287–312.

DiMaggio, P. J. and Powell, W. W. (1991) 'The Iron Cage Revisited: Institutional Isomorphism and Collective Rationality in Organizational Fields', in W. W.

Powell and P. J. DiMaggio (eds) *The New Institutionalism in Organizational Analysis*, Chicago, IL: University of Chicago Press.

Dorf, M. C. and Sabel, C. F. (1998) 'A Constitution of Democratic Experimentalism', *Columbia Law Review*, 98(2): 267–473.

Döring, H. (ed.) (1995) *Parliaments and Majority Rule in Western Europe*, Frankfurt am Main: Campus.

Downey, J. and Koenig, T. (2006) 'Is there a European Public Sphere? The Berlusconi–Schulz Case', *European Journal of Communication*, 21(2): 165–87.

Driessen, B. (2005) 'The Council of the European Union and Access to Documents', *European Law Review*, 30(5): 675–96.

Dryzek, J. S. (1999) 'Transnational Democracy', *Journal of Political Philosophy*, 7(1): 30–51.

—— (2000) *Deliberative Democracy and Beyond: Liberals, Critics, Contestations*, Oxford: Oxford University Press.

Dubiel, H. (1999) *Niemand ist frei von der Geschichte: Die nationalsozialistische Herrschaft in den Debatten des Deutschen Bundestages*, München: Hanser.

Ebbinghausen, R. and Neckel, S. (1989) *Anatomie des politischen Skandals*, Frankfurt am Main: Suhrkamp.

Eder, K. (1995) 'Die Dynamik demokratischer Institutionenbildung: Strukturelle Voraussetzungen deliberativer Demokratie in fortgeschrittenen Industriegesellschaften', in B. Nedelmann (ed.) 'Politische Institutionen im Wandel', *Kölner Zeitschrift für Soziologie und Sozialpsychologie*, Special Issue, 35: 327–45.

—— (2000) 'Zur Transformation nationalstaatlicher Öffentlichkeit in Europa: Von der Sprachgemeinschaft zur issuespezifischen Kommunikationsgemeinschaft', *Berliner Journal für Soziologie*, 10: 167–284.

—— (2003a) 'Demokratie und Öffentlichkeit', in M. Jachtenfuchs and B. Kohler-Koch (eds) *Europäische Integration*, Opladen: Leske und Budrich.

—— (2003b) 'Die Besonderheit kollektiver Identitätsbildung in Europa: Eine Suchstrategie zur Antwort auf die Frage nach der 'Einheit' in der 'Vielfalt' Europas', Berlin: Humboldt University Berlin.

—— (2004) 'From the Common Market to the Political Union: The Shifting Opportunity Structure of Contentious Politics in Europe', in C. Tilly and M. Kousis (eds) *Threats and Opportunities in Contentious Politics*, Boulder, CO: Paradigm Publishers.

Eder, K. and Giesen, B. (2001) 'Citizenship and the Making of a European Society', in K. Eder and B. Giesen (eds) *European Citizenship between National Legacies and Postnational Projects*, Oxford: Oxford University Press.

Eder, K. and Kantner, C. (2000) 'Transnationale Resonanzstrukturen in Europa: Eine Kritik der Rede vom Öffentlichkeitsdefizit in Europa', *Kölner Zeitschrift für Soziologie und Sozialpsychologie*, Special Issue, 40: 306–31.

Eder, K. and Trenz, H.-J. (2003) 'The Making of a European Public Space: The Case of Justice and Home Affairs', in B. Kohler-Koch (ed.) *Linking EU and National Governance*, Oxford: Oxford University Press.

Eilders, C. (1997) 'The Impact of Editorial Content on the Political Agenda in Germany: Theoretical Assumptions and Open Questions Regarding a Neglected Subject in Mass Communication Research', Discussion Paper FS III 97–102, Berlin: Wissenschaftszentrum Berlin für Sozialforschung.

Eilders, C. and Voltmer, K. (2003) 'Zwischen Deutschland und Europa: Eine empirische Untersuchung zum Grad von Europäisierung und

Unterstützung der meinungsführenden deutschen Tageszeitungen', *Medien und Kommunikationswissenschaft*, 51(2): 250–70.

Eilders, C., Neidhardt, F. and Pfetsch, B. (2004) *Die Stimme der Medien: Pressekommentare und politische Öffentlichkeit in der Bundesrepublik*, Wiesbaden: VS Verlag für Sozialwissenschaften.

Eisenstadt, S. N., Roniger, L. and Seligman, A. (1984) *Centre Formation, Protest Movements and Class Structure in Europe and the United States*, New York, NY: New York University Press.

Elazar, D. (1987) *Exploring Federalism*, Tuscaloosa, AL: University of Alabama Press.

Elias, N. (1982) *Über den Prozess der Zivilisation*, Frankfurt am Main: Suhrkamp.

Elster, J. (1983) *Sour Grapes*, Cambridge: Cambridge University Press.

—— (1989) *Vitenskap og Politikk*, Oslo: Universitetsforlaget.

—— (ed.) (1998) *Deliberative Democracy*, Cambridge: Cambridge University Press.

Enzensberger, H.-M. (1962) *Einzelheiten 1. Bewusstseinsindustrie*, Frankfurt am Main: Suhrkamp.

Eriksen, E. O. (2000) 'Deliberative Supranationalism in the EU', in E. O. Eriksen and J. E. Fossum (eds) *Democracy in the European Union: Integration Through Deliberation?*, London: Routledge.

—— (2001) 'Democratic or Technocratic Governance?', in C. Joerges, Y. Mény and J. H. H. Weiler (eds) 'Mountain or Molehill? A Critical Appraisal of the Commission White Paper on Governance', Jean Monnet Working Paper 6/01, Florence, Italy: European University Institute/New York: NYU School of Law. Available at: www.iue.it/RSCAS/Research/OnlineSymposia/Eriksen.pdf.

—— (2005) 'Reflexive Integration in Europe', in. E. O. Eriksen (ed.) *Making the European Polity: Reflexive Integration in the EU*, London: Routledge.

—— (2006) 'Deliberation und demokratische Legitimität in der EU – Zwischen Konsens und Kompromiss', in P. Niesen and B. Herborth (eds) *Anarchie der kommunikativen Freiheit: Jürgen Habermas und die Theorie der internationalen Politik*, Frankfurt am Main: Suhrkamp.

Eriksen, E. O. and Fossum, J. E. (eds) (2000) *Democracy in the European Union: Integration Through Deliberation?*, London: Routledge.

—— (2002) 'Democracy Through Strong Publics in the EU?', *Journal of Common Market Studies*, 40(3): 401–23.

—— (2004) 'Europe in Search of Legitimacy: Strategies of Legitimation Assessed', *International Political Science Review*, 25(4): 435–59.

Eriksen, E. O. and Weigård, J. (2003) *Understanding Habermas: Communicative Action and Deliberative Democracy*, London: Continuum.

Eriksen, E. O., Fossum, J. E. and Menéndez, A. J. (eds) (2004) *Developing a Constitution for Europe*, London: Routledge.

Eriksen, E. O., Joerges, C. and Neyer, J. (eds) (2003) 'European Governance, Deliberation and the Quest for Democratisation', ARENA Report 02/03, Oslo: ARENA.

Etzioni, A. (1997) *The New Golden Rule: Community and Morality in a Democratic Society*, New York, NY: Basic Books.

European Commission (1996) 'Ouverture et transparence dans l'Union européenne', Brussels.

—— (2001a) European Governance: A White Paper, COM (2001) 428 final, Brussels, 25 July 2001.

—— (2001b) White Paper on Governance, Work area 1: Broadening and Enriching the Public Debate on European Matters, Report of the working group

'Democratising expertise and establishing scientific reference systems' (Group 1b), rapporteur A. Liberatore, Brussels. Available at: ec.europa.eu/governance/areas/group2/index_en.htm.

—— (2003) Report from the Commission on the application in 2002 of Regulation (EC) No 1049/2001 of the European Parliament and the Council regarding public access to European Parliament, Council and Commission documents, COM (2003) 216 final, Brussels, 29 April 2003.

—— (2004) Report from the Commission on the implementation of the principles in EC Regulation No 1049/2001 regarding public access to European Parliament, Council and Commission documents, COM (2004) 45 final, Brussels, 30 January 2004.

—— (2005) Plan-D for Democracy, Dialogue and Debate, COM (2005) 494 final, Brussels, 13 October 2005.

—— (2006) White Paper on a European Communication Policy, COM (2006) 35 final, Brussels, 1 February 2006.

European Parliament (2001) Resolution on the Constitutional Process and the Future of the Union, 2001/2180(INI), Brussels, 29 November 2001.

Fischer, F. (1990) *Technocracy and the Politics of Expertise*, Newbury Park, CA: Sage.

Foret, F. (2001) 'L'Europe en représentations: Eléments pour une analyse de la politique symbolique de l'Union européenne', PhD thesis, Université de Paris 1.

—— (2003) 'Espace public européen et mise en scène du pouvoir', in E. Dacheux (ed.) *L'Europe qui se construit*, Sainte-Etienne: Publications de l'Université de Saint-Etienne.

Foret, F. and Soulez, G. (eds) (2004) 'Europe, la quête d'un espace médiatique?' *Médiamorphoses*, 12(3): 21–91.

Fossum, J. E. (2000) 'Constitution-making in the European Union', in E. O. Eriksen and J. E. Fossum (eds) *Democracy in the European Union: Integration Through Deliberation?*, London: Routledge.

—— (2003) 'The European Union in Search of an Identity', *European Journal of Political Theory*, 2(3): 319–40.

—— (2004) 'Still a Union of Deep Diversity? The Convention and the Constitution for Europe', in E. O. Eriksen, J. E. Fossum and A. J. Menéndez (eds) *Developing a Constitution for Europe*, London: Routledge.

Fossum, J. E. and Menéndez, A. J. (2005) 'The Constitution's Gift? A Deliberative Democratic Analysis of Constitution Making in the European Union', *European Law Journal*, 11(4): 382–412.

Fossum, J. E. and Trenz, H.-J. (2006) 'The EU's Fledgling Society: From Deafening Silence to Critical Voice in European Constitution-making', *Journal of Civil Society*, 2(1): 57–77.

Fouilleux, E., De Maillard, J. and Smith, A. (forthcoming) 'The Role of Council Working Groups in Shaping European Problems and Policies', in T. Christiansen, T. Laarsen and G. Schaefer (eds) *Committees in EU Governance*, Manchester: Manchester University Press.

Fraser, N. (1992) 'Rethinking the Public Sphere: A Contribution to the Critique of Actually Existing Democracy', in C. Calhoun (ed.) *Habermas and the Public Sphere*, Cambridge, MA: MIT Press.

—— (2005) 'Transnationalizing the Public Sphere', in M. Pensky (ed.) *Globalizing Critical Theory*, Lanham, MD: Rowman and Littlefield.

Fung, A. (2003) 'Survey Article: Recipes for Public Spheres: Eight Institutional

Design Choices and Their Consequences', *Journal of Political Philosophy*, 11(3): 338–67.

Gabel, M. J. and Hix, S. (2004) 'Defining the EU Political Space: An Empirical Study of the European Election Manifestos, 1979–99', in G. Marks and M. R. Steenbergen (eds) *European Integration and Political Conflict*, Cambridge: Cambridge University Press.

Gallie, W. B. (1956) 'Essentially Contested Concepts', *Proceedings of the Aristotelian Society*, 56: 167–98.

Garnham, N. (1986) 'The Media and the Public Sphere', in P. Golding, G. Murdock and P. Schlesinger (eds) *Communicating Politics: Mass Communications and Political Process*, Leicester: University of Leicester Press.

—— (2000a) *Emancipation, the Media and Modernity: Arguments about the Media and Social Theory*, Oxford: Oxford University Press.

—— (2000b) 'La théorie del la société de l'information en tant qu'idéologie: une critique', *Réseaux*, 18(101): 53–91.

Gavin, N. T. (forthcoming) *Media, Economy and Democracy: Press and Television in British Politics*, London: Palgrave Macmillan.

Gaxie, D. (1993) *La démocratie représentative*, Paris: Montchrestien.

Geertz, C. (1980) *Negara: The Theatre State in Nineteenth Century Bali*, Princeton, NJ: Princeton University Press.

Gellner, E. (1983) *Nations and Nationalism*, Oxford: Blackwell.

Gerhards, J. (1992) 'Europäische Öffentlichkeit durch Massenmedien?', in B. Schäfers (ed.) *Lebensverhältnisse und soziale Konflikte im neuen Europa: Verhandlungen des 26. Deutschen Soziologentages in Düsseldorf 1992*, Frankfurt: Campus.

—— (2001) 'Missing a European Public Sphere', in M. Kohli and M. Novak (eds) *Will Europe Work? Integration, Employment and the Social Order*, London: Routledge.

Gerstenberg, O. and Sabel, C. F. (2002) 'Directly Deliberative Polyarchy: An Institutional Ideal for Europe?', in C. Joerges and R. Dehousse (eds) *Good Governance in Europe's Integrated Market*, Oxford: Oxford University Press.

Giesen, B. (1999) 'Europa als Konstruktion der Intellektuellen', in R. Viehoff and R. T. Segers (eds) *Kultur, Identität, Europa: Über die Schwierigkeiten und Möglichkeiten einer Konstruktion*, Frankfurt am Main: Suhrkamp.

—— (2002) 'Constitutional Practice or Community of Memory? Some Remarks on the Collective Identity of Europe', in D. Sachsenmaier and J. Riedel (with S. N. Eisenstadt) (eds) *Reflections on Multiple Modernities*, Leiden: Brill.

Gleissner, M. and de Vreese, C. H. (2005) 'News about the EU Constitution: Journalistic Challenges and Media Portrayal of the European Union Constitution', *Journalism*, 6(2): 221–41.

Goffman, E. (1974) *Frame Analysis: An Essay on the Organization of Experience*, Cambridge, MA: Harvard University Press.

Golding, P. (2007) 'European Journalism and the European Public Sphere: Some Thoughts on Practice and Prospects', in H. Bohrmann, E. Klaus and M. Machill (eds) *Media Industry, Journalism Culture and Communication Policies in Europe*, Köln: Herbert von Halem.

Graddol, D. (1997) *The Future of English? A Guide to Forecasting the Popularity of the English Language in the 21st Century*, London: The British Council.

Grimm, D. (1995) 'Does Europe Need a Constitution?', *European Law Journal*, 1(3): 282–302.

—— (2004) 'Treaty or Constitution? The Legal Basis of the European Union after

Maastricht', in E. O. Eriksen, J. E. Fossum and A. J. Menéndez (eds) *Developing a Constitution for Europe*, London: Routledge.

Grossman, E. and Saurugger, S. (2006) *Les groupes d'intérêt: Action collective et stratégies de représentation*, Paris: Armand Colin.

Grunberg, G. and Moschonas, G. (2002) 'The Disillusionment of European Socialists', in P. Perrineau, G. Grunberg and C. Ysmal (eds) *Europe at the Polls: The European Elections of 1999*, New York: Palgrave.

Grundmann, R. (1999) 'The European Public Space and the Deficit of Democracy', in D. Smith and S. Wright (eds) *Whose Europe? The Turn Towards Democracy*, Oxford: Blackwell.

Guéhenno, J. M. (1996) 'Europea Demokratie erneuern – Stärkung der gemein-schaftsbildende Kraft der Politik', in W. Weidenfeld (ed.) *Demokratie am Wendepunkt*, Berlin: Siedler.

Gutmann, A. and Thompson, D. (1996) *Democracy and Disagreement*, Cambridge, MA: Belknap Press of Harvard University Press.

Haas, E. B. (1961) 'International Integration: The European and the Universal Process', *International Organization*, 15(3): 366–92.

Haas, P. M. (1992) 'Introduction: Epistemic Communities and International Policy Coordination', *International Organization*, 46(1): 1–35.

Habermas, J. (1989) *The Structural Transformation of the Public Sphere*, Cambridge, MA: MIT Press.

—— (1992a) 'Further Reflections on the Public Sphere', in C. Calhoun (ed.) *Habermas and the Public Sphere*, Cambridge, MA: MIT Press.

—— (1992b) 'Drei normative Modelle der Demokratie: Zum Begriff deliberativer Politik', in H. Münkler (ed.) *Die Chancen der Freiheit. Grundprobleme der Demokratie*, München: Piper.

—— (1996a) *Between Facts and Norms: Contributions to a Discourse Theory of Law and Democracy*, Cambridge, MA: MIT Press.

—— (1996b) 'Reply to Symposium Participants, Benjamin N. Cardozo School of Law', *Cardozo Law Review*, 17: 1456–557.

—— (1998) *The Inclusion of the Other: Studies in Political Theory*, Cambridge, MA: MIT Press.

—— (2001) *The Postnational Constellation: Political Essays*, Cambridge: Polity Press.

—— (2004) 'Why Europe Needs a Constitution', in E. O. Eriksen, J. E. Fossum and A. J. Menéndez (eds) *Developing a Constitution for Europe*, London: Routledge. Originally published in *New Left Review*, 11, 2001: 5–26.

—— (2006) 'Political Communication in Media Society – Does Democracy Still Enjoy An Epistemic Dimension?', paper presented at the 56th Annual Conference of the International Communication Association, Dresden, 19–23 June 2006.

Habermas, J. and Derrida, J. (2003) 'February 15, or, What Binds Europeans Together', in G. Borradori (ed.) *Philosophy in a Time of Terror: Dialogues with Jürgen Habermas and Jacques Derrida*, Chicago, IL: University of Chicago Press.

Hall, S., Critcher, C., Jefferson, T. and Clarke, J. (1978) *Policing the Crisis: Mugging, the State, and Law and Order*, London: Macmillan.

Hanák, P. (1992) 'Les traces culturelles d'une histoire discontinue', *Liber*, March: 14–16.

Hannay, A. (2005) *On The Public*, London: Routledge.

Hedström, P. and Swedberg, R. (ed.) (1998) *Social Mechanisms: An Analytical Approach to Social Theory*, Cambridge: Cambridge University Press.

Held, D. (1995) *Democracy and the Global Order: From the Modern State to Cosmopolitan Governance*, Cambridge: Polity Press.
—— (2004) *Global Covenant: The Social Democratic Alternative to the Washington Consensus*, Cambridge: Polity Press.
Heller, M. and Rényi, Á. (1996) 'Discourse Strategies in the New Hungarian Public Sphere: From the Populist–Urban Controversy to the Hungarian–Jewish Confrontation', in K. Mänicke-Gyöngyösi (ed.) *Öffentliche Konfliktdiskurse um Restitution von Gerechtigkeit, Politische Verantwortung und Nationale Identität*, Frankfurt am Main: Peter Lang.
—— (2003a) 'Public Debate in Hungary on the NATO Alliance', in A. Kovács and R. Wodak (eds) *NATO, Neutrality and National Identity: The Case of Austria and Hungary*, Wien: Böhlau.
—— (2003b) 'Joining Nato: The Analysis of a TV-debate on Hungary's Alliance with NATO', in A. Kovács and R. Wodak (eds) *NATO, Neutrality and National Identity: The Case of Austria and Hungary*, Wien: Böhlau.
Heller, M., Némedi, D. and Rényi, Á. (1994) 'Structural Changes in the Hungarian Public Sphere under State Socialism', in A. B. Seligman (ed.) *Comparative Social Research, Vol. 14*, London: JAI Press.
Hermet, G. (2004) 'Un régime à pluralisme limité? À propos de la gouvernance démocratique', *Revue Française de Science Politique*, 54(1): 159–78.
Hix, S. and Lord, C. (1997) *Political Parties in the European Union*, New York, NY: St Martin's Press.
Hix, S., Noury, A. and Roland, G. (2005) 'Power to the Parties: Cohesion and Competition in the European Parliament, 1979–2001', *British Journal of Political Science*, 35: 209–34.
Hix, S., Tapio, R. and Scully, R. (2003) 'Fifty Years On: Research on the European Parliament', *Journal of Common Market Studies*, 41(2): 191–202.
Hjarvard, S. (2001) 'News Media and the Globalization of the Public Sphere', in S. Hjarvard (ed.) *Media in a Globalized Society*, Göteborg: Nordicom.
Holmes, D. R. (2000) *Integral Europe: Fast-capitalism, Multiculturalism and Neofascism*, Princeton, NJ: Princeton University Press.
Holzner, B. and Marx, J. H. (1979) *Knowledge Application*, Boston, MA: Allyn and Bacon.
Hooghe, L. and Marks, G. (2003) 'Unraveling the Central State, but How? Types of Multi-level Governance', *American Political Science Review*, 97(2): 233–43.
Hooghe, L., Marks, G. and Wilson, C. J. (2004) 'Does Left/Right Structure Party Positions on European Integration?', in G. Marks and M. R. Steenbergen (eds) *European Integration and Political Conflict*, Cambridge: Cambridge University Press.
Imig, D. and Tarrow, S. (eds) (2001) *Contentious Europeans: Protest and Politics in an Emerging Polity*, Lanham, MD: Rowman and Littlefield.
Ipsen, H. P. (1972) *Europäisches Gemeinschaftsrecht*, Tübingen: Mohr.
Jachtenfuchs, M., Diez, T. and Jung, S. (1998) 'Which Europe? Conflicting Models of a Legitimate European Order', *European Journal of International Relations*, 4(4): 409–45.
Jentges, E., Löken, G. O. and Vetters, R. (2006) 'Constitutional Claims-making in Quality Newspapers: A Comparative Assessment of Germany, France, Norway', paper presented at the workshop Constitutional Ratification Crisis: Exploring the European Public Sphere, European University Institute, Florence, 19–20 May 2006.

Jepperson, R. L. (2000) 'Institutional Logics: On the Constitutive Dimensions of the Modern Nation-State Polities', EUI Working Paper RSC 2000/36, Florence, Italy: European University Institute.

Joana, J. and Smith, A. (2002) *Les commissaires européens: Technocrates, diplomates ou politiques?*, Paris: Presses de Sciences Po.

Joerges, C. and Neyer, J. (1997) 'From Intergovernmental Bargaining to Deliberative Political Processes: The Constitutionalisation of Comitology', *European Law Journal*, 3(3): 273–99.

Joerges, C. and Vos, E. (eds) (1999) *EU Commitees: Social Regulation, Law and Politics*, Oxford: Hart.

Joerges, C., Mény, Y. and Weiler, J. H. H. (eds) (2000) *What Kind of Constitution for What Kind of Polity? Responses to Joschka Fischer*, Florence, Italy: European University Institute.

John Paul II (2003) 'Post-Synodal Apostolic Exhortation, Ecclesia in Europa', Rome: Libreria Editrice Vaticana. Available at: www.vatican.va/holy_father/john_paul_ii/apost_exhortations/documents/hf_jp-ii_exh_20030628_ecclesia-in-europa_en.html.

Johnson, S. (1987) *The Commissioner*, London: Century.

Jönssen, C., Tägil, S. and Törnqvist, G. (2000) *Organizing European Space*, London: Sage.

Jouët, J. and Pasquier, D. (eds) (2001) 'Médias et Migrations', *Réseaux*, 19(107).

Judge, D. (1995) 'The Failure of National Parliaments?' *West European Politics*, 18(3): 79–100.

Judge, D. and Earnshaw, D. (2003) *The European Parliament*, Basingstoke: Palgrave Macmillan.

Julliard, J. (1999) *La mort du roi. Autour de François Mitterrand. Essai d'ethnographie politique comparée*, Paris: Gallimard.

Kalinowski, W. (2002) 'Les institutions communautaires et L'Ame de l'Europe: La mémoire religieuse en jeu dans la construction européenne', in Commissariat Général du Plan, *Croyances religieuses, morales et éthiques dans le processus de construction européenne*, Paris: La Documentation Française.

Kant, I. (1996 [1797]) 'The Metaphysics of Morals', in I. Kant (ed.) *Practical Philosophy*, Cambridge: Cambridge University Press.

Kantner, C. (2002) 'Europäische Öffentlichkeit: Eine hermeneutisch-pragmatische Perspektive', PhD thesis, Humboldt University Berlin.

Kantorowicz, E. (1957) *The King's Two Bodies: A Study in Mediaeval Political Theology*, Princeton, NJ: Princeton University Press.

Keane, J. (1995) 'Structural Transformation of the Public Sphere', *The Communication Review*, 1(1): 1–22.

Kepplinger, H. M. (1998) *Die Demontage der Politik in der Informationsgesellschaft*, Freiburg: Alber.

Kettner, M. (1998) 'John Deweys demokratische Experimentiergemeinschaft', in H. Brunkhorst (ed.) *Demokratischer Experimentalismus*, Frankfurt am Main: Suhrkamp.

Kevin, D. (2003) *Europe in the Media: A Comparison of Reporting, Representation, and Rhetoric in National Media Systems in Europe*, Mahwah, NJ: Lawrence Erlbaum.

Kingdon, J. W. (1984) *Agendas, Alternatives, and Public Policies*, Boston, MA: Little, Brown and Company.

Klaic, D. (ed.) (2005) *Europe as a Cultural Project: Final Report of the Reflection Group of the European Cultural Foundation (2002–2004)*, Amsterdam: European Cultural Foundation.

Kleger, H. (1998) 'Wie is Mehrfachidentität lebbar? Deutschland zwishen Sub- und Transnationalität', in V. Rüdiger (ed.) *Der Neue Nationalstaat*, Baden-Baden: Nomos.

Kloss, H. and McConnell, G. D. (1989) *The Written Languages of the World: A Survey of the Degree and Modes of Use*, Québec: Presses de l'Université de Laval.

Koopmans, R. (2002) 'Codebook for the Analysis of Political Mobilisation and Communication in European Public Spheres', Europub.com project codebook, 15 April 2002. Available at: europub.wz-berlin.de.

—— (2007) 'Who Inhabits the European Public Sphere? Winners and Losers, Supporters and Opponents in Europeanised Political Debates', *European Journal of Political Research*, 46.

Koopmans, R. and Erbe, J. (2004) 'Towards a European Public Sphere? Vertical and Horizontal Dimensions of Europeanized Political Communication', *Innovation*, 17(2): 97–118.

Koopmans, R. and Pfetsch, B. (2003) 'Towards a Europeanised Public Sphere: Comparing Political Actors and the Media in Germany', ARENA Working Paper 23/03, Oslo: ARENA.

Koopmans, R. and Statham, P. (1999) 'Political Claims Analysis: Integrating Protest Event and Political Discourse Approaches', *Mobilization*, 4(2): 203–21.

—— (2000) 'Political Claims-making Against Racism and Discrimination in Britain and Germany', in J. ter Wal and M. Verkuyten (eds) *Comparative Perspectives on Racism*, Aldershot: Ashgate.

—— (2001) 'The Transformation of Political Mobilisation and Communication in European Public Spheres: A Research Outline', proposal for the research project Europub.com, funded by the European Commission's Fifth Framework Programme. Available at: europub.wz-berlin.de.

Koopmans, R., Statham, P., Giugni, M. and Passy, F. (2005) *Contested Citizenship: Immigration and Cultural Diversity in Europe*, Minneapolis, MN: Minnesota University Press.

Kovács, A. and Wodak, R (eds) (2003) *NATO, Neutrality and National Identity: The Case of Austria and Hungary*, Wien: Böhlau.

Kreppel, A. (2002) 'Moving Beyond Procedure: An Empirical Analysis of European Parliament Legislative Influence', *Comparative Political Studies*, 35(7): 784–813.

Kriesi, H. (2001) 'Die Rolle der Öffentlichkeit im politischen Entscheidungsprozess: Ein konzeptueller Rahmen für ein international vergleichendes Forschungsprojekt', Discussion Paper P01–701, Berlin: Wissenschaftszentrum Berlin für Sozialforschung.

Kriesi, H., Koopmans, R., Duyvendak, J. W. and Giugni, M. G. (1995) *New Social Movements in Western Europe: A Comparative Analysis*, London: UCL Press.

Kymlicka, W. (2001) *Politics in the Vernacular*, Oxford: Oxford University Press.

Lagroye, J. (1985) 'La légitimation', in M. Grawitz and J. Leca (eds) *Traité de science politique*, Paris: PUF.

Laitin, D. (2000) 'The Power of Language and the Language of Power: Language Conflict and Violence: The Straw that Strenghtens the Camel's Back', *Archives Européennes de Sociologie*, 41(1): 97–137.

Lange, A. (2003) 'Amenaza a la diversidad cultural europea: La circulación europea de programas de televisión sigue siendo baja', *Telos*, 55: 17–22.

Lefort, C. (1988) *Democracy and Political Theory*, Cambridge: Polity Press.

Lenaerts, K. and van Nuffel, P. (2005) *Constitutional Law of the European Union*, London: Sweet and Maxwell.

Liebert, U. (1995) 'Parliamentary Lobby Regimes', in H. Döring (ed.) *Parliaments and Majority Rule in Western Europe*, Frankfurt/New York: Campus/St Martins.

—— (2001) 'Constructing the EMU: Euro-Scepticism and the Emergence of a European Public Space', in B. Stråth and L. Magnusson (eds) *From the Werner Plan to EMU: In Search of a Political Economy for Europe*, Brussels: Peter Lang.

—— (2006) 'If Not a Federal Republic of Europe – What Then? A Framework for Comparative Discourse Analysis', paper presented at the workshop 'Constitutional Ratification Crisis: Exploring the European Public Sphere', European University Institute, Florence, 19–20 May 2006.

Liebert, U., Falke, J. and Maurer, A. (eds) (2006) *Postnational Constitutionalisation in the New Europe*, Baden-Baden: Nomos.

Lipset, S. M. (1994) 'The Social Requisites of Democracy Revisited', *American Sociological Review*, 59(1): 1–22.

Loftager, J. (1994) 'Den Politiske Offentlighed i Teori og i Praksis', in E. O. Eriksen (ed.) *Den Politiske Orden*, Oslo: Tano.

—— (2005) *Politisk Offentlighed og Demokrati i Danmark*, Aarhus: Aarhus Universitetsforlag.

Longman, C. (2007), 'Deliberating in Many Tongues: The Convention's Language Regime', in J. Schönlau, M. Aziz, D. Castiglione, E. Lombardo, C. Longman and M. Pérez-Solórzano (eds) *Constitutional Politics in the EU: The Convention Moment and its Aftermath*, Basingstoke: Palgrave Macmillan.

Lorcerie, F. (ed.) (2005) *La politisation du voile – en France, en Europe et dans le monde arabe*, Paris: L'Harmattan.

Lord Nolan, M. (1995) First Report of the Committee on Standards in Public Life, Cm 2850, London: Her Majesty's Stationary Office (HMSO).

Lord, C. (2002) 'The New European Parliament', in P. Perrineau, G. Grunberg and C. Ysmal (eds) *Europe at the Polls: The European Elections of 1999*, New York: NY: Palgrave.

Luhmann, N. (1990) *Essays on Self-Reference*, New York: Columbia University Press.

—— (1995) *Social Systems*, Stanford, CA: Stanford University Press.

—— (1996) *Die Realität der Massenmedien*, Opladen: Westdeutscher Verlag.

—— (2000) *Die Politik der Gesellschaft*, Frankfurt am Main: Suhrkamp.

Madeley, J. T. S. (2003) 'A Framework for the Comparative Analysis of Church-State Relations in Europe', in J. T. S. Madeley and Z. Enyedi (eds) *Church and State in Contemporary Europe: The Chimera of Neutrality*, London: Frank Cass.

Madeley, J. T. S. and Enyedi, Z. (eds) (2003) *Church and State in Contemporary Europe: The Chimera of Neutrality*, London: Frank Cass.

Magnette, P. (1999) 'L'Union européenne: Un régime semi-parlementaire', in P. Delwit, J.-M. De Waele and P. Magnette (eds) *A quoi sert le Parlement européen? Stratégies et pouvoirs d'une assemblée transnationale*, Brussels: Complexe.

—— (2001) 'Appointing and Censuring the European Commission: The Adaptation of Parliamentary Institutions to the Community Context', *European Law Journal*, 7(3): 292–310.

—— (2003) 'Between Parliamentary Control and the Rule of Law: The Political Role of the Ombudsman in the European Union', *Journal of European Public Policy*, 10(5): 677–94.

—— (2004) 'Deliberation or Bargaining? Coping with Constitutional Conflicts in the Convention on the Future of Europe', in E. O. Eriksen, J. E. Fossum and A. J. Menéndez (eds) *Developing a Constitution for Europe*, London: Routledge.

Magnette, P. and Nicolaïdis, K. (2004) 'The European Convention: Bargaining in the Shadow of Rhetoric', *West European Politics*, 27(3): 381–404.

Mair, P. (2005) 'Popular Democracy and the European Union Polity', European Governance Papers (EUROGOV) C-05–03. Available at: www.connex-network. org/eurogov/pdf/egp-connex-C-05–03.pdf.

—— (2006) 'Political Parties and Party Systems', in P. Graziano and M. Vink (eds) *Europeanization: New Research Agendas*, Basingstoke: Palgrave.

Majone, G. (1994) 'The Rise of the Regulatory State in Europe', *West European Politics*, 17(3): 77–101.

—— (1996) *Regulating Europe*, London: Routledge.

Mamadouh, V. (1995) 'De talen in het Europees Parlement', Amsterdamse sociaal-geografische studies, 52, Amsterdam: Instituut voor Sociale Geografie, Unversiteit van Amsterdam.

Mänicke-Gyöngyösi, K. (ed.) (1996) *Öffentliche Konfliktdiskurse um Restitution von Gerechtigkeit, Politische Verantwortung und Nationale Identität*, Frankfurt am Main: Peter Lang.

Manners, I. (2002) 'Normative Power Europe – A Contradiction in Terms?' *Journal of Common Market Studies*, 40(2): 235–58.

Mansbridge, J. (2003) 'Rethinking Representation', *American Political Science Review*, 97(4): 515–28.

March, J. G. (1994) 'Decision Engineering', in J. G. March *A Primer on Decision Making: How Decisions Happen*, New York: The Free Press.

March, J. G. and Olsen, J. P. (1995) *Democratic Governance*, New York: The Free Press.

Marsh, M. and Norris, P. (1997) 'Political Representation in the European Parliament', *European Journal of Political Research*, 32(2): 153–63.

Martin, P. (1999) 'Stand Up if You're European: Football and the Development of a Sense of European Identity', paper presented at the Fourth European Conference of Sociology, Amsterdam, 18–21 August 1999.

Massignon, B. (2002) 'Les relations des organismes européens religieux et humanistes avec les institutions de l'Union européenne: logiques nationales et confessionnelles et dynamiques d'européanisation', in Commissariat Général du Plan, *Croyances religieuses, morales et éthiques dans le processus de construction européenne*, Paris: La Documentation Française.

—— (2005) 'La construction européenne: Un laboratoire de gestion de la pluralité religieuse et philosophique: Clivages nationaux et confessionnels et dynamiques d'européanisation', PhD thesis, L'École des hautes études en sciences sociales (EHESS), Paris.

Mattelart, A. (2000) 'L'âge de l'information: Genèse d'une appelation non contrôlée', *Réseaux*, 18(101): 19–52.

Maurer, A. (1999) *What Next for the European Parliament?* London: Kogan Page.

—— (2002) *Parlamentarische Demokratie in der Europäischen Union: Der Beitrag des Europäischen Parlaments und der nationalen Parlamente*, Baden-Baden: Nomos.

—— (2005) 'Der Vertrag über eine Verfassung für Europa: Die neuen Handlungsermächtigungen der Organe', Discussion Paper FG 1 2005/03, Berlin: Wissenschaftszentrum Berlin für Sozialforschung.

Maurer, A. and Wessels, W. (eds) (2001) *National Parliaments on their Ways to Europe: Losers or Latecomers?* Baden-Baden: Nomos.

—— (2003) *Das Europäische Parlament nach Amsterdam und Nizza: Akteur, Arena oder Alibi?*, Baden-Baden: Nomos.

Mayhew, L. (1997) *The New Public*, Cambridge: Cambridge University Press

McAdam, D., Tarrow, S. and Tilly, C. (2001) *Dynamics of Contention*, New York: Cambridge University Press.

McNair, B. (2000) *Journalism and Democracy: An Evaluation of the Political Public Sphere*, London: Routledge.

Medrano, J. D. (2003) 'Qualitätspresse und politische Integration', in A. Klein and R. Koopmans (eds) *Bürgerschaft, Öffentlichkeit und Demokratie in Europa*, Opladen: Leske und Budrich.

Mercier, A. (ed.) (2003) *Vers un espace public européen?*, Paris: L'Harmattan.

Meyer, C. O. (2000) 'Towards a European Public Sphere? Transnational Investigative Journalism and the European Commission's Resignation', in B. Baerns and J. Raupp (eds) *Information and Transnational Communication in Europe: Practice and Research*, Berlin: Vistas.

—— (2002) *Europäische Öffentlichkeit als Kontrollsphäre: Die Europäische Kommission, die Medien und politische Verantwortung*, Berlin: Vistas.

Miller, D. (1995) *On Nationality*, Oxford: Oxford University Press.

Moragas Spà, M., Garitaonandía, C. and López, B. (1999) *Television on Your Doorstep: Decentralization Experiences in the European Union*, Luton: University of Luton Press.

Morgan, D. (1999) *The European Parliament, Mass Media and the Search for Power and Influence*, Aldershot: Ashgate.

Nassehi, A. (2002) 'Politik des Staates oder Politik der Gesellschaft: Kollektivität als Problemformel des Politischen', in K.-U. Hellmann and R. Schmalz-Bruns (eds) *Niklas Luhmanns politische Soziologie*, Frankfurt am Main: Suhrkamp.

Neveu, C. (2000) 'Citizens of Europe and European Citizens: Exploring European Citizenship', in I. Bellier and T. Wilson (eds) *An Anthropology of the European Union: Building, Imagining and Experiencing the New Europe*, Oxford: Berg.

—— (2002) '"Devenir européen": entre individuation et emprise des cadres nationaux', *Anthropologie et Sociétés*, 26(1): 127–38.

Neveu, E. (2002) 'Europe as an "Un-imaginable Community"? The Failure of the French News-Magazine L'Européen', *Journal of European Area Studies*, 10(2): 283–300.

Neyer, J. (2000) 'Justifying Comitology: The Promise of Deliberation', in K. Neunreither and A. Wiener (eds) *European Integration After Amsterdam: Institutional Dynamics and Prospects for Democracy*, Oxford: Oxford University Press.

—— (2003) 'Discourse and Order in the EU: A Deliberative Approach to Multi-level Governance', *Journal of Common Market Studies*, 41(4): 687–706.

Norris, P. (2000) 'Blaming the Messenger? Political Communications and Turnout in EU Elections', in H. Agné *et al.*, 'Citizen Participation in European Politics', SOU 1999: 151, Demokratiutredningens skrift nr 32 [Commission of Democracy in Sweden], Stockholm: Statens Offentliga Utredningar.

Offe, C. (1990) 'Reflections on the Institutional Self-transformation of Movement Politics: A Tentative Stage Model', in R. J. Dalton and M. Kuechler (eds) *Challenging the Political Order*, Cambridge: Polity Press.

—— (1998) '"Homogeneity" and Constitutional Democracy: Coping with Identity Conflicts through Group Rights', *Journal of Political Philosophy*, 6(2): 113–41.

Oleszek, W. J. (2001) *Congressional Procedures and the Policy Process*, Washington, DC: Congressional Quarterly Press.

Olsen, J. P. (1983) 'Citizens Initiatives and the Organization of Representation', in J. P. Olsen *Organized Democracy*, Bergen: Universitetsforlaget.

Padioleau, J.-G. (2006) '"Les médias" face à la destruction créatrice', *Le Débat*, 139.

Pateman, C. (1974) *Participation and Democratic Theory*, 4th edn, New York: Cambridge University Press.

Peters, A. (2003) 'A Plea for a European Semi-Parliamentary and Semi-Consociational Democracy', European Integration online Papers (EIoP) 7(3). Available at: eiop.or.at/eiop/texte/2003–003a.htm.

Peters, B. (1993) *Die Integration moderner Gesellschaften*, Frankfurt am Main: Suhrkamp.

—— (2005) 'Public Discourse, Identity, and the Problem of Democratic Legitimacy', in Erik O. Eriksen (ed.) *Making the European Polity: Reflexive Integration in the EU*, London: Routledge.

Peters, B., Sifft, S., Wimmel, A., Brüggemann, M. and Kleinen-von Königslöw (2005) 'National and Transnational Public Spheres: The Case of the EU', in S. Leibfried and M. Zürn (eds) *Transformations of the State?*, Cambridge: Cambridge University Press.

Peters, G. and Barker, A. (1993) *Advising West European Government: Inquiries, Expertise and Public Policy*, Pittsburgh, PA: University of Pittsburgh Press.

Pinder, J. (ed.) (1999) *Foundations of Democracy in the European Union: From the Genesis of Parliamentary Democracy to the European Parliament*, New York: Palgrave Macmillan.

Pollack, M. A. (2003) *The Engines of European Integration: Delegation, Agency, and Agenda Setting in the EU*, Oxford: Oxford University Press.

Price, G. (1998) *Encyclopedia of the Languages of Europe*, Oxford: Blackwell.

Putnam, R. D. (2000) *Bowling Alone: The Collapse and Revival of American Community*, New York: Simon and Schuster.

—— (with R. Leonardi and R. Y. Nanetti) (1993) *Making Democracy Work: Civic Traditions in Modern Italy*, Princeton, NJ: Princeton University Press.

Radaelli, C. (1999) *Technocracy in the European Union*, Harlow: Addison Wesley Longman.

Ragnemalm, H. (1999) 'The Community Courts and Openness within the European Union', in A. Dashwood and A. Ward (eds) *The Cambridge Yearbook of European Legal Studies, Volume 2*, Cambridge: Centre for European Legal Studies.

Rawls, J. (1971) *A Theory of Justice*, Cambridge, MA: Harvard University Press.

Ricoeur, P. (1992) 'Personal Identity and Narrative Identity', in P. Ricoeur *Oneself as Another*, Chicago, IL: University of Chicago Press.

Risse-Kappen, T. (1996) 'Exploring the Nature of the Beast: International Relations Theory and Comparative Policy Analysis Meet the European Union', *Journal of Common Market Studies*, 34(1): 53–79.

Rittberger, B. (2000) 'Impatient Legislators and New Issue-Dimensions: A Critique of the Garrett-Tsebelis "Standard Version" of Legislative Politics', *Journal of European Public Policy*, 7(4): 554–75.

—— (2003) 'The Creation and Empowerment of the European Parliament', *Journal of Common Market Studies*, 41(2): 203–25.

—— (2005) *Building Europe's Parliament*, Oxford: Oxford University Press.

Robert, C. (2004) 'Doing Politics and Pretending Not To: The Commission's Role in Distributing Aid to Eastern Europe', in A. Smith (ed.) *Politics and the European Commission*, London: Routledge.

Rosenau, J. N. (1997) *Along the Domestic-Foreign Frontier: Exploring Governance in a Turbulent World*, Cambridge: Cambridge University Press.

—— (1998) 'Governance and Democracy in a Globalizing World', in D. Archibugi, D. Held and M. Köhler (eds) *Re-imagining Political Community*, Oxford: Polity Press.

Ross, G. (1995) *Jacques Delors and European Integration*, Cambridge: Blackwell.

Rucht, D., Koopmans, R. and Neidhardt, F. (eds) (1998) *Acts of Dissent: New Developments in the Study of Protest*, Berlin: Sigma.

Sandel, M. J. (1998) *Liberalism and the Limits of Justice*, 2nd edn, Cambridge: Cambridge University Press.

Scharpf, F. W. (1994) 'Community and Autonomy: Multi-level Policy-making in the European Union', *Journal of European Public Policy*, 1(2): 219–42.

—— (1999) *Governing in Europe: Effective and Democratic*, Oxford: Oxford University Press.

Schlesinger, P. (1999) 'Changing Spaces of Political Communication: The Case of the European Union', *Political Communication*, 16(3): 263–79.

—— (2000) 'The Nation and Communicative Space', in H. Tumber (ed.) *Media Power, Professionals and Politics*, London: Routledge.

—— (2002) 'Media and Belonging: The Changing Shape of Political Communication in the European Union', in U. Hedetoft and M. Hjort (eds) *The Postnational Self: Belonging and Identity*, Minneapolis, MN: University of Minnesota Press.

—— (2003) 'The Babel of Europe? An Essay on Networks and Communicative Spaces', ARENA Working Paper 22/03, Oslo: ARENA.

—— (2006) 'Is there a Crisis in British Journalism?' *Media, Culture and Society*, 28(2): 299–307.

Schlesinger, P. and Foret, F. (2006) 'Political Roof and Sacred Canopy? Religion and the EU Constitution', *European Journal of Social Theory*, 9(1): 59–81.

Schlesinger, P. and Kevin, D. (2000) 'Can the European Union Become a Sphere of Publics?', in E. O. Eriksen and J. E. Fossum (eds) *Democracy in the European Union: Integration Through Deliberation?*, London: Routledge.

Schlossmacher, M. (1994) 'Die Arbeitssprachen in den Organen der Europäischen Gemeinschaft. Methoden und Ergebnisse einer empirischen Untersuchung', in U. Ammon, K. J. Mattheier and P. H. Nelde (eds) *Sociolinguistica: International Yearbook of European Sociolinguistics. Vol. 8: English Only? in Europe*, Tübingen: Max Niemeyer.

Schmitter, P. C. (2000) *How to Democratize the European Union – and Why Bother?*, Lanham: Rowman & Littlefield.

Schmitter, P. C. and Kim, S. (2005) 'Prospects for Northeast Asian Integration: Lessons from Europe', paper presented at the conference 'The European Union and the World: Asia, Enlargement and Constitutional Change', Beijing, 5–6 May 2005.

Sennett, R. (1977) *The Fall of Public Man*, New York: Knopf.

Shaw, J. (2000) 'Importing Gender: The Challenge of Feminism and the Analysis of the EU Legal Order', *Journal of European Public Policy*, 7(3): 406–31.

—— (2003) 'Process, Responsibility and Inclusion in EU Constitutionalism', *European Law Journal*, 9(1): 45–68.

Shore, C. (2000) *Building Europe: The Cultural Politics of European Integration*, London: Routledge.

Siedentop, L. (2000) *Democracy in Europe*, London: Penguin.

Sinclair, J. (2004) 'Globalization, Supranantional Institutions, and Media', in J. Downing, D. McQuail, P. Schlesinger and E. Wartella (eds) *The SAGE Handbook of Media Studies*, Thousand Oaks, CA: Sage.

Sjursen, H. (ed.) (2006) 'What Kind of Power? European Foreign Policy in Perspective', *Journal of European Public Policy*, Special Issue, 13(2): 169–81.

Slaatta, T. (2006) 'Europeanization and the News Media: Issues and Research Imperatives', *Javnost – The Public*, 13(1): 5–24.

Smith, A. (2003) 'Why European Commissioners Matter', *Journal of Common Market Studies*, 41(1): 37–55.

—— (2004a) *Le gouvernement de l'Union européenne: Une sociologie politique*, Paris: Librairie Générale de Droit et de Jurisprudence.

—— (2004b) 'Conclusion: Politics and the European Union', in A. Smith (ed.) *Politics and the European Commission*, London: Routledge.

Smith, A. D. (1986) *The Ethnic Origins of Nations*, Oxford: Blackwell.

Smith, D. (1999) 'Making Europe – Processes of Europe-formation since 1945', in D. Smith and S. Wright (eds) *Whose Europe? The Turn Towards Democracy*, Oxford: Blackwell.

Snow, D. A. and Benford, R. D. (1999) 'Alternative Types of Cross-National Diffusion in the Social Movement Arena', in D. della Porta, H. Kriesi and D. Rucht (eds) *Social Movements in a Globalizing World*, New York: St Martin's Press.

Söderman, J. (1998) 'The Citizen, the Administration and Community Law', General Report for the XVIII Congress of FIDE (Fédération internationale de droit européen), Stockholm, 3–6 June 1998.

Soysal, Y. (2002) 'Locating Europe', *European Societies*, 4(3): 265–84.

Splichal, S. (1999) *Public Opinion: Developments and Controversies in the Twentieth Century*, New York: Rowman & Littlefield.

Statham, P. (2003) 'National Report on Political Claims-making Data-set for Britain', UNEMPOL Research Report (The Contentious Politics of Unemployment in Europe: Political Claim-making, Policy Deliberation and Exclusion from the Labour Market). Available at: ics.leeds.ac.uk/eurpolcom/unempol/reports. cfm.

Statham, P. and Gray, E. (2005) 'The Public Sphere and Debates about Europe in Britain: Internalized and Conflict-Driven?', *Innovation*, 18(1): 61–81.

Stie, A. E. (2002) 'Preconditions for Democracy: National Identity versus Constitutional Patriotism. A Theoretical Analysis of the German Federal Constitutional Court's Maastricht Judgement', ARENA Report 9/02, Oslo: ARENA.

Stone Sweet, A. and Brunell, T. L. (1998) 'Constructing a Supranational Constitution: Dispute Resolution and Governance in the European Community', *American Political Science Review*, 92(1): 63–81.

Street, J. (2001) *Mass Media, Politics and Democracy*, Basingstoke: Palgrave Macmillan.

Szücs, J. (1988) 'Three Historical Regions of Europe', in J. Keane (ed.) *Civil Society and the State*, London: Verso.

Taggart, P. (1998) 'A Touchstone of Dissent: Euroscepticism in Contemporary Western European Party Systems', *European Journal of Political Research*, 33(3): 363–88.

Talberg, J. (2004) 'The Power of the Presidency: Brokerage, Efficiency and Distribution in EU Negotiations', *Journal of Common Market Studies*, 42(5): 999–1022.

Taylor, C. (1989) *Sources of the Self: The Making of the Modern Identity*, Cambridge, MA: Harvard University Press.

—— (1993) *Reconciling the Solitudes: Essays on Canadian Federalism and Nationalism*, Montreal: McGill-Queens' University Press.

—— (1995) *Philosophical Arguments*, Cambridge, MA: Harvard University Press.

Therborn, G. (2002) 'The World's Trader, the World's Lawyer: Europe and Current Global Processes', *European Journal of Social Theory*, 5(4): 403–17.

Tilly, C. (1986) 'European Violence and Collective Action since 1700', *Social Research*, 53: 158–84.

Touraine, A. (1981) *The Voice and the Eye*, Cambridge: Cambridge University Press.

Trenz, H.-J. (2002a) *Zur Konstitution politischer Öffentlichkeit in der Europäischen Union*, Baden-Baden: Nomos.

—— (2002b) 'Ein Rauschen geht durch den europäischen Blätterwald: Kommissionspräsident Prodi und die Entstehung einer europäischen Publizistik', *Berliner Debatte Initial*, 13(5/6): 24–35.

—— (2004a) 'Europäische Integration und Öffentlichkeit: Institutionelle Selbstdarstellung und mediale Repräsentation der politischen Gesellschaft Europas', habilitation thesis, Humboldt University Berlin.

—— (2004b) 'Media Coverage on European Governance: Exploring the European Public Sphere in National Quality Newspapers', *European Journal of Communication*, 19(3): 291–319.

—— (2005a) *Europa in den Medien: Die europäische Integration im Spiegel nationaler Öffentlichkeit*, Frankfurt am Main: Campus.

—— (2005b) 'Die mediale Ordnung des politischen Europas: Formen und Dynamiken der Europäiserung politischer Kommunikation in der Qualitetspresse', *Zeitschrift für Soziologie*, 34(3): 188–206.

Trenz, H.-J. and Eder, K. (2004) 'The Democratising Dynamics of a European Public Sphere: Towards a Theory of Democratic Functionalism', *European Journal of Social Theory*, 7(1): 5–25.

Trenz, H.-J. and Vetters, R. (2006) 'No News from Brussels: Comment on the Commission's White Paper on a European Communication Policy', The Federal Trust European Newsletter, March/April 2006: 3–4.

Trenz, H.-J., Conrad, M. and Rosén, G. (2006) 'The Interpretative Moment of European Journalism: The Impact of Media Voice in the Ratification Process', paper presented at the workshop 'Constitutional Ratification Crisis: Exploring the European Public Sphere', European University Institute, Florence, 19–20 May 2006.

Trumpf, J. and Piris, C. (1999) 'Operation of the Council with an Enlarged Union in Prospect', Report by the Working Party set up by the Secretary-General of the Council, March 1999. Available at: www.consilium.europa.eu/ueDocs/cms_Data/docs/pressdata/en/misc/02139.EN9.htm.

Tsebelis, G. (1994) 'The Power of the European Parliament as a Conditional Agenda Setter', *American Political Science Review*, 88(1): 128–42.

Tsoukalis, J. (2003) *What Kind of Europe?* Oxford: Oxford University Press.

Tumber, H. (1995) 'Marketing Maastricht: The EU and News Management', *Media, Culture and Society*, 17: 511–19.

Urwin, D. (1995) *The Community of Europe*, London: Longman.

Van de Steeg, M. (2002) 'Rethinking the Conditions for a Public Sphere in the European Union', *European Journal of Social Theory*, 5(4): 499–519.

—— (2004) 'Does a Public Sphere Exist in the EU? An Analysis of the Content of the Debate on the Haider-Case', EUI Working Paper SPS 2004/5, Florence: European University Institute.

Van Dijk, T. A. (1985) *Handbook of Discourse Analysis*, New York: Academic Press.

Van der Eijk, C. and Franklin, M. N. (2004) 'Potential for Contestation on European Matters at National Elections in Europe', in G. Marks and M. R. Steenbergen (eds) *European Integration and Political Conflict*, Cambridge: Cambridge University Press.

Vesterdorf, B. (1999) 'Transparency – Not Just a Vogue Word', *Fordham International Law Journal*, 22(3): 902–29.

Von Beyme, K. (1999) *Die Parlamentarische Demokratie: Entstehung und Funktionswandel 1789–1999*, Opladen: Westdeutscher Verlag.

Waldron, J. (1994) 'Vagueness in Law and Language: Some Philosophical Issues', *California Law Review*, 82: 509–39.

—— (2002) 'Is the Rule of Law an Essentially Contested Concept (in Florida)?', *Law and Philosophy*, 21(2): 137–64.

Wallace, W. and Smith, J. (1995) 'Democracy or Technocracy? European Integration and the Problem of Popular Consent', *West European Politics*, 18(3): 137–57.

Wallis, R. and Bruce, S. (1992) 'Secularization: The Orthodox Model', in S. Bruce (ed.) *Religion and Modernization: Sociologists and Historians Debate the Secularization Thesis*, Oxford: Clarendon Press.

Weber, M. (1971) *Economie et société*, Paris: Plon.

Weiler, J. H. H. (1999) *The Constitution of Europe: Essays on the Ends and Means of European Integration*, Cambridge, MA: Cambridge University Press.

Weiler, J. H. H., Haltern, U. and Mayer, F. C. (1995) 'European Democracy and Its Critique: Five Uneasy Pieces', *West European Politics*, 18(3): 4–39.

Welch, E. W. and Wong, W. (2001) 'Global Information Technology Pressure and Government Accountability: The Mediating Effect of Domestic Context on Website Openness', *Journal of Public Administration Research and Theory*, 11: 509–38.

Wessels, B. (2004) 'Contestation Potential of Interests Groups in the EU: Emergence, Structure, and Political Alliances', in G. Marks and M. R. Steenbergen (eds) *European Integration and Political Conflict*, Cambridge: Cambridge University Press.

Wessels, W. (1991) 'The EC Council: The Community's Decision-making Centre', in R. O. Keohane and S. Hoffmann (eds) *The New European Community: Decision-making and Institutional Change*, Boulder, CO: Westview.

Whitely, P. F. (1995) 'Rational Choice and Political Participation: Evaluating the Debate', *Political Research Quarterly*, 48: 211–34.

Wickham, J. (2004) 'Something New in Old Europe? Innovations in EU-funded Social Research', *Innovation*, 17(3): 187–204.

Willaime, J.-P. (2004) *Europe et religions: Les enjeux du XXIe siècle*, Paris: Fayard.

Williams, R. (1981) *Culture*, London: Fontana Paperbacks.

Wodak, R. (1998) *Zur diskursiven Konstruktion nationaler Identität*, Frankfurt am Main: Suhrkamp.

—— (1991) *Language, Power and Ideology*, Amsterdam: John Benjamins.

Wodak, R. and Van Dijk, T. A. (eds) (2000) *Racism at the Top: Parliamentary Discourses on Ethnic Issues in Six European States*, Klagenfurt: Drava.

Young, I. M. (1996) 'Communication and the Other: Beyond Deliberative Democracy', in S. Benhabib (ed.) *Democracy and Difference: Contesting the Boundaries of the Political*, Princeton, NJ: Princeton University Press.

Zürn, M. (1999) 'The State in the Post-National Constellation: Societal Denationalization and Multi-Level Governance', ARENA Working Paper 35/99, Oslo: ARENA.

Index

Tables are indicated by italic type and figures by bold.